GLIDER FLYING HANDBOOK

2003

U.S. DEPARTMENT OF TRANSPORTATION
FEDERAL AVIATION ADMINISTRATION
Flight Standards Service

PREFACE

The *Glider Flying Handbook* is designed as a technical manual for applicants who are preparing for glider category rating and for currently certificated glider pilots who wish to improve their knowledge. Certificated flight instructors will find this handbook a valuable training aid, since detailed coverage of aeronautical decision making, components and systems, aerodynamics, flight instruments, performance limitations, ground operations, flight maneuvers, traffic patterns, emergencies, soaring weather, soaring techniques, and cross-country is included. Topics, such as radio navigation and communication, use of flight information publications, and regulations are available in other Federal Aviation Administration (FAA) publications.

This handbook conforms to pilot training and certification concepts established by the FAA. There are different ways of teaching, as well as performing flight procedures and maneuvers, and many variations in the explanations of aerodynamic theories and principles. This handbook adopts a selective method and concept to flying gliders. The discussion and explanations reflect the most commonly used practices and principles. Occasionally, the word "must" or similar language is used where the desired action is deemed critical. The use of such language is not intended to add to, interpret, or relieve a duty imposed by Title 14 of the Code of Federal Regulations (14 CFR).

It is essential for persons using this handbook to also become familiar with and apply the pertinent parts of 14 CFR and the *Aeronautical Information Manual (AIM)*. Performance standards for demonstrating competence required for pilot certification are prescribed in the appropriate glider practical test standard.

This handbook contains all or part of the information found in AC 61-94, *Pilot Transition Course for Self-Launching or Powered Sailplanes (Motorgliders)*. This publication may be purchased from the Superintendent of Documents, U.S. Government Printing Office (GPO), Washington, DC 20402-9325, or from U.S. Government Bookstores located in major cities throughout the United States.

The current Flight Standards Service airman training and testing material and subject matter knowledge codes for all airman certificates and ratings can be obtained from the Flight Standards Services web site at **http://av-info.faa.gov.**

The FAA gratefully acknolwedges the valuable assistance provided by many individuals and organizations throughout the aviation community who contributed their time and talent in publishing this handbook.

Comments regarding this handbook should be sent to U.S. Department of Transportation, Federal Aviation Administration, Airman Testing Standards Branch, AFS-630, P.O. Box 25082, Oklahoma City, OK 73125.

AC 00-2, *Advisory Circular Checklist*, transmits the current status of FAA advisory circulars and other flight information publications. This checklist is free of charge and may be obtained by sending a request to U.S. Department of Transportation, Subsequent Distribution Office, SVC-121.23, Ardmore East Business Center, 3341 Q 75th Avenue, Landover, MD 20785. The checklist also is available on the Internet at: **http://www.faa.gov/aba/html_policies/ac00_2.html**

CONTENTS

Chapter 10—Soaring Techniques

Chapter 11—Cross-Country Soaring

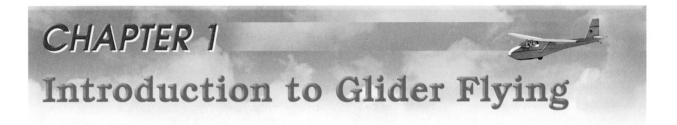

CHAPTER 1
Introduction to Glider Flying

Welcome to the world of soaring. The *Glider Flying Handbook* is designed to help you achieve your goals in aviation and to provide you with the knowledge and practical information needed to attain private, commercial, and flight instructor category ratings in gliders.

GLIDERS — THE EARLY YEARS

The fantasy of flight led people to dream up intricate designs in an attempt to imitate the flight of birds. Leonardo da Vinci sketched a vision of flying machines in his 15th century manuscripts. His work consisted of a number of wing designs including a human-powered ornithopter, derived from the Greek word for bird. Centuries later, when others began to experiment with his designs, it became apparent that the human body could not sustain flight by flapping wings like birds. [Figure 1-1]

GLIDER OR SAILPLANE?

The Federal Aviation Administration (FAA) defines a **glider** as a heavier-than-air aircraft that is supported in flight by the dynamic reaction of the air against its lifting surfaces, and whose free flight does not depend on an engine. The term glider is used to designate the rating that can be placed on a pilot certificate once a person successfully completes required glider knowledge and practical tests.

Another widely accepted term used in the industry is **sailplane**. Soaring refers to the sport of flying sailplanes, which usually includes traveling long distances and remaining aloft for extended periods of time. Gliders were designed and built to provide short flights off a hill down to a landing area. Since their wings provided relatively low lift and high drag, these simple gliders were generally unsuitable for sustained flight using atmospheric lifting forces. The most well known example of a glider is the space shuttle, which literally glides back to earth. The space shuttle, like gliders, cannot sustain flight for long periods of time. Early gliders were easy and inexpensive to build, and they played an important role in flight training.

Self-launch gliders are equipped with engines, but with the engine shut down, they display the same flight characteristics as non-powered gliders. The engine allows them to be launched under their own power. Once aloft, pilots of self-launch gliders can shut down the engine and fly with the power off. The additional training and procedures required to earn a self-launch endorsement are covered later in this handbook.

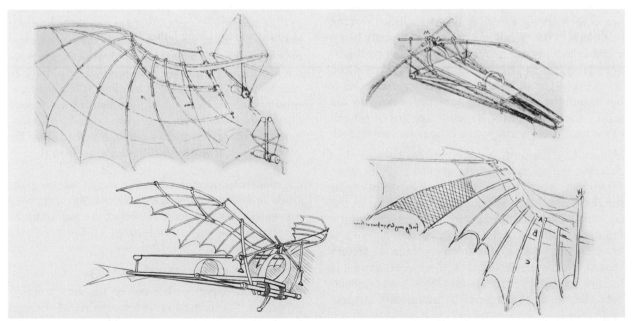

Figure 1-1. A human-powered ornithopter is virtually incapable of flight due to the dramatic difference in the strength-to-weight ratio of birds compared to humans.

GLIDER CERTIFICATE ELIGIBILITY REQUIREMENTS

To be eligible to fly a glider solo, you must be at least 14 years of age and demonstrate satisfactory aeronautical knowledge on a test developed by your instructor. You also must have received and logged flight training for the maneuvers and procedures in Title 14 of the Code of Federal Aviation Regulations (14 CFR) part 61 that are appropriate to the make and model of aircraft to be flown, as well as demonstrate satisfactory proficiency and safety. Only after all of these requirements are met, can your instructor endorse your student certificate and logbook for solo flight.

To be eligible for a private pilot certificate with a glider rating, you must be at least 16 years of age, complete the specific training and flight time requirements described in 14 CFR part 61, pass a knowledge test, and successfully complete a practical test.

To be eligible for a commercial or flight instructor glider certificate, you must be 18 years of age, complete the specific training requirements described in 14 CFR part 61, pass the required knowledge tests, and pass another practical test. If you currently hold a pilot certificate for a powered aircraft and are adding a glider category rating on that certificate, you are exempt from the knowledge test but must satisfactorily complete the practical test. Certificated glider pilots are not required to hold an airman medical certificate to operate a glider.

AERONAUTICAL DECISION MAKING

Aeronautical decision making (ADM) is a systematic approach to the mental process used by pilots to consistently determine the best course of action in response to a given set of circumstances. The importance of learning effective ADM skills cannot be overemphasized. While progress is continually being made in the advancement of pilot training methods, aircraft equipment and systems, and services for pilots, accidents still occur. Despite all the changes in technology to improve flight safety, one factor remains the same—the human factor. It is estimated that 65 percent of the total glider accidents are **human factors** related.

Historically, the term "pilot error" has been used to describe the causes of these accidents. Pilot error means that an action or decision made by the pilot was the cause of, or a contributing factor that lead to, the accident. This definition also includes the pilot's failure to make a decision or take action. From a broader perspective, the phrase "human factors related" more aptly describes these accidents since it is usually not a single decision that leads to an accident, but a chain of events triggered by a number of factors.

The poor judgment chain, sometimes referred to as the "error chain," is a term used to describe this concept of contributing factors in a human factors related accident. Breaking one link in the chain normally is all that is necessary to change the outcome of the sequence of events. The following is an example of the type of scenario illustrating the poor judgment chain.

An experienced glider pilot returning from a cross-country flight is approaching a jagged mountain ridge that lies between him and his home airport located in the valley below. As he nears the ridge he sees people on the top waving to him in excitement. Overjoyed with having flown over 400 kilometers, he decides to do a low pass over the peak. He is flying into a 30 knot headwind that is blowing across the peak. Holding what he feels is adequate airspeed as he nears the lee side of the peak, he realizes his altitude is not very high in relation to the peak of the ridge. As he nears the peak he finds himself in a strong downdraft created by the strong wind blowing over the ridge. In an attempt to make a 180° turn to avoid contacting the ridge, the pilot puts his glider into a steep right turn and pulls back hard on the control stick resulting in an accelerated stall/spin. In the ensuing crash, the pilot is fatally injured and the glider is completely destroyed.

By discussing the events that led to this accident, we can understand how a series of judgmental errors contributed to the final outcome of this flight. For example, one of the first elements that affected the pilot's flight was his inability to realize that his decision-making skills were probably dulled by the long distance flight, which preceded the accident. The pilot had flown over this ridge a number of times and was aware that downdrafts are often present on the lee side of the peak but had never had problems in the past.

Next, he let his desire to show-off for the people on the mountain peak override his concern for arriving safely at his home airport, and he failed to recognize the threat posed by the strong wind blowing over the ridge. Rather than heading straight for the airport, he decided to make a low pass over the ridge with insufficient altitude to maintain the FAA mandatory minimums in dangerous wind conditions. Next, rather than aborting his attempt to make the pass over the peak when he realized his altitude was not sufficient, he continued to fly toward the peak rather than making a 180° turn away from it.

On numerous occasions during the flight, the pilot could have made effective decisions that may have prevented this accident. However, as the chain of events unfolded, each poor decision left him with fewer and fewer options.

ORIGINS OF ADM TRAINING

The airlines developed some of the first training programs that focused on improving ADM. Human factors-related accidents motivated the airline industry to implement crew resource management (CRM) training for flight crews. The focus of CRM programs is the effective use of all available resources—human resources, hardware, and information. Human resources include all groups routinely working with the cockpit crew (or pilot) who are involved in decisions required to operate a flight safely. These groups include, but are not limited to: ground, maintenance, and flight personnel. Although the CRM concept originated as airlines developed ways of facilitating crew cooperation to improve decision making in the cockpit, CRM principles, such as workload management, situational awareness, communication, the leadership role of the captain, and crewmember coordination have direct application to the general aviation cockpit. This also includes single pilot operations, since pilots of small aircraft, as well as crews of larger aircraft, must make effective use of all available resources—human

resources, hardware, and information. You can also refer to AC 60-22, *Aeronautical Decision Making*, which provides background references, definitions, and other pertinent information about ADM training in the general aviation environment. [Figure 1-2]

THE DECISION-MAKING PROCESS

An understanding of the decision-making process provides you with a foundation for developing ADM skills. Some situations, such as towrope breaks, require you to respond immediately, using established procedures, with little time for detailed analysis. Traditionally, pilots have been well trained to react to emergencies, but are not as well prepared to make decisions that require a more reflective response. Typically during a flight, you have time to examine any changes that occur, gather information, and assess risk before

---

DEFINITIONS

ADM is a systematic approach to the mental process used by pilots to consistently determine the best course of action in response to a given set of circumstances.

ATTITUDE is a personal motivational predisposition to respond to persons, situations, or events in a given manner that can, nevertheless, be changed or modified through training as sort of a mental shortcut to decision making.

ATTITUDE MANAGEMENT is the ability to recognize hazardous attitudes in oneself and the willingness to modify them as necessary through the application of an appropriate antidote thought.

CREW RESOURCE MANAGEMENT (CRM) is the application of team management concepts in the flight deck environment. It was initially known as cockpit resource management, but as CRM programs evolved to include cabin crews, maintenance personnel, and others, the phrase crew resource management was adopted. This includes single pilots, as in most general aviation aircraft. Pilots of small aircraft, as well as crews of larger aircraft, must make effective use of all available resources; human resources, hardware, and information. A current definition includes all groups routinely working with the cockpit crew who are involved in decisions required to operate a flight safely. These groups include, but are not limited to: pilots, dispatchers, cabin crewmembers, maintenance personnel, and air traffic controllers. CRM is one way of addressing the challenge of optimizing the human/machine interface and accompanying interpersonal activities.

HEADWORK is required to accomplish a conscious, rational thought process when making decisions. Good decision making involves risk identification and assessment, information processing, and problem solving.

JUDGMENT is the mental process of recognizing and analyzing all pertinent information in a particular situation, a rational evaluation of alternative actions in response to it, and a timely decision on which action to take.

PERSONALITY is the embodiment of personal traits and characteristics of an individual that are set at a very early age and extremely resistant to change.

POOR JUDGMENT CHAIN is a series of mistakes that may lead to an accident or incident. Two basic principles generally associated with the creation of a poor judgment chain are: (1) one bad decision often leads to another; and (2) as a string of bad decisions grows, it reduces the number of subsequent alternatives for continued safe flight. ADM is intended to break the poor judgment chain before it can cause an accident or incident.

RISK ELEMENTS IN ADM take into consideration the four fundamental risk elements: the pilot, the aircraft, the environment, and the type of operation that comprise any given aviation situation.

RISK MANAGEMENT is the part of the decision making process which relies on situational awareness, problem recognition, and good judgment to reduce risks associated with each flight.

SITUATIONAL AWARENESS is the accurate perception and understanding of all the factors and conditions within the four fundamental risk elements that affect safety before, during, and after the flight.

SKILLS and PROCEDURES are the procedural, psychomotor, and perceptual skills used to control a specific aircraft or its systems. They are the airmanship abilities that are gained through conventional training, are perfected, and become almost automatic through experience.

STRESS MANAGEMENT is the personal analysis of the kinds of stress experienced while flying, the application of appropriate stress assessment tools, and other coping mechanisms.

Figure 1-2. These terms are used in AC 60-22 to explain concepts used in ADM training.

reaching a decision. The steps leading to this conclusion constitute the decision-making process.

DEFINING THE PROBLEM

Problem definition is the first step in the decision-making process. Defining the problem begins with recognizing that a change has occurred or that an expected change did not occur. A problem is perceived first by the senses, then is distinguished through insight and experience. These same abilities, as well as an objective analysis of all available information, are used to determine the exact nature and severity of the problem.

While going through your pre-landing checklist, you discover that your landing gear is stuck in the retracted position.

CHOOSING A COURSE OF ACTION

After the problem has been identified, you must evaluate the need to react to it and determine the actions that need to be taken to resolve the situation in the time available. The expected outcome of each possible action should be considered and the risks assessed before you decide on a response to the situation.

Your first thought was to try to thermal back up to buy yourself some time and see if you could get the landing gear freed. After weighing the consequences of not finding lift and not focusing on flying the glider, you realize your only course is to make a gear-up landing. You plan to land on the grass runway to the east of the paved runway to avoid causing extensive damage to your glider and allow for a softer touchdown.

IMPLEMENTING THE DECISION AND EVALUATING THE OUTCOME

Although a decision may be reached and a course of action implemented, the decision-making process is not complete. It is important to think ahead and determine how the decision could affect other phases of the flight. As the flight progresses, you must continue to evaluate the outcome of the decision to ensure that it is producing the desired result.

As you make your turn to downwind, you realize a tractor mowing the field is in the middle of the grass runway. At this point you make the decision to land on the paved runway with as smooth a touchdown as possible. You make a normal pattern and approach to landing and perform a minimum energy touchdown, at which point the glider's belly contacts the pavement and grinds to a stop wings level, causing only minor damage to the glider's underside.

The decision making process normally consists of several steps before you choose a course of action. To help you remember the elements of the decision-making process, a six-step model has been developed using the acronym "DECIDE." [Figure 1-3]

DECIDE MODEL
Detect the fact that a change has occurred.
Estimate the need to counter or react to the change.
Choose a desirable outcome for the success of the flight.
Identify actions which could successfully control the change.
Do the necessary action to adapt to the change.
Evaluate the effect of the action.

Figure 1-3. The DECIDE model can provide a framework for effective decision making.

RISK MANAGEMENT

During each flight, decisions must be made regarding events that involve interactions between the four risk elements—the pilot in command, the aircraft, the environment, and the operation. The decision-making process involves an evaluation of each of these risk elements to achieve an accurate perception of the flight situation. [Figure 1-4]

One of the most important decisions that a pilot in command must make is the go/no-go decision. Evaluating each of these risk elements can help you decide whether a flight should be conducted or continued. Let us evaluate the four risk elements and how they affect our decision making regarding the following situations.

Pilot—As a pilot, you must continually make decisions about your own competency, condition of health, mental and emotional state, level of fatigue, and many other variables. For example, you plan for an extended cross-country flight. You have had only a few hours of sleep, and you are concerned that the congestion you feel could be the onset of a cold. Are you safe to fly?

Aircraft—You will frequently base decisions on your evaluations of the aircraft, such as performance, equipment, or airworthiness. Picture yourself in the following situation. You are on a cross-country flight and have begun to fly over extremely rugged terrain, which covers the next 20 miles of your planned route and will not allow you to land safely should the need arise. The thermals are beginning to dissipate and your altitude is 3,000 feet above ground level (AGL). Should you continue to fly over this terrain?

Environment—This encompasses many elements not pilot or aircraft related. It can include such factors as weather, air traffic control, navaids, terrain, takeoff and landing areas, and surrounding obstacles. Weather is one element that can change drastically over time and distance. Imagine you are flying on a cross-country flight when you encounter unexpected snow squalls and

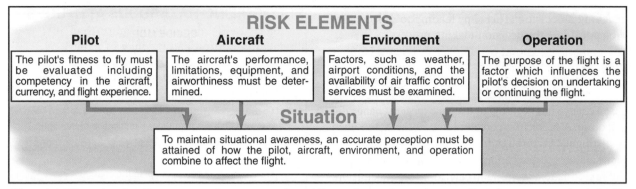

RISK ELEMENTS

Pilot	Aircraft	Environment	Operation
The pilot's fitness to fly must be evaluated including competency in the aircraft, currency, and flight experience.	The aircraft's performance, limitations, equipment, and airworthiness must be determined.	Factors, such as weather, airport conditions, and the availability of air traffic control services must be examined.	The purpose of the flight is a factor which influences the pilot's decision on undertaking or continuing the flight.

Situation

To maintain situational awareness, an accurate perception must be attained of how the pilot, aircraft, environment, and operation combine to affect the flight.

Figure 1-4. When situationally aware, you have an overview of the total operation and are not fixated on one perceived significant factor.

declining visibility in an area of rising terrain. Do you try to stay aloft and stay clear of the snow or land at the airport located in the valley below as soon as possible?

Operation—The interaction between you as the pilot, your aircraft, and the environment is greatly influenced by the purpose of each flight operation. You must evaluate the three previous areas to decide on the desirability of undertaking or continuing the flight as planned. It is worth asking yourself why the flight is being made, how critical is it to maintain the schedule, and is the trip worth the risks? For instance, you are giving glider rides at a busy commercial glider operation located near a mountain range on an extremely windy and turbulent day with strong downdrafts. Would it be better to wait for better conditions to ensure safe flight? How would your priorities change if your boss told you he only wanted you to take one more flight and then you could call it a day?

ASSESSING RISK

Examining National Transportation Safety Board (NTSB) reports and other accident research can help you to assess risk more effectively. For example, studies indicate the types of flight activities that are most likely to result in the most serious accidents. For gliders, takeoff and landing accidents consistently account for over 90 percent of the total number of accidents in any given year.

Causal factors for takeoff accidents are evenly divided between loss of directional control, collision with obstructions during takeoff, mechanical factors, and a premature termination of the tow. Accidents occurring during the landing phase of flight consistently account for an overwhelming majority of injury to pilots and damage to aircraft. This has proven to be especially true during recent years in which approximately 80 percent of all glider accidents occurred during the landing phase of flight. Accidents are more likely during takeoff and landing because the tolerance for error is greatly diminished and opportunities for pilots to overcome errors in judgment and decision-making become increasingly limited. The most common causal factors for landing accidents include collision with obstructions in the intended landing area. [Figure 1-5]

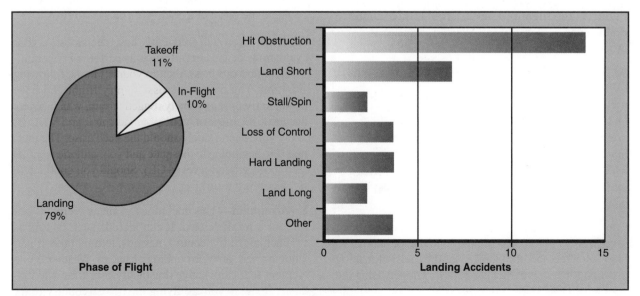

Figure 1-5. Statistical data can identify operations that have the highest risk.

FACTORS AFFECTING DECISION MAKING

It is important to point out the fact that being familiar with the decision-making process does not ensure that you will have the good judgment to be a safe pilot. The ability to make effective decisions as pilot in command depends on a number of factors. Some circumstances, such as the time available to make a decision, may be beyond your control. However, you can learn to recognize those factors that can be managed and learn skills to improve decision-making ability and judgment.

PILOT SELF-ASSESSMENT

The pilot in command of an aircraft is directly responsible for, and is the final authority as to, the operation of that aircraft. In order to effectively exercise that responsibility and make effective decisions regarding the outcome of a flight, you must have an understanding of your limitations. Your performance during a flight is affected by many factors, such as health, recency of experience, knowledge, skill level, and attitude.

Exercising good judgment begins prior to taking the controls of an aircraft. Often, pilots thoroughly check their aircraft to determine airworthiness, yet do not evaluate their own fitness for flight. Just as a checklist is used when preflighting an aircraft, a personal checklist based on such factors as experience, currency, and comfort level can help determine if you are prepared for a particular flight. Specifying when refresher training should be accomplished and designating weather minimums, which may be higher than those listed in Title 14 of the Code of Federal Regulations (14 CFR) part 91, are elements that may be included on a personal checklist. In addition to a review of personal limitations, you should use the I'M SAFE Checklist to further evaluate your fitness for flight. [Figure 1-6]

I'M SAFE CHECKLIST

Illness—Do I have any symptoms?

Medication—Have I been taking prescription or over-the-counter drugs?

Stress—Am I under psychological pressure from the job? Worried about financial matters, health problems, or family discord?

Alcohol—Have I been drinking within 8 hours? Within 24 hours?

Fatigue—Am I tired and not adequately rested?

Eating—Am I adequately nourished?

Figure 1-6. Prior to flight, you should assess your fitness, just as you evaluate the aircraft's airworthiness.

RECOGNIZING HAZARDOUS ATTITUDES

Being fit to fly depends on more than just your physical condition and recency of experience. For example, attitude affects the quality of your decisions. Attitude can be defined as a personal motivational predisposition to respond to persons, situations, or events in a given manner. Studies have identified five hazardous attitudes that can interfere with your ability to make sound decisions and exercise authority properly. [Figure 1-7]

HAZARDOUS ATTITUDES	ANTIDOTES
Macho—Brenda often brags to her friends about her skills as a pilot and wants to impress them with her abilities. During her third solo flight she decides to take a friend for a glider ride.	**Taking chances is foolish.**
Anti-authority—In the air, she thinks "It's great to be up here without an instructor criticizing everything I do. His do-it-by-the-book attitude takes all of the fun out of flying."	**Follow the rules. They are usually right.**
Invulnerability—Brenda soon realizes that the lift is not as strong as she had thought. But she feels confident that her skill in thermaling will still allow a long flight several miles from the gliderport so she can show her friend the countryside. She thinks, "It's no more difficult than many of the flights with my instructor."	**It could happen to me.**
Impulsivity—While returning to the gliderport, Brenda notices a lot of her glider friends sitting outside watching the activities. She decides to "buzz" the field and impress her fiends, as well as Sarah, her passenger. As she pulls up from her performance she realizes she is running out of airspeed, altitude and ideas.	**Not so fast. Think first.**
Resignation—After returning at a low altitude during a local soaring flight Brenda does not realize that she is landing with a tailwind. Brenda makes a fast approach followed by a hard landing and nearly hits the fence before the glider stops. As she and her passenger exit the glider, she says to herself, "Oh well, it's all part of learning to fly."	**I'm not helpless. I can make a difference.**

Figure 1-7. You must be able to identify hazardous attitudes and apply the appropriate antidote when needed.

Hazardous attitudes can lead to poor decision making and actions that involve unnecessary risk. You must examine your decisions carefully to ensure your choices have not been influenced by hazardous attitudes, and you must be familiar with positive alternatives to counteract the hazardous attitudes. These substitute attitudes are referred to as antidotes. During a flight operation, it is important to be able to recognize a hazardous attitude, correctly label the thought, and then recall its antidote. [Figure 1-8]

1. Anti-Authority: "Don't tell me."	This attitude is found in people who do not like anyone telling them what to do. In a sense, they are saying, "No one can tell me what to do." They may be resentful of having someone tell them what to do, or may regard rules, regulations, and procedures as silly or unnecessary. However, it is always your prerogative to question authority if you feel it is in error.
2. Impulsivity: "Do it quickly."	This is the attitude of people who frequently feel the need to do something, anything, immediately. They do not stop to think about what they are about to do; they do not select the best alternative, and they do the first thing that comes to mind.
3. Invulnerability: "It won't happen to me."	Many people feel that accidents happen to others, but never to them. They know accidents can happen, and they know that anyone can be affected. They never really feel or believe that they will be personally involved. Pilots who think this way are more likely to take chances and increase risk.
4. Macho: "I can do it."	Pilots who are always trying to prove that they are better than anyone else are thinking, "I can do it —I'll show them." Pilots with this type of attitude will try to prove themselves by taking risks in order to impress others. While this pattern is thought to be a male characteristic, women are equally susceptible.
5. Resignation: "What's the use?"	Pilots who think, "What's the use?" do not see themselves as being able to make a great deal of difference in what happens to them. When things go well, the pilot is apt to think that it is good luck. When things go badly, the pilot may feel that someone is out to get him, or attribute it to bad luck. The pilot will leave the action to others, for better or worse. Sometimes, such pilots will even go along with unreasonable requests just to be a "nice guy."

Figure 1-8. You should examine your decisions carefully to ensure that your choices have not been influenced by a hazardous attitude.

STRESS MANAGEMENT

Everyone is stressed to some degree all the time. A certain amount of stress is good since it keeps a person alert and prevents complacency. However, effects of stress are cumulative and, if not coped with adequately, eventually add up to an intolerable burden. Performance generally increases with the onset of stress, peaks, and then begins to fall off rapidly as stress levels exceed a person's ability to cope. The ability to make effective decisions during flight can be impaired by stress. Factors, referred to as stressors, can increase a pilot's risk of error in the cockpit. [Figure 1-9]

There are several techniques to help manage the accumulation of life stresses and prevent stress overload. For example, including relaxation time in a busy schedule and maintaining a program of physical fitness can help reduce stress levels. Learning to manage time more effectively can help you avoid heavy pressures imposed by getting behind schedule and not meeting deadlines.

Take an assessment of yourself to determine your capabilities and limitations and then set realistic goals. In addition, avoiding stressful situations and encounters can help you cope with stress.

USE OF RESOURCES

To make informed decisions during flight operations, you must be aware of the resources found both inside and outside the cockpit. Since useful tools and sources of information may not always be readily apparent, learning to recognize these resources is an essential part of ADM training. Resources must not only be identified, but you must develop the skills to evaluate whether you have the time to use a particular resource and the impact that its use will have upon the safety of flight. For example, the assistance of air traffic control (ATC) may be very useful if you are not sure of your location. However, in an emergency situation when action needs be taken quickly, time may not be available to contact ATC immediately.

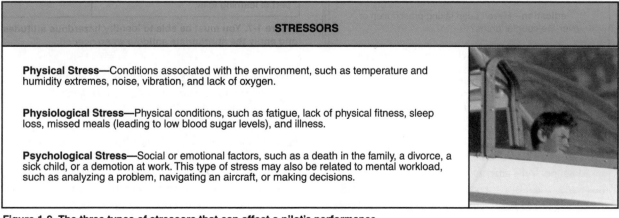

STRESSORS

Physical Stress—Conditions associated with the environment, such as temperature and humidity extremes, noise, vibration, and lack of oxygen.

Physiological Stress—Physical conditions, such as fatigue, lack of physical fitness, sleep loss, missed meals (leading to low blood sugar levels), and illness.

Psychological Stress—Social or emotional factors, such as a death in the family, a divorce, a sick child, or a demotion at work. This type of stress may also be related to mental workload, such as analyzing a problem, navigating an aircraft, or making decisions.

Figure 1-9. The three types of stressors that can affect a pilot's performance.

INTERNAL RESOURCES

Internal resources are found in the cockpit during flight. Since some of the most valuable internal resources are ingenuity, knowledge, and skill, you can expand cockpit resources immensely by improving these capabilities. This can be accomplished by frequently reviewing flight information publications, such as the CFRs and the *Aeronautical Information Manual* (AIM), as well as by pursuing additional training.

A thorough understanding of all the equipment and systems in the aircraft is necessary to fully utilize all resources. For example, satellite navigation systems are valuable resources. However, if pilots do not fully understand how to use this equipment, or they rely on it so much that they become complacent, it can become a detriment to safe flight.

Checklists are essential cockpit resources for verifying that the aircraft instruments and systems are checked, set, and operating properly, as well as ensuring that the proper procedures are performed if there is a system malfunction or in-flight emergency. Other valuable cockpit resources include current aeronautical charts, and publications, such as the *Airport/Facility Directory* (A/FD).

Passengers can also be a valuable resource. Passengers can help watch for traffic and may be able to provide information in an irregular situation, especially if they are familiar with flying. A strange smell or sound may alert a passenger to a potential problem. As pilot in command, you should brief passengers before the flight to make sure they are comfortable voicing any concerns.

EXTERNAL RESOURCES

Possibly the greatest external resources during flight are air traffic controllers and flight service specialists. ATC can help decrease pilot workload by providing traffic advisories, radar vectors, and assistance in emergency situations. Flight service stations can provide updates on weather, answer questions about airport conditions, and may offer direction-finding assistance. The services provided by ATC can be invaluable in enabling you to make informed in-flight decisions.

WORKLOAD MANAGEMENT

Effective workload management ensures that essential operations are accomplished by planning, prioritizing, and sequencing tasks to avoid work overload. As experience is gained, you learn to recognize future workload requirements and can prepare for high workload periods during times of low workload. Reviewing the appropriate chart and setting radio frequencies well in advance of when they are needed helps reduce workload as your flight nears the airport.

In addition, you should listen to the Automatic Terminal Information Service (ATIS), Automated Surface Observing System (ASOS), or Automated Weather Observing System (AWOS), if available, and then monitor the tower frequency or the Common Traffic Advisory Frequency (CTAF) to get a good idea of what traffic conditions to expect. Checklists should be performed well in advance so there is time to focus on traffic and ATC instructions. These procedures are especially important prior to entering a high-density traffic area, such as Class B airspace.

To manage workload, items should be prioritized. For example, during any situation, and especially in an emergency, you should remember the phrase "aviate, navigate, and communicate." This means that the first thing you should do is make sure the glider is under control. Then begin flying to an acceptable landing area. Only after the first two items are assured, should you try to communicate with anyone.

Another important part of managing workload is recognizing a work overload situation. The first effect of high workload is that you begin to work faster. As workload increases, attention cannot be devoted to several tasks at one time, and you may begin to focus on one item. When you become task saturated, there is no awareness of inputs from various sources, so decisions may be made on incomplete information, and the possibility of error increases.

Accidents often occur when flying task requirements exceed pilot capabilities. The difference between these two factors is called the margin of safety. Note that in this example, the margin of safety is minimal during the approach and landing. At this point, an emergency or distraction could overtax pilot capabilities, causing an accident. [Figure 1-10]

When becoming overloaded, you should stop, think, slow down, and prioritize. It is important that you understand options that may be available to decrease workload.

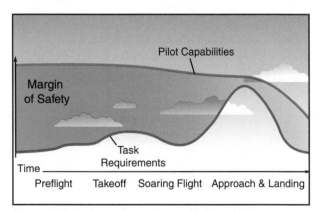

Figure 1-10. Task requirements vs. pilot capabilities.

SITUATIONAL AWARENESS

Situational awareness is the accurate perception of the operational and environmental factors that affect the aircraft, pilot, and passengers during a specific period of time. Maintaining situational awareness requires an understanding of the relative significance of these factors and their future impact on the flight. When situationally aware, you have an overview of the total operation and are not fixated on one perceived significant factor. Some of the elements inside the aircraft to be considered are the status of aircraft systems, you as the pilot, and passengers. In addition, an awareness of the environmental conditions of the flight, such as spatial orientation of the glider, and its relationship to terrain, traffic, weather, and airspace must be maintained.

To maintain situational awareness, all of the skills involved in aeronautical decision making are used. For example, an accurate perception of your fitness can be achieved through self-assessment and recognition of hazardous attitudes. A clear assessment of the status of navigation equipment can be obtained through workload management, and establishing a productive relationship with ATC can be accomplished by effective resource use.

OBSTACLES TO MAINTAINING SITUATIONAL AWARENESS

Fatigue, stress, and work overload can cause you to fixate on a single perceived important item rather than maintaining an overall awareness of the flight situation. A contributing factor in many accidents is a distraction that diverts the pilot's attention from monitoring the instruments or scanning outside the aircraft. Many cockpit distractions begin as a minor problem, such as a gauge that is not reading correctly, but result in accidents as the pilot diverts attention to the perceived problem and neglects to properly control the aircraft.

Complacency presents another obstacle to maintaining situational awareness. When activities become routine, you may have a tendency to relax and not put as much effort into performance. Like fatigue, complacency reduces your effectiveness in the cockpit. However, complacency is harder to recognize than fatigue, since everything is perceived to be progressing smoothly. For example, you have been flying multiple glider rides out of an uncontrolled airport. The wind has been calm, and you have been using the same runway all day. Without thinking, you enter downwind without taking the wind direction into account. As you make your turn to final, you realize that your groundspeed is extremely fast. You overshoot the runway and collide with a fence, causing extensive damage to the glider and injuring your passenger.

OPERATIONAL PITFALLS

There are a number of classic behavioral traps into which pilots have been known to fall. Pilots, particularly those with considerable experience, as a rule, always try to complete a flight as planned, please passengers, and meet schedules. The basic drive to meet or exceed goals can have an adverse effect on safety, and can impose an unrealistic assessment of piloting skills under stressful conditions. These tendencies ultimately may bring about practices that are dangerous and often illegal, and may lead to a mishap. You will develop awareness and learn to avoid many of these operational pitfalls through effective ADM training. [Figure 1-11]

OPERATIONAL PITFALLS

Peer Pressure—Poor decision making may be based upon an emotional response to peers, rather than an objective evaluation of a situation.

Mind Set—A pilot displays mind set through an inability to recognize and cope with changes in a given situation.

Get-There-Itis—This disposition impairs pilot judgment through a fixation on the original goal or destination, combined with a disregard for any alternative course of action.

Scud Running—This occurs when a pilot tries to maintain visual contact with the terrain at low altitudes while instrument conditions exist.

Continuing VFR into Instrument Conditions—Spatial disorientation or collision with ground/obstacles may occur when a pilot continues VFR into instrument conditions. This can be even more dangerous if the pilot is not instrument-rated or current.

Getting Behind the Aircraft—This pitfall can be caused by allowing events or the situation to control pilot actions. A constant state of surprise at what happens next may be exhibited when the pilot is getting behind the aircraft.

Loss of Positional or Situational Awareness—In extreme cases, when a pilot gets behind the aircraft, a loss of positional or situational awareness may result. The pilot may not know the aircraft's geographical location, or may be unable to recognize deteriorating circumstances.

Flying Outside the Envelope—The assumed high performance capability of a particular aircraft may cause a mistaken belief that it can meet the demands imposed by a pilot's overestimated flying skills.

Neglect of Flight Planning, Preflight Inspections, and Checklists—A pilot may rely on short- and long-term memory, regular flying skills, and familiar routes instead of established procedures and published checklists. This can be particularly true of experienced pilots.

Figure 1-11. All experienced pilots have fallen prey to, or have been tempted by, one or more of these tendencies in their flying careers.

Medical Factors Associated with Glider Flying

A number of physiological effects can be linked to flying. Some are minor, while others are important enough to require special attention to ensure safety of flight. In some cases, physiological factors can lead to in-flight emergencies. Some important medical factors that you should be aware of as a glider pilot include hypoxia, hyperventilation, middle ear and sinus problems, spatial disorientation, motion sickness, carbon monoxide poisoning, stress and fatigue, dehydration, and heatstroke. Other subjects include the effects of alcohol and drugs, and excess nitrogen in the blood after scuba diving.

HYPOXIA

Hypoxia occurs when the tissues in the body do not receive enough oxygen. The symptoms of hypoxia vary with the individual. Hypoxia can be caused by several factors, including an insufficient supply of oxygen, inadequate transportation of oxygen, or the inability of the body tissues to use oxygen. The forms of hypoxia are divided into four major groups based on their causes; hypoxic hypoxia, hypemic hypoxia, stagnant hypoxia, and histotoxic hypoxia.

HYPOXIC HYPOXIA

Although the percentage of oxygen in the atmosphere is constant, its partial pressure decreases proportionately as atmospheric pressure decreases. As you ascend during flight, the percentage of each gas in the atmosphere remains the same, but there are fewer molecules available at the pressure required for them to pass between the membranes in your respiratory system. This decrease of oxygen molecules at sufficient pressure can lead to hypoxic hypoxia.

HYPEMIC HYPOXIA

When your blood is not able to carry a sufficient amount of oxygen to the cells in your body, a condition called hypemic hypoxia occurs. This type of hypoxia is a result of a deficiency in the blood, rather than a lack of inhaled oxygen, and can be caused by a variety of factors. For example, if you have anemia, or a reduced number of healthy functioning blood cells for any reason, your blood has a decreased capacity for carrying oxygen. In addition, any factor that interferes or displaces oxygen that is attached to the blood's hemoglobin can cause hypemic hypoxia. The most common form of hypemic hypoxia is carbon monoxide poisoning, which is discussed later. Hypemic hypoxia also can be caused by the loss of blood that occurs during a blood donation. Your blood can take several weeks to return to normal following a donation. Although the effects of the blood loss are slight at ground level, there are risks when flying during this time.

STAGNANT HYPOXIA

Stagnant hypoxia is an oxygen deficiency in the body due to the poor circulation of the blood. Several different situations can lead to stagnant hypoxia, such as shock, the heart failing to pump blood effectively, or a constricted artery. During flight, stagnant hypoxia can be the result of pulling excessive positive Gs. Cold temperatures also can reduce circulation and decrease the blood supplied to extremities.

HISTOTOXIC HYPOXIA

The inability of the cells to effectively use oxygen is defined as histotoxic hypoxia. The oxygen may be inhaled and reach the cell in adequate amounts, but the cell is unable to accept the oxygen once it is there. This impairment of cellular respiration can be caused by alcohol and other drugs, such as narcotics and poisons. Research has shown that drinking one ounce of alcohol can equate to about an additional 2,000 feet of physiological altitude.

High-altitude flying, which glider pilots encounter when mountain wave soaring or thermal soaring at high elevations, can place you in danger of becoming hypoxic. Oxygen starvation causes the brain and other vital organs to become impaired. One particularly noteworthy attribute of the onset of hypoxia is the fact that the first symptoms are euphoria and a carefree feeling. With increased oxygen starvation, your extremities become less responsive, and your flying becomes less coordinated. The following are common symptoms of hypoxia.

- Headache
- Decreased Reaction Time
- Impaired Judgment
- Euphoria
- Visual Impairment
- Drowsiness
- Lightheaded or Dizzy Sensation
- Tingling in Fingers and Toes
- Numbness
- Blue Fingernails and Lips (Cyanosis)
- Limp Muscles

As hypoxia worsens, your field of vision begins to narrow, and instruments can start to look fuzzy. Even with all these symptoms, the intoxicating effects of hypoxia can cause you to have a false sense of security and deceive you into believing you are flying as well as ever. The treatment for hypoxia includes flying at lower altitudes and/or using supplemental oxygen.

All pilots are susceptible to the effects of oxygen starvation, regardless of your physical endurance or acclimatization. When flying at high altitudes, it is paramount that you carry aviator's breathing oxygen in your glider and have it readily accessible. The term "time of useful consciousness" is used to describe the maximum time you have to make rational, life-saving decisions and carry them out at a given altitude without supplemental oxygen. As altitude increases above 10,000 feet, the symptoms of hypoxia increase in severity, while the time of useful consciousness rapidly decreases. [Figure 1-12]

Altitude	Time of Useful Consciousness
45,000 ft. MSL	9 to 15 seconds
40,000 ft. MSL	15 to 20 seconds
35,000 ft. MSL	30 to 60 seconds
30,000 ft. MSL	1 to 2 minutes
28,000 ft. MSL	2 1/2 to 3 minutes
25,000 ft. MSL	3 to 5 minutes
22,000 ft. MSL	5 to 10 minutes
20,000 ft. MSL	30 minutes or more

Figure1-12. This illustration shows the symptoms of hypoxia and time of useful consciousness as altitude increases.

Since symptoms of hypoxia vary in an individual, the ability to recognize hypoxia can be greatly improved by experiencing and witnessing the effects of it during an altitude chamber "flight." The FAA provides this opportunity through aviation physiology training, which is conducted at the FAA Civil Aerospace Medical Institute (CAMI) and at many military facilities across the United States. To attend the Physiological Training Program at CAMI telephone (405) 954-6212 or write:

FAA/AAM-400
Aerospace Medical Education Division
P.O. Box 25082
Oklahoma City, OK 73125

HYPERVENTILATION

Hyperventilation occurs when you are experiencing emotional stress, fright, or pain, and your breathing rate and depth increase although the carbon dioxide is already at a reduced level in the blood. The result is an excessive loss of carbon dioxide from your body, which can lead to unconsciousness due to the respiratory system's overriding mechanism to regain control of breathing.

Glider pilots encountering extreme, unexpected turbulence, or strong areas of sink over rough terrain or water, may unconsciously increase their breathing rate. If you are flying at higher altitudes, either with or without oxygen, you may have a tendency to breathe more rapidly than normal, which often leads to hyperventilation.

Since many of the symptoms of hyperventilation are similar to those of hypoxia, it is important to correctly diagnose and treat the proper condition. If you are using supplemental oxygen, check the equipment and flow rate to ensure you are not suffering from hypoxia. The following are common symptoms of hyperventilation.

- Headache
- Decreased Reaction Time
- Impaired Judgment
- Euphoria
- Visual Impairment
- Drowsiness
- Lightheaded or Dizzy Sensation
- Tingling in Fingers and Toes
- Numbness
- Pale, Clammy Appearance
- Muscle Spasms

Hyperventilation may produce a pale, clammy appearance and muscle spasms compared to the cyanosis and limp muscles associated with hypoxia. The treatment for hyperventilation involves restoring the proper carbon dioxide level in the body. Breathing normally is both the best prevention and the best cure for hyperventilation. In addition to slowing the breathing rate, you also can breathe into a paper bag or talk aloud to overcome hyperventilation. Recovery is usually rapid once the breathing rate is returned to normal.

MIDDLE EAR AND SINUS PROBLEMS

Since gliders are not pressurized, pressure changes affect glider pilots flying to high altitudes. Inner ear pain and a temporary reduction in your ability to hear is caused by the ascents and descents of the glider. The physiological explanation for this discomfort is a difference between the pressure of the air outside your body and that of the air inside your middle ear. The middle ear cavity is a small cavity located in the bone of the skull. While the external ear canal is always at the same pressure as the outside air, the pressure in the middle ear often changes more slowly. Even a slight difference between external pressure and middle ear pressure can cause discomfort.

During a climb, as the glider ascends, middle ear air pressure may exceed the pressure of the air in the external ear canal, causing the eardrum to bulge outward. You become aware of this pressure change when you experience alternate sensations of "fullness" and "clearing." During descent, the reverse happens. While the pressure of the air in the external ear canal increases, the middle ear cavity, which equalized with the lower pressure at altitude, is at lower pressure than the external ear canal. This results in the higher outside pressure, causing the eardrum to bulge inward.

This condition can be more difficult to relieve due to the fact that air must be introduced into the middle ear through the eustachian tube to equalize the pressure. The fact that the inner ear is a partial vacuum tends to constrict the walls of the eustachian tube. To remedy this often painful condition, which causes temporary reduction in hearing sensitivity, pinch your nostrils shut, close your mouth and lips, and blow slowly and gently in the mouth and nose.

This procedure, which is called the Valsalva maneuver, forces air up the eustachian tube into the middle ear. If you have a cold, an ear infection, or sore throat, you may not be able to equalize the pressure in your ears. A flight in this condition can be extremely painful, as well as damaging to your eardrums. If you are experiencing minor congestion, nose drops or nasal sprays may reduce the chance of a painful ear blockage. Before you use any medication, check with an aviation medical examiner to ensure that it will not affect your ability to fly.

During ascent and descent, air pressure in the sinuses equalizes with the pressure in the cockpit through small openings that connect the sinuses to the nasal passages. Either an upper respiratory infection, such as a cold or sinusitis, or a nasal allergic condition can produce enough congestion around an opening to slow equalization and, as the difference in pressure between the sinus and the cockpit mounts, eventually plug the opening. This "sinus block" occurs most frequently during descent. Slow descent rates can reduce the associated pain. A sinus block can occur in the frontal sinuses, located above each eyebrow, or in the maxillary sinuses, located in each upper cheek. It will usually produce excruciating pain over the sinus area. A maxillary sinus block can also make the upper teeth ache. Bloody mucus may discharge from the nasal passages.

You can prevent a sinus block by not flying with an upper respiratory infection or nasal allergic condition. Adequate protection is usually not provided by decongestant sprays or drops to reduce congestion around the sinus openings. Oral decongestants have side effects that can impair pilot performance. If a sinus block does not clear shortly after landing, a physician should be consulted.

SPATIAL DISORIENTATION

Spatial disorientation specifically refers to the lack of orientation with regard to position in space and to other objects. Orientation is maintained through the body's sensory organs in three areas: visual, vestibular, and postural. The eyes maintain visual orientation; the motion sensing system in the inner ear maintains vestibular orientation; and the nerves in the skin, joints, and muscles of the body maintain postural orientation.

During flight in **visual meteorological conditions (VMC)**, the eyes are the major orientation source and usually prevail over false sensations from other sensory systems. When these visual cues are taken away, as they are in **instrument meteorological conditions (IMC)**, false sensations can cause the pilot to quickly become disoriented.

The vestibular system in the inner ear allows you to sense movement and determine your orientation in the surrounding environment. In both the left and right inner ear, three semi-circular canals are positioned at approximate right angles to each other. Each canal is filled with fluid and has a section full of fine hairs. Acceleration of the inner ear in any direction causes the tiny hairs to deflect, which in turn stimulates nerve impulses, sending messages to the brain. The vestibular nerve transmits the impulses from the utricle, saccule, and semicircular canals to the brain to interpret motion. [Figure 1-13]

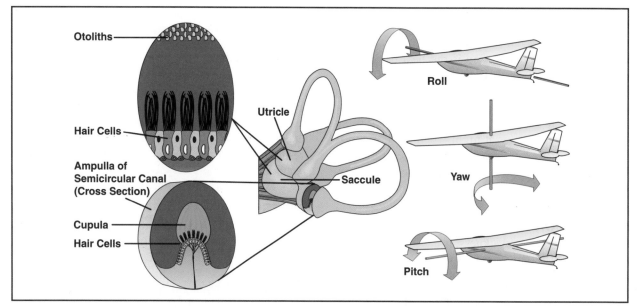

Figure 1-13. The semicircular canals lie in three planes, and sense the motions of roll, pitch, and yaw.

The postural system sends signals from the skin, joints, and muscles to the brain that are interpreted in relation to the Earth's gravitational pull. These signals determine posture. Inputs from each movement update the body's position to the brain on a constant basis. "Seat of the pants" flying is largely dependent upon these signals. Used in conjunction with visual and vestibular clues, these sensations can be fairly reliable. However, because of the forces acting upon the body in certain flight situations, many false sensations can occur due to acceleration forces overpowering gravity.

Under normal flight conditions, when you have reference to the horizon and ground, these sensitive hairs allow you to identify the pitch, roll, and yaw movement of the glider. When you become disoriented and lose visual reference to the horizon and ground, the sensory system in your inner ear is no longer reliable. Lacking visual reference to the ground, your vestibular system may lead you to believe you are in level flight, when, in reality, you are in a turn. As the airspeed increases, you may experience a postural sensation of a level dive and pull back on the stick. This increased back-pressure on the control stick tightens the turn and creates ever-increasing g-loads. If recovery is not initiated, a steep spiral will develop. This is sometimes called the graveyard spiral, because if the pilot fails to recognize that the aircraft is in a spiral and fails to return the aircraft to wings-level flight, the aircraft will eventually strike the ground. If the horizon becomes visible again, you will have an opportunity to return the glider to straight-and-level flight. Continued visual contact with the horizon will allow you to maintain straight-and-level flight. However, if you lose contact with the horizon again, your inner ear may fool you into thinking you have started a bank in the other direction, causing the graveyard spiral to begin all over again.

For glider pilots, prevention is the best remedy for spatial disorientation. If the glider you are flying is not equipped for instrument flight, and you do not have many hours of training in controlling the glider by reference to instruments, you should avoid flight in reduced visibility or at night when the horizon is not visible. You can reduce your susceptibility to disorienting illusions through training and awareness, and learning to rely totally on your flight instruments.

MOTION SICKNESS

Motion sickness, or airsickness, is caused by the brain receiving conflicting messages about the state of the body. You may experience motion sickness during initial flights, but it generally goes away within the first 10 lessons. Anxiety and stress, which you may feel as you begin flight training, can contribute to motion sickness. Symptoms of motion sickness include general discomfort, nausea, dizziness, paleness, sweating, and vomiting.

It is important to remember that experiencing air sickness is no reflection on your ability as a pilot. Let your flight instructor know if you are prone to motion sickness since there are techniques that can be used to overcome this problem. For example, you may want to avoid lessons in turbulent conditions until you are more comfortable in the glider, or start with shorter flights and graduate to longer instruction periods. If you experience symptoms of motion sickness during a lesson, you can alleviate some of the discomfort by opening fresh air vents or by focusing on objects outside the glider. Although medication like Dramamine can prevent airsickness in passengers, it is not recommended while you are flying since it can cause drowsiness.

CARBON MONOXIDE POISONING

One factor that can affect your vision and consciousness in flight and poses a danger to self-launch glider pilots is carbon monoxide poisoning. Since it attaches itself to the hemoglobin about 200 times more easily than does oxygen, carbon monoxide (CO) prevents the hemoglobin from carrying oxygen to the cells. It can take up to 48 hours for the body to dispose of carbon monoxide. If the poisoning is severe enough, it can result in death. Carbon monoxide, produced by all internal combustion engines, is colorless and odorless. Aircraft heater vents and defrost vents may provide carbon monoxide a passageway into the cabin, particularly if the engine exhaust system is leaky or damaged. If you detect a strong odor of exhaust gases, you can assume that carbon monoxide is present. However, carbon monoxide may be present in dangerous amounts even if you cannot detect exhaust odor. Disposable, inexpensive carbon monoxide detectors are widely available. In the presence of carbon monoxide, these detectors change color to alert you to the presence of carbon monoxide. Some effects of carbon monoxide poisoning include headache, blurred vision, dizziness, drowsiness, and/or loss of muscle power. Anytime you smell exhaust odor, or any time you experience these symptoms, immediate corrective actions should be taken. These include turning off the heater, opening fresh air vents, windows and using supplemental oxygen, if available.

STRESS

Stress can be defined as the body's response to physical and psychological demands placed upon it. Reactions of your body to stress include the release of chemical hormones (such as adrenaline) into the blood and the speeding of the metabolism to provide energy to the muscles. In addition, blood sugar, heart rate, respiration, blood pressure, and perspiration all increase. The term stressor is used to describe an element that causes you to experience stress.

Stress falls into two categories: acute stress (short-term) and chronic stress (long-term). Acute stress involves an immediate threat that is perceived as danger. This is the type of stress that often involves a "fight or flight" response in an individual, whether the threat is real or imagined. Stressors are categorized on page 1-7 within the stress management discussion. Examples include noise (physical stress), fatigue (physiological stress), and difficult work or personal situations (psychological stress). Normally, a healthy person can cope with acute stress and prevent stress overload. However, on-going acute stress can develop into chronic stress.

Chronic stress can be defined as a level of stress that presents an intolerable burden, exceeds the ability of an individual to cope, and causes performance to fall sharply. Unrelenting psychological pressures such as loneliness, financial worries, and relationship or work problems, can produce a cumulative level of stress that exceeds a person's ability to cope with the situation. When stress reaches these levels, performance falls off rapidly. Pilots experiencing this level of stress are not safe and should not exercise their airman privileges. The stress management discussion on page 1-7 contains several recommendations for coping with stress. If you suspect you are suffering from chronic stress, consult your doctor.

FATIGUE
Fatigue is frequently associated with pilot error. Some of the effects of fatigue include degradation of attention and concentration, impaired coordination, and decreased ability to communicate. These factors can seriously influence your ability to make effective decisions. Physical fatigue can result from sleep loss, exercise, or physical work. Factors, such as stress and prolonged performance of cognitive work, can result in mental fatigue.

Fatigue falls into two broad categories; acute fatigue (short-term) and chronic fatigue (long-term). Acute fatigue is short-lived and is a normal occurrence in everyday living. It is the kind of tiredness people feel after a period of strenuous effort, excitement, or lack of sleep. Rest after exertion and eight hours of sound sleep ordinarily cures this condition.

A special type of acute fatigue, skill fatigue has two main effects on performance:

- Timing disruption—You appear to perform a task as usual, but the timing of each component is slightly off. This makes the pattern of the operation less smooth, because you perform each component as though it were separate, instead of part of an integrated activity.

- Disruption of the perceptual field—You concentrate your attention upon movements or objects in the center of your vision and neglect those in the periphery. This may be accompanied by loss of accuracy and smoothness in control movements.

Acute fatigue has many causes, but the following are among the most important for the pilot.

- Mild hypoxia (oxygen deficiency)
- Physical stress
- Psychological stress
- Depletion of physical energy resulting from psychological stress

Acute fatigue can be prevented by a proper diet and adequate rest and sleep. A well-balanced diet prevents the body from having to consume its own tissues as an energy source. Adequate rest maintains the body's store of vital energy.

Sustained psychological stress accelerates the glandular secretions that prepare the body for quick reactions during an emergency. These secretions make the circulatory and respiratory systems work harder, and the liver releases energy to provide the extra fuel needed for brain and muscle work. When this reserve energy supply is depleted, the body lapses into chronic fatigue.

Chronic fatigue, extending over a long period of time, usually has psychological roots, although an underlying disease is sometimes responsible. Continuous high stress levels, for example, can produce chronic fatigue. Chronic fatigue is not relieved by proper diet and adequate rest and sleep, and usually requires treatment from your doctor. You may experience this condition in the form of weakness, tiredness, palpitations of the heart, breathlessness, headaches, or irritability. Sometimes chronic fatigue even creates stomach or intestinal problems and generalized aches and pains throughout the body. When the condition becomes serious enough, it can lead to emotional illness.

If you find yourself suffering from acute fatigue, stay on the ground. If you become fatigued in the cockpit, no amount of training or experience can overcome the detrimental effects. Getting adequate rest is the only way to prevent fatigue from occurring. You should avoid flying when you have not had a full night's rest, when you have been working excessive hours, or have had an especially exhausting or stressful day. If you suspect you are suffering from chronic fatigue, consult your doctor.

DEHYDRATION AND HEATSTROKE
Dehydration is the term given to a critical loss of water from the body. The first noticeable effect of dehydration is fatigue, which in turn makes top physical and

mental performance difficult, if not impossible. As a glider pilot, you often fly for a long period of time in hot summer temperatures or at high altitudes. This makes you particularly susceptible to dehydration for two reasons: the clear canopy offers no protection from the sun and, at high altitude, there are fewer air pollutants to diffuse the sun's rays. The result is that you are continually exposed to heat that your body attempts to regulate by perspiration. If this fluid is not replaced, fatigue progresses to dizziness, weakness, nausea, tingling of hands and feet, abdominal cramps, and extreme thirst.

Heatstroke is a condition caused by any inability of the body to control its temperature. Onset of this condition may be recognized by the symptoms of dehydration, but also has been known to be recognized only by complete collapse. To prevent these symptoms, it is recommended that you carry an ample supply of water and use it at frequent intervals on any long flight, whether you are thirsty or not. Wearing light colored, porous clothing and a hat provides protection from the sun, and keeping the cockpit well ventilated aids in dispelling excess heat.

ALCOHOL

Everyone knows that alcohol impairs the efficiency of the human mechanism. Studies have positively proven that drinking and performance deterioration are closely linked. Pilots must make hundreds of decisions, some of them time-critical, during the course of a flight. The safe outcome of any flight depends on your ability to make the correct decisions and take the appropriate actions during routine occurrences, as well as abnormal situations. The influence of alcohol drastically reduces the chances of completing your flight without incident. Even in small amounts, alcohol can impair your judgement, decrease your sense of responsibility, affect your coordination, constrict your visual field, diminish your memory, reduce your reasoning power, and lower your attention span. As little as one ounce of alcohol can decrease the speed and strength of your muscular reflexes, lessen the efficiency of your eye movements while reading, and increase the frequency at which you commit errors. Impairments in vision and hearing occur at alcohol blood levels as low as .01 percent.

The alcohol consumed in beer and mixed drinks is simply ethyl alcohol, a central nervous system depressant. From a medical point of view, it acts on your body much like a general anesthetic. The "dose" is generally much lower and more slowly consumed in the case of alcohol, but the basic effects on the system are similar. Alcohol is easily and quickly absorbed by the digestive tract. The bloodstream absorbs about 80 to 90 percent of the alcohol in a drink within 30 minutes on an empty stomach. The body requires about three hours to rid itself of all the alcohol contained in *one* mixed drink or *one* beer.

When you have a hangover, you are still under the influence of alcohol. Although you may think that you are functioning normally, the impairment of motor and mental responses still remains. Considerable amounts of alcohol can remain in the body for over 16 hours, so you should be cautious about flying too soon after drinking.

The effect of alcohol is greatly multiplied when a person is exposed to altitude. Two drinks on the ground are equivalent to three or four at altitude. The reason for this is that, chemically, alcohol interferes with the brain's ability to utilize oxygen. The effects are rapid because alcohol passes so quickly into the bloodstream. In addition, the brain is a highly vascular organ that is immediately sensitive to changes in the blood's composition. For a pilot, the lower oxygen availability at altitude, along with the lower capability of the brain to use what oxygen *is* there, adds up to a deadly combination.

Intoxication is determined by the amount of alcohol in the bloodstream. This is usually measured as a percentage by weight in the blood. 14 CFR part 91 requires that your blood alcohol level be less than .04 percent and that eight hours pass between drinking alcohol and piloting an aircraft. If you have a blood alcohol level of .04 percent or greater after eight hours, you cannot fly until your blood alcohol falls below that amount. Even though your blood alcohol may be well below .04 percent, you cannot fly sooner than eight hours after drinking alcohol. Although the regulations are quite specific, it is a good idea to be more conservative than the regulations.

DRUGS

Pilot performance can be seriously degraded by both prescribed and over-the-counter medications, as well as by the medical conditions for which they are taken. Many medications, such as tranquilizers, sedatives, strong pain relievers, and cough-suppressants, have primary effects that may impair judgment, memory, alertness, coordination, vision, and the ability to make calculations. Others, such as antihistamines, blood pressure drugs, muscle relaxants, and agents to control diarrhea and motion sickness, have side effects that may impair the same critical functions. Any medication that depresses the nervous system, such as a sedative, tranquilizer, or antihistamine, can make a pilot much more susceptible to hypoxia.

Pain killers can be grouped into two broad categories: analgesics and anesthetics. Over-the-counter analgesics, such as aspirin and codeine, are drugs that decrease pain. The majority of the drugs that contain acetylsalicylic acid (Aspirin), acetaminophen (Tylenol), and ibuprofen (Advil) have few side effects when taken in the correct dosage. Although some people are allergic to certain analgesics or may suffer from stomach irritation, flying usually is not restricted when taking these drugs. However, flying is almost always precluded while using prescription analgesics, such as Darvon, Percodan, Demerol, and codeine, since these drugs may cause side effects such as mental confusion, dizziness, headaches, nausea, and vision problems.

Anesthetics are drugs that deaden pain or cause a loss of consciousness. These drugs are commonly used for dental and surgical procedures. Most local anesthetics used for minor dental and outpatient procedures wear off within a relatively short period of time. The anesthetic itself may not limit flying so much as the actual procedure and subsequent pain.

Stimulants are drugs that excite the central nervous system and produce an increase in alertness and activity. Amphetamines, caffeine, and nicotine are all forms of stimulants. Common uses of these drugs include appetite suppression, fatigue reduction, and mood elevation. Some of these drugs may cause a stimulant reaction, even though this reaction is not their primary function. In some cases, stimulants can produce anxiety and mood swings, both of which are dangerous when you fly.

Depressants are drugs that reduce the body's functioning in many areas. These drugs lower blood pressure, reduce mental processing, and slow motor and reaction responses. There are several types of drugs that can cause a depressing effect on the body, including tranquilizers, motion sickness medication, some types of stomach medication, decongestants, and antihistamines. The most common depressant is alcohol.

Some drugs, which can neither be classified as stimulants nor depressants, have adverse effects on flying. For example, some forms of antibiotics can produce dangerous side effects, such as balance disorders, hearing loss, nausea, and vomiting. While many antibiotics are safe for use while flying, the infection requiring the antibiotic may prohibit flying. In addition, unless specifically prescribed by a physician, you should not take more than one drug at a time, and you should never mix drugs with alcohol, because the effects are often unpredictable.

The danger of illegal drugs also are well documented. Certain illegal drugs can have hallucinatory effects that occur days or weeks after the drug is taken. Obviously, these drugs have no place in the aviation community.

Federal Aviation Regulations prohibit pilots from performing crewmember duties while using any medication that affects the faculties in any way contrary to safety. The safest rule is not to fly as a crewmember while taking any medication, unless approved to do so by the FAA. If there is any doubt regarding the effects of any medication, consult an Aviation Medical Examiner (AME) before flying.

SCUBA DIVING

The reduction of atmospheric pressure that accompanies flying can produce physical problems for scuba divers. This is because the increased pressure of the water during a dive causes excess nitrogen to be absorbed into the body tissues and bloodstream. When flying, reduced atmospheric pressures at altitude allow this nitrogen to come out of solution in the bloodstream and body tissues at a rapid rate. This rapid outgassing of nitrogen is called the bends and is painful and incapacitating. The bends can be experienced from as low as 8,000 feet mean sea level (MSL), with increasing severity as altitude increases. As noted in the AIM, the minimum recommended time between scuba diving on nondecompression stop dives and flying is 12 hours, while the minimum time recommended between decompression stop diving and flying is 24 hours. [Figure 1-14]

Figure 1-14. Scuba divers must not fly for specific time periods following dives to avoid the bends.

CHAPTER 2
Components and Systems

Although gliders come in an array of shapes and sizes, the basic design features of most gliders are fundamentally the same. All gliders conform to the aerodynamic principles that make flight possible. When air flows over the wings of a glider, the wings produce a force called lift that allows the aircraft to stay aloft. Glider wings are designed to produce maximum lift with minimum drag.

Glider airframes are designed with a fuselage, wings, and empennage or tail section. Self-launch gliders are equipped with an engine that enables them to launch without assistance and return to an airport under engine power if soaring conditions deteriorate.

THE FUSELAGE
The fuselage is the portion of the airframe to which the wings and empennage are attached. The fuselage houses the cockpit and contains the controls for the glider, as well as a seat for each occupant. Glider fuselages can be formed from wood, fabric over steel tubing, aluminum, fiberglass, kevlar or carbon fiber composites, or a combination of these materials. [Figure 2-1]

WINGS AND COMPONENTS
Glider wings incorporate several components, which help the pilot in maintaining the attitude of the glider

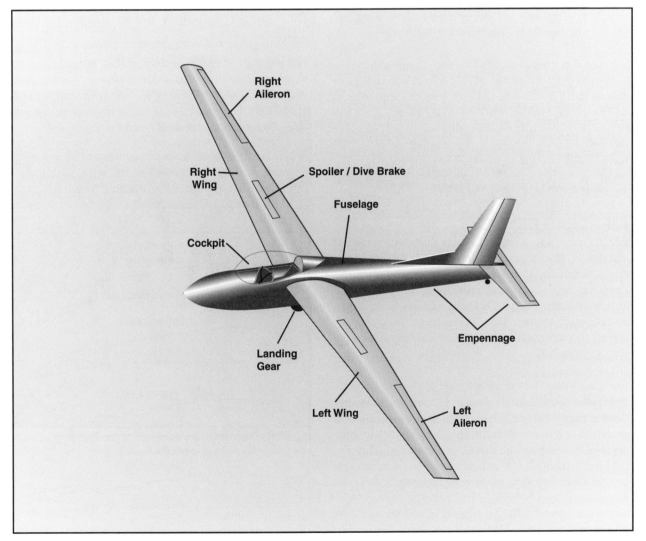

Figure 2-1. Components of a glider.

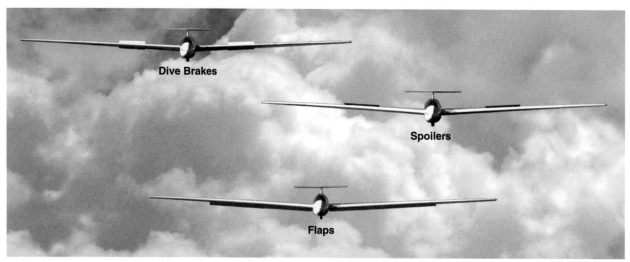

Figure 2-2. Types of lift/drag devices.

and controlling lift and drag. These include **ailerons**, as well as lift and drag devices, such as spoilers, dive brakes, and flaps.

The ailerons control movement around the longitudinal axis. This is known as roll. The ailerons are attached to the outboard tailing edge of each wing and move in the opposite direction from each other.

Moving the control stick to the right causes the right aileron to deflect upward and the left aileron to deflect downward. The upward deflection of the right aileron decreases the camber resulting in decreased lift on the right wing. The corresponding downward deflection of the left aileron increases the camber resulting in increased lift on the left wing. Thus, the increased lift on the left wing and decreased lift on the right wing causes the glider to roll to the right.

LIFT/DRAG DEVICES

Gliders are equipped with devices that modify the lift and drag of the wing. High drag devices include spoilers, dive brakes, and flaps. **Spoilers** extend from the upper surface of the wing interrupting or *spoiling* the airflow over the wings. This action causes the glider to descend more rapidly. Dive brakes extend from both the upper and lower surfaces of the wing and help to increase drag. [Figure 2-2]

Flaps are located on the trailing edge of the wing, inboard of the ailerons, and can be used to increase lift, drag, and descent rate. When the glider is cruising at moderate airspeeds in wings-level flight, the flaps are set to zero degree deflection and are in trail with the wing. When the flap is extended downward, wing camber is increased, and the lift and the drag of the wing increase.

There are several different types of flaps. [Figure 2-3] The plain flap is the simplest of the four types. When deflected downward, it increases the effective camber

and changes the wing's chord line. Both of these factors increase the lifting capacity of the wing. The slotted flap is similar to the plain flap. In addition to changing the wing's camber and chord line, it also allows a portion of the higher pressure air beneath the wing to travel through a slot. This increases the velocity of the airflow over the flap and provides additional lift.

Another type of flap is the Fowler flap. When extended, it moves rearward as well as down. This rearward motion increases the total wing area, as well as the camber and chord line. Negative flap is used at high speeds where wing lift reduction is desired to reduce drag.

When the flaps are extended in an upward direction, or negative setting, the camber of the wing is reduced, resulting in a reduction of lift produced by the wing at a fixed angle of attack and airspeed.

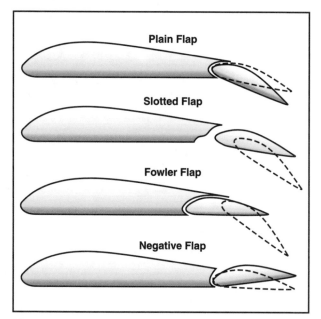

Figure 2-3. The four different types of flaps.

Figure 2-4. The empennage components.

THE EMPENNAGE

The **empennage** includes the entire tail section, consisting of fixed surfaces, such as the horizontal stabilizer and the vertical fin, or stabilizer. These two fixed surfaces act like the feathers on an arrow to steady the glider and help maintain a straight path through the air. The movable surfaces include the elevator and the rudder. [Figure 2-4]

The **elevator** is attached to the back of the horizontal stabilizer. The elevator controls movement around the lateral axis. This is known as pitch. During flight, the elevator is used to move the nose up and down, which controls the pitch attitude of the glider. The trim tab normally located on the elevator of the glider lessens the resistance you feel on the flight controls due to the airflow over the associated control surface.

The **rudder** is attached to the back of the vertical stabilizer. The rudder controls movement about the vertical axis. This is known as yaw. The rudder is used in combination with the ailerons and elevator to coordinate turns during flight.

Some gliders use a **stabilator**, which is a one-piece horizontal stabilizer used in lieu of an elevator. The stabilator pivots up and down on a central hinge point. When you pull back on the control stick, the nose of the glider moves up; when you push forward, the nose moves down. Stabilators sometimes employ an anti-servo trim tab to achieve pitch trim. The anti-servo tab provides a control feel comparable to that of an elevator. [Figure 2-5]

Trim devices reduce pilot workload by relieving the pressure required on the controls to maintain a desired airspeed. One type of trim device found on gliders is called an elevator trim tab. The elevator trim tab is a small, hinged, cockpit-adjustable tab on the trailing edge of the elevator. Other types of elevator trim devices include bungee spring systems and ratchet trim systems. In these systems, fore and aft control stick pressure is applied by an adjustable spring or bungee cord.

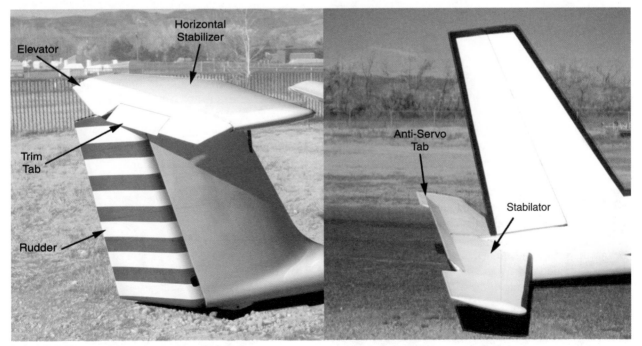

Figure 2-5. Empennage components and trim tabs.

Over the years, the shape of the empennage has seen different forms. Early gliders were most often built with the horizontal stabilizer mounted at the bottom of the vertical stabilizer. This type of tail arrangement is called the **conventional tail**. Other gliders were designed with a **T-tail**, and still others were designed with **V-tail**. T-tail gliders have the horizontal stabilizer mounted on the top of the vertical stabilizer, forming a T. V-tails have two tail surfaces mounted to form a V. V-tails combine elevator and rudder movements.

TOWHOOK DEVICES

An approved towhook is a vital part of glider equipment. The **towhook** is designed for quick release when the pilot applies pressure to the release handle. As a safety feature, if back pressure from either getting out of position during the tow or over running the towrope, the release will automatically open. Part of the glider pilot's preflight is to ensure the towhook releases properly with applied forward and back pressure.

The glider may have a towhook located on or under the nose and/or under the center of gravity (CG), near the main landing gear. The forward towhook is used for aerotow. The CG hook is used for ground launch. If the glider has only a CG hook, it may be approved for aerotow in accordance with the Glider Flight Manual/Pilot's Operating Handbook. [Figure 2-6]

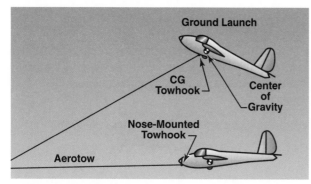

Figure 2-6. Towhook locations.

POWERPLANT

Self-launch gliders are equipped with engines powerful enough to enable them to launch without external assistance. The engines also may be used to sustain flight if the soaring conditions deteriorate. Self-launch gliders differ widely in terms of engine location and type of propeller.

Some are equipped with a fixed, nose-mounted engine and a full feathering propeller. On other types of self-launch gliders, the engine and propeller are located aft of the cockpit. When the engine and propeller are not in use, they are retracted into the fuselage, reducing drag and increasing soaring performance. These types of self-launch engines are usually coupled to a folding propeller, so the entire powerplant can be retracted and the bay doors closed and sealed. [Figure 2-7]

Some gliders are equipped with sustainer engines to assist in remaining aloft long enough to return to an airport. However, sustainer engines do not provide sufficient power to launch the glider from the ground without external assistance. A more detailed explanation of engine operations can be found in Chapter 7—Launch and Recovery Procedures and Flight Maneuvers.

LANDING GEAR

Gliders feature a nose skid or wheel, a swiveling tail wheel, and wheels or protective metal brackets at the wingtips. Gliders designed for high speed and low drag often feature a fully retractable main landing gear and a small break away tail wheel or tail skid. Break away tail skids are found on high performance gliders, and are designed to break off when placed under side loads. [Figure 2-8]

WHEEL BRAKES

The wheel brake, mounted on the main landing gear wheel, helps the glider slow down or stop after touchdown. The type of wheel brake often depends on the design of the glider. Many early gliders relied on friction between the nose skid and the ground to come to a stop. Current models of gliders are fitted with drum brakes, disc brakes, and friction brakes. The most common type of wheel brake found in modern gliders is the disc brake, which is very similar to the disc brake on the front wheels of most cars. Most glider disc brakes are hydraulically operated to provide maximum braking capability. Wheel brake controls vary from one glider type to another.

Figure 2-7. Self-launch gliders are different in performance, as well as appearance.

Figure 2-8. Some gliders have fixed main wheels, others have retractable main wheels. Nose skids, or nose wheels, tail wheels and wing tip wheels are found on many gliders.

CHAPTER 3
Aerodynamics of Flight

To understand what makes a glider fly, you need to have an understanding of aerodynamics. This chapter discusses the fundamentals of the aerodynamics of flight.

AIRFOIL

Airfoil is the term used for surfaces on a glider that produce lift. Although many different airfoil designs exist, all airfoils produce lift in a similar manner.

Some airfoils are designed with an equal amount of curvature on the top and bottom surface. These are called symmetrical airfoils. Airfoils that have a different curvature on the bottom of the wing when compared to the top surface are asymmetrical.

The term **camber** refers to the curvature of a wing when looking at a cross section. A wing possesses upper camber on its top surface and lower camber on its bottom surface. The term leading edge is used to describe the forward edge of the airfoil. The rear edge of the airfoil is called the trailing edge. The **chord line** is an imaginary straight line drawn from the leading edge to the trailing edge.

Relative wind is created by the motion of an airfoil through the air. Relative wind may be affected by movement of the glider through the air, as well as wind sheer. When a glider is flying through undisturbed air, the relative wind is represented by its forward velocity and is parallel to and opposite of the direction of flight.

ANGLE OF ATTACK

The **angle of attack** is the angle formed between the relative wind and the chord line of the wing. You have direct control over angle of attack. By changing the **pitch attitude** of the glider in flight through the use of the elevator/stabilator, you are changing the angle of attack of the wings. [Figure 3-1]

ANGLE OF INCIDENCE

The wings are usually mounted to the fuselage with the chord line inclined upward at a slight angle. This angle, called the **angle of incidence**, is built into the

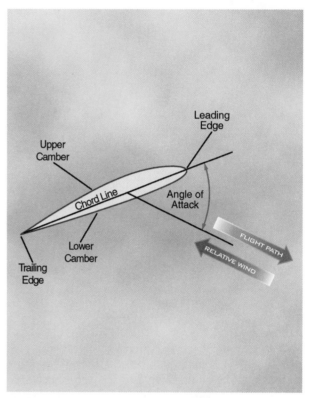

Figure 3-1. Aerodynamic terms of an airfoil.

glider by the manufacturer and cannot be adjusted by the pilot's movements of the controls. It is represented by the angle between the chord line of the wing and the longitudinal axis of the glider.

CENTER OF PRESSURE

The point along the wing chord line where lift is considered to be concentrated is called the **center of pressure**. For this reason, the center of pressure is sometimes referred to as the center of lift. On a typical **asymmetrical airfoil**, this point along the chord line changes position with different flight attitudes. It moves forward as the angle of attack increases and aft as the angle of attack decreases.

FORCES OF FLIGHT

Three forces act on an unpowered glider while in flight—lift, drag, and weight. Thrust is another force of flight that enables self-launch gliders to launch on their own and stay aloft when soaring conditions subside. The theories that explain how these forces work include

Figure 3-2. The forces that act on a glider in flight.

Magnus Effect, Bernoulli's Principle, and Newton's laws of motion. [Figure 3-2]

LIFT

Lift opposes the downward force of weight and is produced by the dynamic effects of the surrounding airstream acting on the wing. Lift acts perpendicular to the flight path through the wing's center of lift. There is a mathematical relationship between lift, angle of attack, airspeed, altitude, and the size of the wing. In the lift equation, these factors correspond to the terms coefficient of lift, velocity, air density, and wing surface area. The relationship is expressed in Figure 3-3.

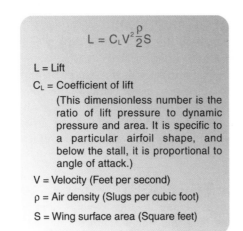

$$L = C_L V^2 \frac{\rho}{2} S$$

L = Lift

C_L = Coefficient of lift

(This dimensionless number is the ratio of lift pressure to dynamic pressure and area. It is specific to a particular airfoil shape, and below the stall, it is proportional to angle of attack.)

V = Velocity (Feet per second)

ρ = Air density (Slugs per cubic foot)

S = Wing surface area (Square feet)

Figure 3-3. The lift equation is mathematically expressed by the above formula.

This shows that for lift to increase, one or more of the factors on the other side of the equation must increase. Lift is proportional to the square of the velocity, or airspeed, therefore, doubling airspeed quadruples the amount of lift if everything else remains the same. Likewise, if other factors remain the same while the coefficient of lift increases, lift also will increase. The coefficient of lift goes up as the angle of attack is increased. As **air density** increases, lift increases. However, you will usually be more concerned with how lift is diminished by reductions in air density on a hot day, or as you climb higher.

MAGNUS EFFECT

The explanation of lift can best be explained by looking at a cylinder rotating in an airstream. The local velocity near the cylinder is composed of the airstream velocity and the cylinder's rotational velocity, which decreases with distance from the cylinder. On a cylinder, which is rotating in such a way that the top surface area is rotating in the same direction as the airflow, the local velocity at the surface is high on top and low on the bottom.

As shown in Figure 3-4, at point "A," a stagnation point exists where the airstream line meets on the surface and then splits; some air goes over and some under. Another stagnation point exists at "B," where the two air streams rejoin and resume at identical velocities. We now have upwash ahead of the rotating cylinder and downwash at the rear.

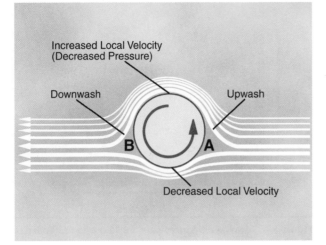

Figure 3-4. Magnus Effect.

The difference in surface velocity accounts for a difference in pressure, with the pressure being lower on the top than the bottom. This low pressure area produces an upward force known as the "Magnus Effect." This mechanically induced circulation illustrates the relationship between circulation and lift.

BERNOULLI'S PRINCIPLE

An airfoil with a positive angle of attack develops air circulation as its sharp trailing edge forces the rear stagnation point to be aft of the trailing edge, while the front stagnation point is below the leading edge. [Figure 3-5]

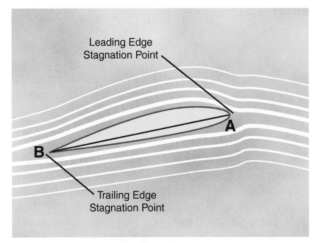

Figure 3-5. Stagnation points on an airfoil.

Air flowing over the top surface accelerates. The airfoil is now subjected to Bernoulli's Principle, or the "venturi effect." As air velocity increases through the constricted portion of a venturi tube, the pressure decreases. Compare the upper surface of an airfoil with the constriction in a venturi tube that is narrower in the middle than at the ends. [Figure 3-6]

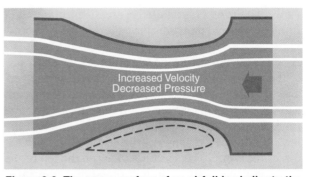

Figure 3-6. The upper surface of an airfoil is similar to the constriction in a venturi tube.

The upper half of the venturi tube can be replaced by layers of undisturbed air. Thus, as air flows over the upper surface of an airfoil, the camber of the airfoil causes an increase in the speed of the airflow. The increased speed of airflow results in a decrease in pressure on the upper surface of the airfoil. At the same time, air flows along the lower surface of the airfoil, building up pressure. The combination of decreased pressure on the upper surface and increased pressure on the lower surface results in an upward force. [Figure 3-7]

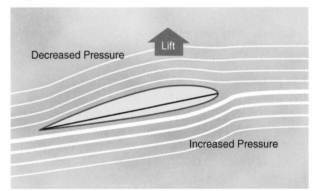

Figure 3-7. Lift is produced when there is decreased pressure above and increased pressure below an airfoil.

As angle of attack is increased, the production of lift is increased. More upwash is created ahead of the airfoil as the leading edge stagnation point moves under the leading edge, and more downwash is created aft of the trailing edge. Total lift now being produced is perpendicular to relative wind. In summary, the production of lift is based upon the airfoil creating circulation in the airstream (Magnus Effect) and creating differential pressure on the airfoil (Bernoulli's Principle).

NEWTON'S THIRD LAW OF MOTION

According to Newton's Third Law of Motion, "for every action there is an equal and opposite reaction." Thus, the air that is deflected downward also produces an upward (lifting) reaction. The wing's construction is designed to take advantage of certain physical laws that generate two actions from the airmass. One is a positive pressure lifting action from the airmass below the wing, and the other is a negative pressure lifting action from the lowered pressure above the wing.

As the airstream strikes the relatively flat lower surface of the wing when inclined at a small angle to its direction of motion, the air is forced to rebound downward, causing an upward reaction in positive lift. At the same time, airstream striking the upper curve section of the leading edge of the wing is deflected upward, over the top of the wing. The speed up of air on the top of the wing produces a sharp drop in pressure. Associated with the lowered pressure is downwash, a downward-backward flow. In other words, a wing shaped to cause an action on the air, and forcing it downward, will provide an equal reaction from the air, forcing the wing upward. If a wing is constructed in such form that it will cause a lift force greater than the weight of the glider, the glider will fly.

If all the required lift was obtained from the deflection of air by the lower surface of the wing, a glider would need only a flat wing like a kite. This, of course, is not the case at all. The balance of the lift needed to support the glider comes from the flow of air above the wing. Herein lies the key to flight. The fact that the most lift is the result of the airflow downwash from above the wing, forcing the wing upward, must be thoroughly understood in order to continue further in the study of flight.

It is neither accurate nor does it serve a useful purpose, however, to assign specific values to the percentage of lift generated by the upper surface of the airfoil versus that generated by the lower surface. These are not constant values, and will vary, not only with flight conditions, but also with different wing designs.

DRAG

The force that resists the movement of the glider through the air is called **drag**. Two different types of drag combine to form total drag—parasite and induced.

PARASITE DRAG

Parasite drag is caused by any aircraft surface, which deflects or interferes with the smooth airflow around the glider. Parasite drag is divided into three types— form drag, interference drag, and skin friction drag. [Figure 3-8]

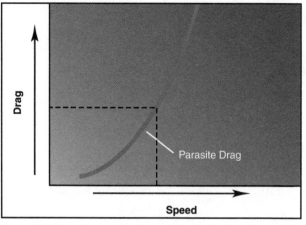

Figure 3-8. Parasite drag increases fourfold when airspeed is doubled.

FORM DRAG

Form drag results from the turbulent wake caused by the separation of airflow from the surface of a structure. The amount of drag is related to both the size and shape of the structure protruding into the relative wind. [Figure 3-9]

INTERFERENCE DRAG

Interference drag occurs when varied currents of air over a glider meet and interact. Placing two objects adjacent to one another may produce turbulence 50 percent to 200 percent greater than the parts tested separately. An example of interference drag is the mixing of air over structures, such as the wing, tail surfaces, and wing struts.

SKIN FRICTION DRAG

Skin friction drag is caused by the roughness of the glider's surfaces. Even though the surfaces may appear smooth, they may be quite rough when viewed under a microscope. This roughness allows a thin layer of air to cling to the surface and create small eddies, which contribute to drag.

INDUCED DRAG

The airflow circulation around the wing generates **induced drag** as it creates lift. The high-pressure air beneath the wing joins the low-pressure air above the wing at the trailing edge of the wingtips. This causes a spiral or vortex that trails behind each wingtip whenever lift is being produced. These wingtip

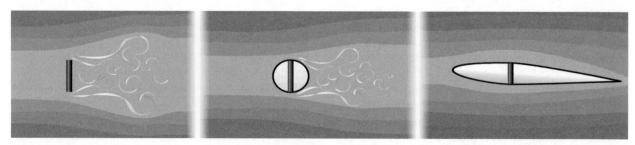

Figure 3-9. Streamlined airfoil designs greatly reduce form drag by reducing the amount of airflow separation.

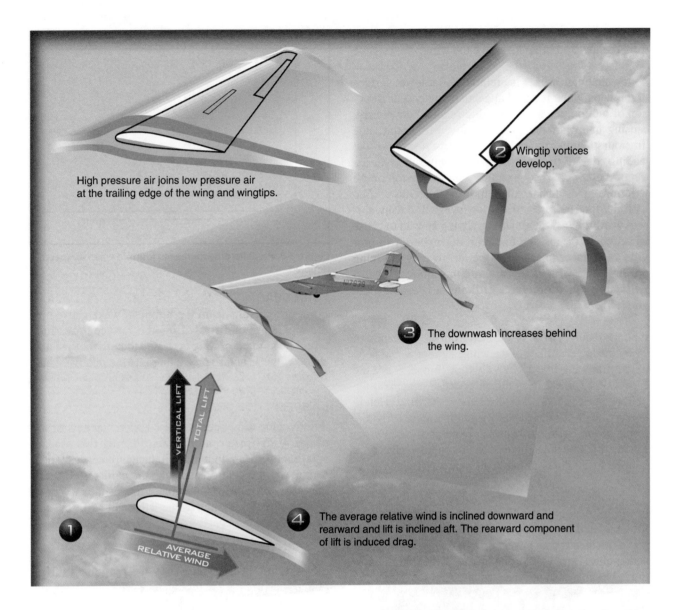

High pressure air joins low pressure air at the trailing edge of the wing and wingtips.

2 Wingtip vortices develop.

3 The downwash increases behind the wing.

VERTICAL LIFT

TOTAL LIFT

1

AVERAGE RELATIVE WIND

4 The average relative wind is inclined downward and rearward and lift is inclined aft. The rearward component of lift is induced drag.

vortices have the effect of deflecting the airstream downward in the vicinity of the wing, creating an increase in downwash. Therefore, the wing operates in an average relative wind, which is deflected downward and rearward near the wing. Because the lift produced by the wing is perpendicular to the relative wind, the lift is inclined aft by the same amount. The component of lift acting in a rearward direction is induced drag. [Figure 3-10]

As the air pressure differential increases with an increase in the angle of attack, stronger vortices form and induced drag is increased. The wings of a glider are at a high angle of attack at low speed and at a low angle of attack at high speed.

TOTAL DRAG

Total drag on a glider is the sum of parasite and induced drag. The total drag curve represents these combined forces and is plotted against airspeed. [Figure 3-11]

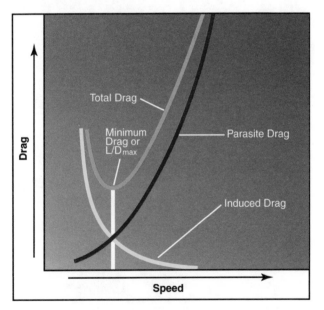

Figure 3-11. The low point on the total drag curve shows the airspeed at which drag is minimized.

L/D_{max} is the point, where lift-to-drag ratio is greatest. At this speed, the total lift capacity of the glider, when compared to the total drag of the glider, is most favorable. In calm air, this is the airspeed you can use to obtain maximum glide distance.

DRAG EQUATION

To help explain the force of drag, the mathematical equation $D=C_DqS$ is used. In this equation drag (D) is the product of drag coefficient (C_D), dynamic pressure (q), and surface area (S). The drag coefficient is the ratio of drag pressure to dynamic pressure. The drag coefficient is represented graphically by Figure 3-12. This graph shows that at higher angles of attack, the drag coefficient is greater than at low angles of attack. At high angles of attack, drag increases significantly with small increases in angle of attack. During a stall, the wing experiences a sizeable increase in drag. [Figure 3-12]

WING PLANFORM

The shape, or planform, of the wings also has an effect on the amount of lift and drag produced. The four most common wing planforms used on gliders are elliptical, rectangular, tapered, and swept-forward wing. [Figure 3-13]

Elliptical wings produce the least amount of induced drag for a given wing area. This design of wing is difficult to manufacture. The elliptical wing is more efficient in terms of L/D, but stall characteristics are not as good as the rectangular wing.

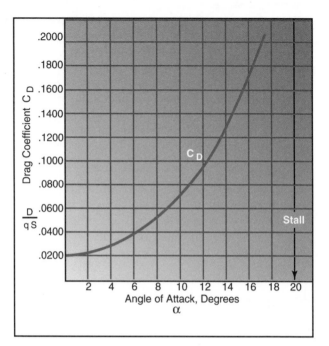

Figure 3-12. This graph shows drag characteristics in terms of angle of attack. As the angle of attack becomes greater, the amount of drag increases.

The rectangular wing is similar in efficiency to the elliptical wing but is much easier to build. Rectangular wings have very gentle stall characteristics with a warning buffet prior to stall and are easier to manufacture than elliptical wings. One drawback to this wing design is that rectangular wings create more induced drag than an elliptical wing of comparable size.

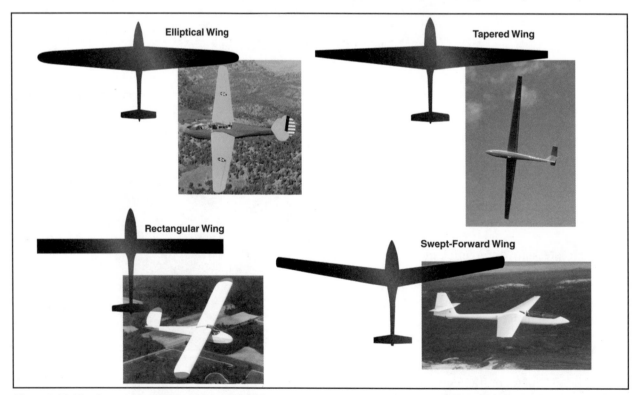

Figure 3-13. Planform refers to the shape of the glider's wing when viewed from above or below. There are advantages and disadvantages to each planform design.

The tapered wing is the planform found most frequently on gliders. Assuming equal wing area, the tapered wing produces less drag than the rectangular wing because there is less area at the tip of the tapered wing. If speed is the prime consideration, a tapered wing is more desirable than a rectangular wing, but a tapered wing with no twist has undesirable stall characteristics.

Swept-forward wings are used to allow for the lifting area of the wing to move forward while keeping the mounting point aft of the cockpit. This wing configuration is used on some tandem two-seat gliders to allow for a small change in center of gravity with the rear seat occupied or while flying solo.

Washout is built into wings by putting a slight twist between the wing root and wing tip. When washout is designed into the wing, the wing displays very good stall characteristics. As you move outward along the span of the wing, the trailing edge moves up in reference to the leading edge. This twist causes the wing root to have a greater angle of attack than the tip, and as a result stall first. This provides ample warning of the impending stall, and at the same time allows continued aileron control.

Dihedral is the angle at which the wings are slanted upward from the root to the tip. The stabilizing effect of dihedral occurs when the airplane sideslips slightly as one wing is forced down in turbulent air. This sideslip results in a difference in the angle of attack between the higher and lower wing with the greatest angle of attack on the lower wing. The increased angle of attack produces increased lift on the lower wing with a tendency to return the airplane to wings level flight.

ASPECT RATIO

The aspect ratio is another factor that affects the lift and drag created by a wing. **Aspect ratio** is determined by dividing the wingspan (from wingtip to wingtip), by the average wing chord. Glider wings have a high aspect ratio as shown in Figure 3-14. High-aspect ratio wings produce a comparably high amount of lift at low angles of attack with less induced drag.

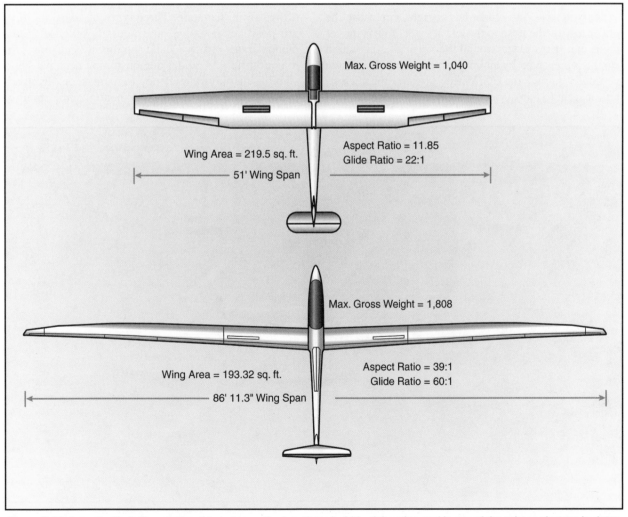

Max. Gross Weight = 1,040

Wing Area = 219.5 sq. ft.

Aspect Ratio = 11.85
Glide Ratio = 22:1

51' Wing Span

Max. Gross Weight = 1,808

Wing Area = 193.32 sq. ft.

Aspect Ratio = 39:1
Glide Ratio = 60:1

86' 11.3" Wing Span

Figure 3-14. Aspect ratio is the relationship between the length and width of the wing and is one of the primary factors in determining lift/drag characteristics.

WEIGHT

Weight is the third force that acts on a glider in flight. **Weight** opposes lift and acts vertically through the center of gravity of the glider. Gravitational pull provides the force necessary to move a glider through the air since a portion of the weight vector of a glider is directed forward.

THRUST

Thrust is the forward force that propels a self-launch glider through the air. Self-launch gliders have engine-driven propellers that provide this thrust. Unpowered gliders have an outside force, such as a tow plane, winch, or automobile to launch the glider.

THREE AXES OF ROTATION

The glider is maneuvered around three axes of rotation. These axes of rotation are the **vertical axis**, the **lateral axis**, and the **longitudinal axis**. They rotate around one central point in the glider called the center of gravity (CG). This point is the center of the glider's total weight and varies with the loading of the glider.

When you move the rudder left or right, you cause the glider to yaw the nose to the left or right. Yaw is movement that takes place around the vertical axis, which can be represented by an imaginary straight line drawn vertically through the CG. When you move the ailerons left or right to bank, you are moving the glider around

the longitudinal axis. This axis would appear if a line were drawn through the center of the fuselage from nose to tail. When you pull the stick back or push it forward, raising or lowering the nose, you are controlling the pitch of the glider or its movement around the lateral axis. The lateral axis could be seen if a line were drawn from one side of the fuselage to the other through the center of gravity. [Figure 3-15]

STABILITY

A glider is in equilibrium when all of its forces are in balance. **Stability** is defined as the glider's ability to maintain a uniform flight condition and return to that condition after being disturbed. Often during flight, gliders encounter equilibrium-changing pitch disturbances. These can occur in the form of vertical gusts, a sudden shift in CG, or deflection of the controls by the pilot. For example, a stable glider would display a tendency to return to equilibrium after encountering a force that causes the nose to pitch up.

Static and dynamic are two types of stability a glider displays in flight. **Static stability** is the initial tendency to return to a state of equilibrium when disturbed from that state. Three types of static stability are positive, negative, and neutral. When a glider demonstrates positive static stability it tends to return to equilibrium. A glider demonstrating negative static stability displays a tendency to increase its displacement. Gliders that demonstrate neutral static stability

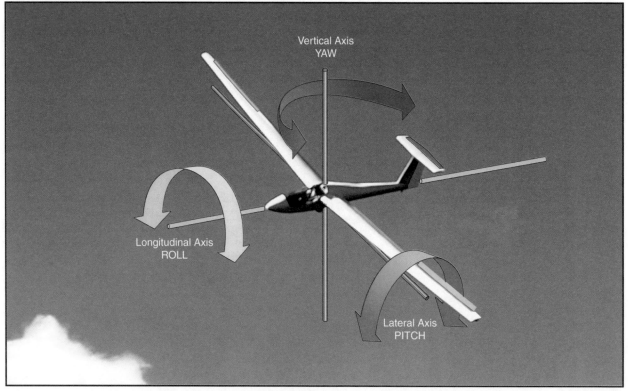

Figure 3-15. The elevator controls pitch movement about the lateral axis, the ailerons control roll movement about the longitudinal axis, and the rudder controls yaw movement about the vertical axis.

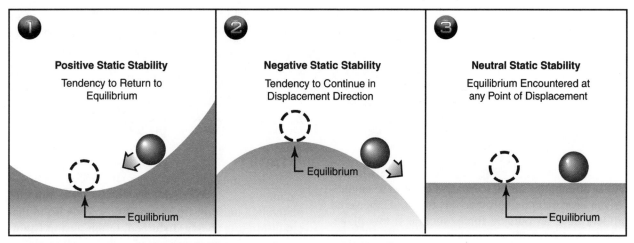

Figure 3-16. The three types of static stability are positive, negative, and neutral.

have neither the tendency to return to equilibrium nor the tendency to continue displacement. [Figure 3-16]

Dynamic stability describes a glider's motion and time required for a response to static stability. In other words, dynamic stability describes the manner in which a glider oscillates when responding to static stability. A glider that displays positive dynamic and static stability will reduce its oscillations with time. A glider demonstrating negative dynamic stability is the opposite situation where its oscillations increase in amplitude with time following a displacement. A glider displaying neutral dynamic stability experiences oscillations, which

remain at the same amplitude without increasing or decreasing over time. Figure 3-17 illustrates the various types of dynamic stability.

Both static and dynamic stability are particularly important for pitch control about the lateral axis. Measurement of stability about this axis is known as longitudinal stability. Gliders are designed to be slightly nose-heavy in order to improve their longitudinal stability. This causes the glider to tend to nose down during normal flight. The horizontal stabilizer on the tail is mounted at a slightly negative angle of attack to offset this tendency. When a dynamically stable

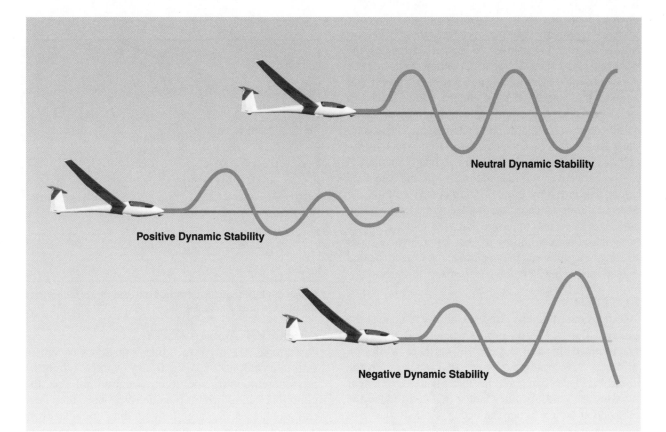

Figure 3-17. The three types of dynamic stability also are referred to as neutral, positive, and negative.

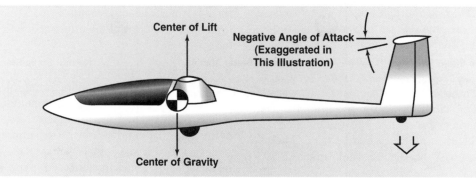

Figure 3-18. The horizontal stabilizer is mounted at a slightly negative angle of attack to offset the glider's natural tendency to enter a dive.

glider oscillates, the amplitude of the oscillations should reduce through each cycle and eventually settle down to a speed at which the downward force on the tail exactly offsets the tendency to dive. [Figure 3-18]

Adjusting the trim assists you in maintaining a desired pitch attitude. A glider with positive static and dynamic longitudinal stability tends to return to the trimmed pitch attitude when the force that displaced it is removed. If a glider displays negative stability, oscillations will increase over time. If uncorrected, negative stability can induce loads exceeding the design limitations of the glider.

Another factor that is critical to the longitudinal stability of a glider is its loading in relation to the center of gravity. The center of gravity of the glider is the point where the total force of gravity is considered to act. When the glider is improperly loaded so it exceeds the aft CG limit it loses longitudinal stability. As airspeed decreases, the nose of a glider rises. To recover, control inputs must be applied to force the nose down to return to a level flight attitude. It is possible that the glider could be loaded so far aft of the approved limits that control inputs are not sufficient to stop the nose from pitching up. If this were the case, the glider could enter a spin from which recovery would be impossible. Loading a glider with the CG too far forward also is hazardous. In extreme cases, the glider may not have enough pitch control to hold the nose up during an approach to a landing. For these reasons, it is important to ensure that your glider is within weight and balance limits prior to each flight. Proper loading of a glider and the importance of CG will be discussed further in Chapter 5–Performance Limitations.

FLUTTER

Another factor that can affect the ability to control the glider is flutter. **Flutter** occurs when rapid vibrations are induced through the control surfaces while the glider is traveling at high speeds. Looseness in the control surfaces can result in flutter while flying near maximum speed. Another factor that can reduce the airspeed at which flutter can occur is a disturbance to the balance of the control surfaces. If vibrations are felt in the control surfaces, reduce the airspeed.

LATERAL STABILITY

Another type of stability that describes the glider's tendency to return to wings-level flight following a displacement is lateral stability. When a glider is rolled into a bank, it has a tendency to sideslip in the direction of the bank. In order to obtain lateral stability, dihedral is designed into the wings. Dihedral increases the stabilizing effects of the wings by increasing the lift differential between the high and low wing during a sideslip. A roll to the left would tend to slip the glider to the left, but since the glider's wings are designed with dihedral, an opposite moment helps to level the wings and stop the slip. [Figure 3-19]

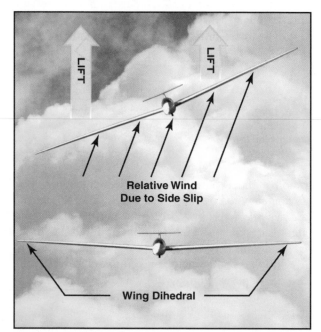

Figure 3-19. Dihedral is designed into the wings to increase the glider's lateral stability.

DIRECTIONAL STABILITY

Directional stability is the glider's tendency to remain stationary about the vertical or yaw axis. When the relative wind is parallel to the longitudinal axis, the glider is in equilibrium. If some force yaws the glider and produces a slip, a glider with directional stability develops a positive yawing moment and returns to equilibrium. In order to accomplish this stability, the vertical tail and the side surfaces of the rear fuselage must counterbalance the side surface area ahead of the center of gravity. The vertical stabilizer is the primary contributor to directional stability and causes a glider in flight to act much like a weather vane. The nose of the glider corresponds to a weather vane's arrowhead, while the vertical stabilizers on the glider act like the tail of the weathervane. When the glider enters a sideslip, the greater surface area behind the CG helps the glider realign with the relative wind. [Figure 3-20]

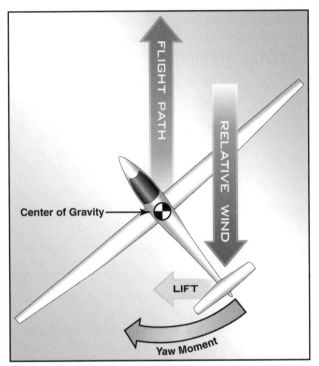

Figure 3-20. During a sideslip, the glider is helped to stay in alignment with the relative wind due to the added surface area behind the CG.

TURNING FLIGHT

Before a glider turns, it must first overcome inertia, or its tendency to continue in a straight line. You create the necessary turning force by using the ailerons to bank the glider so that the direction of total lift is inclined. This is accomplished by dividing the force of lift into two components; one component acts vertically to oppose weight, while the other acts horizontally to oppose centrifical force. The latter is the horizontal component of lift.

To maintain your attitude with the horizon during a turn, you need to increase backpressure on the control stick. The horizontal component of lift creates a force directed inward toward the center of rotation, which is known as centripetal force. This center-seeking force causes the glider to turn. Since centripetal force works against the tendency of the aircraft to continue in a straight line, **inertia** tends to oppose **centripetal force** toward the outside of the turn. This opposing force is known as **centrifugal force**. In reality, centrifugal

force is not a true aerodynamic force; it is an apparent force that results from the effect of inertia during the turn.

If you attempt to improve turn performance by increasing angle of bank while maintaining airspeed, you must pay close attention to glider limitations due to the effects of increasing the load factor. **Load factor** is defined as the ratio of the load supported by the glider's wings to the actual weight of the aircraft and its contents. A glider in stabilized, wings level flight has a load factor of one. Load factor increases rapidly as the angle of bank increases. [Figure 3-21]

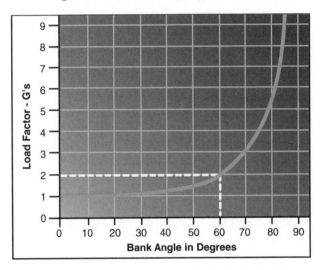

Figure 3-21. The loads placed on a glider increase as the angle of bank increases.

In a turn at constant speed, increasing the angle of attack must occur in order to increase lift. As the bank angle increases, angle of attack must also increase to provide the required lift. The result of increasing the angle of attack will be a stall when the critical angle of attack is exceeded in a turn. [Figure 3-22]

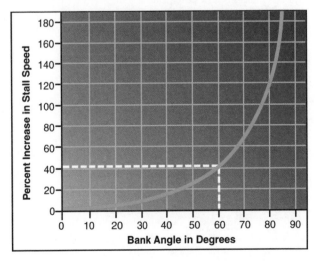

Figure 3-22. A glider's stall speed increases as the bank angle increases. For example, a 60° angle of bank causes a 40 percent increase in the glider's stall speed.

Induced drag also increases as a result of increased lift required to maintain airspeed in the turn. This increased induced drag results in a greater rate of sink during a turn compared to level flight.

RATE OF TURN

Rate of turn refers to the amount of time it takes for a glider to turn a specified number of degrees. If flown at the same airspeed and angle of bank, every glider will turn at the same rate. If airspeed increases and the angle of bank remains the same, the rate of turn will decrease. Conversely, a constant airspeed coupled with an angle of bank increase will result in a faster rate of turn.

RADIUS OF TURN

The amount of horizontal distance an aircraft uses to complete a turn is referred to as the **radius of turn**. The radius of turn at any given bank angle varies directly with the square of the airspeed. Therefore, if the airspeed of the glider were doubled, the radius of the turn would be four times greater. Although the radius of turn is also dependent of a glider's airspeed and angle of bank, the relationship is the opposite of rate of turn. As the glider's airspeed is increased with the angle of bank held constant, the radius of turn increases. On the other hand if the angle of bank increases and the airspeed remains the same, the radius of turn is decreased. [Figure 3-23]

TURN COORDINATION

It is important that rudder and aileron inputs are coordinated during a turn so maximum glider performance can be maintained. If too little rudder is applied or if rudder is applied too late, the result will be a slip. Too much rudder or rudder applied before aileron results in a skid. Both skids and slips swing the fuselage of the glider into the relative wind, creating additional parasite drag, which reduces lift and airspeed. Although this increased drag caused by a slip can be useful during approach to landing to steepen the approach path and counteract a crosswind, it decreases glider performance during other phases of flight.

When you roll into a turn, the aileron on the inside of the turn is raised and the aileron on the outside of the turn is lowered. The lowered aileron on the outside increases the angle of attack and produces more lift for that wing. Since induced drag is a by-product of lift, the outside wing also produces more drag than the inside wing. This causes a yawing tendency toward the outside of the turn called adverse yaw. Coordinated use of rudder and aileron corrects for adverse yaw and aileron drag.

SLIPS

A **slip** is a descent with one wing lowered and the glider's longitudinal axis at an angle to the flight path. It may be used for either two purposes, or both of them combined. A slip may be used to steepen the approach path without increasing the airspeed, as would be the case if a dive were used. It can also be used to make the glider move sideways through the air to counteract the drift, which results from a crosswind.

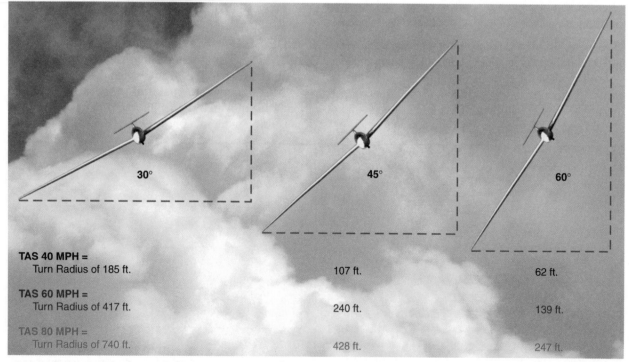

TAS 40 MPH =
  Turn Radius of 185 ft.   107 ft.   62 ft.

TAS 60 MPH =
  Turn Radius of 417 ft.   240 ft.   139 ft.

TAS 80 MPH =
  Turn Radius of 740 ft.   428 ft.   247 ft.

Figure 3-23. The radius of a turn is directly related to airspeed and bank angle.

Formerly, slips were used as a normal means of controlling landing descents to short or obstructed fields, but they are now primarily used in the performance of crosswind and short-field landings. With the installation of wing flaps and effective spoilers on modern gliders, the use of slips to steepen or control the angle of descent is no longer a common procedure. However, the pilot still needs skill in performance of forward slips to correct for possible errors in judgment of the landing approach.

The use of slips has definite limitations. Some pilots may try to lose altitude by violent slipping rather than by smoothly maneuvering and exercising good judgment and using only a slight or moderate slip. In short-field landings, this erratic practice invariably will lead to trouble since enough excess speed may result to prevent touching down anywhere near the proper point, and very often will result in overshooting the entire field.

If a slip is used during the last portion of a final approach, the longitudinal axis of the glider must be aligned with the runway just prior to touchdown so that the glider will touch down headed in the direction in which it is moving over the runway. This requires timely action to discontinue the slip and align the glider's longitudinal axis with its direction of travel over the ground at the instant of touchdown. Failure to accomplish this imposes severe sideloads on the landing gear and imparts violent groundlooping tendencies.

Discontinuing the slip is accomplished by leveling the wings and simultaneously releasing the rudder pressure while readjusting the pitch attitude to the normal glide attitude. If the pressure on the rudder is released abruptly the nose will swing too quickly into line and the glider will tend to acquire excess speed.

Because of the location of the pitot tube and static vents, airspeed indicators in some gliders may have considerable error when the glider is in a slip. The pilot must be aware of this possibility and recognize a properly performed slip by the attitude of the Glider, the sound of the airflow, and the feel of the flight controls.

FORWARD SLIP

The primary purpose of a **forward slip** is to dissipate altitude without increasing the glider's speed, particularly in gliders not equipped with flaps or if the spoilers are inoperative. There are many circumstances requiring the use of forward slips, such as in a landing approach over obstacles and in making short-field landings, when it is always wise to allow an extra margin of altitude for safety in the original estimate of the approach. In the latter case, if the inaccuracy of the approach is confirmed by excess altitude when nearing the boundary of the selected field, slipping can dissipate the excess altitude.

The "forward slip" is a slip in which the glider's direction of motion continues the same as before the slip was begun. [Figure 3-24] If there is any crosswind, the slip will be much more effective if made toward the wind.

Assuming the glider is originally in straight flight, the wing on the side toward which the slip is to be made should be lowered by use of the ailerons. Simultaneously, the airplane's nose must be yawed in the opposite direction by applying opposite rudder so that the glider's longitudinal axis is at an angle to its original flight path. The degree to which the nose is yawed in the opposite direction from the bank should be such that the original ground track is maintained. The nose should also be raised as necessary to prevent the airspeed from increasing.

Forward slips with wing flaps extended should not be done in gliders wherein the manufacturer's operating instructions prohibit such operation.

SIDE SLIP

A **side slip**, as distinguished from a forward slip [Figure 3-24], is one during which the glider's longitudinal axis remains parallel to the original flight path but in which the flight path changes direction according to the steepness of the bank. To perform a

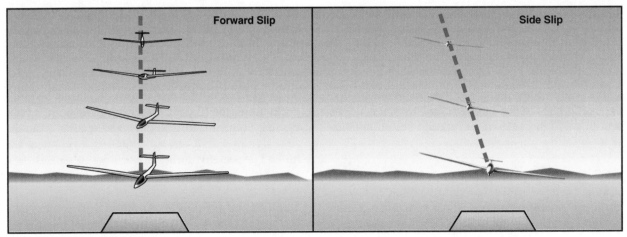

Figure 3-24. Two types of slips.

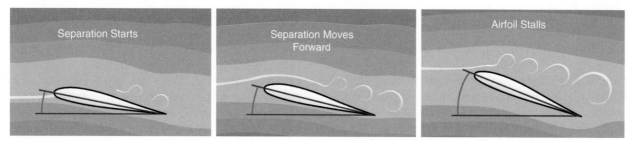

Figure 3-25. Increasing the pitch attitude beyond the critical angle of attack or C_{Lmax} causes progressive disruption of the airflow from the upper surface of the wing. At first the airflow begins to separate at the trailing edge. As the angle of attack is further increased, the airflow separation progresses forward until the wing is fully stalled.

sideslip, the upwind wing is lowered and simultaneously the opposite rudder is applied to maintain the landing area alignment. The sideslip is important in counteracting wind drift during crosswind landings and is discussed in a later chapter.

STALLS

It is important to remember that a **stall** can occur at any airspeed and at any flight attitude. A stall will occur when the **critical angle of attack** is exceeded. [Figure 3-25] The stall speed of a glider can be affected by many factors including weight, load factor due to maneuvering, and environmental conditions. As the weight of the glider increases, a higher angle of attack is required to maintain the same airspeed since some of the lift is sacrificed to support the increase in weight. This is why a heavily loaded glider will stall at a higher airspeed than it will when lightly loaded. The manner in which this weight is distributed also affects stall speed. For example, a forward CG creates a situation that requires the tail to produce a greater downforce to balance the aircraft. The result of this configuration requires the wings to produce more lift than if the CG were located further aft. Therefore, a more forward CG also increases stall speed.

Environmental factors also can affect stall speed. Snow, ice, or frost accumulation on the wing's surface can increase the weight of the wing in addition to changing the shape and disrupting the airflow, all of which will increase stall speed. Turbulence is another environmental factor that can affect a glider's stall speed. The unpredictable nature of turbulence can cause a glider to stall suddenly and abruptly at a higher airspeed than it would in stable conditions. The reason turbulence has such a strong impact on the stall speed of a glider is that the vertical gusts change the direction of the relative wind and abruptly increase the angle of attack. During landing in gusty conditions, it is important that you increase your airspeed in order to maintain a wide margin above stall.

SPINS

A **spin** can be defined as an aggravated stall that results in the glider descending in a helical, or corkscrew, path. A spin is a complex, uncoordinated flight maneuver in which the wings are unequally stalled. Upon entering a

spin, the wing that is more completely stalled will drop before the other, and the nose of the aircraft will yaw in the direction of the low wing.

The cause of a spin is exceeding the critical angle of attack while performing an uncoordinated maneuver. The lack of coordination is normally caused by either too much or not enough rudder control for the amount of aileron being used. If the stall recovery is not promptly initiated, the glider is likely to enter a full stall that may develop into a spin. Spins that occur as the result of uncoordinated flight usually rotate in the direction of the rudder being applied, regardless of the raised wing. When you enter a slipping turn, holding opposite aileron and rudder, the resultant spin usually occurs in the opposite direction of the aileron already applied. In a skidding turn where both aileron and rudder are applied in the same direction, rotation will also be in the direction of rudder application.

Spins are normally placed in three categories as shown in Figure 3-26. The most common is the upright, or erect, spin, which is characterized by a slightly nose down rolling and yawing motion in the same direction. An inverted spin involves the aircraft spinning upside down with the yaw and roll occurring in opposite directions. A third type of spin, the flat spin, is the most hazardous of all spins. In a flat spin, the glider yaws around the vertical axis at a pitch attitude nearly level with the horizon. A flat spin often has a very high rate of rotation; the recovery is difficult, and sometimes impossible. If your glider is properly loaded within its CG limits, entry into a flat spin should not occur.

Since spins normally occur when a glider is flown in an uncoordinated manner at lower airspeeds, coordinated use of the flight controls is important. It is critical that you learn to recognize and recover from the first sign of a stall or spin. Entering a spin near the ground, especially during the landing pattern, is most often fatal. [Figure 3-27]

GROUND EFFECT

Ground effect is a reduction in induced drag for the same amount of lift produced. Within one wingspan

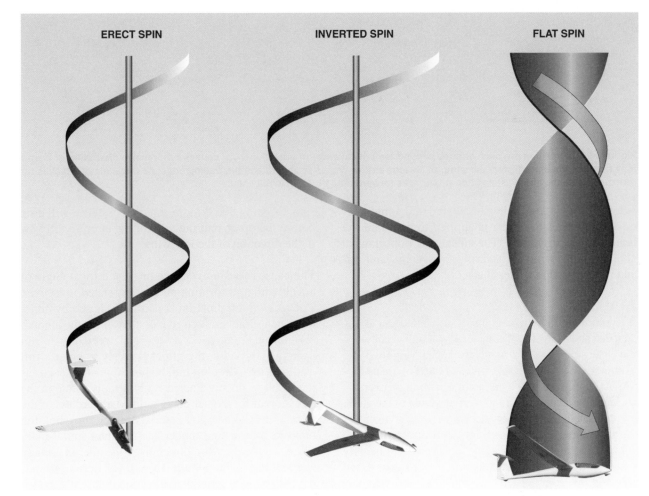

ERECT SPIN   INVERTED SPIN   FLAT SPIN

Figure 3-26. A spin can be upright or erect, inverted, or flat, depending on the roll and yaw motion of the glider.

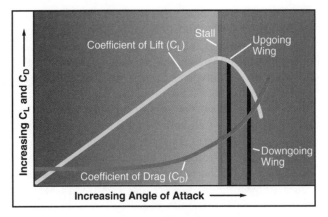

Figure 3-27. This graph depicts the relative coefficients of lift and drag for each wing during a spin. Note that the ascending wing experiences more lift and less drag. The opposite wing is forced down and back due to less lift and increased drag.

above the ground, the decrease in induced drag enables the glider to fly at a slower airspeed. In ground effect, a lower angle of attack is required to produce the same amount of lift. Ground effect enables the glider to fly near the ground at a slower airspeed. It is ground effect that causes the glider to float as you approach the touchdown point.

During takeoff and landing, the ground alters the three-dimensional airflow pattern around the glider. The result is a decrease in upwash, downwash, and a reduction in wingtip vortices. Upwash and downwash refer to the effect an airfoil has on the free airstream. Upwash is the deflection of the oncoming airstream upward and over the wing. Downwash is the downward deflection of the airstream as it passes over the wing and past the trailing edge.

During flight, the downwash of the airstream causes the relative wind to be inclined downward in the vicinity of the wing. This is called the average relative wind. The angle between the free airstream relative wind and the average relative wind is the induced angle of attack. In effect, the greater the downward deflection of the airstream, the higher the induced angle of attack and the higher the induced drag. Ground effect restricts the downward deflection of the airstream, decreasing both induced angle of attack and induced drag.

Flight instruments in the glider cockpit provide information regarding the glider's direction, altitude, airspeed, and performance. These instruments are categorized according to their method of operation. The categories include pitot-static, magnetic, gyroscopic, electrical, or self-contained. Examples of self-contained instruments and indicators that are useful to the pilot include the yaw string, inclinometer, and outside air temperature gauge (OAT).

Gyroscopic instruments, including the attitude indicator, turn coordinator, and heading indicator, are discussed in this chapter to give you an understanding of how they function. Self-launch gliders often have one or more gyroscopic instruments on the panel. Gliders without power rarely have gyroscopic instruments installed.

PITOT-STATIC INSTRUMENTS

There are two major parts of the **pitot-static system**: (1) impact pressure lines; and (2) static pressure lines, which provide the source of ambient air pressure for the operation of the altimeter, variometer, and the airspeed indicator.

IMPACT AND STATIC PRESSURE LINES

The impact air pressure (air striking the glider because of its forward motion) is taken from a pitot tube, which is mounted either on the nose or the vertical stabilizer, and aligned with the relative wind. These locations minimize disturbance or turbulence caused by the motion of the glider through the air.

The static pressure (pressure of the still air) is taken from the static line, which is attached to a vent or vents mounted flush with the side of the fuselage or tube mounted on the vertical stabilizer. Gliders using a flush-type static source with two vents, have one vent on each side of the fuselage. This compensates for any possible variation in static pressure due to erratic changes in glider attitude.

The openings of both the pitot tube and the static vent(s) should be checked during the preflight inspection to enure they are free from obstructions. Clogged or partially clogged openings should be cleaned by a certificated mechanic. Blowing into these openings is not recommended because this could damage any of the three instruments.

AIRSPEED INDICATOR

The airspeed indicator displays the speed of the glider through the air. Some airspeed indicator dials provide color-coded arcs that depict permissible airspeed ranges for different phases of flight. The upper and lower limits of the arcs correspond to airspeed limitations specific to the glider in which the instrument is mounted. [Figure 4-1]

The airspeed indicator is the only instrument that depends on both pitot pressure and static pressure. When pitot pressure and static pressure are the same, zero airspeed is indicated. As pitot pressure becomes progressively greater than static pressure, indicated airspeed increases. The airspeed indicator contains a small diaphragm that drives the needle on the face of the instrument.

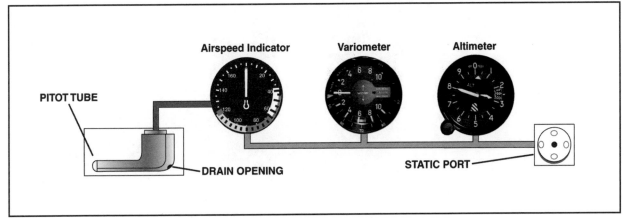

Figure 4-1. The airspeed indicator uses both the pitot and static system.

TYPES OF AIRSPEED

There are three kinds of airspeed that the pilot should understand: indicated airspeed, calibrated airspeed, and true airspeed. [Figure 4-2]

INDICATED AIRSPEED

Indicated airspeed (IAS) is the direct instrument reading obtained from the airspeed indicator, uncorrected for variations in atmospheric density, installation error, or instrument error.

CALIBRATED AIRSPEED

Calibrated airspeed (CAS) is indicated airspeed corrected for installation and instrument error. Although manufacturers attempt to keep airspeed errors to a minimum, it is impossible to eliminate all errors throughout the airspeed operating range. At certain airspeeds and with certain flap/spoiler settings, the installation and instrument error may be significant. The error is generally greatest at low airspeeds. In the cruising and higher airspeed ranges, indicated airspeed and calibrated airspeed are approximately the same.

It is important to refer to the airspeed calibration chart to correct for possible airspeed errors because airspeed limitations, such as those found on the color-coded face of the airspeed indicator, on placards in the cockpit, or in the Glider Flight Manual or Pilot's Operating Handbook (GFM/POH), are usually calibrated airspeeds. Some manufacturers use indicated rather than calibrated airspeed to denote the airspeed limitations mentioned. The airspeed indicator should be calibrated periodically.

Dirt, dust, ice, or snow collecting at the mouth of the tube may obstruct air passage and prevent correct indications, and also vibrations may destroy the sensitivity of the diaphragm.

TRUE AIRSPEED

The airspeed indicator is calibrated to indicate true airspeed only under standard atmospheric conditions at sea level (29.92 inches of mercury and 15° C or 59°F). Because air density decreases with an increase in altitude, the glider has to be flown faster at higher altitudes to cause the same pressure difference between pitot impact pressure and static pressure. Therefore, for a given true airspeed, indicated airspeed decreases as altitude increases or for a given indicated airspeed, true airspeed increases with an increase in altitude.

A pilot can find true airspeed by two methods. The first method, which is more accurate, involves using a computer. In this method, the calibrated airspeed is corrected for temperature and pressure variation by using the airspeed correction scale on the computer.

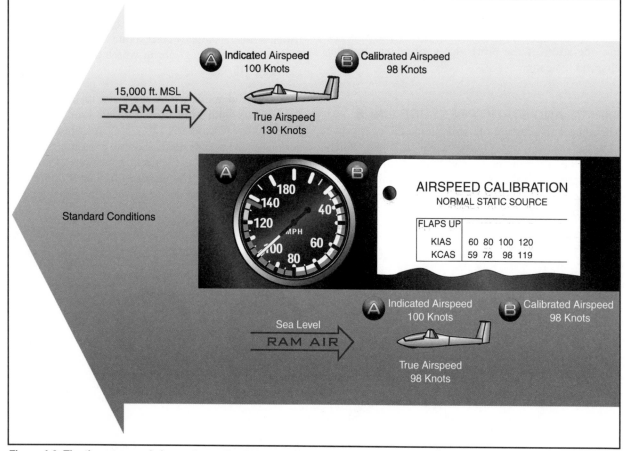

Figure 4-2. The three types of airspeed you should know include calibrated airspeed, indicated airspeed, and true airspeed.

A second method, which is a "rule of thumb," can be used to compute the approximate true airspeed. This is done by adding to the indicated airspeed 2 percent of the indicated airspeed for each 1,000 feet of altitude.

AIRSPEED INDICATOR MARKINGS

Aircraft weighing 12,500 pounds or less, manufactured after 1945 and certificated by the FAA, are required to have airspeed indicators that conform to a standard color-coded marking system. This system enables the pilot to determine at a glance certain airspeed limitations, which are important to the safe operation of the aircraft. For example, if during the execution of a maneuver, the pilot notes that the airspeed needle is in the yellow arc and is rapidly approaching the red line, immediate corrective action to reduce the airspeed should be taken. It is essential that the pilot use smooth control pressure at high airspeeds to avoid severe stresses upon the glider structure. [Figure 4-3]

Figure 4-3. Airspeed indicator with color markings.

The following is a description of the standard color-code markings on airspeed indicators.

- FLAP OPERATING RANGE (the white arc).

- STALLING SPEED WITH THE WING FLAPS AND LANDING GEAR IN THE LANDING POSITION (the lower limit of the white arc).

- MAXIMUM FLAPS EXTENDED SPEED (the upper limit of the white arc). This is the highest airspeed at which the pilot should extend full flaps. If flaps are operated at higher airspeeds, severe strain or structural failure could result.

- NORMAL OPERATING RANGE (the green arc).

- STALLING SPEED WITH THE WING FLAPS AND LANDING GEAR RETRACTED (the lower limit of the green arc).

- MAXIMUM STRUCTURAL CRUISING SPEED (the upper limit of the green arc). This is the maximum speed for normal operation.

- CAUTION RANGE (the yellow arc). The pilot should avoid this area unless in smooth air.

- NEVER-EXCEED SPEED (the red line). This is the maximum speed at which the glider can be operated in smooth air. This speed should never be exceeded intentionally.

OTHER AIRSPEED LIMITATIONS

There are other important airspeed limitations not marked on the face of the airspeed indicator. These speeds are generally found on placards in view of the pilot and in the GFM/POH.

MANEUVERING SPEED is the maximum speed at which the **limit load** can be imposed (either by gusts or full deflection of the control surfaces) without causing structural damage. If during flight, rough air or severe turbulence is encountered, the airspeed should be reduced to maneuvering speed or less to minimize the stress on the glider structure. Maneuvering speed is not marked on the airspeed indicator.

Other important airspeeds include LANDING GEAR OPERATING SPEED, the maximum speed for extending or retracting the landing gear if using glider equipped with retractable landing gear; the MINIMUM SINK SPEED, important when thermaling; and the BEST GLIDE SPEED, the airspeed that results in the least amount of altitude loss over a given distance not considering the effects of wind. MAXIMUM AEROTOW or GROUND LAUNCH SPEED is the maximum airspeed that the glider may safely be towed without causing structural damage.

The following are abbreviations for performance speeds.

V_A—design maneuvering speed.
V_C—design cruising speed.
V_F—design flap speed.
V_{FE}—maximum flap extended speed.
V_{LE}—maximum landing gear extended speed.
V_{LO}—maximum landing gear operating speed.
V_{NE}—never-exceed speed.
V_S—the stalling speed or the minimum steady flight speed at which the glider is controllable.
V_{S0}—the stalling speed or the minimum steady flight speed in the landing configuration.

V$_{S1}$—the stalling speed or the minimum steady flight speed obtained in a specified configuration.

ALTIMETER

The altimeter measures the height of the glider above a given level. Since it is the only instrument that gives altitude information, the altimeter is one of the most important instruments in the glider. To use the altimeter effectively, the pilot must thoroughly understand its principle of operation and the effect of atmospheric pressure and temperature on the altimeter. [Figure 4-4]

PRINCIPLE OF OPERATION

The pressure altimeter is simply an aneroid barometer that measures the pressure of the atmosphere at the level where the altimeter is located, and presents an altitude indication in feet. The altimeter uses static pressure as its source of operation. Air is denser at the surface of the Earth than aloft, therefore as altitude increases, atmospheric pressure decreases. This difference in pressure at various levels causes the altimeter to indicate changes in altitude.

The presentation of altitude varies considerably between different types of altimeters. Some have one pointer while others have more. Only the multi-pointer type will be discussed in this handbook.

The dial of a typical altimeter is graduated with numerals arranged clockwise from 0 to 9 inclusive as shown in Figure 4-4. Movement of the aneroid element is transmitted through a gear train to the three hands, which sweep the calibrated dial to indicate altitude. The shortest hand indicates altitude in tens of thousands of feet; the intermediate hand in thousands of feet; and the longest hand in hundreds of feet, subdivided into 20-foot increments.

The altitude indicated on the altimeter is correct only if the sea level barometric pressure is standard (29.92 in. Hg.), the sea level free air temperature is standard (+15° C or 59° F), and the pressure and temperature decrease at a standard rate with an increase in altitude. Since atmospheric pressure continually changes, a means is provided to adjust the altimeter to compensate for nonstandard conditions. This is accomplished through a system by which the altimeter setting (local station barometric pressure reduced to sea level) is set to a barometric scale located on the face of the altimeter. Only after the altimeter is set properly will it indicate the correct altitude.

EFFECT OF NONSTANDARD PRESSURE AND TEMPERATURE

If no means were provided for adjusting altimeters to nonstandard pressure, flight could be hazardous. For example, if a flight is made from a high-pressure area to a low-pressure area without adjusting the altimeter, the actual altitude of the glider will be LOWER than the indicated altitude. When flying from a low-pressure area to a high-pressure area, the actual altitude of the glider will be HIGHER than the indicated altitude. Fortunately, this error can be corrected by setting the altimeter properly.

Variations in air temperature also affect the altimeter. On a warm day, the expanded air is lighter in weight per unit volume than on a cold day, and consequently the pressure levels are raised. For example, the pressure level where the altimeter indicates 10,000 feet will be HIGHER on a warm day than under standard conditions. On a cold day, the reverse is true, and the 10,000 foot level would be LOWER. The adjustment made by the pilot to compensate for nonstandard pressures does not compensate for nonstandard temperatures. Therefore, if terrain or obstacle clearance is a factor in the selection of a cruising altitude, particularly at higher altitudes, remember to anticipate that COLDER-THAN-STANDARD TEMPERATURE will place the glider LOWER than the altimeter indicates. Therefore, a higher altitude should be used to provide adequate terrain clearance. A memory aid in applying the above is "from a high to a low or hot to cold, look out below." [Figure 4-5]

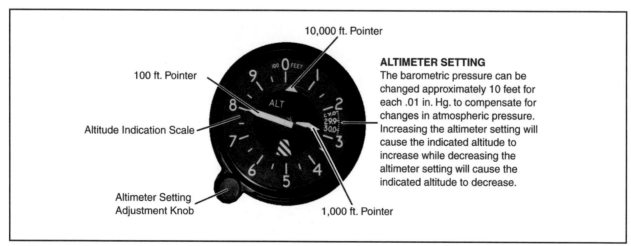

100 ft. Pointer

10,000 ft. Pointer

Altitude Indication Scale

Altimeter Setting Adjustment Knob

1,000 ft. Pointer

ALTIMETER SETTING
The barometric pressure can be changed approximately 10 feet for each .01 in. Hg. to compensate for changes in atmospheric pressure. Increasing the altimeter setting will cause the indicated altitude to increase while decreasing the altimeter setting will cause the indicated altitude to decrease.

Figure 4-4. The altimeter indicator.

SETTING THE ALTIMETER

To adjust the altimeter for variation in atmospheric pressure, the pressure scale in the altimeter setting window, calibrated in inches of mercury (in. Hg.), is adjusted to correspond with the given altimeter setting. Altimeter settings can be defined as station pressure reduced to sea level, expressed in inches of mercury.

The station reporting the altimeter setting takes an hourly measurement of the station's atmospheric pressure and corrects this value to sea level pressure. These altimeter settings reflect height above sea level only in the vicinity of the reporting station. Therefore, it is necessary to adjust the altimeter setting as the flight progresses from one station to the next.

Title 14 of the Code of Federal Regulations (14 CFR) part 91 provides the following concerning altimeter settings. The cruising altitude of an aircraft below 18,000 feet mean sea level (MSL) shall be maintained by reference to an altimeter that is set to the current reported altimeter setting of a station located along the route of flight and within 100 nautical miles (NM) of the aircraft. If there is no such station, the current reported altimeter setting of an appropriate available station shall be used. In an aircraft having no radio, the altimeter shall be set to the elevation of the departure airport or an appropriate altimeter setting available before departure.

Many pilots confidently expect that the current altimeter setting will compensate for irregularities in atmospheric pressure at all altitudes. This is not always true because the altimeter setting broadcast by ground stations is the station pressure corrected to mean sea level. The altimeter setting does not account for the irregularities at higher levels, particularly the effect of nonstandard temperature.

It should be pointed out, however, that if each pilot in a given area were to use the same altimeter setting, each altimeter will be equally affected by temperature and pressure variation errors, making it possible to maintain the desired separation between aircraft.

When flying over high mountainous terrain, certain atmospheric conditions can cause the altimeter to indicate an altitude of 1,000 feet, or more, HIGHER than the actual altitude. For this reason, a generous margin of altitude should be allowed—not only for possible altimeter error, but also for possible downdrafts that are particularly prevalent if high winds are encountered.

To illustrate the use of the altimeter setting system, follow a cross-country flight from TSA Gliderport, Midlothian, Texas, to Winston Airport, Snyder, Texas, via Stephens County Airport, Breckenridge, Texas. Before takeoff from TSA Gliderport, the pilot receives a current local altimeter setting of 29.85 from the Fort

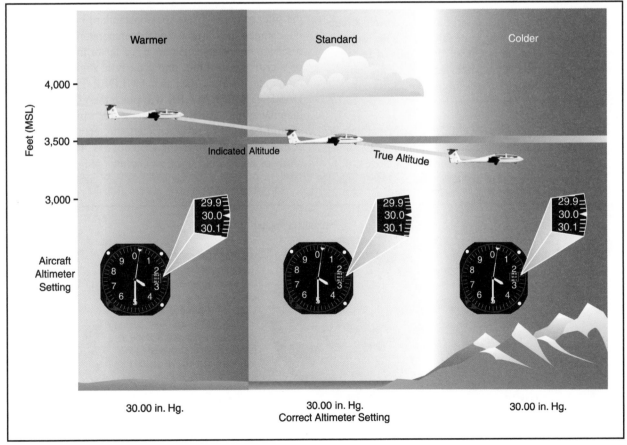

Figure 4-5. Nonstandard pressure and temperature.

Worth AFSS. This value is set in the altimeter setting window of the altimeter. The altimeter indication should then be compared with the known airport elevation of 660 feet. Since most altimeters are not perfectly calibrated, an error may exist. If an altimeter indication varies from the field elevation more than 75 feet, the accuracy of the instrument is questionable and it should be referred to an instrument repair station.

When over Stephens County Airport, assume the pilot receives a current area altimeter setting of 29.94 and applies this setting to the altimeter. Before entering the traffic pattern at Winston Airport, a new altimeter setting of 29.69 is received from the Automated Weather Observing System (AWOS), and applied to the altimeter. If the pilot desires to enter the traffic pattern at approximately 1,000 feet above terrain, and the field elevation of Winston Airport is 2,430 feet, an indicated altitude of 3,400 feet should be used (2,430 feet + 1000 feet = 3,420 feet, rounded to 3,400 feet).

The importance of properly setting and reading the altimeter cannot be overemphasized. Let us assume that the pilot neglected to adjust the altimeter at Winston Airport to the current setting, and uses the Stephens CO area setting of 29.94. If this occurred, the glider, when entering the Winston Airport traffic pattern, would be approximately 250 feet below the proper traffic pattern altitude of 3,200 feet, and the altimeter would indicate approximately 250 feet more than the field elevation (2,430 feet) upon landing.

Actual altimeter setting	29.94
Correct altimeter setting	29.69
Difference	.25

(1 inch of pressure is equal to approximately 1,000 feet of altitude—.25 x 1,000 feet = 250 feet)

The previous calculation may be confusing, particularly in determining whether to add or subtract the amount of altimeter error. The following additional explanation is offered and can be helpful in finding the solution to this type of problem.

There are two means by which the altimeter pointers can be moved. One utilizes changes in air pressure while the other utilizes the mechanical makeup of the altimeter setting system.

When the glider altitude is changed, the changing pressure within the altimeter case expands or contracts the aneroid barometer that through linkage rotates the pointers. A decrease in pressure causes the altimeter to indicate an increase in altitude, and an increase in pressure causes the altimeter to indicate a decrease in altitude. It is obvious then that if the glider is flown from a pressure level of 28.75 in. Hg. to a pressure level of 29.75 in. Hg., the altimeter would show a decrease of approximately 1,000 feet in altitude. [Figure 4-6]

The other method of moving the pointers does not rely on changing air pressure, but the mechanical construction of the altimeter. When the knob on the altimeter is rotated, the altimeter setting pressure scale moves simultaneously with the altimeter pointers. This may be confusing because the numerical values of pressure indicated in the window increase while the altimeter indicates an increase in altitude; or decrease while the altimeter indicates a decrease in altitude. This is contrary to the reaction on the pointers when air pressure changes, and is based solely on the mechanical makeup of the altimeter. To further explain this point, assume that the correct altimeter setting is 29.50 or a .50 difference. This would cause a 500-foot error in altitude. In this case if the altimeter setting is adjusted from 30.00 to 29.50, the numerical value decreases and the altimeter indicates a decrease of 500

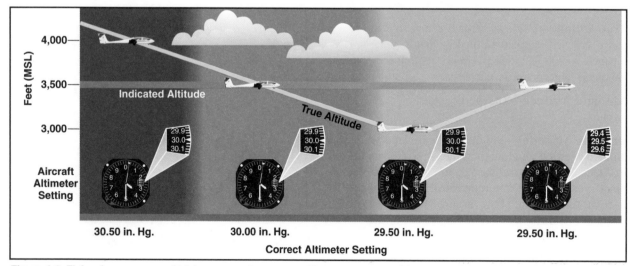

Figure 4-6. Flying from an area of high pressure to an area of lower pressure, without resetting your altimeter, results in your glider's true altitude being lower than indicated.

feet in altitude. Before this correction was made, the glider was flying at an altitude of 500 feet lower than was shown on the altimeter.

TYPES OF ALTITUDE

Knowing the glider's altitude is vitally important to the pilot for several reasons. The pilot must be sure that the glider is flying high enough to clear the highest terrain or obstruction along the intended route; this is especially important when visibility is restricted. To keep above mountain peaks, the pilot must be aware of the glider's altitude and elevation of the surrounding terrain at all times. Knowledge of the altitude is necessary to calculate true airspeeds.

Altitude is vertical distance above some point or level used as a reference. There may be as many kinds of altitude as there are reference levels from which altitude is measured and each may be used for specific reasons.

The following are the four types of altitude that affect glider pilots. [Figure 4-7]

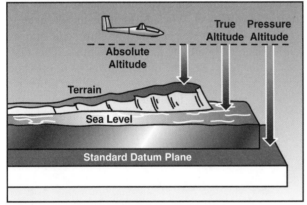

Figure 4 -7. Types of altitude.

Indicated Altitude—That altitude read directly from the altimeter (uncorrected) after it is set to the current altimeter setting.

True Altitude—The true vertical distance of the glider above sea level—the actual altitude. (Often expressed in this manner: 10,900 feet MSL.) Airport, terrain, and obstacle elevations found on aeronautical charts are true altitudes.

Absolute Altitude—The vertical distance above the terrain.

Pressure Altitude—The altitude indicated when the altimeter setting window (barometric scale) is adjusted to 29.92. This is the standard datum plane, a theoretical plane where air pressure (corrected to 15° C or 59° F) is equal to 29.92 in. Hg. Pressure altitude is used for computer solutions to determine density altitude, true altitude, true airspeed, etc.

Density Altitude—This altitude is pressure altitude corrected for nonstandard temperature variations. When conditions are standard, pressure altitude and density altitude are the same. Consequently, if the temperature is above standard, the density altitude will be higher than pressure altitude. If the temperature is below standard, the density altitude will be lower than pressure altitude. This is an important altitude because it is directly related to the glider's takeoff and climb performance.

VARIOMETER

The **variometer** gives the glider pilot information on performance of the glider while flying through the atmosphere. The variometer operates on the same principle as the altimeter, however, it indicates rate of climb or descent instead of vertical distance. The variometer depends upon the pressure lapse rate in the atmosphere to derive information about rate of climb or rate of descent. Most non-electrical variometers use a separate insulated tank, such as a Thermos or capacity flask, as a reference chamber. The tubing is plumbed from the reference chamber through the variometer to an outside static port. By using different hairsprings, the sensitivity of the variometer can be controlled. The variometer has a very rapid response due to the small mass and lightweight construction of the moving parts.

Pressure differences between the air inside the variometer/reference chamber system and the air outside of the system tend to equalize as air flows from high pressure areas to low pressure areas. When pressure inside the reference chamber is greater than the pressure outside, air flows out of the reference chamber through the mechanical variometer to the outside environment, displacing a vane inside the variometer. The vane, in turn, drives the needle to display a climb indication. When air pressure outside the reference chamber is greater than pressure inside, air flows through the variometer and into the reference chamber until pressure is equalized. The variometer needle indicates a descent. [Figure 4-8]

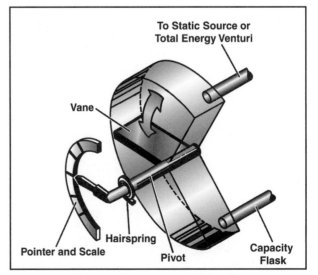

Figure 4-8. The mechanics of a variometer allow the instrument face to display small changes in pressure.

Electric powered variometers offer several advantages over the non-electric variety. These advantages include more rapid response rates and separate audible signals for climb and descent.

Some electric variometers operate by the cooling effect of airflow on an element called a thermistor, a heat-sensitive electrical resistor. The electrical resistance of the thermistor changes when temperature changes. As air flows into or out of the reference chamber, it flows across two thermistors in a bridge circuit. An electrical meter measures the imbalance across the bridge circuit and calculates the rate of climb or descent. It then displays the information on the variometer.

Newer electric variometers operate on the transducer principle. A tiny vacuum cavity on a circuit board is sealed with a flexible membrane. Variable resistors are embedded in the membrane. When pressure outside the cavity changes, minute alterations in the shape of the membrane occur. As a result, electrical resistance in the embedded resistors changes. These changes in electrical resistance are interpreted by a circuit board and indicated on the variometer dial as climb or descent.

Many electrical variometers provide audible tones or beeps that indicate the rate of climb or rate of descent of the glider. Audio variometers enhance safety of flight because they make it unnecessary for the glider pilot to look at the variometer to discern the rate of climb or rate of descent. Instead, the pilot can hear the rate of climb or rate of descent. This allows the pilot to minimize time spent looking at the flight instruments and maximize time spent looking outside for other air traffic. [Figure 4-9]

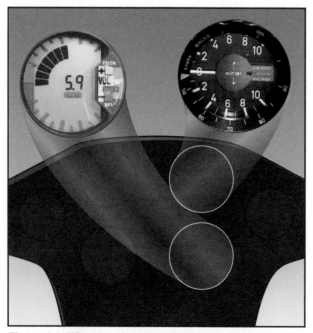

Figure 4-9. When an electric variometer is mounted in the glider a non-electric variometer is usually installed as a backup.

Some variometers are equipped with a rotatable rim speed scale called a MacCready ring. This scale indicates the optimum airspeed to fly when traveling between thermals for maximum cross-country performance. During the glide between thermals, the index arrow is set at the rate of climb expected in the next thermal. On the speed ring, the variometer needle points to the optimum speed to fly between thermals. If expected rate of climb is slow, optimum inter-thermal cruise airspeed will be relatively slow. When expected lift is strong, however, optimum inter-thermal cruise airspeed will be much faster. [Figure 4-10]

Figure 4-10. The MacCready ring.

Variometers are sensitive to changes in pressure altitude caused by airspeed. In still air, when the glider dives, the variometer indicates a descent. When the glider pulls out of the dive and begins a rapid climb, the variometer indicates an ascent. This indication is sometimes called a "stick thermal." A glider lacking a compensated variometer must be flown at a constant airspeed to receive an accurate variometer indication.

TOTAL ENERGY SYSTEM

A variometer with a total energy system senses changes in airspeed and tends to cancel out the resulting climb and dive indications (stick thermals). This is desirable because the glider pilot wants to know how rapidly the airmass is rising or descending despite changes in airspeed.

A popular type of total energy system consists of a small venturi mounted in the air stream and connected to the static outlet of the variometer. When airspeed increases, more suction from the venturi moderates the pressure at the static outlet of the variometer. Similarly, when airspeed decreases, reduced suction from the venturi moderates the pressure at the static outlet of the variometer. If the venturi is properly designed and installed, the net effect is to reduce climb and dive indications caused by airspeed changes.

Another type of total energy system is designed with a diaphragm-type compensator placed in line from the pitot tube to the line coming from the capacity flask. Deflection of the diaphragm is proportional to the effect the airspeed change has on pitot pressure. In

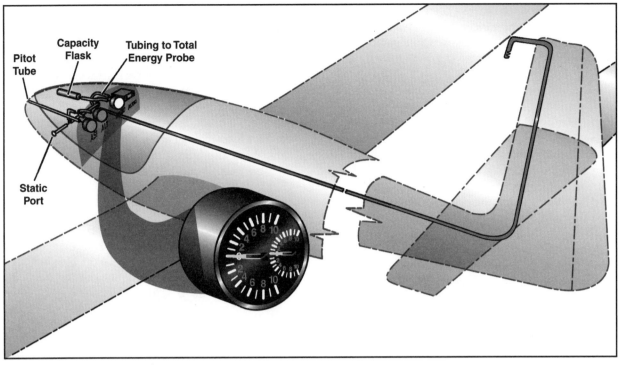

Figure 4-11. A total energy variometer system.

effect, the diaphragm modulates pressure changes in the capacity flask. When properly adjusted, the diaphragm compensator does an adequate job of masking stick thermals. [Figure 4-11]

NETTO

A variometer that indicates the vertical movement of the airmass, regardless of the sailplane's climb or descent rate, is called a NETTO variometer system. Some NETTO variometer systems employ a calibrated capillary tube that functions as a tiny valve. Pitot pressure pushes minute quantities of air through the valve and into the reference chamber tubing. The effect is to remove the glider's sink rate at various airspeeds from the variometer indication (polar sink rate). [Figure 4-12]

Electronic, computerized NETTO variometers employ a different method to remove the glider performance polar sink rate from the variometer indication. In this type of system, sensors for both pitot pressure and static pressure provide airspeed information to the computer. The sink rate of the glider at every airspeed is stored in the computer memory. At any given airspeed, the sink rate of the glider is mathematically removed, and the variometer displays the rate of ascent or descent of the airmass itself.

ELECTRONIC FLIGHT COMPUTERS

Electronic flight computers are found in the cockpits of gliders that are flown in competition and cross-country soaring. Since non-powered gliders lack a generator or alternator, electrical components, such as the flight computer and VHF transceiver, draw power from the

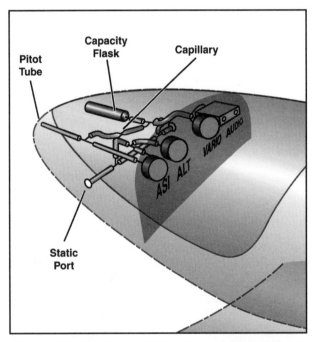

Figure 4-12. This is an example of a NETTO variometer system.

glider battery or batteries. The battery is usually a 12 or 14 volt sealed battery. Solar cells are sometimes arrayed behind the pilot or on top of the instrument panel cover to supply additional power to the electrical system during flight in sunny conditions.

The primary components of most flight computer systems are an electric variometer, a coupled Global Positioning Satellite (GPS) receiver, and a microprocessor. The variometer measures rate of climb and descent. The GPS provides position information. The microprocessor interprets altitude, speed, and position information. The microprocessor output aids the pilot in cross-country decision-making. [Figure 4-13]

The GPS-coupled flight computer can provide you with the following information.

- Where you are.
- Where you have been.
- Where you are going.
- How fast you are going there.
- How high you need to be to glide there.
- How fast you are climbing or descending.
- The optimum airspeed to fly to the next area of anticipated lift.
- The optimum airspeed to fly to a location on the ground, such as the finish line in a race, or the airport of intended landing at the end of a cross-country flight.

The primary benefits of the flight computer can easily be divided into two areas: navigation assistance and performance (speed) enhancement.

Fundamental to the use of the flight computer is the concept of waypoint. A waypoint is simply a point in space. The three coordinates of the point are latitude, longitude, and altitude. Glider races and cross-country glider flights frequently involve flight around a series of waypoints called turnpoints. The course may be an out-and-return course, a triangle, a quadrilateral or other type of polygon, or a series of waypoints laid out more or less in a straight line. The glider pilot must navigate from point to point, using available lift sources to climb periodically so that that flight can continue to the intended goal. The GPS-enabled flight computer aids in navigation and in summarizing how the flight is going. When strong lift is encountered, and

if the pilot believes it is likely that the strong lift source may be worth returning to after rounding a turnpoint, the flight computer can "mark" the location of the thermal. Then the glider pilot can round a nearby turnpoint and use the flight computer to guide the return to the marked thermal in the hopes of making a rapid climb and heading out on course toward the next turnpoint.

During the climb portion of the flight, the flight computer's variometer constantly updates the achieved rate of climb. During cruise, the GPS-coupled flight computer aids in navigating accurately to the next turnpoint. The flight computer also suggests the optimum cruise airspeed for the glider to fly, based on the expected rate of climb in the next thermal.

During final glide to a goal, the flight computer can display glider altitude, altitude required to reach the goal, distance to the goal, the strength of the headwind or tailwind component, optimum airspeed to fly, glider groundspeed, and the amount of time it will take to reach the goal.

Most flight computers incorporate an electronic audiovisual variometer. The rate of climb or descent can be viewed on the computer's visual display. The variometer also provides audible rate of climb information through a small loudspeaker. The loudspeaker allows the pilot to hear how fast the glider is climbing or descending. Because this information is received through hearing, the pilot's vision can be constantly directed outside the glider to enhance safety of flight and cross-country performance.

Flight computers also provide information to help the pilot select and fly the optimum airspeed for the weather conditions being encountered. When lift is strong and climbs are fast, higher airspeeds around the course are

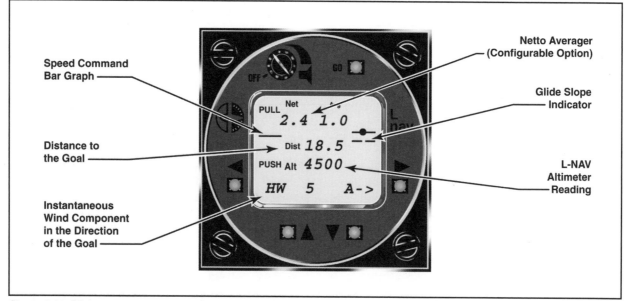

Figure 4-13. Flight computer system display.

possible. The flight computer detects the rapid climbs and suggests very fast cruise airspeeds to enhance performance. When lift is weak and climbs are slow, optimum airspeed will be significantly slower than when conditions are strong. The flight computer, sensing the relatively slow rate of climb on a difficult day, compensates for the weaker conditions and suggests optimum airspeeds that are slower than they would be if conditions were strong. The flight computer relieves the pilot of the chore of making numerous speed-to-fly calculations during cross-country flight. This freedom allows the pilot to look for other air traffic, look for sources of lift, watch the weather ahead, and plot a strategy for the remaining portion of the flight.

The presence of water ballast alters the performance characteristics of the glider. In racing, the ability to make faster glides without excess altitude penalty is very valuable. The additional weight of water in the glider's ballast tanks allows flatter glides at high airspeeds. The water-ballast glider possesses the strongest advantage when lift conditions are strong and rapid climbs are achievable. The flight computer compensates for the amount of water ballast carried, adjusting speed-to-fly computations according to the weight and performance of the glider. Some flight computers require the pilot to enter data regarding the ballast condition of the glider. Other flight computers automatically compensate for the effect of water ballast by constantly measuring the performance of the glider and deducting the operating weight of the glider from these measurements. If the wings of the glider become contaminated with bugs, glider performance will decline. The glide computer can be adjusted to account for the resulting performance degradation.

MAGNETIC COMPASS
The magnetic compass, which is the only direction-seeking instrument in the glider, is simple in construction. It contains two steel magnetized needles fastened to a float around which a compass card is mounted. The needles are parallel, with their north-seeking ends pointed in the same direction. The compass card has letters for cardinal headings, and each 30° interval is represented by a number, the last zero of which is omitted. For example, 30° would appear as a 3 and 300° would appear as 30. Between these numbers, the card is graduated for each 5°. [Figure 4-14]

The float assembly is housed in a bowl filled with acid-free white kerosene. The purposes of the liquid are to dampen out excessive oscillations of the compass card, and relieve by buoyancy part of the weight of the float from the bearings. Jewel bearings are used to mount the float assembly on top of a pedestal. A line (called the lubber line) is mounted behind the glass of the instrument that can be used for a

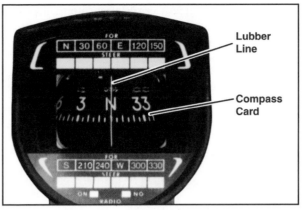
Figure 4-14. A magnetic compass.

reference line when aligning the headings on the compass card.

The magnetic compass works on the principle of magnetism. The glider pilot must have a basic understanding of the principles of operation of the magnetic compass. A simple bar magnet has two centers of magnetism, which are called poles. Lines of magnetic force flow out from each pole in all directions, eventually bending around and returning to the other pole. The area through which these lines of force flow is called the field of the magnet. For the purpose of this discussion, the poles are designated "north" and "south." If two bar magnets are placed near each other, the north pole of one will attract the south pole of the other. There is evidence that there is a magnetic field surrounding the Earth, and this theory is applied in the design of the magnetic compass. It acts very much as though there were a huge bar magnet running along the axis of the Earth, which ends several hundred miles below the surface. [Figure 4-15]

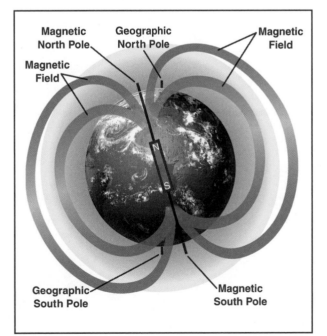
Figure 4-15. Earth magnetic force flow.

The lines of force have a vertical component (or pull), which is zero at the Equator, but builds to 100 percent of the total force at the poles. If magnetic needles, such as the glider magnetic compass bars, are held along these lines of force, the vertical component causes one end of the needle to dip or deflect downward. The amount of dip increases as the needles are moved closer and closer to the poles. It is this deflection or dip that causes some of the larger compass errors.

MAGNETIC VARIATION

Although the magnetic field of the Earth lies roughly north and south, the Earth's magnetic poles do not coincide with its geographic poles, which are used in the construction of aeronautical charts. Consequently, at most places on the Earth's surface, the direction-sensitive steel needles, which seek the Earth's magnetic field, will not point to True North but to Magnetic North. Furthermore, local magnetic fields from mineral deposits and other conditions may distort the Earth's magnetic field and cause an additional error in the position of the compass' north-seeking magnetized needles with reference to True North. The angular difference between True North and the direction indicated by the magnetic compass—excluding deviation error—is variation. Variation is different for different points on the Earth's surface and is shown on the aeronautical charts as broken lines connecting points of equal variation. These lines are isogonic lines. The line where the magnetic variation is zero is an agonic line. [Figure 4-16]

MAGNETIC DEVIATION

A compass is very rarely influenced solely by the Earth's magnetic lines of force. Magnetic disturbances from magnetic fields produced by metals and electrical accessories in a glider disturb the compass needles and produce an additional error known as deviation.

If a glider changes heading, the compass' direction-sensitive magnetized needles will continue to point in about the same direction while the glider turns with relation to it. As the glider turns, metallic and electrical equipment in the glider change their position relative to the steel needles; hence, their influence on the compass needle changes and deviation changes. The deviation depends, in part, on the heading of the glider. Although compensating magnets on the compass are adjusted to reduce this deviation on most headings, it is impossible to eliminate this error entirely on all headings. A deviation card is installed in the cockpit in view of the pilot, enabling the pilot to maintain the desired magnetic headings. [Figure 4-17]

COMPASS ERRORS

Since the compass card is suspended in fluid, the magnetic compass is sensitive to in-flight turbulence. In light turbulence, you may be able to use the compass by averaging the readings. For example, if the compass swings between 40° and 70°, you can estimate the approximate magnetic heading of 55°. In

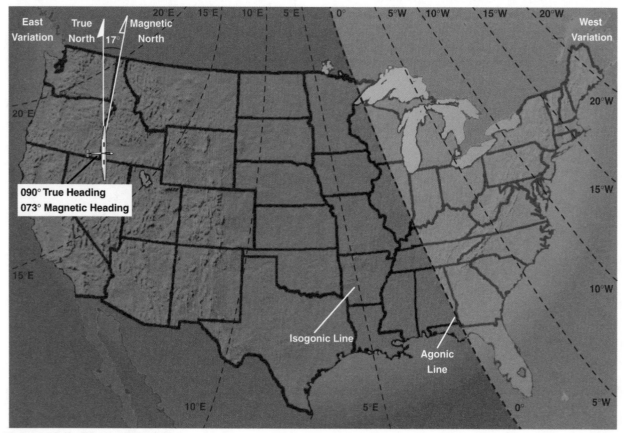

Figure 4-16. Earth's magnetic field.

FOR (MH)	0°	30°	60°	90°	120°	150°	180°	210°	240°	270°	300°	330°
STEER (CH)	359°	30°	60°	88°	120°	152°	183°	212°	240°	268°	300°	329°
RADIO ON ☑						RADIO OFF ☐						

Figure 4-17. Compass correction card.

severe turbulence, however, the magnetic compass may be so disturbed that is unusable for navigation.

Since the magnetic compass is the only direction-seeking instrument in most gliders, the pilot must be able to turn the glider to a magnetic compass heading and maintain this heading. It will help to remember the following characteristics of the magnetic compass, which are caused by magnetic dip. These characteristics are only applicable in the Northern Hemisphere. In the Southern Hemisphere the opposite is true.

ACCELERATION ERROR
When on an east or west heading, no error is apparent while entering a turn to north or south. However, an increase in airspeed or acceleration will cause the compass to indicate a turn toward north; a decrease in airspeed or acceleration will cause the compass to indicate a turn toward south. On a north or south heading, no error will be apparent because of acceleration or deceleration. [Figure 4-18]

TURNING ERROR
The turning error is directly related to magnetic dip; the greater the dip, the greater the turning error. It is most pronounced when you are turning to or from headings of north or south. When you begin a turn from a heading of north, the compass starts to turn in the opposite direction and it lags behind the actual heading. As the turn continues, the amount of lag decreases, then disappears, as the glider reaches a heading of east or west.

When initiating a turn from a heading of east or west to a heading of north, there is no error as you begin the turn. As the heading approaches north, the compass increasingly lags behind the glider's actual heading.

When you turn from a heading of south, the compass initially indicates a turn in the proper direction but at a faster rate, and leads the glider's actual heading. This error also cancels out as the glider reaches a heading of east or west. Turning from east or west to a heading of south causes the compass to move correctly at the start

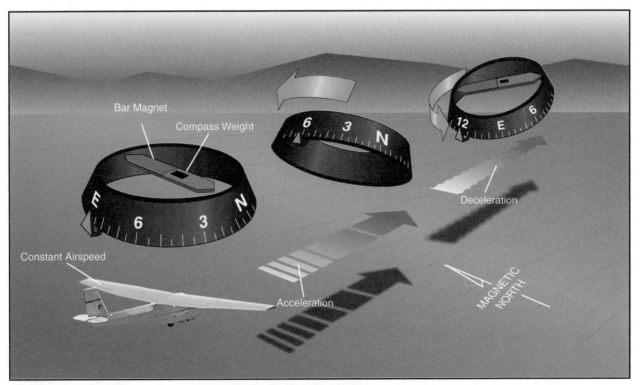

Figure 4-18. Acceleration error on a compass in the Northern Hemisphere.

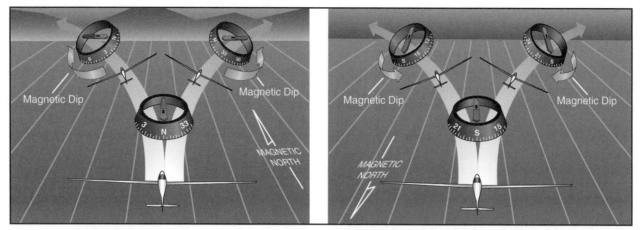

Figure 4-19. The left side of this figure shows the initial turning error that occurs during a turn from a northerly heading. The initial tendency of the magnetic compass in a turn from a southerly heading is shown on the right.

of a turn, but then it increasingly leads the actual heading as the glider nears a southerly direction. [Figure 4-19]

The amount of lead or lag is approximately equal to the latitude of the glider. For example, if you are turning from a heading of south to a heading of west while flying at 35° north latitude, the compass will rapidly turn to a heading of 215° (180°+35°). At the midpoint of the turn, the lead will decrease to approximately half (17.5°), and upon reaching a heading of west, it will be zero. The lead and lag errors discussed here are only valid in the Northern Hemisphere. Lead and lag errors in the Southern Hemisphere act in opposite directions.

YAW STRING

The most effective, yet least expensive, slip/skid indicator is made from a piece of yarn mounted in the free airstream in a place easily visible to the pilot as shown in Figure 4-20. The yaw string helps you coordinate rudder and aileron inputs. When the controls are properly coordinated, the yarn points straight back, aligned with the longitudinal axis of the glider. During a slipping turn, the tail of the yaw string will be offset toward the outside of the turn. To center the yaw string in a slipping turn, add pressure to the rudder pedal that is opposite the tail of the yaw string. During a skidding turn, the tail of the yaw string will be offset toward the inside of the turn. To center the yaw string in a skidding turn, add pressure to the rudder pedal that is opposite the tail of the yaw string.

INCLINOMETER

Another type of slip/skid indicator is the inclinometer. Mounted in the bottom of a turn-and-bank indicator or mounted separately in the instrument panel, the inclinometer consists of a metal ball in an oil-filled, curved glass tube. When the glider is flying in coordinated fashion, the ball remains centered at the bottom of the glass tube. The inclinometer differs from the yaw string during uncoordinated flight. The ball moves to the inside of the turn to indicate a slip and to the outside of the turn to indicate a skid. If you remember the phrase

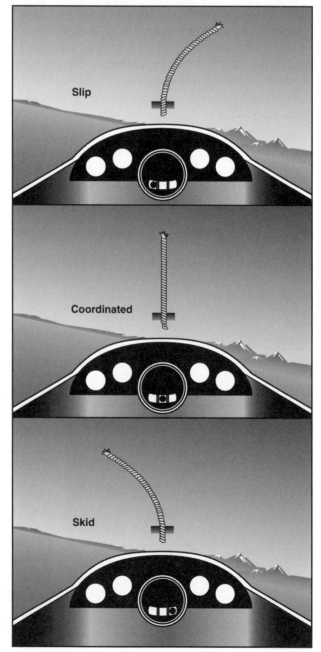

Figure 4-20. The yaw string and Inclinometer.

"step on the ball" in reference to the inclinometer, it will help you coordinate the turn using rudder inputs.

GYROSCOPIC INSTRUMENTS

Gyroscopic instruments are found in virtually all modern airplanes but are infrequently found in gliders. This section is designed to provide you with a basic understanding of how gyroscopic instruments function. The three gyroscopic instruments found most frequently in a glider are the heading indicator, the attitude indicator, and the turn coordinator.

RIGIDITY IN SPACE

Rigidity in space and precession are the two fundamental concepts that affect the operation of gyroscopic instruments. Rigidity in space refers to the principle that a gyroscope remains in a fixed position in the plane in which it is spinning. By mounting this wheel, or gyroscope, on a set of gimbal rings, the gyro is able to rotate freely in any direction. Thus, if the gimbal rings are tilted, twisted, or otherwise moved, the gyro remains in the plane in which it was originally spinning. [Figure 4-21]

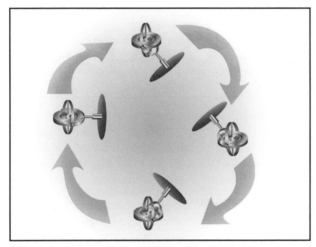

Figure 4-21. Regardless of the position of its base, a gyro tends to remain rigid in space, with its axis of rotation pointed tin a constant direction.

PRECESSION

Precession is the tilting or turning of a gyro in response to a deflective force. The reaction to this force does not occur at the point where it was applied; rather, it occurs at a point that is 90° later in the direction of rotation. This principle allows the gyro to determine a rate of turn by sensing the amount of pressure created by a change in direction. The rate at which the gyro precesses is inversely proportional to the speed of the rotor and proportional to the deflective force. [Figure 4-22]

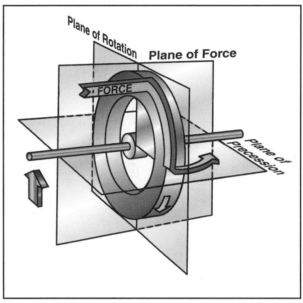

Figure 4-22. Precession of a gyroscope results from an applied deflective force.

Gyroscopic instruments require a power source to keep the gyro rotating at a constant rate. The most common power source for gliders is an electric battery. [Figure 4-23]

The turn coordinator and turn-and-slip indicator both provide an indication of turn direction, rate, and quality. The main difference between the turn coordinator and

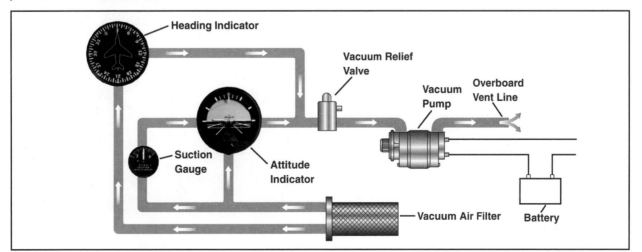

Figure 4-23. Electric powered gyro system.

the turn-and-slip indicator is the manner in which turn information is displayed. The turn coordinator uses a miniature aircraft, while the turn-and-slip indicator utilizes a pointer called a turn needle.

We will discuss the turn coordinator. During a turn, the miniature aircraft in the turn coordinator banks in the same direction the glider is banked. The turn coordinator enables you to establish a standard-rate-turn. You do this by aligning the wing of the miniature aircraft with the turn index. At this rate, the aircraft will turn 3° per second, completing a 360° turn in two minutes. The turn coordinator is designed to indicate the rate of turn, not the angle of bank. The turn coordinator is also equipped with an inclinometer to help you coordinate your turn. [Figure 4-24]

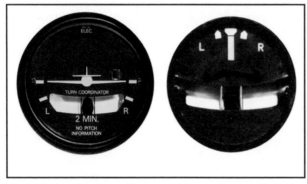

Figure 4-24. A turn coordinator and turn-and-slip indicator.

ATTITUDE INDICATOR
The attitude indicator, with its miniature aircraft and horizon bar, displays a picture of the attitude of the glider. The relationship of the miniature aircraft to the horizon bar is the same as the relationship of the real aircraft to the actual horizon. The instrument gives an instantaneous indication of even the smallest changes in attitude. [Figure 4-25]

The gyro in the attitude indicator is mounted on a horizontal plane and depends upon rigidity in space for its operation. The horizon bar represents the true horizon. This bar is fixed to the gyro and remains in a horizontal plane as the glider is pitched or banked about its lateral or longitudinal axis, indicating the attitude of the glider relative to the true horizon.

An adjustment knob is provided to allow the pilot to move the miniature aircraft up or down to align the miniature aircraft with the horizon bar to suit the pilot's line of vision. Normally, the miniature aircraft is adjusted so the wings overlap the horizon bar when the glider is in straight-and-level cruising flight. The attitude indicator is reliable and the most realistic flight instrument on the instrument panel. Its indications are very close approximations of the actual attitude of the glider.

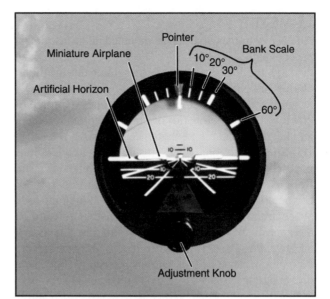

Figure 4-25. Attitude Indicator.

HEADING INDICATOR
The operation of the heading indicator depends upon the principle of rigidity in space. The rotor turns in a vertical plane, and fixed to the rotor is a compass card. Since the rotor remains rigid in space, the points on the card hold the same position in space relative to the vertical plane. As the instrument case and the glider revolve around the vertical axis, the card provides clear and accurate heading information.

Because of precession, caused chiefly by friction, the heading indicator will creep or drift from a heading to which it is set. Among other factors, the amount of drift depends largely upon the condition of the instrument. If the bearings are worn, dirty, or improperly lubricated, the drift may be excessive.

Bear in mind that the heading indicator is not direction seeking, as is the magnetic compass. It is important to check the indications frequently and reset the heading indicator to align it with the magnetic compass when required. Adjusting the heading indicator to the magnetic compass heading should be done only when the glider is in wings-level unaccelerated flight; otherwise erroneous magnetic compass readings may be obtained. [Figure 4-26]

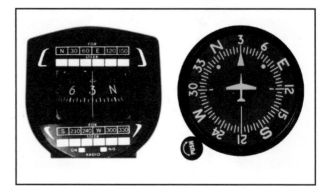

Figure 4-26. Setting the heading indicator.

G-METER

Another instrument that can be mounted in the instrument panel of a glider is a G-meter. The G-meter measures and displays the load imposed on the glider during flight. During straight, unaccelerated flight in calm air, a glider experiences a load factor of 1G (1.0 times the force of gravity). During aerobatics or during flight in turbulent air, the glider and pilot experience G-loads greater than 1G. These additional loads result from accelerations imposed on the glider. Some of these accelerations result from external sources, such as flying into updrafts or downdrafts. Other accelerations arise from pilot input on the controls, such as pulling back or pushing forward on the control stick. G-loads are classified as positive or negative. Positive G is felt when increasing pitch rapidly for a climb. Negative G is felt when pushing over into a dive or during sustained inverted flight. Each glider type is designed to withstand a specified maximum positive G-load and a specified maximum negative G-load. The GFM/POH is the definitive source for this information. Exceeding the allowable limit loads may result in deformation of the glider structure. In extreme cases, exceeding permissible limit loads may cause structural failure of the glider. The G-meter allows the pilot to monitor G-loads from moment to moment. This is useful in aerobatic flight and during flight in rough air. Most G-meters also record and display the maximum positive G-load and the maximum negative G-load encountered during flight. The recorded maximum positive and negative G-loads can be reset by adjusting the control knob of the G-meter. [Figure 4-27]

OUTSIDE AIR TEMPERATURE GAUGE

The outside air temperature gauge (OAT) is a simple and effective device mounted so that the sensing element is exposed to the outside air. The sensing element consists of a bimetallic-type thermometer in which two dissimilar metals are welded together into a single strip and twisted into a helix. One end is anchored into a protective tube, and the other end is affixed to the pointer, which reads against the calibration on a circular face. OAT gauges are calibrated in degrees Celsius, degrees Fahrenheit, or both. An accurate air temperature will provide the glider pilot with useful information about temperature lapse rate with altitude change.

When flying a glider loaded with water ballast, knowledge of the height of the freezing level is important to safety of flight. Extended operation of a glider loaded with water ballast in below-freezing temperatures may result in frozen drain valves, ruptured ballast tanks, and structural damage to the glider. [Figure 4-28]

Figure 4-27. The G-meter.

Figure 4-28. A typical outside air temperature (OAT) gauge.

CHAPTER 5
Glider Performance

Glider performance during launch phase and during free flight phase depends on many factors. The design of the glider itself is one factor. Weather, wind, and other atmospheric phenomena also affect glider performance.

FACTORS AFFECTING PERFORMANCE

Glider performance during launch depends on the power output of the launch mechanism and on the aerodynamic efficiency of the glider itself. The three major factors that affect performance are density altitude, weight, and wind.

DENSITY ALTITUDE

Air density directly affects the launch performance of the glider. As the density of the air increases, the engines power output of the launching vehicle (towplane, ground tow, or self-launch glider) and the aerodynamic lift of the glider's wings increase. When air density is less dense, the launch performance decreases. **Density altitude** is the altitude above mean sea level (MSL) at which a given atmospheric density occurs in the **standard atmosphere**. It can also be interpreted as **pressure altitude** corrected for nonstandard temperature differences.

PRESSURE ALTITUDE

Pressure altitude is displayed as the height above a standard datum plane, which, in this case, is a theoretical plane where air pressure is equal to 29.92 inches of mercury (in. Hg). Pressure altitude is the indicated height value on the altimeter when the altimeter setting is adjusted to 29.92 in. Hg. Pressure altitude, as opposed to **true altitude**, is an important value for calculating performance as it more accurately represents the air content at a particular level.

The difference between true altitude and pressure altitude must be clearly understood. True altitude means the vertical height of the glider above MSL. True altitude is displayed on the altimeter when the altimeter is adjusted to the local atmospheric pressure setting.

For example, if the local altimeter setting is 30.12 in. Hg., and the altimeter is adjusted to this value, the altimeter indicates exact height above sea level. However, this does not reflect conditions found at this height under standard conditions. Since the altimeter setting is more than 29.92 in. Hg., the air in this example has a higher pressure, and is more compressed indicative of the air found at a lower altitude. Therefore, the pressure altitude is lower than the actual height above MSL.

To calculate pressure altitude without the use of an altimeter, remember that the pressure decreases approximately 1 inch of mercury for every 1,000-foot increase in altitude. For example, if the current local altimeter setting at a 4,000-foot elevation were 30.42, the pressure altitude would be 3,500 feet. (30.42 - 29.92 = .50 in. Hg. x 1,000 feet = 500 feet. Subtracting 500 feet from 4,000 equals 3,500 feet).

The four factors that affect density altitude the most are atmospheric pressure, altitude, temperature, and the moisture content of the air.

ATMOSPHERIC PRESSURE

Due to changing weather conditions, atmospheric pressure at a given location changes from day to day. When barometric pressure drops, air density decreases. The reduced density of the air results in an increase in density altitude and decreased glider performance. This reduces takeoff and climb performance and increases the length of runway needed for landing.

When barometric pressure rises, air density increases. The greater density of the air results in lower density altitude. Thus, takeoff and climb performance improves, and the length of runway needed for landing decreases.

ALTITUDE

As altitude increases, air density decreases. At altitude, the atmospheric pressure that acts on a given volume of air is less, allowing the air molecules to space themselves further apart. The result is that a given volume of air at high altitude contains fewer air molecules than the same volume of air at lower altitude. As altitude increases, density altitude increases, and glider takeoff and climb performance is reduced.

TEMPERATURE

Temperature changes have a large affect on density altitude. When air is heated, it expands and the molecules move farther apart, creating less dense air. Takeoff and climb performance is reduced, while the length of runway required for landing is increased.

The effects are different when the air is cool. When air cools, the molecules move closer together, creating denser air. Takeoff and climb performance improves, and the length of runway required for landing decreases.

The effect of temperature on density altitude can be very great. High temperatures cause even low elevations to have high-density altitudes, resulting in reduced takeoff and climb performance. Very cold temperatures, on the other hand, can result in density altitudes that are far below those at sea level. In this dense, cold air, takeoff and climb performance is enhanced considerably.

MOISTURE

The water vapor content of the air affects air density. Water vapor molecules, consisting of two hydrogen atoms and one oxygen atom, have a relatively low molecular weight. Water vapor molecules in the atmosphere displace gas molecules with higher molecular weights. Therefore, as the water vapor content of the air increases, the air becomes less dense. The result is increased density altitude and decreased takeoff and climb performance.

Relative humidity refers to the amount of water vapor contained in the atmosphere. It is expressed as a percentage of the maximum amount of water vapor the air can hold. Perfectly dry air (air that contains no water vapor) has a relative humidity of 0 percent, while saturated air (air that cannot hold any more water vapor) has a relative humidity of 100 percent.

The amount of water vapor that an airmass can sustain is affected by temperature. Cold air can hold a relatively small amount of water as vapor; warm air can hold much more. Increasing the temperature of an airmass by 20°F doubles the amount of water the airmass can hold as water vapor. Increasing the temperature of an airmass by 40°F quadruples the amount of water the airmass can hold. Increasing the temperature of an airmass by 60°F causes an eightfold increase and so on.

By itself, humidity usually is not considered an important factor in calculating density altitude and glider performance. Nevertheless, high humidity does cause a slight decrease in glider takeoff and climb performance. At relatively low temperatures, the effect of humidity is very slight because the total amount of water vapor the airmass can hold is relatively small. At

relatively high temperatures, on the other hand, the effect of humidity is more significant because the total amount of water vapor the airmass can hold is many times larger. There are no rules-of-thumb or charts used to compute the effects of humidity on density altitude. Expect a minor decrease in takeoff performance when humidity is high.

HIGH AND LOW DENSITY ALTITUDE CONDITIONS

Every pilot must understand the terms "high density altitude" and "low density altitude." In general, high density altitude refers to thin air, while low density altitude refers to dense air. Those conditions that result in a high density altitude (thin air) are high elevations, low atmospheric pressure, high temperatures, high humidity, or some combination thereof. Lower elevations, high atmospheric pressure, low temperatures and low humidity are more indicative of low density altitude (dense air). However, high density altitudes may be present at lower elevations on hot days, so it is important to calculate the density altitude and determine performance before a flight.

One way to determine density altitude is to use charts designed for that purpose. [Figure 5-1] For example, assume you are planning to depart an airport where the field elevation is 1,165 feet MSL, the altimeter setting is 30.10, and the temperature is 70°F. What is the density altitude? First, correct for nonstandard pressure (30.10) by referring to the right side of the chart and subtracting 165 feet from the field elevation. The result is a pressure altitude of 1,000 feet. Then, enter the chart at the bottom, just above the temperature of 70°F (21°C). Proceed up the chart vertically until you intercept the diagonal 1,000-foot pressure altitude line, then move horizontally to the left and read the density alti-

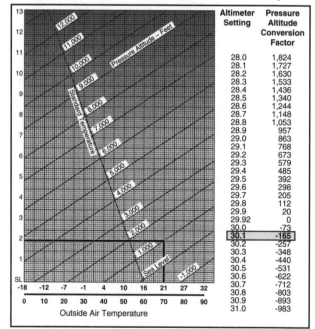

Figure 5-1. Density Altitude Chart.

tude of approximately 2,000 feet. This means your self-launching glider or towplane will perform as if it were at 2,000 feet MSL on a standard day.

Most performance charts do not require you to compute density altitude. Instead, the computation is built into the performance chart itself. All you have to do is enter the chart with the correct pressure altitude and the temperature. Some charts, however, may require you to compute density altitude before entering them. Density altitude may be computed using a density altitude chart or by using a flight computer.

WINDS

Wind affects glider performance in many ways. Headwind during launch results in shorter ground roll, while tailwind causes longer ground roll before takeoff. Crosswinds during launch require proper crosswind procedures. [Figure 5-2]

During cruising flight, headwinds reduce the groundspeed of the glider. A glider flying at 60 knots true airspeed into a headwind of 25 knots has a groundspeed of only 35 knots. Tailwinds, on the other hand, increase the groundspeed of the glider. A glider flying at 60 knots true airspeed with a tailwind of 25 knots has a groundspeed of 85 knots.

Crosswinds during cruising flight cause glider heading (where the glider nose is pointed) and glider track (the path of the glider over the ground) to diverge. When gliding toward an object on the ground in the presence of crosswind, such as on final glide at the end of a cross-country flight, the glider pilot should keep the

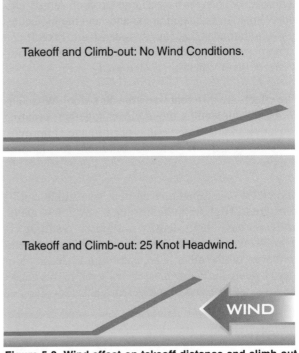

Figure 5-2. Wind effect on takeoff distance and climb-out angle.

nose of the glider pointed somewhat upwind of the target on the ground. For instance, if the crosswind is from the right, during final glide the nose of the glider is pointed a bit to the right of the target on the ground. The glider's heading will be upwind (to the right, in this case) of the target, but if the angle of crab is correct, the glider's track will be straight toward the target on the ground. [Figure 5-3]

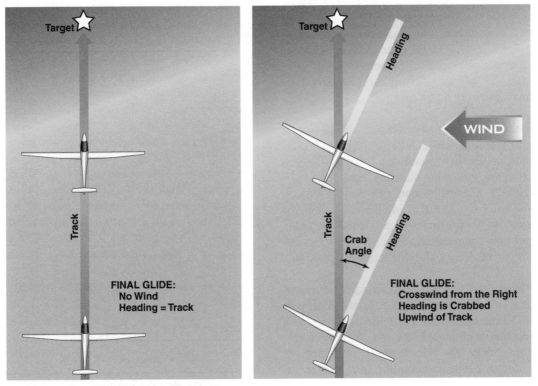

Figure 5-3. Crosswind effect on final glide.

Headwind during landing results in a shortened ground roll and tailwind results in a longer ground roll. Crosswind landings require the pilot to compensate for drift with either a sideslip or a crab. [Figure 5-4]

Some self-launch gliders are designed for extended periods of powered cruising flight. For these self-launch gliders, maximum range (distance) for powered flight and maximum duration (elapsed time aloft) for powered flight is primarily limited by the self-launch glider's fuel capacity. Wind has no effect on flight duration but does have a significant effect on range. During powered cruising flight, a headwind reduces range, and a tailwind increases range. The Glider Flight Manual/Pilot's Operating Handbook (GFM/POH) provides recommended airspeeds and power settings to maximize range when flying in no-win, headwind, or tailwind conditions.

WEIGHT

In gliding, increased weight decreases takeoff and climb performance, but increases high speed cruise performance. During launch, a heavy glider takes longer to accelerate to flying speed. The heavy glider has more inertia making it more difficult to accelerate the mass of a glider to flying speed. After takeoff, the heavier glider takes longer to climb out because the heavier

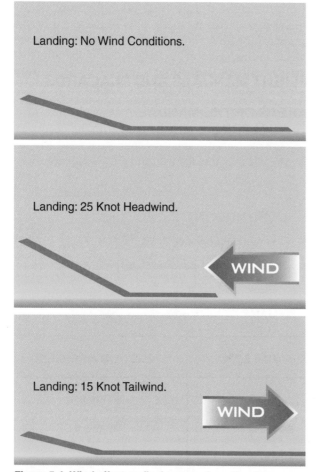

Figure 5-4. Wind effect on final approach and landing distance.

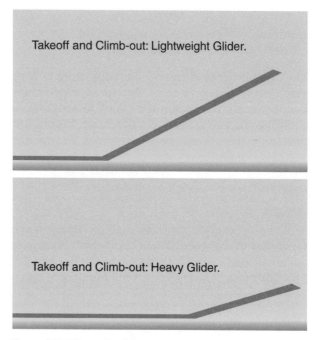

Figure 5-5. Effect of weight on takeoff distance and climbout rate and angle.

glider has more mass to lift to altitude than does the lighter glider (whether ground launch, aerotow launch, or self-launch). [Figure 5-5]

The heavy glider has a higher stall speed and a higher minimum controllable airspeed than an otherwise identical, but lighter, glider. The stall speed of a glider increases with the square root of the increase in weight. If weight of the glider is doubled (multiplied by 2.0), then the stall speed increases by more than 40 percent (1.41 is the approximate square root of 2; 1.41 times the old stall speed results in the new stall speed at the heavier weight).

When circling in thermals to climb, the heavy glider is at a disadvantage relative to the light glider. The increased weight of the heavy glider means stall airspeed and minimum sink airspeed is faster than they would be if the glider were operating at a light weight. At any given bank angle, the heavy glider's faster airspeeds mean the pilot must fly larger diameter thermaling circles than the pilot of the light glider. Since the best lift in thermals is often found in a narrow cylinder near the core of the thermal, larger diameter circles generally mean the heavy glider is unable to exploit the strong lift of the thermal core, as well as the slower, lightweight glider. This results in the heavy glider's inability to climb as fast in a thermal as the light glider. [Figure 5-6]

The heavy glider can fly faster than the light glider while maintaining the same glide ratio as the light glider. The advantage of the heavier weight becomes apparent during cruising flight. The heavy glider can

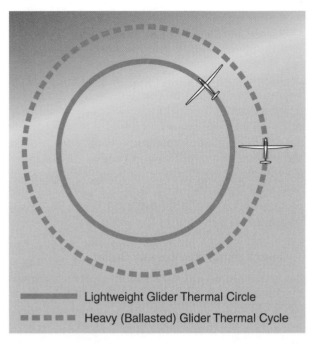

Figure 5-6. Effect and added weight on thermaling turn radius.

fly faster than the light glider and still retains the same lift/drag (L/D) ratio.

If the operating weight of a given glider is increased, the stall airspeed, the minimum controllable airspeed, the minimum sink airspeed, and the **best L/D airspeed** will be increased by a factor equal to the square root of the increase in weight. [Figure 5-7]

The addition of **ballast** to increase weight allows the glider to fly at faster airspeeds while maintaining its L/D ratio. The table in Figure 5-7 shows that adding 400 pounds of water ballast increases the best L/D airspeed from 60 knots to 73 knots. The heavy glider will have more difficulty climbing in thermals than the light glider, but if lift is strong enough for the heavy glider to climb reasonably well, the heavy glider's advantage during the cruising portion of flight will outweigh the heavy glider's disadvantage during climbs.

Water is often used as ballast to increase the weight of the glider. However, the increased weight will require a higher airspeed during the approach and a longer landing roll. Once the cross-country phase is completed, the water ballast serves no further purpose. The pilot should jettison the water ballast prior to entering the traffic pattern. Reducing the weight of the glider prior to landing allows the pilot to make a normal approach and landing. The lighter landing weight also reduces the loads that the landing gear of the glider must support.

RATE OF CLIMB
Rate of climb for the ground-launched glider primarily depends on the strength of the ground-launch equipment. When ground launching, rates-of-climb generally are quite rapid, and can exceed 2,000 feet per minute if the winch or tow vehicle is very powerful.

When aerotowing, rate-of-climb is determined by the power of the towplane. It is important when selecting a towplane, to ensure that it is capable of towing the glider considering the existing conditions and glider weight.

Self-launching glider rate-of-climb is determined by design, powerplant output and glider weight. The rate-of-climb of self-launch gliders may vary from as low as 200 feet per minute to as much as 800 feet per minute or more in others. The pilot should consult the GFM/POH to determine rate-of-climb under the existing conditions.

FLIGHT MANUALS AND PLACARDS

AREAS OF THE MANUAL
The GFM/POH provides the pilot with the necessary performance information to operate the glider safely. A GFM/POH may include the following information.

• Description of glider primary components.

• Glider Assembly.

• Weight and balance data.

• Description of glider systems.

• Glider performance.

• Operating limitations.

OPERATING WEIGHT	STALL AIRSPEED	MINIMUM SINK	BEST L/D AIRSPEED
800 Pounds	36 Knots	48 Knots	60 Knots
1200 Pounds	44 Knots	58 Knots	73 Knots
1600 Pounds	50 Knots	68 Knots	83 Knots

Figure 5-7. Effect of added weight on performance airspeeds.

PLACARDS

Cockpit **placards** provide the pilot with readily available information that is essential for the safe operation of the glider. All required placards are located in the GFM/POH.

The amount of information that placards must convey to the pilot increases as the complexity of the glider increases. High performance gliders may be equipped with wing flaps, retractable landing gear, a water ballast system, drogue chute for use in the landing approach, and other features than are intended to enhance performance. These gliders may require additional placards. [Figure 5-8]

PERFORMANCE INFORMATION

The GFM/POH is the source provided by the manufacturer for glider performance information. In the GFM/POH, glider performance is presented as terms of specific airspeed such as stall speed, minimum sinking airspeed, best L/D airspeed, maneuvering speed, rough air speed, and V_{NE}.

Some performance airspeeds apply only to particular types of gliders. Gliders with wing flaps, for instance, have a maximum permitted flaps extended airspeed (V_{FE}).

Manuals for self-launch gliders include performance information about powered operations. These include rate-of-climb, engine and propeller limitations, fuel consumption, endurance, and cruise.

GLIDER POLARS

In addition, the manufacturer provides information about the rate of sink in terms of airspeed, which is summarized in a graph called a polar curve, or simply a polar. [Figures 5-9].

The vertical axis of the polar shows the sink rate in knots (increasing sink downwards), while the horizontal axis shows airspeed in knots. Every type of glider has a characteristic polar derived either from theoretical calculations by the designer or by actual in-flight measurement of the sink rate at different speeds. The polar of each individual glider will vary (even from other gliders of the same type) by a few percent depending on relative smoothness of the wing surface, the amount of sealing around control surfaces, and even the number of bugs on the wing's leading edge. The polar forms the basis for **speed-to-fly** and final glide tools that will be discussed in Chapter 11–Cross-Country Soaring.

Minimum sink rate is determined from the polar by extending a horizontal line from the top of the polar to the vertical axis. The **minimum sink speed** is found by drawing a vertical line from the top of the polar to the horizontal axis. [Figure 5-10]. In this example, a minimum sink of 1.9 knots occurs at 40 knots. Note that the sink rate increases between minimum sink speed and the stall speed (the left-hand end point of the polar). The best glide speed (best L/D) is found by drawing a tangent to the polar from the origin. The best L/D speed is 50 knots. The glide ratio at best L/D speed is determined by dividing the best L/D speed by the sink rate at that speed, or 50/1.9, which is approximately 26. Thus, this glider has a best glide ratio in calm air (no lift or sink and no headwind or tailwind) of 26:1 at 50 knots.

The best speed-to-fly in a headwind is easily determined from the polar. To do this, shift the origin to the right along the horizontal axis by the speed of the headwind and draw a new tangent line to the polar. From the new tangent point, draw a vertical line to read the best speed-to-fly. An example for a 20 knot headwind is shown in Figure 5-11. The speed-to-fly in a 20 knot headwind is found to be 60 knots. By

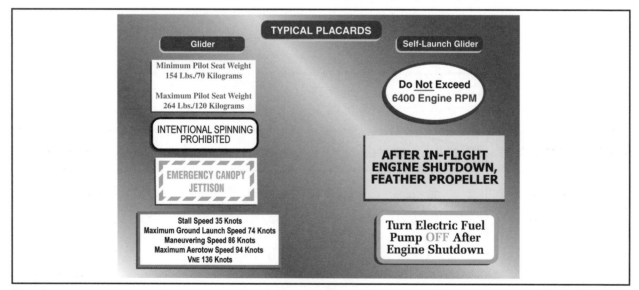

Figure 5-8. Typical placards for non-motorized and self-launch glider.

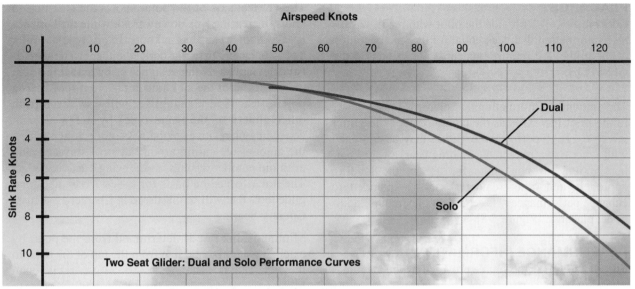

Figure 5-9. Dual and solo performance curves for a two-seat glider.

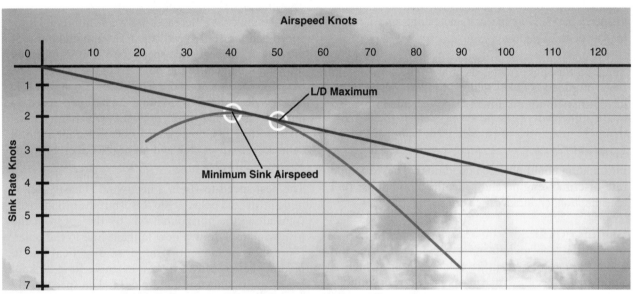

Figure 5-10. Graphic depiction of minimum sink airspeed and maximum L/D speed.

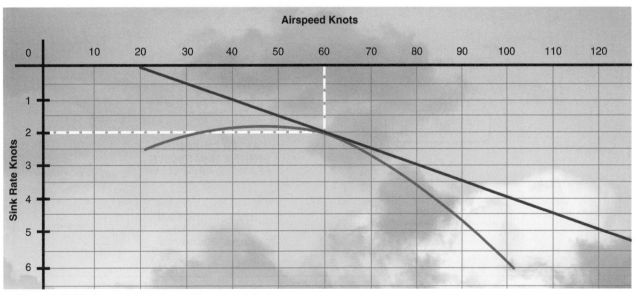

Figure 5-11. Best speed-to-fly in a 20-knot headwind.

repeating the procedure for different headwinds, it is apparent that flying a faster airspeed as the headwind increases will result in the greatest distance over the ground. If this is done for the polar curves from many gliders, a general rule of thumb is found, namely, add half the headwind component to the best L/D for the maximum distance. For tailwinds, shift the origin to the left of the '0' mark on the horizontal axis. The speed-to-fly in a tailwind is found to lie between minimum sink and best L/D but never slower than minimum sink speed.

Sinking air usually exists between thermals, and it is most efficient to fly faster than best L/D in order to spend less time in sinking air. How much faster to fly can be determined by the glider polar, as illustrated in Figure 5-12 for an air mass that is sinking at 3 knots. The polar graph in this figure has its vertical axis extended upwards. Shift the origin vertically by 3 knots and draw a new tangent to the polar, then draw a line vertically to read the best speed-to-fly. For this glider, the best speed-to-fly is found to be 60 knots. Note that the variometer will show the total sink of 5 knots as illustrated in the figure.

If the glider is equipped with water ballast, wing flaps, or wingtip extensions, the performance characteristics of the glider will be depicted in multiple configurations. [Figures 5-13, 5-14, and 5-15]. Comparing the polar with and without ballast [Figure 5-13] it is evident that the minimum sink is higher and occurs at a faster speed. With ballast, therefore, it would be more difficult to work small, weak thermals. The best glide ratio is the same, but it occurs at a higher speed. In addition, the sink rate at higher speeds is lower with ballast. From the polar, then, ballast should be used under stronger thermal conditions for better speed between thermals. Note that the stall speed is higher with ballast as well.

Flaps with a negative setting as opposed to a '0' degree setting during cruise also reduce the sink rate at higher speeds, as shown in the polar [Figure 5-14]. Therefore, when cruising at or above 70 knots, a –8 flap setting would be advantageous for this glider. The polar with flaps set at –8 does not extend to speeds slower than 70 knots since the negative flap setting loses its advantage there.

Wing-tip extensions will also alter the polar, as shown in [Figure 5-15]. The illustration shows that the additional 3 meters of wing span is advantageous at all speeds. In some gliders, the low-speed performance is better with the tip extensions, while high-speed performance is slightly diminished by comparison.

WEIGHT AND BALANCE INFORMATION

The GFM/POH provides information about the weight and balance of the glider. This information is correct when the glider is new as delivered from the factory. Subsequent maintenance and modifications can alter weight and balance considerably. Changes to the glider that affect weight and balance should be noted in the airframe logbook and on appropriate cockpit placards. Maximum Fuselage Weight: 460 pounds

Weight is the force with which gravity attracts a body toward the center of the earth. It is a product of the mass of a body and the acceleration acting on the body. Weight is a major factor in glider construction and operation; it demands respect from all pilots. The pilot of a glider should always be aware of the comsequences of overloading.

LIMITATIONS

Whether the glider is very simple or very complex, designers and manufacturers provide operating limitations which must be complied with to ensure the safety

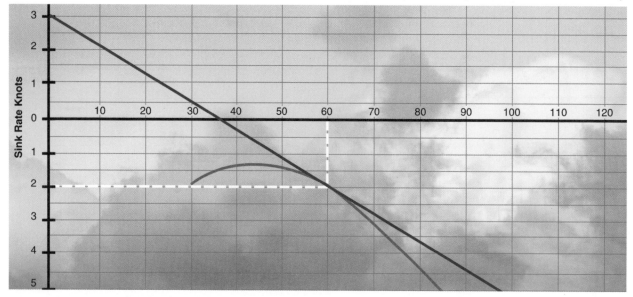

Figure 5-12. Best speed-to-fly in sink.

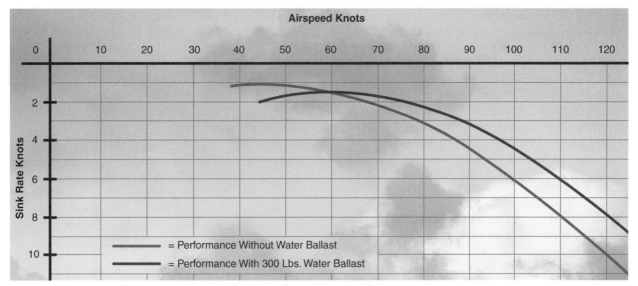

Figure 5-13. Effect of water ballast on performance polar.

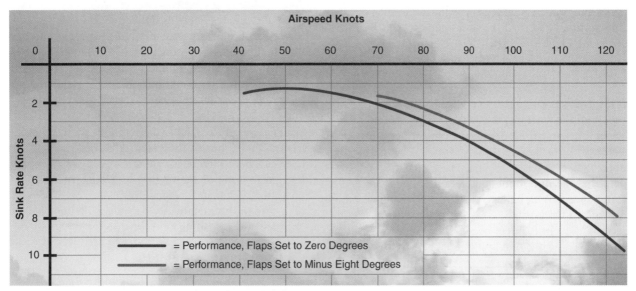

Figure 5-14. Performance polar with flaps at 0° and minus 8°.

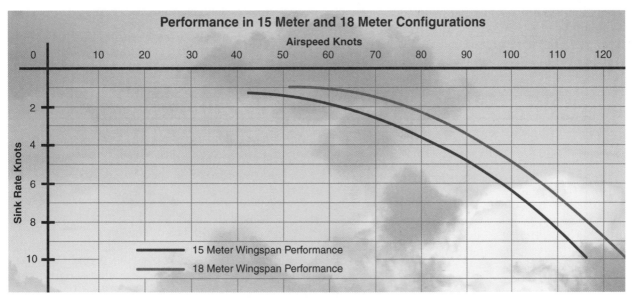

Figure 5-15. Performance polar with 15 meter and 18 meter wingspan configurations.

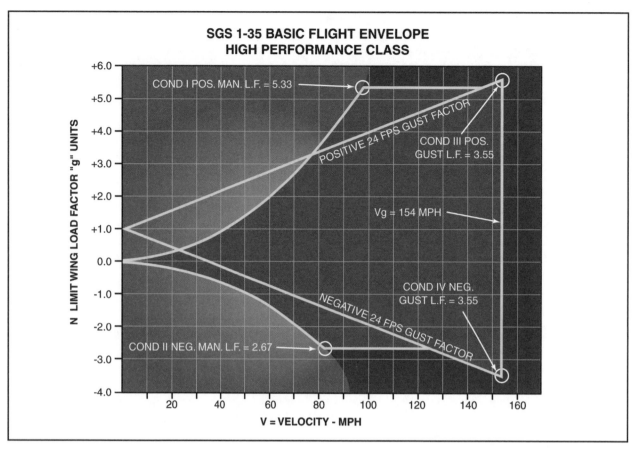

Figure 5-16. VG Diagram.

of flight. Weight is a major factor in glider construction and operation; it demands respect from all pilots. The pilot of a glider should always be aware of the consequences of overloading. The V-G diagram provides the pilot with information on the design limitations of the glider such as limiting airspeeds and load factors. Pilots familiarize themselves with all the operating limitations of each glider they fly. [Figure 5-16]

TERMS AND DEFINITIONS

The pilot should be familiar with terms used in working the problems related to weight and balance. The following list of terms and their definitions is well standardized, and knowledge of these terms will aid the pilot to better understand weight and balance calculations of any glider.

- Arm (moment arm)—is the horizontal distance in inches from the reference datum line to the center of gravity of an item. The algebraic sign is plus (+) if measured aft of the datum, and minus (–) if measured forward of the datum.

- Ballast—is a removable weight installed to meet minimum balance conditions to comply with center of gravity limitations. Ballast may also be in the form of water used to enhance the performance of the glider.

- Center of gravity (CG)—is the point about which a glider would balance if it were possible

to suspend it at that point. It is the mass center of the glider, or the theoretical point at which the entire weight of the glider is assumed to be concentrated. It may be expressed in inches from the reference datum, or in percent of mean aerodynamic chord (MAC).

- Center-of-gravity limits—are the specified forward and aft points within which the CG must be located during flight. These limits are indicated on pertinent glider specifications.

- Center-of-gravity range—is the distance between the forward and aft CG limits indicated on pertinent glider specifications.

- Datum (reference datum)—is an imaginary vertical plane or line from which all measurements of arm are taken. The manufacturer establishes the datum. Once the datum has been selected, all moment arms and the location of CG range are measured from this point.

- Empty weight—is the weight as established by the manufacturer, and which may be modified by addition or deletion of equipment.

- Fuel load—is the expendable part of the load of the self-launch glider. It includes only usable fuel, not fuel required to fill the lines or that which remains trapped in the tank sumps.

- Maximum gross weight—is a weight limitation established by the manufacturer that must not be exceeded. Some gliders may have two maximum gross weights, one with ballast and one without.

- Mean aerodynamic chord (MAC)—is the average distance from the leading edge to the trailing edge of the wing. Some GFM/POHs present the acceptable CG range as a percent of the Mean Aerodynamic Chord (MAC).

- Moment—is the product of the weight of an item multiplied by its arm. Moments are expressed in pound-inches (lb.-in). Total moment is the weight of the airplane multiplied by the distance between the datum and the CG.

- Moment index (or index)—is a moment divided by a constant, such as 100, 1,000, or 10,000. The purpose of using a moment index is to simplify weight and balance computations of gliders where heavy items and long arms result in large, unmanageable numbers.

- Standard weights—have been established for numerous items involved in weight and balance computations. These weights should not be used if actual weights are available. Some of the standard weights are:

  Gasoline..6 lb./US gal
  Oil..7.5 lb./US gal
  Water...8.35 lb./US gal

- Station—is a location in the airplane that is identified by a number designating its distance in inches from the datum. The datum is, therefore, identified as station zero. An item located at station +50 would have an arm of 50 inches.

- Useful load—is the weight of the pilot, passengers, baggage, ballast, usable fuel, and drainable oil. It is the empty weight subtracted from the maximum allowable gross weight.

CENTER OF GRAVITY

Longitudinal balance affects the stability of the longitudinal axis of the glider. To achieve satisfactory pitch attitude handling in a glider, the CG of the properly loaded glider is forward of the Center of Pressure (CP). When a glider is produced the manufacturer provides glider center-of-gravity limitations, which must be complied with. These limitations are generally found in the GFM/POH and may also be found in the glider airframe logbook. Addition or removal of equipment, such as radios, batteries, flight instruments, or airframe repairs, can have an effect on the center of gravity position. Aviation maintenance technicians must record any changes in the weight and balance data in the GFM/POH or glider airframe logbook. Weight and balance placards in the cockpit must also be updated.

PROBLEMS ASSOCIATED WITH CG FORWARD OF FORWARD LIMIT

If the center of gravity is within limits, pitch attitude control stays within acceptable limits. However, if the glider is loaded so the CG is forward of the forward limit, handling will be compromised. Nose heaviness will make it difficult to raise the nose on takeoff and considerable back pressure on the control stick will be required to control the pitch attitude. Stalls will occur at higher than normal airspeeds and will be followed by a rapid nose-down pitch tendency. Restoring a normal flight attitude during stall recoveries will take longer. The landing flare will be more difficult than normal, or perhaps even impossible, due to nose heaviness. Inability to flare could result in a hard nose-first landing.

The following are the most common reasons for CG forward of forward limit.

- Pilot weight exceeds the maximum permitted pilot weight.

- Seat or nose ballast weights are installed but are not required due to the weight of the pilot.

PROBLEMS ASSOCIATED WITH CG AFT OF AFT LIMIT

If the glider is loaded so the CG location is behind the aft limit, handling is compromised. The glider is said to be tail-heavy. Tail heaviness can make pitch control of the glider difficult or even impossible.

When the glider is tail-heavy recovering from a stall may be difficult or impossible. When the stall occurs, the tail-heavy loading tends to make the glider nose continue to pitch upward, increasing angle of attack and complicating stall recovery. In extreme cases, recovery from stall or spin may be difficult or even impossible.

The following are the most common reasons for flight with CG located behind permissible limits.

- Pilot weight is less than the specified minimum pilot seat weight and trim ballast weights necessary for the lightweight pilot are not installed in the glider prior to flight.

- Tailwheel dolly is still attached, far aft on the tail-boom of the glider.

- Foreign matter or debris (water, ice, mud, sand, and nests) has accumulated in the aft fuselage of the glider and was not discovered and removed prior to flight.

- A heavy, non-approved tailwheel or tail skid was installed on the aft tailboom of the glider.

- Improper repair of the aft fuselage of the glider resulted in an increase in aft weight of the fuselage that was not recorded in the glider airframe logbook, or not reflected in cockpit placards, or both.

SAMPLE WEIGHT AND BALANCE PROBLEMS

Some glider manufacturers provide weight and balance information in a graphic presentation. A well-designed graph provides a convenient way to determine whether the glider is within weight and balance limitations.

In Figure 5-17, the chart indicates that the minimum weight for the front seat pilot is 125 pounds, and that the maximum is 250 pounds. It also indicates that the maximum rear seat pilot weight is 225 pounds. If each pilot weighs 150 pounds, the intersection of pilot weights falls within the envelope and the glider load is within the envelope and is safe for flight. If each pilot weights 225 pounds, the rear seat maximum load is exceeded, and the glider load is outside the envelope and not safe for flight.

DETERMINING CG WITHOUT LOADING CHARTS

The CG position can also be determined by calculation using the following formulas:

Weight multiplied by Arm equals Moment

Weight x Arm = Moment

Total Moment divided by Total weight equals CG position in inches aft of the reference datum.

Total Moment ÷ Total Weight = CG

The computational method involves the application of basic math functions. The following is an example of the computational method.

Given:

Maximum Gross Weight	1,100 lb.
Empty Weight	600 lb.
Center-of-Gravity Range	14.8 – 18.6 in.
Front Seat Occupant	180 lb.
Rear Seat Occupant	200 lb.

To determine the loaded weight and CG, follow these steps.

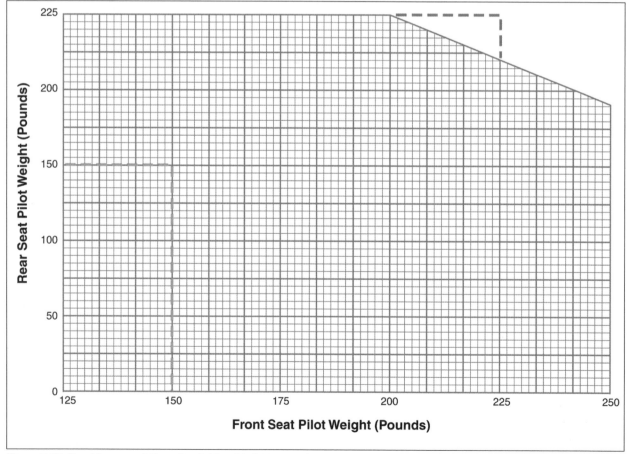

Figure 5-17. Graphic presentation of weight and balance envelope.

Step 1—List the empty weight of the glider and the weight of the occupants.

Step 2—Enter the moment for each item listed. Remember "weight x arm = moment." To simplify calculations, the moments may be divided by 100.

Step 3—Total the weight and moments.

Step 4—To determine the CG, divide the moments by the weight.

NOTE: The weight and balance records for a particular glider will provide the empty weight and moment as well as the information on the arm distance. [Figure 5-18]

In Figure 5-18, the weight of each pilot has been entered into the correct block in the table. For the front seat pilot, multiplying 180 pounds by +30 inches yields a moment of +5400 inch/pounds. For the rear seat pilot, multiplying 200 pounds by -5 inches yields a moment of -1000 inch/pounds.

The next step is to find the sum of all weights, and record it: 980 pounds. Then, find the sum of all moments, and record it: +16,400 inch/pounds.

Now we can find the Arm (the CG position) of the loaded glider. Divide the total moment by the total weight to discover the CG of the loaded aircraftglider. So, +16,400 divided by 980 = +16.73 inches from datum. [Figure 5-20]

We now know the total weight (980 pounds) and the CG location (+16.73 inches from datum) of the loaded glider. The final step is to determine whether these two values are within acceptable limits. The GFM/POH lists the maximum gross weight as 1,100 pounds. The operating weight of 980 pounds is less than 1,100 pounds maximum gross weight. The GFM/POH lists the approved CG range as between +14.80 inches and +18.60 inches from datum. The operating CG is +16.73 inches from datum and is within these limits. We have

determined that the weight and balance are within operating limits.

BALLAST WEIGHT

Ballast weight is non-structural weight that is added to a glider. In gliding, ballast weight is used for two purposes. Trim ballast is used to adjust the location of the center of gravity of the glider so handling characteristics remain within acceptable limits. Performance ballast is loaded into the glider to improve high-speed cruise performance.

Removable trim ballast weights are usually made of metal and are bolted into a ballast receptacle incorporated in the glider structure. The manufacturer generally provides an attachment point well forward in the glider cabin for trim ballast weights. These weights are designed to compensate for a front seat pilot who weighs less than the minimum permissible front seat pilot weight. The ballast weight mounted well forward in the glider cabin helps place the CG within permissible limits.

Some trim ballast weights are in the form of seat cushions, with sand or lead shot sewn into the unit to provide additional weight. This type of ballast, which is installed under the pilot's seat cushion, is inferior to bolted-in ballast because of the propensity to shift position. Seat cushion ballast should never be used during acrobatic or inverted flight.

EFFECTS OF WATER BALLAST

Sometimes trim ballast is water placed in a tail tank in the vertical fin of the fuselage. The purpose of the fin trim ballast tank is to adjust CG location after water is added to, or drained from, the main wing ballast tanks. Unless the main wing ballast tanks are precisely centered on the center of gravity of the loaded aircraftglider, CG location shifts when water is added to the main ballast tanks. CG location shifts again when water is dumped from the main ballast tanks. Adjusting the amount of water in the fin tank compensates for CG shifts resulting from changes in

ITEM	WEIGHT (POUNDS)	ARM (INCHES)	MOMENT (INCH/POUNDS)
EMPTY WEIGHT	600	+20	12,000
FRONT SEAT PILOT	180	+30	+5,400
REAR SEAT PILOT	200	-5	-1,000
	980 Total Weight	+16.73	+16,400 Total Mom.

Figure 5-18. Weight and balance: front and rear seat pilot weights and moments.

the amount of water ballast carried in the main wing ballast tanks. Water weighs 8.35 pounds per gallon. Because the tail tank is located far aft, it does not take much water to have a considerable effect on CG location. For this reason, tail tanks do not need to contain a large volume of water. Tail tank maximum water capacity is generally less than two gallons of water.

Although some older gliders employed bags of sand or bolt-in lead weights as performance ballast, water is used most commonly to enhance high-speed performance in modern sailplanes. Increasing the operating weight of the glider increases the optimum speed-to-fly during wings-level cruising flight. The higher ground-speed that result provide a very desirable advantage in cross-country soaring and in sailplane racing.

Water ballast tanks are located in the main wing panels. Clean water is added through fill ports in the top of each wing. In most gliders, the water tanks or bags can be partially or completely filled, depending on the pilot's choice of operating weight. After water is added, the filler caps are replaced to prevent water from sloshing out of the filler holes.

Drain valves are fitted to the bottom of each tank. The valves are controlled from inside the cockpit. The tanks can be fully or partially drained while the glider is on the ground to reduce the weight of the glider prior to launch, if the pilot so desires. The ballast tanks also can be partially or completely drained in flight—a process called dumping ballast. The long streaks of white spray behind a speeding airborne glider are dramatic evidence that the glider pilot is dumping water ballast, most likely to lighten the glider prior to landing. The filler caps are vented to allow air to enter the tanks to replace the volume of water draining from the tanks. It is important to ensure that the vents are working properly to prevent wing damage when water ballast is drained or jettisoned. [Figures 5-19 and 5-20]

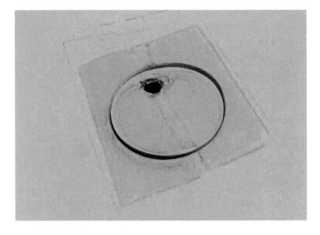

Figure 5-19. Water ballast tank vented filler cap.

It is important to check the drain valves for correct operation prior to flight. Water ballast should drain from each wing tank at the same rate. Unequal draining leads to a wing-heavy condition that makes in-flight handling, as well as landings, more difficult. If the wing-heavy condition is extreme, it is possible the pilot will lose control of the glider.

Ballast drains should also be checked to ensure that water ballast drains properly into the airstream, rather than leaking into the fuselage and pooling in the bottom of the fuselage. Water that is trapped in the fuselage may flow through or over bulkheads, causing dislocation of the CG of the glider. This can lead to loss of control of the glider.

The flight manual provides guidance as to the length of time it takes for the ballast tanks to drain completely. For modern gliders, it takes about 3 to 5 minutes to drain a full tank. When landing is imminent, dump ballast early enough to give the ballast drains sufficient time to empty the tanks.

Use of water ballast when ambient temperatures are low can result in water freezing the drain valve. If the drain valve freezes, dumping ballast is difficult or impossible. If water in the wings is allowed to freeze, serious wing damage is likely to occur. Damage occurs because the volume of water expands during the freezing process. The resulting increased volume can deform ribs and other wing structures, or cause glue bonds to de-laminate. When weather or flight conditions are very cold, do not use water ballast unless anti-freeze has been added to the water. Prior to using an anti-freeze solution, consult the glider flight manual to ensure that anti-freeze compounds are approved for use in the glider.

A glider carrying large amounts of water ballast has noticeably different handling characteristics than the same glider without water ballast. Water ballast:

- Reduces the rate of acceleration of the glider at the beginning of the launch due to the increased glider weight.

- Increases the length of ground roll prior to glider liftoff.

- Increases stall speed.

- Reduces aileron control during the takeoff roll, increasing the chance of uncontrolled wing drop and resultant ground loop.

- Reduces rate of climb during climb-out.

- Reduces aileron response during free flight. The addition of large amounts of water increases lateral stability substantially. This makes quick banking maneuvers difficult or impossible to perform.

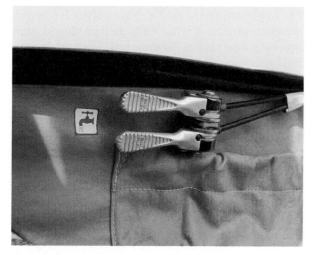 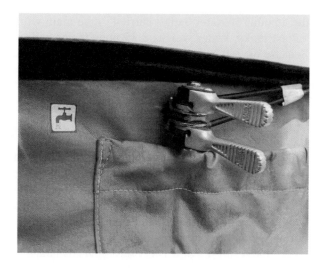

Figure 5-20. Water ballast drain valve handles.

Water ballast is routinely dumped before landing to reduce the weight of the glider. Dumping ballast:

- Decreases stall speed.

- Decreases the optimum airspeed for the landing approach.

- Shortens landing roll.

- Reduces the load that glider structures must support during landing and rollout.

The performance advantage of water ballast during strong soaring conditions is considerable. However, there is a down side. The pilot should be aware that water ballast degrades takeoff performance, climb rate, and low speed handling. Before committing to launching with water ballast aboard, the pilot should review operating limitations to ensure the safety of flight will not be comprised.

CHAPTER 6
Preflight and Ground Operations

Operating a glider requires meticulous assembly and preflight. Proper assembly techniques, followed by a close inspection of the glider using checklists contained in the Glider Flight Manual/Pilot's Operating Handbook (GFM/POH), are essential for flight safety. In order to ensure correct and safe procedures for assembly of a glider, students and pilots unfamiliar with glider assembly should seek instruction from a knowledgable glider flight instructor or certificated private or higher glider pilot. Safely launching a glider requires careful inspection, appropriate use of checklists, and quality teamwork. Launch procedures should be carried out systematically and consistently each time you fly.

ASSEMBLY TECHNIQUES

While preparing to assemble a glider, consider the following elements: location, number of crewmembers, tools and parts necessary, and checklists that detail the appropriate assembly procedures. The GFM/POH should contain checklists for assembling and preflighting your glider. If not, develop your own and follow it every time you fly. Haphazard assembly and preflight procedures can lead to unsafe flying conditions.

Before assembling a glider, find a location that shields the project from the elements and offers enough room for completion. Wind is an important factor to consider during an outdoor assembly. Each wing is an airfoil regardless of whether or not it is connected to the fuselage; even a gentle breeze is enough to produce lift on the wings, making them cumbersome or impossible to handle. If assembling the glider in a spot shielded from the wind, great care must still be taken when handling the wings.

When performing the assembly inside a hangar, ensure there is enough room to maneuver the glider's components throughout the process. Also, consider the length of time you anticipate to complete the entire procedure, and choose an area that allows complete undisturbed assembly. Moving the glider during assembly may cause parts or tools to be misplaced.

Wing stands, pliers, screwdrivers, and lubricants should be on hand when assembling the glider. [Figure 6-1] To stay organized, use a written assembly check-

Figure 6-1. Wing stand used during glider assembly.

list, and keep an inventory of parts and tools. Once the assembly is complete account for all parts and tools. Objects inadvertently misplaced in the glider could become jammed in the flight controls, making control difficult if not impossible.

Depending on the type of glider, two or more people may be required for assembly. It is important for everyone involved to maintain focus throughout the assembly process in order to avoid missed steps. Outside disturbances should also be avoided. Once the assembly is finished, a thorough inspection of all attach points ensures that bolts and pins were installed and secured properly.

TRAILERING

Trailers are used to transport, store, and retrieve gliders. [Figure 6-2] The components of the glider should fit snugly without being forced, be guarded against chafing, and be well secured within the trailer. Once the loading is completed, take a short drive, stop, and check for rubbing or chafing of components.

Figure 6-2. Open and closed trailers.

Prior to taking the trailer on the road, complete a thorough inspection. Inspect the tires for proper inflation and adequate tread; check all lights to make sure they are operating; ensure the hitch is free moving and well lubricated; make sure the vehicle attachment is rated for the weight of the trailer; check the vehicle and trailer brake operation.

When using a trailer, there are other precautions to note. First, avoid towing with too much or too little tongue weight as this causes the trailer to fishtail at certain speeds, and it may become uncontrollable. Second, take care when unloading the glider to avoid damage.

TIEDOWN AND SECURING

Anytime the glider is left unattended it should be tied down. When selecting a tiedown location, choose a spot that faces into the wind if possible. Permanent tiedowns are often equipped with straps, ropes, or chains for the wings and tail, and a release hook for the nose. Check the condition of these tiedowns before use.

If strong winds are expected, tie the spoilers open with seat belts, or place a padded stand under the tail to reduce the angle of attack of the wings. This reduces the pull of the glider against the tiedowns. When securing the glider outside for an extended period of time, install gust locks on the control surfaces to prevent them from banging against their stops in the wind. Cover the pitot tube and the total energy probe to keep spiders, wasps, and other insects or debris from causing an obstruction. [Figure 6-3]

Always use a cover to protect the glider canopy. It can be damaged by blowing dust and sand or scratched by apparel, such as watches or belt buckles. A cover protects the canopy from damage while shielding the interior of the cockpit from ultra-violet (UV) rays. [Figure 6-4]

Figure 6-3. Protecting the pitot tube and total energy probe.

Figure 6-4. Protecting the canopy.

GROUND HANDLING

Moving a glider on the ground requires special handling procedures, especially during high winds. Normally, gliders are pushed or pulled by hand or towed with a vehicle. When moving a glider, ensure that all appropriate personnel have been briefed on procedures and signals.

When using a vehicle to tow a glider, use a towrope that is more than half the wingspan of the glider. If one wingtip stops moving for any reason, this length prevents the glider from pivoting and striking the tow vehicle with the opposite wingtip. One half the wingspan plus 10 feet provides safe operation.

When starting, slowly take up slack in the line with the vehicle to prevent sudden jerking of the glider. The towing speed should be no faster than a brisk walk. When towing a glider, always use at least one wingwalker. The wingwalker and the driver of the tow vehicle function as a team, alert for obstacles, wind, and any other factor that may affect the safety of the glider. The driver should always stay alert for any signals from the wingwalkers. [Figure 6-5]

If it is necessary to move the glider during high winds, use two or more crewmembers placed at the wingtips and tail. Also, have a pilot in the cockpit, with the spoilers deployed, holding the controls appropriately to reduce lift on the glider. Strong winds and gusts can cause damage to the glider during ground handling, so exercise care during these conditions.

LAUNCH EQUIPMENT INSPECTION

Prior to making a flight, it is important to inspect the condition of the towrope. The towrope should be free from excess wear; all strands should be intact, and the rope should be free from knots. [Figure 6-6]

Figure 6-5. Positioning the glider for the tow vehicle.

Title 14 of the Code of Federal Regulations (14 CFR) part 91, section 91.309 requires that the strength of the towrope be within a range of 80 to 200 percent of the maximum certificated weight of the glider. A knot in the towrope reduces its strength by up to 50 percent, and causes a high spot in the rope that is more susceptible to wear. Pay particular attention to the ring area that the glider attaches to because this is also a high wear area.

If the towrope exceeds the required strength it is necessary to use a weak link, or safety link, at both ends of

the towrope. The safety link is constructed of towrope with a towring on one end and the other end spliced into a loop. The weak link at the glider attach end of the towrope must be 80 to 200 percent of the maximum certificated operating weight of the glider. The safety link at the tow plane attach end must be of greater strength than the safety link at the glider attach end of the towrope, but not more than 25 percent greater nor greater than 200 percent of the maximum certificated weight of the glider. Towropes and weak links are assembled using a towring that is appropriate for the operation. [Figure 6-7]

The towhooks on both the glider and the towplane need to be inspected. The two most common types of towhook are an over-the-top design, such as a

Figure 6-6. Inspecting the towrope.

Figure 6-7. The weak link.

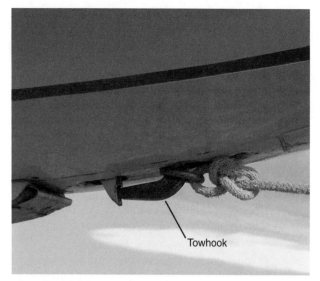

Figure 6-8. Schweizer-type towhook.

Schweizer hook, or a grasping style, such as a Tost hook. Any towhook must be freely operating, and free from damage. [Figure 6-8]

GLIDER PREFLIGHT INSPECTION
A thorough inspection of the glider should be accomplished before launch. A preflight checklist for a glider should be in the GFM/POH. If not, develop a checklist using the guidelines contained in Appendix A— Preflight Checklist.

COCKPIT MANAGEMENT
Prior to launch, passengers should be briefed on the use of safety belts, shoulder harnesses, and emergency procedures. If ballast is used, it must be properly secured. Organize the cockpit so items needed in flight are accessible. All other items must be securely stowed. The necessary charts and cross-country aids should be stowed within easy reach of the pilot.

PERSONAL EQUIPMENT
If a parachute is to be used, 14 CFR part 91 requires that a certified rigger repack it within the preceding 120 days. The packing date information is usually found on a card contained in a small pocket on the body of the parachute.

14 CFR part 91 also requires that the pilot in command (PIC) use supplemental oxygen for flights more than 30 minutes in duration above 12,500 feet, and at all times during a flight above 14,000 feet. If supplemental oxygen is used, the system should be checked for flow and availability.

The glider pilot should carry water on every flight to prevent dehydration. The effects of dehydration on a pilot's performance are subtle, but can be dangerous and are especially a factor in warmer climates.

PRELAUNCH CHECKLIST
Adjustments to the pilot or passenger seats, as well as the pedals, should be made prior to buckling in. At this point, especially if the glider has just been assembled, it is appropriate to do a positive control check with the help of one crewmember. While the pilot moves the control stick, the crewmember alternately holds each aileron and the elevator to provide resistance. This also applies to the spoilers and flaps. This ensures that the control connections are correct and secure. If the stick moves freely while the control surfaces are being restricted, the connections are not secure, and the glider is not airworthy. [Figure 6-9]

Figure 6-9. Positive control check of spoilers.

If the GFM/POH does not provide a specific prelaunch checklist, then a good generic checklist is ABCC-CDD, which stands for:

A—Altimeter set to correct elevation.

B—Seat belts and shoulder harnesses fastened and tightened.

C—Controls checked for full and free movement.

C—Cable or towrope properly connected to the correct hook.

C—Canopy closed, locked, and checked.

D—Dive brakes closed and locked.

D—Direction of wind checked and emergency plan reviewed.

APPENDIX A—Preflight Checklist

Add to this list any items that are appropriate for your particular glider.

- Begin by assessing the overall condition of the fiberglass or fabric.

- Be alert for signs of damage or excessive wear.

- Check that the canopy is clean and free from damage.

- Verify the interior wing and control connections are safe and secure.

- If a battery is used, ensure that it is charged, and safely fastened in the proper spot.

- Check that seat harnesses are free from excessive wear.

- To prevent it from inadvertently interfering with the controls, buckle and tighten any harness that will not be used.

- Test the tow hook to make sure it is operating correctly.

- Inspect top, bottom, and leading edge of wings, making sure they are free from excess dirt, bugs, and damage.

- Inspect spoilers/dive brakes for mechanical damage. They should be clear of obstructions.

- Inspect the wingtip and wingtip skid or wheel for general condition.

- Inspect ailerons for freedom of movement, the condition of hinges and connections, and the condition of the gap seal.

- Check the condition of flaps for freedom from damage and appropriate range of motion.

- Inspect the general condition of the empennage.

- Check static ports, pitot tube, total energy probe to ensure they are free from obstruction.

- Check top, bottom, and leading edge of tailplane for freedom of bugs, dirt, and damage.

- Check the landing gear for signs of damage or excessive wear. The brake pads should be checked if they are visible, otherwise the brakes can be checked by pulling the glider forward and applying the brakes. It should be noted that the landing gear is frequently a problem area for gliders used in training.

- Check elevator and trim tab for condition of connections, freedom of movement, and condition of gap seal.

- Check rudder freedom of movement and condition of connections.

CHAPTER 7
Launch and Recovery Procedures and Flight Maneuvers

This chapter discusses glider launch and takeoff procedures, traffic patterns, landing and recovery procedures, and flight maneuvers.

AEROTOW LAUNCH SIGNALS

Launching a non-powered glider requires the use of visual signals for communication and coordination between the glider pilot, towpilot, and launch crewmembers. If the aircraft and launch crewmembers are equipped with compatible radios, communication is enhanced over hand signals. Aerotow launch signals consist of pre-launch signals and in-flight signals.

PRE-LAUNCH SIGNALS FOR AEROTOW LAUNCHES

Aerotow pre-launch signals facilitate communication between pilots and launch crewmembers preparing for the launch. These signals are shown in Figure 7-1.

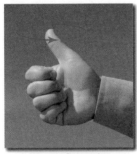
Check Controls
(Thumb moves thru circle.)

Open Towhook

Close Towhook

Raise Wingtip to Level Position

Take Up Slack
(Arm moves slowly back and forth thru arc.)

Hold
(Arms straight out and held steady.)

Begin Takeoff!
(Arm makes rapid circles.)

Stop Operation Immediately!
(Wave arms.)

Stop!

Release Towrope or Stop Engine Now
(Draw arm across throat.)

Figure 7-1. Aerotow pre-launch signals.

IN-FLIGHT AEROTOW VISUAL SIGNALS

Visual signals allow the towpilot and the glider pilot to communicate with each other. The signals are divided into two types: those from the towpilot to the glider pilot, and those from the glider pilot to the towpilot. These signals are shown in Figure 7-2.

TAKEOFF PROCEDURES AND TECHNIQUES

Takeoff procedures for gliders require close coordination between launch crewmembers and pilots. Both the glider and towpilot must be familiar with the appropriate tow procedures.

AEROTOW TAKEOFFS

Normal takeoffs are made into the wind. Prior to takeoff, the towpilot and glider pilot must reach an agreement on the plan for the aerotow. The glider pilot should ensure that the launch crewmember is aware of safety procedures concerning the tow. Some of these items would be proper runway and pattern clearing procedures and glider configuration checks (spoilers closed, tailwheel dolly removed, canopy secured). When the required checklists have been completed and

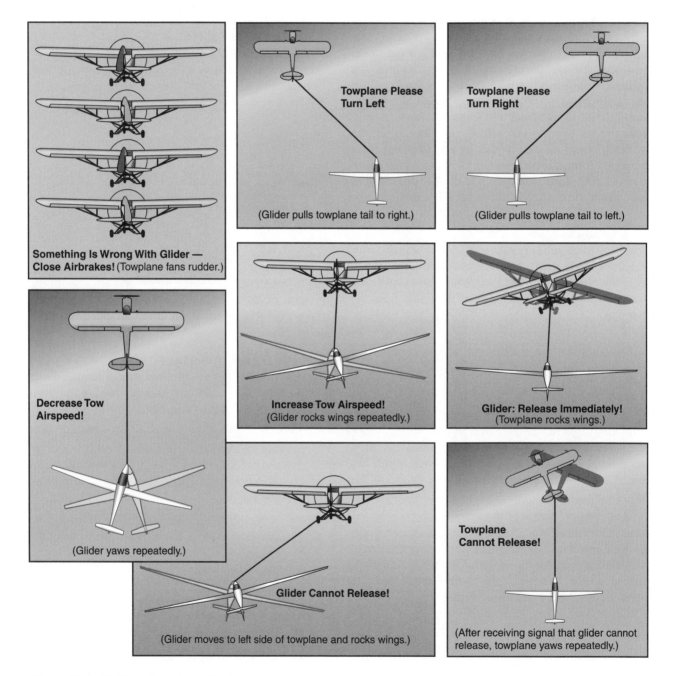

Figure 7-2. In-flight aerotow visual signals.

both the glider and towplane are ready for takeoff, the glider pilot signals the launch crewmember to hook the towrope to the glider.

NORMAL TAKEOFFS

The hook-up should be done deliberately and correctly, and the release mechanism should be checked for proper operation. The launch crewmember applies tension to the towrope and signals the glider pilot to activate the release. The launch crewmember should verify that the release works properly and signals the glider pilot. When the towline is hooked up to the glider again, the launch crewmember repositions to the wing that is down. When the glider pilot signals "ready for takeoff" the launch crewmember clears both the takeoff and landing area, then signals the towpilot to "take up slack" in the towrope. Once the slack is out of the towrope, the launch crewmember verifies that the glider pilot is ready for takeoff, then raises the wings to a level position. With the wings raised, the launch crewmember does a final traffic pattern check and signals the towpilot to takeoff. At the same time, the glider pilot signals the towpilot by wagging the rudder back and forth, concurring with the launch crewmember's takeoff signal. The procedures may differ somewhat from site to site, so follow local convention.

As the launch begins and the glider accelerates, the launch crewmember runs alongside the glider, holding the wing level. If there is a crosswind, the launch crewmember should hold the wing down into the wind, but not in a way as to steer the glider from the wingtip.

When the glider achieves lift-off airspeed, the glider pilot eases the glider off the ground and climbs to an altitude within three to five feet of the runway surface, while the towplane continues to accelerate to lift-off speed. The glider pilot should maintain this altitude by applying forward stick pressure, as necessary, while the glider is accelerating. Once the towplane lifts off, it accelerates in ground effect to the desired climb airspeed, then the climb begins for both the glider and the towplane.

During the takeoff roll, use the rudder pedals to steer the glider. Control the bank angle of the wings with aileron. Full deflection of the flight controls may be necessary at low airspeeds, but the flight controls become more effective as airspeed increases. [Figure 7-3]

In most takeoffs, the glider achieves flying airspeed before the towplane. However, if the glider is a heavily ballasted glider, the towplane may be able to achieve liftoff airspeed before the glider. In such a situation,

Crab into the wind to track the runway centerline until clear of obstacles and terrain features.

Figure 7-3. Tracking the runway centerline.

the towplane should remain in ground effect until the glider is off the ground. Climb-out must not begin until the previously agreed upon climb airspeed has been achieved.

CROSSWIND AEROTOW TAKEOFFS

Crosswind takeoff procedures are a modification of the normal takeoff procedure. The following are the main differences in crosswind takeoffs.

- The glider tends to yaw, or weathervane, into the wind any time the main wheel is touching the ground. The stronger the crosswind, the greater the tendency of the glider to turn into the wind.

- After liftoff, the glider tends to drift toward the downwind side of the runway. The stronger the crosswind, the greater the glider's tendency to drift downwind.

Prior to takeoff, the glider pilot should coordinate with the launch crewmember to hold the upwind wing slightly low during the initial takeoff roll. If a crosswind is indicated, full aileron should be held into the wind as the takeoff roll is started. This control position should be maintained while the glider is accelerating

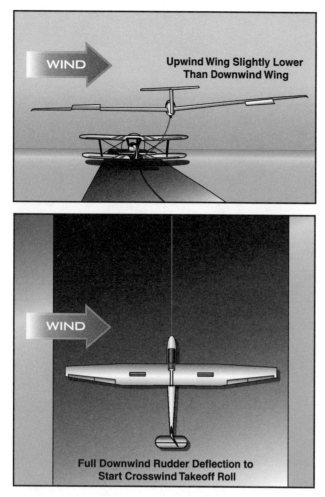

Figure 7-4. Crosswind correction or takeoff.

and lifting it. If the downwind wingtip touches the ground, the resulting friction may cause the glider to yaw in the direction of the dragging wingtip. This could lead to loss of directional control.

While on the runway throughout the takeoff, the glider pilot uses the rudder to maintain directional control and alignment behind the towplane. Yawing back and forth behind the towplane should be avoided, as this effects the ability of the towplane pilot to maintain control. If glider controllability becomes a problem, the glider pilot must release and stop the glider on the remaining runway. Remember, as the glider slows, the crosswind may cause it to weathervane into the wind.

Prior to the towplane becoming airborne and after the glider lifts off, the glider pilot should turn into the wind and establish a wind correction angle to remain behind the towplane. This is accomplished by using coordinated control inputs to turn the glider. Once the towplane becomes airborne and establishes a wind correction angle, the glider pilot repositions to align behind the towplane.

COMMON ERRORS
- Improper glider configuration for takeoff.
- Improper initial positioning of flight controls.
- Improper use of visual launch signals.
- Failure to maintain alignment behind towplane before towplane becomes airborne.
- Improper alignment with the towplane after becoming airborne.
- Climbing too high after liftoff and causing a towplane upset.

TAKEOFF EMERGENCY PROCEDURES
The most common emergency situations on takeoff develop when a towrope breaks, there is an inadvertent towrope release, or towplane loses power. There are five planning situations regarding in-motion towrope breaks, uncommanded release, or power loss of the towplane. While the best course of action depends on many variables, such as runway length, airport environment, and wind, all tow failures have one thing in common: the need to maintain control of the glider. Two possibilities are stalling the glider, or dragging a wingtip on the ground during a low altitude turn and cartwheeling the glider. [Figure 7-5]

Situation 1. If the towrope breaks or is inadvertently released prior to the towplane's liftoff, the standard procedure is for the towplane to continue the takeoff and clear the runway, or abort the takeoff and remain on the left side of the runway. If the towplane loses power during the takeoff, the towpilot should maneuver the towplane to the left side of the runway. If the glider is still on the runway, the glider pilot should pull

and until the ailerons start becoming sufficiently effective for maneuvering the glider about its longitudinal (roll) axis. With the aileron held into the wind, the takeoff path must be held straight with the rudder. This requires application of downwind rudder pressure, since the glider tends to weathervane into the wind while on the ground. [Figure 7-4]

As the forward speed of the glider increases and the crosswind becomes more of a relative headwind, the many mechanical application of full aileron into the wind should be reduced. It is when increasing pressure is being felt on the aileron control that the ailerons are becoming more effective. Because the crosswind component effect does not completely dissipate, some aileron pressure must be maintained throughout the takeoff roll to prevent the crosswind from raising the upwind wing. If the upwind wing rises, exposing more surface to the crosswind, a "skipping" action may result, as indicated by a series of small bounces occurring when the glider attempts to fly and then settles back onto the runway. This side skipping imposes side loads on the landing gear. Keeping the upwind wingtip slightly lower than the downwind wingtip prevents the crosswind from getting underneath the upwind wing

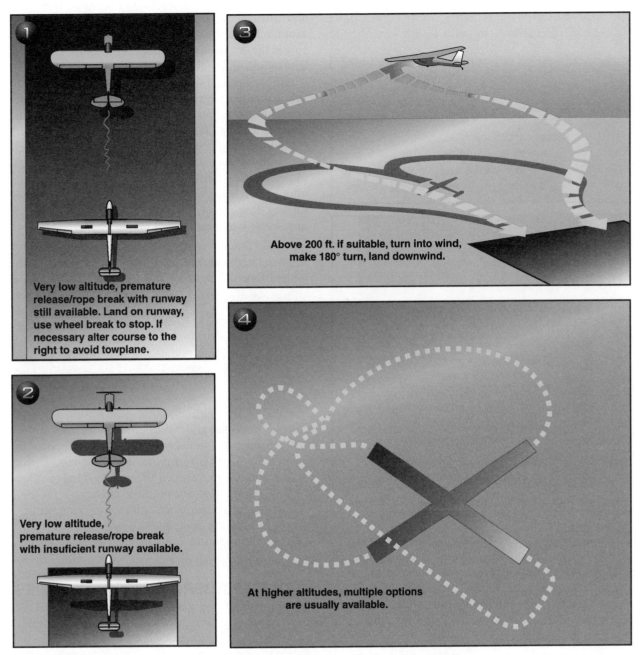

Figure 7-5. Situations for towline break, uncommanded release, or power loss of the towplane.

the release, decelerate using the wheel brake, and be prepared to maneuver to the right side of the runway. If the rope breaks, is inadvertently released, or the towplane loses power after the glider is airborne, the glider pilot should pull the towrope release, land straight ahead, and be prepared to maneuver to the right side of the runway. Pulling the towrope release in either case ensures that the rope is clear of the glider. Since local procedures vary, both the glider and towpilot must be familiar with the specific gliderport/airport procedures.

Situation 2. This situation occurs when both the towplane and glider are airborne and at a low altitude. If an inadvertent release, towrope break, or a signal to release from the towplane occurs at a point in which

the glider has insufficient runway directly ahead and has insufficient altitude to make a safe turn, the best course of action is to land the glider straight ahead. After touchdown, use wheel brake, as necessary, to slow and stop as conditions permit. At low altitude, attempting to turn prior to landing is very risky because of the likelihood of dragging a wingtip on the ground and cartwheeling the glider. Slowing the glider as much as possible prior to touching down and rolling onto unknown terrain generally is the safest course of action. Low speed means low impact forces, which reduce the likelihood of injury and reduce the risk of significant damage to the glider.

Situation 3. If an inadvertent release, towrope break, or a signal to release from the towplane occurs after the towplane and glider are airborne, and the glider possesses sufficient altitude to make a 180° turn, then a downwind landing on the departure runway may be attempted.

The 180° turn and downwind landing option should be used only if the glider is within gliding distance of the airport or landing area. In ideal conditions, a minimum altitude of 200 feet above ground level is required to complete this maneuver safely. Such things as a hot day, weak towplane, strong wind, or other traffic may require a greater altitude to make a return to the airport a viable option.

The responsibility of the glider pilot is to avoid the towplane or other aircraft. If the tow was terminated because the towplane was in distress, the towpilot is also dealing with an emergency situation and may maneuver the aircraft abruptly.

After releasing from the towplane at low altitude, if the glider pilot chooses to make a 180° turn and a downwind landing, the first responsibility is to maintain flying speed. The pilot must immediately lower the nose to achieve the proper pitch attitude necessary to maintain the appropriate approach airspeed.

Make the initial turn into the wind. Use a medium bank angle to align the glider with the landing area. Using too shallow a bank angle may not allow enough time for the glider to align with the landing area. Too steep a bank angle may result in an accelerated stall. If the turn is made into the wind, only minor course corrections should be necessary to align the glider with the intended landing area. Throughout the maneuver the pilot must maintain the appropriate approach speed and proper coordination.

Downwind landings result in higher groundspeed due to the effect of tailwind. The glider pilot must maintain the appropriate approach airspeed. During the straight-in portion of the approach, spoilers/dive breaks should be used as necessary to control the descent path. Landing downwind requires a shallower than normal approach. Groundspeed will be higher during a downwind landing and especially noticeable during the flare. After touchdown, spoilers/dive breaks, and wheel brakes should be used as necessary to slow and stop the glider as quickly as possible. During the later part of the roll-out, the glider will feel unresponsive to the controls despite the fact that it is rolling along the runway at a higher than normal groundspeed. It is important to stop the glider before any loss of directional control.

Situation 4. When the emergency occurs at or above 800 feet above the ground, the glider pilot may have more time to assess the situation. Depending on gliderport/airport environment, the pilot may choose to land on a cross runway, land into the wind on the departure runway, or land on a taxiway. In some situations an off gliderport/airport landing may be safer than attempting to land on the gliderport/airport.

Situation 5. If an emergency occurs above the traffic pattern altitude, the glider pilot should maneuver away from the towplane, release the towrope if still attached, and turn toward the gliderport/airport. The glider pilot should evaluate the situation to determine if there is sufficient altitude to search for lift or if it is necessary to return to the gliderport/airport for a landing.

AEROTOW CLIMB-OUT AND RELEASE PROCEDURES

Once airborne and climbing, the glider can fly one of two tow positions. High tow is aerotow flight with the glider positioned above the wake of the towplane. Low tow is aerotow flight with the glider positioned below the wake of the towplane. [Figure 7-6] Climbing turns are made with shallow bank angles and the glider in the high tow position.

High tow is the preferred position for climbing out because the glider is above the turbulence of the towplane wake. High tow affords the glider pilot an ample view of the towplane and provides a measure of protection against fouling if the towrope breaks or is released by the towplane because the towrope falls below the glider in this position.

Low tow offers the glider pilot a better view of the towplane, but puts the glider at risk from towrope fouling if the towrope breaks or is released by the towplane. Low tow is used for cross-country and level flight aerotows.

During level flight aerotows, positioning the glider above the wake of the towplane has several disadvantages. One is that the towplane wake is nearly level rather than trailing down and back as it does during climbing aerotow operations. Because the towplane wake is nearly level, the glider must take a higher position relative to the towplane to ensure the glider stays above the wake. This higher position makes it difficult to see the towplane over the nose of the glider. Easing the stick forward to get a better view of the towplane accelerates the glider toward the towplane, causing the towrope slack. Positioning the glider beneath the wake of the towplane in level flight offers an excellent view of the towplane, but the danger of fouling from a

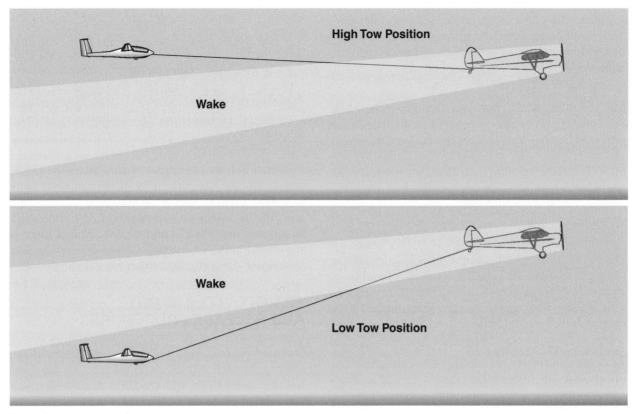

High Tow Position

Wake

Wake

Low Tow Position

Figure 7-6. Aerotow climb-out.

towrope failure or inadvertent release is greater when flying in the low tow position. Gliders using a center of gravity (CG) tow hook during low tow position on level flight aerotows may encounter the towrope sliding up and to the side of the glider nose, causing possible damage.

Straight ahead climbs are made with the glider in the high tow position. The towpilot should maintain a steady pitch attitude and a constant power setting to maintain the desired climb airspeed. The glider pilot uses visual references on the towplane to maintain lateral and vertical position.

Climbing turns are made with shallow bank angles in the high tow position. During turns, the glider pilot observes and matches the bank angle of the towplane's wings. In order to stay in the same flight path of the towplane, the glider pilot must aim the nose of the glider at the outside wingtip of the towplane. This allows the glider's flight path to coincide with the towplane's flight path. [Figure 7-7]

If the glider's bank is steeper than the towplane's bank, the glider's turn radius is smaller than the towplane's turn radius. [Figure 7-8 on page 7-8] If this occurs, the reduced tension on the towrope causes it to bow and slack, allowing the glider's airspeed to slow. As a

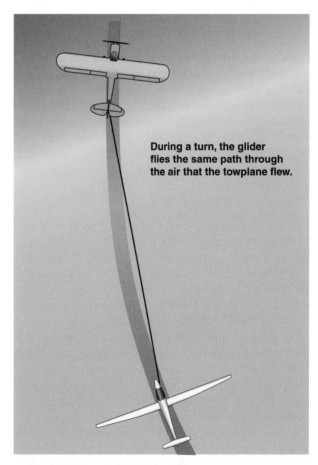

During a turn, the glider flies the same path through the air that the towplane flew.

Figure 7-7. Aerotow climbing turns.

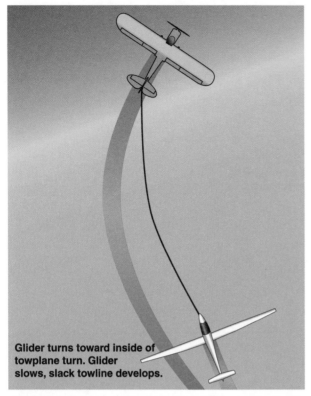

Glider turns toward inside of towplane turn. Glider slows, slack towline develops.

Figure 7-8. Aerotow induced slack towline by turning inside towplane.

result, the glider begins to sink, relative to the towplane. The correct course of action is to reduce the glider's bank angle so the glider flies the same radius of turn as the towplane. If timely corrective action is not

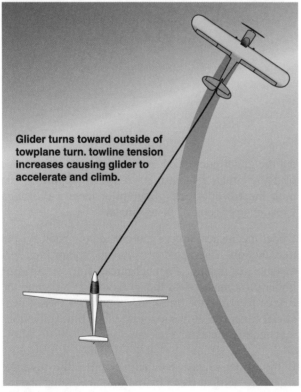

Glider turns toward outside of towplane turn. towline tension increases causing glider to accelerate and climb.

Figure 7-9. Glider bank too shallow, causing turn outside towplane turn.

taken, and if the glider slows and sinks below the towplane, the towplane may rapidly pull the towrope taut and possibly cause it to fail and/or cause structural damage to both aircraft.

If the glider's bank is shallower than the towplane, the glider's turn radius is larger than the towplane's turn radius. [Figure 7-9] If this occurs, the increased tension on the towrope causes the glider to accelerate and climb. The correct course of action to take when the glider is turning outside the towplane radius of turn is to increase the glider's bank angle, so the glider eases back into position behind the towplane and flies the same radius of turn as the towplane. If timely corrective action is not taken, and if the glider accelerates and climbs above the towplane, the towplane may lose rudder and elevator control. In this situation, the glider pilot should release the towrope and turn to avoid the towplane.

COMMON ERRORS

- Faulty procedures maintaining vertical and lateral positions during high and/or low tow.
- Inadvertent entry into towplane wake.
- Failure to maintain glider alignment during turns on aerotow.

AEROTOW RELEASE

Standard aerotow release procedures provide safety benefits for both the glider pilot and the towpilot. When the aerotow has reached a predetermined altitude, the glider pilot should clear the area for other aircraft in all directions, especially to the right. When ready to release, the glider pilot should pull the release handle, and visually confirm that towrope has released from the glider as shown in Figure 7-10, item 1. Next, bank to the right, accomplishing 90° of heading change, then level the wings and fly straight, away from the release point. [Item 2] This 90° change of heading achieves maximum separation between towplane and glider in minimum time. After confirming that the glider has released and has turned away from the towplane, the towpilot should turn left away from the release point. [Item 3] Once clear of the glider and other aircraft, the towpilot then begins a descent.

COMMON ERRORS

- Lack of proper tension on towrope.
- Failure to clear the area prior to release.
- Failure to make turn in proper direction after release.
- Release in close proximity of other aircraft.

AEROTOW ABNORMAL PROCEDURES

Mechanical equipment failure, environmental factors, and pilot errors can cause abnormal aerotow occurrences during climb-out.

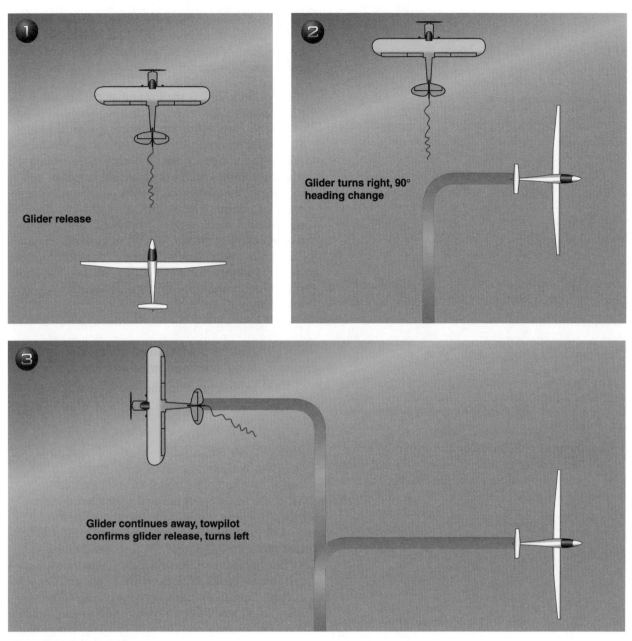

Figure 7-10. Aerotow release.

Mechanical equipment failures can be caused by towrope and towhook failures, towplane mechanical failures, and/or glider mechanical failures. Towrope failure (one that breaks unexpectedly) can result from using an under-strength or worn towrope. Towrope failures can be avoided by using appropriately rated towrope material, weak links when necessary, proper towrings, and proper towrope maintenance.

Towhook system failures include uncommanded towrope releases or the inability to release. These failures can occur in either the towplane or the glider towhook system. Proper preflight and maintenance of these systems should help to avoid these types of failures. Towplane mechanical failures can involve the powerplant and/or flight control. When the towpilot encounters a mechanical failure, he or she should sig-

nal the glider pilot to release immediately. This is one of many situations that make it vitally important that both the towpilot and glider pilot have a thorough knowledge of aerotow visual signals.

Glider mechanical failure can include towhook system malfunctions, flight control problems, and/or improper assembly or rigging. If a mechanical failure occurs, the glider pilot must assess the situation to determine the best course of action. In some situations, it may be beneficial to remain on the aerotow, while other situations may require immediate release.

If the glider release mechanism fails, the towpilot should be notified either by radio or tow signal and the glider should maintain the high tow position. The towpilot should tow the glider over the gliderport/airport and release the glider from the towplane. The towrope should fall back and below the glider. The design of the towhook mechanism is such that the rope pulls free from the glider by it's own weight. Since some gliders do not "back release," the glider pilot should pull the release to ensure the towrope is in fact released.

Failure of both the towplane and glider release mechanisms is extremely rare. If it occurs, however, radio or tow signals between the glider and towpilot should verify this situation. The glider pilot should move down to the low tow position once the descent has started to the gliderport/airport. The glider pilot needs to use spoilers/dive breaks to maintain the low tow position and to avoid over taking the towplane. The towpilot should plan the approach to avoid obstacles. The approach should be shallow enough so that the glider touches down first. The glider pilot should use the spoilers/dive breaks to stay on the runway, and use the wheel brake as necessary to avoid overtaking the towplane. Excessive use of the glider wheel break may result in the towplane landing hard.

Environmental factors include encountering clouds, mountain rotors, or restricted visibility. Any of these factors also may require the glider pilot to release from the aerotow. During the aerotow, each pilot is responsible for avoiding situations that would place the other pilot at risk. For the towplane pilot, examples of pilot error include deliberately starting the takeoff before the glider pilot has signaled the glider is ready for launch, using steep banks during the aerotow without prior consent of the glider pilot, or frivolous use of aerotow signals, such as "release immediately!" For the glider pilot, examples of pilot error include rising high above the towplane during takeoff and climb, or leaving airbrakes open during takeoff and climb.

One of the most dangerous occurrences during the aerotow is allowing the glider to rise high above and losing sight of the towplane. The tension on the towrope by the glider pulls the towplane tail up, lowering its nose. If the glider continues to rise pulling the towplane tail higher, the towpilot may not be able to raise the nose. Ultimately, the towpilot may run out of up elevator authority. Additionally, the towpilot may not be able to release the towrope from the towplane. This situation can be critical if it occurs at altitudes below 500 feet AGL. Upon losing sight of the towplane, the glider pilot must release immediately.

SLACK LINE
Slack line is a reduction of tension in the towrope. If the slack is severe enough it might entangle the glider, or cause damage to the glider or towplane. The following situations may result in a slack line.

- Abrupt power reduction by the towplane.

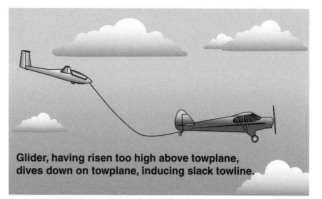
Glider, having risen too high above towplane, dives down on towplane, inducing slack towline.

Figure 7-11. Diving on towplane.

- Aerotow descents.
- Turning the glider inside the towplane turn radius. [Figure 7-8]
- Turbulence.
- Abrupt recovery from a high tow position. [Figure 7-11]

Slack line recovery procedures should be initiated as soon as the glider pilot becomes aware of the situation. The pilot's initial action should be to yaw away from the bow in the line. In the event the yawing motion fails to reduce the slack sufficiently, careful use of spoilers/dive brakes can be used to decelerate the glider and take up the slack. When the towline tightens, stabilize the tow, then gradually resume the desired aerotow position. When the slack in the line is excessive, or beyond the pilot's capability to safely recover, the pilot should immediately release from the aerotow.

COMMON ERRORS
- Failure to take corrective action at the first indication of a slack line.
- Use of improper procedure to correct slack line, causing excessive stress on tow rope, towplane, and glider.

BOXING THE WAKE
Boxing the wake is a performance maneuver designed to demonstrate a pilot's ability to accurately maneuver the glider around the towplane's wake during aerotow. [Figure 7-12]

Boxing the wake requires flying a rectangular pattern around the towplane's wake. Before starting the maneuver, the glider should descend through the wake to the center low tow position as a signal to the towpilot that the maneuver is about to begin. The pilot uses coordinated control inputs to move the glider out to one side of the wake and holds that lower corner of the rectangle momentarily with rudder pressure. Applying back pressure to the control stick starts a vertical ascent, then rudder pressure is used to maintain equal

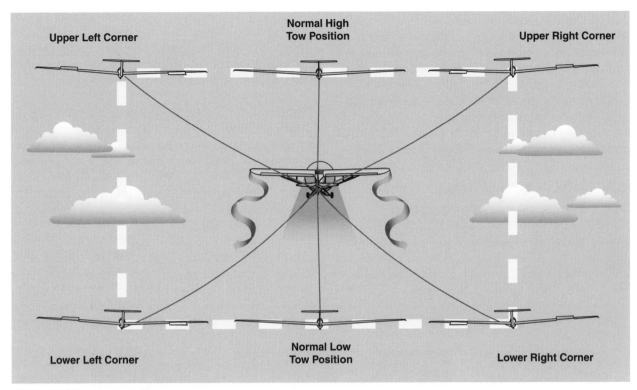

Figure 7-12. Boxing the wake.

distance from the wake. The pilot holds the wings level with the ailerons to parallel the towplane's wings. When the glider has attained high corner position, the pilot momentarily maintains this position.

As the maneuver continues, the pilot reduces the rudder pressure and uses coordinated flight controls to bank the glider to fly along the top side of the box. The glider should proceed to the opposite corner using aileron and rudder pressure, as appropriate. The pilot maintains this position momentarily with rudder pressure, then begins a vertical descent by applying forward pressure to the control stick. Rudder pressure is used to maintain glider position at an equal distance from the wake. The pilot holds the wings level with the ailerons to parallel the towplane's wings. When the glider has attained low corner position, the pilot momentarily maintains this position. The pilot releases the rudder pressure and, using coordinated flight controls, banks the glider to fly along the bottom side of the box until reaching the original center low tow position. From center low tow position, the pilot maneuvers the glider through the wake to the center high tow position, completing the maneuver.

COMMON ERRORS
- Performing an excessively large rectangle around the wake.
- Improper control coordination and procedure
- Abrupt or rapid changes of position.

If pulling the towline release handle fails to release the towline, cycle release handle and try again several times. If handle still fails to release, fly over winch/auto and allow the back release to function.

Figure 7-13. Testing the towhook.

GROUND LAUNCH TAKEOFF

When ground launching, it is essential to use a tow hook that has an automatic back-release feature. This protects the glider if the pilot is unable to release the towline during the launch. The failure of the tow release could cause the glider to be pulled to the ground as it flies over the launching vehicle or winch. Since the back-release feature of the tow hook is so important, it should be tested prior to every flight. [Figure 7-13]

GROUND LAUNCH SIGNALS

PRE-LAUNCH SIGNALS FOR GROUND LAUNCHES (WINCH/AUTOMOBILE)

Pre-launch visual signals for a ground launch operation allow the glider pilot, the glider wing runner, the safety officer, and the launch crew to communicate over considerable distances. When ground launching with an automobile, the glider and launch automobile may be 1,000 or more feet apart. When launching with a winch, at the beginning of the launch the glider may be 4,000 feet or more from the winch. Because of the great distances involved, members of the ground launch crew use colored flags or large paddles to enhance visibility as shown in Figure 7-14.

When complex information must be relayed over great distances, visual pre-launch signals can be augmented with direct voice communications between crewmember stations. Hard-wired ground telephones, two-way radios, or wireless telephones can be used to communicate between stations, adding protection against premature launch and facilitating an aborted launch if an unsafe condition arises.

IN-FLIGHT SIGNALS FOR GROUND LAUNCHES

Since ground launches are of short duration, in-flight signals for ground launches are limited to signals to the winch operator or ground vehicle driver to increase or decrease speed. [Figure 7-15]

Check Controls
(Thumb moves thru circle.)

Open Towhook

Close Towhook

**Raise Wingtip
to Level Position**

Take Up Slack
(Arm moves slowly back
and forth thru arc.)

Hold
(Arms straight out and held steady.)

Begin Takeoff!
(Arm makes rapid circles.)

Stop Operation Immediately!
(Wave arms.)

Release Towrope or Cut Towline Now
(Draw arm across throat.)

Figure 7-14. Winch and aerotow pre-launch signals.

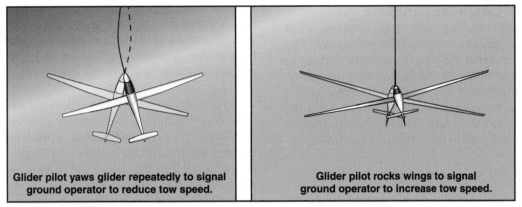

Glider pilot yaws glider repeatedly to signal ground operator to reduce tow speed.	Glider pilot rocks wings to signal ground operator to increase tow speed.

Figure 7-15. In-flight signals for ground launch.

TOW SPEEDS

Proper ground launch tow speed is critical for a safe launch. Figure 7-16 compares various takeoff profiles that result when tow speeds vary above or below the correct speed.

Each glider certified for ground launch operations has a placarded maximum ground launch tow speed. This speed is normally the same for automobile or winch launches. The glider pilot should fly the launch staying at or below this speed to prevent structural damage to the glider during the ground tow.

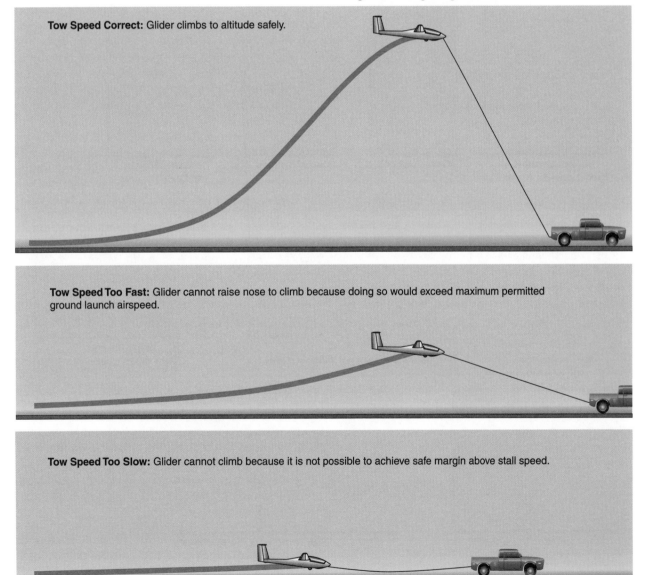

Tow Speed Correct: Glider climbs to altitude safely.

Tow Speed Too Fast: Glider cannot raise nose to climb because doing so would exceed maximum permitted ground launch airspeed.

Tow Speed Too Slow: Glider cannot climb because it is not possible to achieve safe margin above stall speed.

Figure 7-16. Ground launch tow speed.

AUTOMOBILE LAUNCH

During automobile ground launches, the glider pilot and driver should have a thorough understanding of what ground speeds are to be used prior to any launch. Before the first launch, the pilot and vehicle driver should determine the appropriate vehicle ground tow speeds considering the surface wind velocity, the glider speed increase during launch, and the wind gradient encountered during the climb. They should include a safety factor so as not to exceed this maximum vehicle ground tow speed.

The tow speed can be determined by using the following calculations.

1. Subtract the surface winds from the maximum placarded ground launch tow speed for the particular glider.
2. Subtract an additional five miles per hour for the airspeed increase during the climb.
3. Subtract the estimated wind gradient increase encountered during the climb.
4. Subtract a 5 MPH safety factor.

Maximum ground launch speed	**75 MPH**
1. Surface winds 10 MPH	**65 MPH**
2. Airspeed increase during climb 5 MPH	**60 MPH**
3. Estimated climb wind gradient 5 MPH	**55 MPH**
4. Safety factor of 5 MPH	**50 MPH**
Automobile tow speed	**50 MPH**

During winch launches, the winch operator applies full power smoothly and rapidly until the glider reaches an angle of 30° above the horizon. At this point, the operator should start to reduce the power until the glider is about 60° above the horizon where only about 20 percent of the power is needed. As the glider reaches the 70° point above the horizon, the power is reduced to idle. The winch operator monitors the glider continuously during the climb for any signals to increase or decrease speed from the glider pilot. [Figure 7-17]

NORMAL INTO-THE-WIND GROUND LAUNCH

Normal takeoffs are made into the wind. Prior to launch, the glider pilot, ground crew, and launch equipment operator must be familiar with the launch signals and procedures. When the required checklists for the glider and ground launch equipment have been completed and the glider pilot, ground crew, and launch equipment operator are ready for takeoff, the glider pilot should signal the ground crewmember to hook the towline to the glider. The hook-up must be done deliberately and correctly. The release mechanism should be checked for proper operation. To accomplish this, the ground crewmember should apply tension to the towrope and signal the glider pilot to activate the release. The ground crewmember should verify that the release has worked properly and signal the glider pilot. When the towline is hooked up to the glider again, the ground crewmember takes a position at the wingtip of the down wing. When the glider pilot signals "ready for takeoff," the ground crewmember clears both the take-off and landing area. When the ground crewmember has assured the traffic pattern is clear, the ground crewmember then signals the launch equipment operator to "take up slack" in the towline. Once the slack is out of the towline, the ground crewmember again verifies that the glider pilot is ready for takeoff. Then ground crewmember raises the wings to a level position, does a final traffic pattern check, and signals to the launch equipment operator to begin the takeoff.

NOTE: The glider pilot should be prepared for a takeoff anytime the towline is attached to the glider.

The length, elasticity, and mass of the towline used for ground launching has several effects on the glider being launched. First, it is difficult or impossible to prevent the glider from moving forward as the long towline is tautened. Elasticity in the towline causes the glider to creep forward as the towline is tightened. For this reason, the towline is left with a small amount of slack prior to beginning the launch. It is important for the pilot to be prepared for the launch prior to giving the launch signal. If the launch is begun before the pilot gives the launch signal, the glider pilot should pull the towline release handle promptly. In the first several seconds of the launch, the glider pilot should hold the stick forward to avoid kiting.

During the launch, the glider pilot tracks down the runway centerline and monitors the airspeed. (Figure 7-18, item 1) When the glider accelerates and attains liftoff speed the glider pilot eases the glider off the ground. The

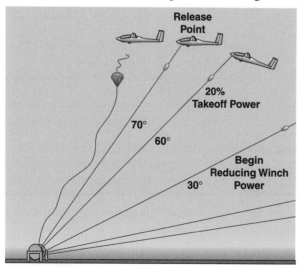

Figure 7-17. Winch procedures.

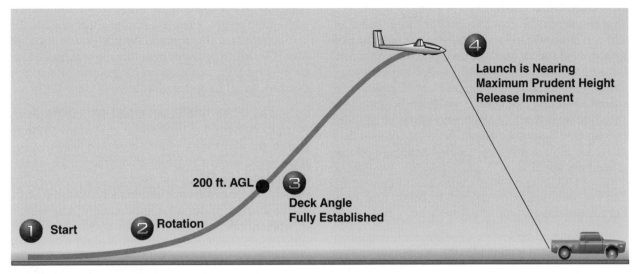

Figure 7-18. Ground launch takeoff profile.

1 Start
2 Rotation
200 ft. AGL
3 Deck Angle Fully Established
4 Launch is Nearing Maximum Prudent Height Release Imminent

time interval from standing start to liftoff may be as short as three to five seconds. After the initial liftoff, the pilot should smoothly raise the nose to the proper pitch attitude, watching for an increase in airspeed. If the nose is raised too soon, or too steeply, the pitch attitude will be excessive while the glider is still at low altitude. If the towline breaks or the launching mechanism loses power, recovery from such a high pitch attitude may be difficult or impossible. Conversely, if the nose is raised too slowly, the glider may gain excessive airspeed, and may exceed the maximum ground launch tow speed. The shallow climb may result in the glider not attaining planned release altitude. If this situation occurs, the pilot should pull the release, and land straight ahead, avoiding obstacles and equipment.

As the launch progresses, the pilot should ease the nose up gradually (item 2), while monitoring the airspeed to ensure that it is adequate for launch but does not exceed the maximum permitted ground launch tow airspeed. When optimum pitch attitude for climb is attained (item 3), the glider should be approximately 200 feet above ground level. The pilot must monitor the airspeed during this phase of the climb-out to ensure the airspeed is adequate to provide a safe margin above stall speed but below the maximum ground launch airspeed. If the towline breaks or if the launching mechanism loses power at or above this altitude, the pilot will have sufficient altitude to release the towline and lower the nose from the climb attitude to the approach attitude that provides an appropriate airspeed for landing straight ahead.

As the glider nears its maximum altitude (item 4), it begins to level off above the launch winch or tow vehicle, and the rate of climb decreases. In this final phase of the ground launch, the towline is pulling steeply down on the glider. The pilot should gently lower the nose of the glider to reduce tension on the towline, and

then pull the towline release two or three times to ensure the towline has released. The pilot will feel the release of the towline as it departs the glider. The pilot should enter a turn to visually confirm the fall of the towline. If only a portion of the towline is seen falling to the ground, it is possible that the towline is broken and a portion of the towline is still attached to the glider.

If pulling the tow release handle fails to release the towline, the back-release mechanism of the towhook automatically releases the towline as the glider overtakes and passes the launch vehicle or winch.

CROSSWIND TAKEOFF AND CLIMB—GROUND LAUNCH

The following are the main differences between crosswind takeoffs and climb procedures and normal takeoff and climb procedures.

- During the takeoff roll, the weathervaning tendency, although present, is much less due to the rapid acceleration to liftoff airspeed.

- After liftoff, the glider tends to drift toward the downwind side of the runway. The stronger the crosswind, the greater the glider's tendency to drift downwind.

After liftoff, the glider pilot should establish a wind correction angle toward the upwind side of the runway to prevent drifting downwind. This prevents downwind drift and allows the glider to work upwind of the runway during the climb-out. When the towline is released at the top of the climb, it will tend to drift back toward the centerline of the launch runway, as shown in Figure 7-19 on the next page. This helps keep the towline from fouling nearby wires, poles, fences, aircraft, and other obstacles on the side of the launching runway. Should

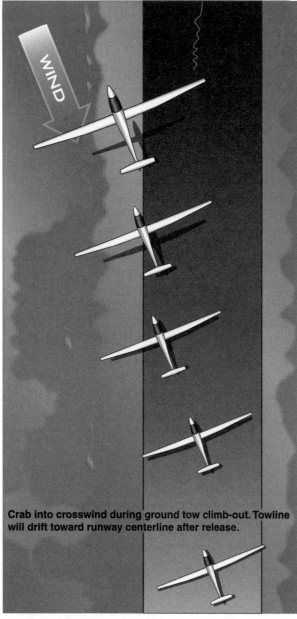

Crab into crosswind during ground tow climb-out. Towline will drift toward runway centerline after release.

Figure 7-19. Ground launch crosswind drift correction.

the glider drift to the downwind side of the runway, the towline may damage items, such as other aircraft, runway lights, nearby fences, structures, and obstacles.

GROUND TOW LAUNCH—
CLIMB-OUT AND RELEASE PROCEDURES

The pitch attitude/airspeed relationship during ground launch is unique. During the launch, pulling back on the stick tends to increase airspeed, and pushing forward tends to reduce airspeed. This is opposite of the normal pitch/airspeed relationship. The wings of the glider divert the towing force of the launch vehicle in an upward direction, enabling rapid climb. The greater the diversion from horizontal pulling power to vertical lifting power, the faster the airspeed. This is true, provided the tow vehicle is powerful enough to meet the energy demands the glider is making on the launch system.

COMMON ERRORS
- Improper glider configuration for takeoff.
- Improper initial positioning of flight controls.
- Improper use of visual launch signals.
- Improper crosswind procedure.
- Improper climb profile.
- Faulty corrective action for adjustment of air speed and porpoising.
- Exceeding maximum launch airspeed.
- Improper towline release procedure.

ABNORMAL PROCEDURES, GROUND LAUNCH

The launch equipment operator manages ground launch towline speed. Because the launch equipment operator is remote from the glider, it is not uncommon for initial tow speed to be too fast or too slow. If the towline speed is too fast, the glider will not be able to climb very high because of excessive airspeed. If the towline speed is too slow, the glider may be incapable of liftoff, possibly stall after becoming airborne or once airborne be incapable of further climb. The pilot should use appropriate signals to direct the launch operator to increase or decrease speed. The pilot must anticipate and be prepared to deal with these situations. In the event these abnormal situations develop, the pilot's only alternative may be to release the towline and land straight ahead.

Wind gradient (a sudden increase in wind speed with height) can have a noticeable effect on ground launches. If the wind gradient is significant or sudden, or both, and the pilot maintains the same pitch attitude the indicated airspeed will increase, possibly exceeding the maximum ground launch tow speed. The pilot must adjust the airspeed to deal with the effect of the gradient. When encountering a wind gradient the pilot should push forward on the stick to reduce the indicated airspeed. [Figure 7-20] The only way for the glider to resume climb without exceeding the maximum ground launch airspeed is for the pilot to signal the launch operator to reduce tow speed. After the reduction of the towing speed, the pilot can resume normal climb. If the tow speed is not reduced, the glider may be incapable of climbing to safe altitude.

Ground launch may be interrupted by a ground launch mechanism malfunction. A gradual deceleration in rate of climb and/or airspeed may be an indication of such a malfunction. If you suspect a launch mechanism malfunction, release and land straight ahead.

EMERGENCY PROCEDURES—
GROUND LAUNCH

The most common type of problem is a broken towline. [Figure 7-21] When there is a towline failure, the glider pilot must pull the release handle and immediately lower the nose of the glider to achieve and maintain a safe airspeed. The distinguishing features of the

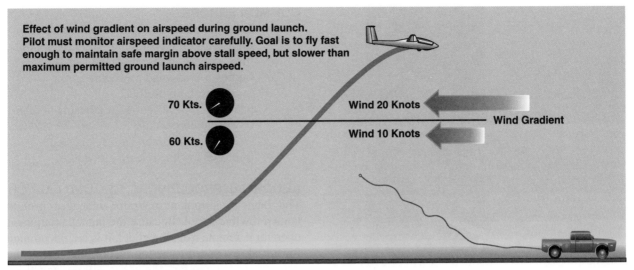

Effect of wind gradient on airspeed during ground launch. Pilot must monitor airspeed indicator carefully. Goal is to fly fast enough to maintain safe margin above stall speed, but slower than maximum permitted ground launch airspeed.

70 Kts.

60 Kts.

Wind 20 Knots

Wind 10 Knots

Wind Gradient

Figure 7-20. Ground launch wind gradient.

ground launch are nose-high pitch attitude and a relatively low altitude for a significant portion of the launch and climb. If a towline break occurs and the glider pilot fails to respond promptly, the nose-high attitude of the glider may result in a stall. Altitude may be insufficient for recovery unless the pilot recognizes and responds to the towline break by lowering the nose.

If the glider tow release mechanism fails, the pilot should fly at an airspeed no slower than best lift/drag (L/D) airspeed over and away from the ground launch equipment, allowing the back release to activate or the weak link to fail. The ground launch equipment is also equipped with an emergency release mechanism in the event the glider tow release fails. If a winch is used, it

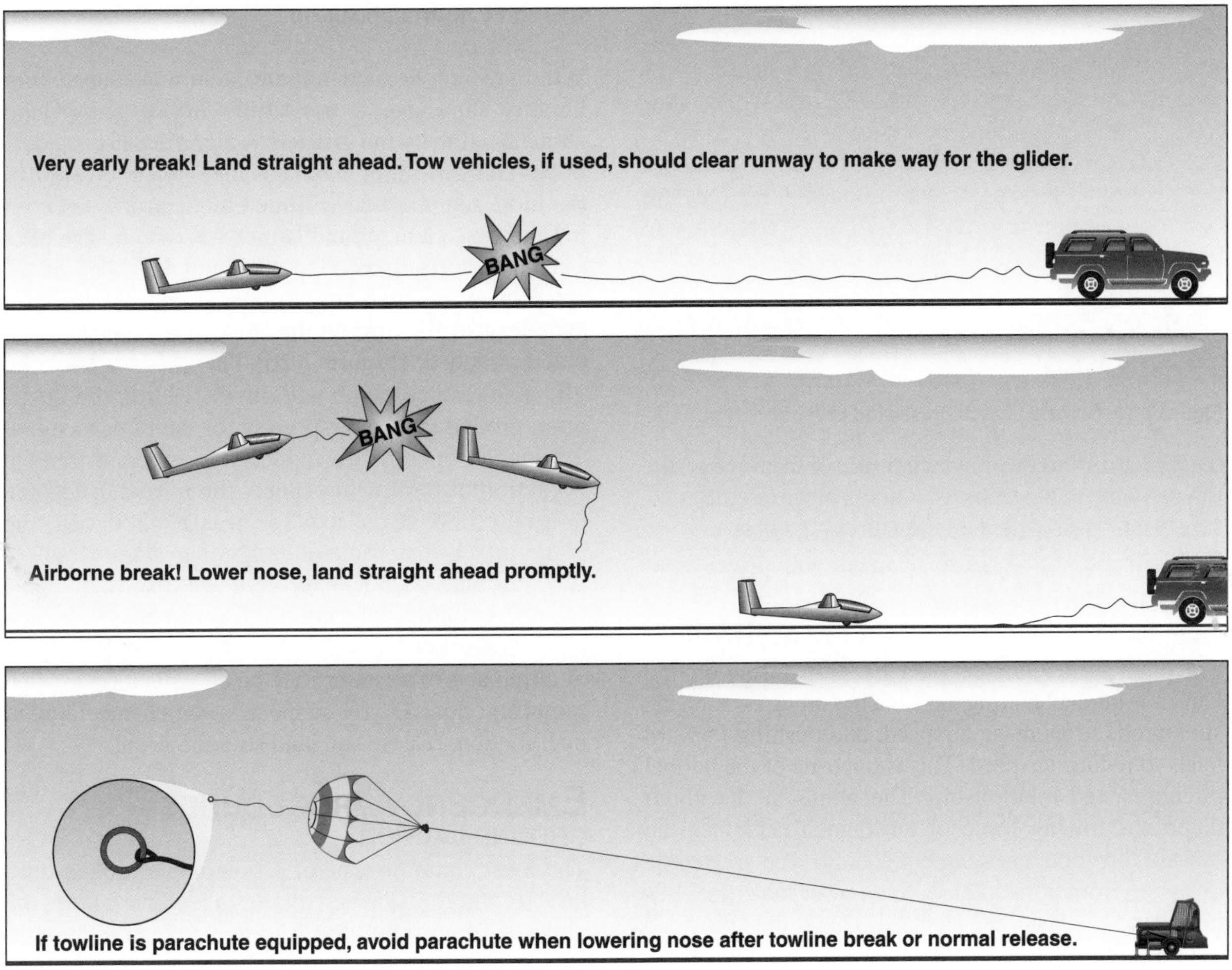

Very early break! Land straight ahead. Tow vehicles, if used, should clear runway to make way for the glider.

BANG

Airborne break! Lower nose, land straight ahead promptly.

BANG

If towline is parachute equipped, avoid parachute when lowering nose after towline break or normal release.

Figure 7-21. Ground launch towline break.

will be equipped with a guillotine to cut the towline. An automobile used for ground launch is normally equipped with some form of backup release mechanism.

SELF-LAUNCH TAKEOFF PROCEDURES

PREPARATION AND ENGINE START

The self-launching glider has many more systems than a non-motorized glider, so the preflight inspection is more complex. A positive control check is just as critical as it is in any other glider. Ailerons, elevator, rudder, elevator trim tab, flaps, and spoiler/dive breaks must all be checked. In addition, numerous other systems must be inspected and readied for flight. These include the fuel system, the electrical system, the engine, the propeller, the cooling system, and any mechanisms and controls associated with extending or retracting the engine or propulsion system. Instruments, gauges, and all engine and propulsion system controls must be inspected for proper operation.

After preflighting the self-launching glider and clearing the area, start the engine in accordance with the manufacturer's instructions. Typical items on a self-launching glider engine-start checklist include fuel mixture control, fuel tank selection, fuel pump switch, engine priming, propeller pitch setting, cowl flap setting (if cowl flaps are fitted), throttle setting, magneto or ignition switch setting, and electric starter activation. After starting the oil pressure, oil temp, alternator/generator charging, and suction instruments should be checked. If the engine and propulsion systems are operating within normal limits, taxi operations can begin.

COMMON ERRORS

- Failure to use or improper use of checklist.
- Improper or unsafe starting procedures.
- Excessively high RPM after starting.
- Failure to ensure proper clearance of propeller.

TAXIING THE SELF-LAUNCHING GLIDER

Self-launching gliders are designed with a variety of landing gear configurations. These include tricycle-landing gear and tailwheel-landing gear. Other types of self-launch gliders rest primarily on the main landing gear wheel in the center of the fuselage and depend on outrigger wheels or skids to prevent the wingtips from contacting the ground. These types of gliders often feature a retractable powerplant for drag reduction. After the launch, the powerplant is retracted into the fuselage and stowed.

Due to the long wingspan and low wingtip ground clearance, many airport taxiways, and some runways, may not be wide enough to accommodate a self-launch glider. Additionally, limited crosswind capability may lead to directional control difficulties during taxi operations.

Taxiing on soft ground requires additional power. Self-launch gliders with outrigger wingtip wheels may lose directional control if a wingtip wheel bogs down. Well-briefed wing walkers should hold the wings level during low-speed taxi operations on soft ground.

COMMON ERRORS

- Improper use of brakes.
- Failure to comply with airport markings, signals, and clearances.
- Taxiing too fast for conditions.
- Improper control positioning for wind. conditions.
- Failure to consider wingspan and space required to maneuver during taxiing.

BEFORE TAKEOFF CHECK— SELF-LAUNCHING GLIDER

The manufacturer provides a takeoff checklist. As shown in Figure 7-22, the complexity of many self-launching gliders makes a written takeoff checklist an essential safety item. Before takeoff items on a self-launch glider may include fuel quantity check, fuel pressure check, oil temperature check, oil pressure check, engine run-up, throttle/RPM check, propeller pitch setting, cowl flap setting, and vacuum check. In addition, other items also must be completed. These include making sure seat belts and shoulder harnesses are latched or secured, doors and windows are closed and locked, canopies are closed and locked, airbrakes are closed and locked, altimeter is set, VHF radio transceiver is set, and the directional gyros is set.

COMMON ERRORS

- Improper positioning of the self-launch glider for run-up.
- Failure to use or improper use of checklist.
- Improper check of flight controls.
- Failure to review takeoff emergency procedures.

NORMAL TAKEOFF— SELF-LAUNCHING GLIDER

When the before takeoff checklist is complete, the pilot should check for traffic and prepare for takeoff. If operating from an airport with an operating control tower, request and receive an ATC clearance prior to taxi. The pilot should make a final check for conflicting traffic, then taxi out on to the active runway and align the glider with the centerline.

Complexity of the self-launching glider requires a complex instrument panel and a lengthy pre-takeoff checklist.

Figure 7-22. Self-launch glider instrument panels.

The pilot should smoothly apply full throttle and begin the takeoff roll, tracking down the centerline of the runway, easing the self-launch glider off the runway at the recommended lift-off airspeed, and allowing the glider to accelerate in ground effect until reaching the appropriate climb airspeed. If the runway has an obstacle ahead, this will be best angle of climb airspeed (Vx) until the obstacle is cleared. If no obstacle is present, the preferred airspeed will be either best rate of climb airspeed (Vy), or the airspeed for best engine cooling during climb. The pilot should monitor the engine and instrument systems during climb out. If the self-launch glider has a time limitation on full throttle operation, the throttle should be adjusted as necessary during the climb.

CROSSWIND TAKEOFF— SELF-LAUNCHING GLIDER

The long wingspan and low wingtip clearance of the typical self-launch glider makes it vulnerable to wing tip strikes on runway border markers, light stanchions, and other obstacles along the edge of the runway. The takeoff roll should be started with upwind aileron and downwind rudder. In a right crosswind, for example, the control stick should be held to the right and the rudder held to the left. The aileron input keeps the crosswind from lifting the upwind wing, and the downwind rudder minimizes the weathervaning tendency of the self-launch glider in a crosswind. As airspeed increases, control effectiveness will improve, and the pilot can gradually decrease some of the control. The self-launch glider should be lifted off at the appropriate lift-off airspeed, and accelerate to climb airspeed. During the climb, a wind correction angle should be established so that the self-launch glider will track the extended centerline of the takeoff runway. [Figure 7-23]

COMMON ERRORS

- Improper initial positioning of flight controls.

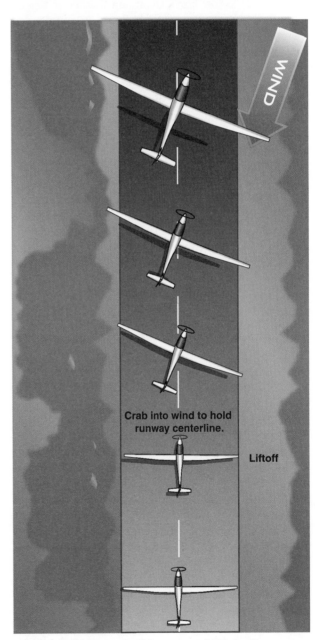

Figure 7-23. Self-launch glider—crosswind takeoff.

- Improper power application.
- Inappropriate removal of hand from throttle.
- Poor directional control.
- Improper use of flight controls.
- Improper pitch attitude during takeoff.
- Failure to establish and maintain proper climb attitude and airspeed.
- Improper crosswind control technique.

SELF-LAUNCH—CLIMB-OUT AND SHUTDOWN PROCEDURES

Self-launch gliders have powerplant limitations, as well as aircraft performance and handling limitations. Powerplant limits include temperature limits, maximum RPM limit, maximum manifold pressure limit, useable fuel limit, and similar items. The Glider Flight Manual (GFM) or Pilot's Operating Handbook (POH) provides useful information about recommended power settings and target airspeed for best angle of climb, best rate-of-climb, best cooling performance climb, and level flight cruise operation while under power. If full-throttle operation is time limited to reduce engine wear, the GFM/POH describes the recommended operating procedures. Aircraft performance limits include weight and balance limits, minimum and maximum front seat weight restrictions, maximum permitted airspeed with engine extended, maximum airspeed to extend or retract the engine, flap operating airspeed range, airbrake operating airspeed range, maneuvering speed, rough air speed limitations, and never exceed speed.

The engine heats up considerably during takeoff and climb, so cooling system mismanagement or failure can lead to dangerously high temperatures in a short time. An overheated engine cannot supply full power, meaning climb performance will be reduced. Extended overheating can cause an in-flight fire. To minimize the chances of engine damage or fire, monitor engine temperatures carefully during high power operations, and observe the engine operating limits described in the GFM/POH.

Many self-launch gliders have a time limitation on full throttle operation to prevent overheating and premature engine wear. If the self-launch glider is equipped with cowl flaps for cooling, make certain the cowl flaps are set properly for high-power operations. In some self-launch gliders, operating at full power with cowl flaps closed can result in an overheated, ruined engine in as little as 2 minutes. If abnormally high engine system temperatures are encountered, follow the procedures described in the GFM/POH. Typically, these require reduced power along with higher airspeed to enhance engine cooling. Cowl flap instructions may be provided as well. If these measures are ineffective in reducing

high temperatures, the safest course of action may be to shut down the engine and make a precautionary landing. A safe landing, whether on or off the airport, is always preferable to an in-flight fire.

Handling limitations for a given self-launch glider may be quite subtle and may include minimum controllable airspeed with power on, minimum controllable airspeed with power off, and other limitations described in the GFM/POH. Self-launch gliders come in many configurations. Those with a top-mounted retractable engine and/or propeller have a thrust line that is quite distant from the longitudinal axis of the glider. The result is that significant changes of power settings tend to cause substantial pitch attitude changes. For instance, full power setting in these self-launch gliders introduces a nose-down pitching moment because the thrust line is high above the longitudinal axis of the glider. To counteract this pitching moment, the pilot should hold the control stick back. If power is quickly reduced from full power to idle power while the control stick is held steady, these gliders tend to pitch up considerably. The nose-up pitching moment may be vigorous enough to induce a stall!

During climb-out, the pilot should hold a pitch attitude that results in climbing out at the desired airspeed, adjusting elevator trim as necessary. Climbs in self-launch gliders are best managed with smooth control inputs and, when power changes are necessary, smooth and gradual throttle adjustments.

When climbing under power, most self-launch gliders exhibit a left- or right-turning tendency (depending on whether the propeller is turning clockwise or counterclockwise) due to P-factor. P-factor is caused by the uneven distribution of thrust caused by the difference in the angle of attack of the ascending propeller blade and the descending propeller blade. Use the rudder to counteract P-factor during climbs with power.

Turns are accomplished with a shallow bank angle because steep banks result in a much-reduced rate of climb. As with all turns in a glider, properly coordinating aileron and rudder results in more efficient flight and a faster climb rate. The pilot should clear for other air traffic before making any turn.

Detailed engine shutdown procedures are described in the GFM/POH. A guide to shutdown procedures is described below, but the GFM/POH is the authoritative source for any self-launch glider.

Engines reach high operating temperatures during extended high-power operations. To reduce or eliminate shock cooling, and to reduce the possibility of in-flight fire, the manufacturer provides engine cool-down procedures to reduce engine system temperatures prior to shutdown. Reducing throttle setting allows the engine to begin a gradual cool down. The GFM/POH may also instruct the pilot to adjust propeller pitch at this time. Lowering the nose to increase airspeed provides faster flow of cooling air to the engine cooling system. Several minutes of reduced throttle and increased cooling airflow are enough to allow the engine to be shut down. If the engine is retractable, additional time after engine shutdown may be necessary to reduce engine temperature to acceptable limits prior to retracting and stowing the engine in the fuselage. Consult the GFM/POH for details. [Figure 7-24]

Retractable-engine self-launch gliders are aerodynamically efficient when the engine is stowed, but produce high-drag when the engine is extended and not providing thrust. Stowing the engine is critical to efficient soaring flight. Prior to stowing, the propeller must be aligned with the longitudinal axis of the glider, so the propeller blades do not interfere with the engine bay doors. Since the engine/propeller installation in these gliders is aft of the pilot's head, these gliders usually have a mirror, enabling the pilot to perform a visual propeller alignment check prior to stowing the engine/propeller pod. Detailed instructions for stowing the engine and propeller are found in the GFM/POH for the particular glider. If a malfunction occurs during engine shutdown and stowage, the pilot cannot count on being able to get the engine restarted. The pilot should have a landing area within power-off gliding distance in anticipation of this eventuality.

Some self-launch gliders use a nose-mounted engine/propeller installation that resembles the typical installation found on single-engine airplanes. In these self-launch gliders, the shutdown procedure usually consists of operating the engine for a short time at reduced power to cool the engine down to acceptable shutdown temperature. After shutdown, the cowl flaps, if installed, should be closed to reduce drag and increase gliding efficiency. The manufacturer may recommend a time interval between engine shutdown and cowl flap closure, to prevent excess temperatures from developing in the confined, tightly cowled engine compartment. These temperatures may not be harmful to the engine itself, but may degrade the structures around the engine, such as composite engine mounts or installed electrical components. Excess engine heat may result in fuel vapor lock.

If the propeller blade pitch can be controlled by the pilot while in flight, the propeller is usually set to coarse pitch, or if possible, feathered, to reduce propeller drag during non-powered flight. Some self-launch gliders require the pilot to set the propeller to coarse pitch prior to engine shutdown. Other self-launch gliders require the pilot to shut down the engine first, then adjust propeller blade pitch to coarse pitch or to feathered position. As always, follow the shutdown procedures described in the GFM/POH.

COMMON ERRORS

- Failure to follow manufacturer's recommended procedure for engine shutdown, feathering, and stowing procedure (if applicable).
- Failure to maintain positive aircraft control while performing engine shutdown procedures.

LANDINGS

If the self-launch glider is to land under power, the pilot should perform the engine restart procedures at a safe altitude to allow time to reconfigure. The pilot should follow the manufacturer's recommended pre-starting checklist. Once the engine is started, the pilot should allow time for it to warm up. After the engine is started the pilot should ensure that all systems necessary for landing are operational, such as the electrical system and landing gear.

The pilot should fly the traffic pattern so as to land into the wind and plan the approach path to avoid all obstacles. The landing area should be of sufficient length to allow for touchdown and roll-out within the performance limitations of the particular self-launch glider. The pilot should also take into consideration any

Figure 7-24. Types of self-launch gliders.

crosswind conditions and the landing surface. After touchdown, the pilot should maintain direction control, and slow the self-launch glider so as to clear the landing area. The after landing checklist should be completed when appropriate.

COMMON ERRORS

- Poor judgment of approach path.
- Improper use of flaps, spoilers, and/or dive brakes.
- Improper approach and landing speed.
- Improper crosswind correction.
- Improper technique during roundout and touchdown.
- Poor directional control after landing.
- Improper use of brakes.
- Failure to use the appropriate checklist.

EMERGENCY PROCEDURES

SELF-LAUNCHING GLIDER

The pilot of a self-launching glider should formulate emergency plans for any type of failure that might occur. Thorough knowledge of aircraft performance data, normal takeoff/landing procedures, and emergency procedures, as outlined in the GFM/POH, is essential to the successful management of any emergency situation. Mismanagement of the aircraft systems through lack of knowledge may cause serious difficulty. For instance, if the spoilers/dive brakes are allowed to open during takeoff and climbout, the self-launch glider may be incapable of generating sufficient power to continue climbing. Other emergency situations may include in-flight fire, structural failure, encounters with severe turbulence/wind shear, canopy failure, and inadvertent encounter with instrument meteorological conditions.

Possible options for handling emergencies are influenced by the altitude above the terrain, wind, weather conditions, density altitude, glider performance, takeoff runway length, landing areas near the gliderport, and other air traffic. Emergency options may include landing straight ahead on the remaining runway, landing off-field, or returning to the gliderport to land on an available runway. The appropriate emergency procedures may be found in the GFM/POH for the specific self-launch glider.

PERFORMANCE MANEUVERS

STRAIGHT GLIDES

To perform a straight glide the glider pilot must hold a constant heading and airspeed. The heading reference should be some prominent point in front of the glider on the Earth's surface. The pilot will also note that during a straight glide each wingtip should be an equal distance above the earth surface. With the wings level, the pitch attitude is established with reference to a point on or below the horizon to establish a specified airspeed. Any change in pitch attitude will result in a change in airspeed. There will be a pitch attitude reference for best glide speed, another for the minimum sink speed, and another for slow flight. The pitch attitude is adjusted with the elevator to hold the specific airspeed. The glider elevator trim control allows the pilot to trim the glider to hold a constant pitch attitude, therefore a constant airspeed. Straight glides should be coordinated as indicated by a centered yaw string or slip-skid ball.

The glider pilot should also stay alert to airflow noise changes. At a constant airspeed in coordinated flight, wind noise should be constant. Any changes in airspeed or coordination cause a change in the wind noise. Gusts that cause the airspeed to change momentarily can be ignored. Holding a constant pitch attitude results in maintaining the desired airspeed.

The glider pilot should learn to fly throughout a wide range of airspeeds; from minimum controllable airspeed to maximum allowable airspeed. This enables the pilot to learn the feel of the controls of the glider throughout its speed range. If the glider is equipped with spoilers/dive brakes and/or flaps, the glider pilot should become familiar with the changes that occur in pitch attitude and airspeed when these controls are used.

COMMON ERRORS

1. Rough or erratic pitch attitude and airspeed control.
2. Rough, uncoordinated, or inappropriate control applications.
3. Failure to use the trim or improper use of trim.
4. Improper use of controls when using spoilers, dive breaks and/or flaps.

TURNS

The performance of turns involves coordination of all three flight controls: ailerons, rudder, and elevator. For purposes of this discussion, turns are divided into the following three classes as shown in Figure 7-25.

- Shallow turns are those in which the bank (less than approximately 20°) is so shallow that the inherent lateral stability of the glider is acting to level the wings unless some aileron is applied to maintain the bank.

- Medium turns are those resulting from a degree of bank (approximately 20° to 45°) at which the lateral stability is overcome by the overbanking tendency, resulting in no control

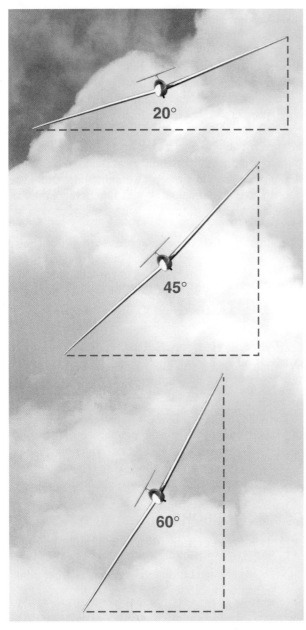

Figure 7-25. Shallow, medium, and steep turns.

inputs (other than elevator) being required to maintain the angle.

- Steep turns are those resulting from a degree of bank (45° or more) at which the "overbank ing tendency" of a glider overcomes stability, and the bank increases unless aileron is applied to prevent it.

Before starting any turn, the pilot must clear the airspace in the direction of the turn. A glider is turned by banking (lowering the wing in the direction of the desired turn, thus raising the other). When the glider is flying straight, the total lift is acting perpendicular to the wings and to the earth. As the glider is banked into a turn, total lift becomes the resultant of two components. One, the vertical lift component, continues to

act perpendicular to the earth and opposes gravity. Second, the horizontal lift component (centripetal) acts parallel to the earth's surface and opposes inertia (apparent centrifugal force). These two lift components act at right angles to each other, causing the resultant total lifting force to act perpendicular to the banked wing of the glider. It is the horizontal lift component that actually turns the glider, not the rudder.

When applying aileron to bank the glider, the aileron on the rising wing is lowered produces a greater drag than the raised aileron on the lowering wing. This increased drag causes the glider to yaw toward the rising wing, or opposite to the direction of turn. To counteract this adverse yawing moment, rudder pressure must be applied in the desired direction of turn simultaneously with aileron pressure. This action is required to produce a coordinated turn.

After the bank has been established in a medium banked turn, all pressure applied to the aileron may be relaxed. The glider will remain at the selected bank with no further tendency to yaw since there is no longer a deflection of the ailerons. As a result, pressure may also be relaxed on the rudder pedals, and the rudder allowed to streamline itself with the direction of the slipstream. Rudder pressure maintained after establishing the turn will cause the glider to skid to the outside of the turn. If a definite effort is made to center the rudder rather than let it streamline itself to the turn, it is probable that some opposite rudder pressure will be exerted inadvertently. This will force the glider to yaw opposite its turning path, causing the glider to slip to the inside of the turn. The yaw string or ball in the slip indicator will be displaced off-center whenever the glider is skidding or slipping sideways. In proper coordinated flight, there is no skidding or slipping.

In all gliding, constant airspeed turns, it is necessary to increase the angle of attack of the wing as the bank progresses by adding nose-up elevator pressure. This is required because the total lift must be equal to the vertical component of lift plus the horizontal lift component. To stop the turn, coordinated use of the aileron and rudder pressure are added to bring the wings back to level flight, and elevator pressure is relaxed.

There is a direct relationship between, airspeed, bank angle, and rate and radius of turn. The rate of turn at any given true airspeed depends on the horizontal lift component. The horizontal lift component varies in proportion to the amount of bank. Therefore, the rate of turn at a given true airspeed increases as the angle of bank is increased. On the other hand, when a turn is made at a higher true airspeed at a given bank angle, the inertia is greater and the horizontal lift component required for the turn is greater, causing the turning rate to become slower. Therefore, at a given angle of bank, a higher true airspeed will make the radius of turn larger because the glider will be turning at a slower rate.

As the angle of bank is increased from a shallow bank to a medium bank, the airspeed of the wing on the outside of the turn increases in relation to the inside wing. The additional lift so developed balances the lateral stability of the glider. No aileron pressure is required to maintain the bank. At any given airspeed, aileron pressure is not required to maintain the bank.

If the bank is increased from a medium bank to a steep bank, the radius of turn decreases even further. The greater lift of the outside wing then causes the bank to steepen and opposite aileron is necessary to keep the bank constant.

As the radius of the turn becomes smaller, a significant difference develops between the speed of the inside wing and the speed of the outside wing. The wing on the outside of the turn travels a longer circuit than the inside wing, yet both complete their respective circuits in the same length of time. Therefore, the outside wing travels faster than the inside wing, and as a result, it develops more lift. This creates an overbanking tendency that must be controlled by the use of the ailerons. Because the outboard wing is developing more lift, it also has more induced drag. This causes a slip during steep turns that must be corrected by rudder usage.

To establish the desired angle of bank, the pilot should use visual reference points on the glider, the Earth's surface, and the natural horizon. The pilot's posture while seated in the glider is very important, particularly during turns. It will affect the interpretation of outside visual references. The beginning pilot may lean away from or into the turn rather than ride with the glider. This should be corrected immediately if the pilot is to properly learn to use visual references.

Applications of large aileron and rudder produces rapid roll rates and allow little time for corrections before the desired bank is reached. Slower (small control displacement) roll rates provide more time to make necessary pitch and bank corrections. As soon as the glider rolls from the wings-level attitude, the nose will start to move along the horizon, increasing its rate of travel proportionately as the bank is increased.

COMMON ERRORS

- Failure to clear turn.
- Nose starts to move before the bank starts—rudder is being applied too soon.
- Bank starts before the nose starts turning, or the nose moves in the opposite direction—the rudder is being applied too late.

- Nose moves up or down when entering a bank—excessive or insufficient elevator is being applied.

As the desired angle of bank is established, aileron and rudder pressures should be relaxed. This stops the bank from increasing because the aileron and rudder control surfaces will be neutral in their streamlined position. The up-elevator pressure should not be relaxed, but should be held constant to maintain the desired airspeed. Throughout the turn, the pilot should crosscheck the airspeed indicator to verify the proper pitch is being maintained. The crosscheck should also include outside visual references. If gaining or losing airspeed, the pitch attitude should be adjusted in relation to the horizon.

During all turns, the ailerons, rudder, and elevator are used to correct minor variations in pitch and bank just as they are in straight glides.

The roll-out from a turn is similar to the roll-in except the flight controls are applied in the opposite direction. Aileron and rudder are applied in the direction of the roll-out or toward the high wing. As the angle of bank decreases, the elevator pressure should be relaxed, as necessary, to maintain airspeed.

Since the glider will continue turning as long as there is any bank, the roll-out must be started before reaching the desired heading. The amount of lead required to roll-out on the desired heading depends on the degree of bank used in the turn. Normally, the lead is one half the degrees of bank. For example, if the bank is 30°, lead the roll-out by 15°. As the wings become level, the control pressures should be smoothly relaxed so the controls are neutralized as the glider returns to straight flight. As the roll-out is being completed, attention should be given to outside visual references, as well as the airspeed and heading indicators to determine that the wings are being leveled and the turn stopped.

COMMON ERRORS

- Rough or uncoordinated use of controls during the roll-in and roll-out.
- Failure to establish and maintain the desired angle of bank.
- Overshooting/undershooting the desired heading.

In a slipping turn, the glider is not turning at the rate appropriate to the bank being used, since the glider is yawed toward the outside of the turning flight path. The glider is banked too much for the rate of turn, so the horizontal lift component is greater than the centrifugal force. Equilibrium between the horizontal lift component and centrifugal force is reestablished either by decreasing the bank (ailerons), increasing yaw (rudder), or a combination of the two. [Figure 7-26]

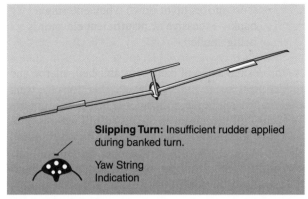

Figure 7-26. Slipping turn.

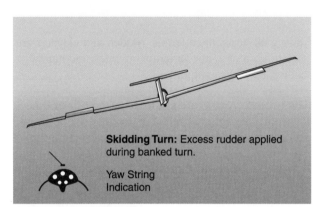

Figure 7-27. Skidding turn.

A skidding turn results from an excess of centrifugal force over the horizontal lift component, pulling the glider toward the outside of the turn. The rate of turn is too great for the angle of bank. Correction of a skidding turn thus involves a decrease in yaw (rudder), an increase in bank (aileron), or a combination of the two changes. [Figure 7-27]

The yaw string identifies slips and skids. In flight, the rule to remember is simple: step away from the tail of the yaw string. If the tail of the yaw string is to the left of center, press the right rudder pedal to coordinate the glider and center the yaw string. If the tail of the yaw string is right of center, pressure the left rudder pedal to coordinate the glider and center the yaw string. [Figure 7-28]

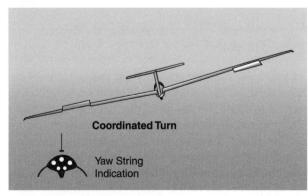

Figure 7-28. Coordinated turn.

The ball in the slip/skid indicator also indicates slips and skids. When using this instrument for coordination, you should apply rudder pressure on the side that the ball is offset (step on the ball).

Correction for uncoordinated condition should be accomplished by using appropriate rudder and aileron control pressures simultaneously to coordinate the glider.

STEEP TURNS
Soaring flight requires competence in steep turns. In thermalling flight, small-radius turns are often necessary to keep the glider in or near the core of the thermal updraft, where lift is usually strongest and rapid climbs are possible. At any given airspeed, increasing the angle of bank will decrease the radius of the turn and increase the rate of turn. The radius of a turn at any given bank angle varies directly with the square of the airspeed at which the turn is made, therefore the slower the airspeed the smaller the turn radius. To keep the radius of turn small, it is necessary to bank steeply, while maintaining an appropriate airspeed, such as minimum sink or best glide speed. The pilot must be aware that as the bank angle increases, the stall speed increases.

Before starting the steep turn, the pilot should ensure that the area is clear of other traffic since the rate of turn will be quite rapid. After establishing the appropriate airspeed, the glider should be smoothly rolled into a coordinated steep turn with at least 45° of bank. The pilot should use outside visual reference to establish and maintain the desired bank angle. If the pilot does not add back pressure to maintain the desired airspeed after the bank is established, the glider will have a tendency to enter a spiral. To counteract the overbanking tendency caused by the steep turn, the pilot should apply top aileron pressure. Because the top aileron pressure pulls the nose away from the direction of the turn, the pilot also has to apply bottom rudder pressure. A coordinated (no slip or skid) steep turn requires back pressure on the elevator for airspeed control, top aileron pressure for bank control, and bottom rudder pressure to stream line the fuselage with the flight path.

COMMON ERRORS
- Failure to clear turn.
- Uncoordinated use of controls.
- Loss of orientation.
- Failure to maintain airspeed within tolerance.
- Unintentional stall or spin.
- Excessive deviation from desired heading during roll-out.

SPIRAL DIVE
Allowing the nose of the glider to get excessively low during a steep turn may result in a significant increase

in airspeed and loss in altitude. This is known as a spiral dive. If the pilot attempts to recover from this situation by only applying back elevator pressure, the limiting load factor may be exceeded, causing structural failure. To properly recover from a spiral dive, the pilot should first reduce the angle of bank with coordinated use of the rudder and aileron, then smoothly increase pitch to the proper attitude.

COMMON ERRORS

- Failure to recognize when a spiral dive is developing.
- Rough, abrupt, and/or uncoordinated control application during recovery.
- Improper sequence of control applications.

MANEUVERING AT MINIMUM CONTROL AIRSPEED, STALLS, AND SPINS

All pilots must be proficient in maneuvering at minimum controllable airspeed and stall recognition and recovery. In addition, all flight instructor applicants must be proficient in spins entries, spins, and spin recovery.

MANEUVERING AT MINIMUM CONTROLLABLE AIRSPEED

Maneuvering during slow flight demonstrates the flight characteristics and degree of controllability of a glider at minimum speeds. By definition, the term "flight at minimum controllable airspeed" means a speed at which any further increase in angle of attack or load factor causes an immediate stall. Pilots must develop an awareness of the particular glider flight characteristics in order to recognize and avoid stalls, which may inadvertently occur during the slow airspeeds used in takeoffs, climbs, thermalling, and approaches to landing.

The objective of maneuvering at minimum controllable airspeed is to develop the pilot's sense of feel and ability to use the controls correctly, and to improve proficiency in performing maneuvers that require slow airspeeds. Maneuvering at minimum controllable airspeed should be performed using outside visual reference. It is important that pilots form the habit of frequently referencing the pitch attitude of the glider for airspeed control while flying at slow speeds.

The maneuver is started from either best glide or minimum sink speed. The pitch attitude is smoothly and gradually increased. While the glider is losing airspeed, the position of the nose in relation to the horizon should be noted and should be adjusted as necessary until the minimum controllable airspeed is established. During these changing flight conditions, it is important to re-trim the glider, as necessary, to compensate for changes in control pressures. Excessive or too aggressive back pressure on the elevator control

may result in an abrupt increase in pitch attitude and a rapid decrease in airspeed, which leads to a higher angle of attack and a possible stall. When the desired pitch attitude and airspeed have been established, it is important to continually crosscheck the pitch attitude on the horizon and the airspeed indicator to ensure accurate control is being maintained.

When minimum controllable airspeed is established in straight flight, turns should be practiced to determine the glider's controllability characteristics at this selected airspeed. During the turns the pitch attitude may need to be decreased in order to maintain the airspeed. If a steep turn is encountered, and the pitch attitude is not decreased, the increase in load factor may result in a stall. A stall may also occur as a result of abrupt or rough control movements resulting in momentary increases in load factor. Abruptly raising the flaps during minimum controllable airspeed will result in sudden loss of lift, possibly causing a stall.

Minimum controllable airspeed should also be practiced with extended spoilers/dive breaks. This will provide additional understanding of the changes in pitch attitude caused by the increase in drag from the spoilers/dive breaks.

Actual minimum controllable airspeed depends upon various conditions, such as the gross weight and CG location of the glider and the maneuvering load imposed by turns and pull-ups. Flight at minimum controllable airspeed requires positive use of rudder and ailerons. The diminished effectiveness of the flight controls during flight at minimum controllable airspeed will help pilots develop the ability to estimate the margin of safety above the stalling speed.

COMMON ERRORS

- Failure to establish or to maintain minimum controllable airspeed.
- Improper use of trim.
- Rough or uncoordinated use of controls.
- Failure to recognize indications of a stall.

STALL RECOGNITION AND RECOVERY

A stall can occur at any airspeed and in any attitude. In the case of the self-launch glider under power, a stall can also occur with any power setting. A stall occurs when the smooth airflow over the glider's wing is disrupted and the lift decreases rapidly. This occurs when the wing exceeds its critical angle of attack.

The practice of stall recovery and the development of awareness of stalls are of primary importance in pilot training. The objectives in performing intentional stalls are to familiarize the pilot with the conditions that produce stalls, to assist in recognizing an approaching stall, and to develop the habit of taking prompt preventive or corrective action.

Intentional stalls should be performed so the maneuver is completed by 1,500 feet above the ground for recovery and return to normal, wings-level flight. Though it depends on the degree to which a stall has progressed, most stalls require some loss of altitude during recovery. The longer it takes to recognize the approaching stall, the more complete the stall is likely to become, and the greater the loss of altitude to be expected.

Pilots must recognize the flight conditions that are conducive to stalls and know how to apply the necessary corrective action since most gliders do not have an electrical or mechanical stall warning device. Pilots should learn to recognize an approaching stall by sight, sound, and feel. The following cues may be useful in recognizing the approaching stall.

Vision is useful in detecting a stall condition by noting the attitude of the glider. This sense can only be relied on when the stall is the result of an unusual attitude of the glider. Since the glider can also be stalled from a normal attitude, vision in this instance would be of little help in detecting the approaching stall.

Hearing is also helpful in sensing a stall condition. In the case of a glider, a change in sound due to loss of airspeed is particularly noticeable. The lessening of the noise made by the air flowing along the glider structure as airspeed decreases is also quite noticeable, and when the stall is almost complete, aerodynamic vibration and incident noises often increase greatly.

Kinesthesia, or the sensing of changes in direction or speed of motion, is probably the most important and the best indicator to the trained and experienced pilot. If this sensitivity is properly developed, it will warn of a decrease in speed or the beginning of a settling or mushing of the glider.

The feeling of control pressures is also very important. As speed is reduced, the resistance to pressures on the controls become progressively less. Pressures exerted on the controls tend to become movements of the control surfaces. The lag between these movements and the response of the glider becomes greater, until in a complete stall all controls can be moved with almost no resistance, and with little immediate effect on the glider.

Signs of an impending stall include the following.
- High nose attitude.
- Low airspeed indication.
- Low airflow noise.
- Back pressure on sticks.
- Mushy controls, especially ailerons.
- Buffet.

Always make clearing turns before performing stalls. During the practice of intentional stalls, the real objective is not to learn how to stall a glider, but to learn how to recognize an approaching stall and take prompt corrective action. The recovery actions must be taken in a coordinated manner.

First, at the indication of a stall, the pitch attitude and angle of attack must be decreased positively and immediately. Since the basic cause of a stall is always an excessive angle of attack, the cause must first be eliminated by releasing the back-elevator pressure that was necessary to attain that angle of attack or by moving the elevator control forward. This lowers the nose and returns the wing to an effective angle of attack. The amount of elevator control pressure or movement to use depends on the design of the glider, the severity of the stall, and the proximity of the ground. In some gliders, a moderate movement of the elevator control—perhaps slightly forward of neutral—is enough, while in others a forcible push to the full forward position may be required. An excessive negative load on the wings caused by excessive forward movement of the elevator may impede, rather than hasten, the stall recovery. The object is to reduce the angle of attack, but only enough to allow the wing to regain lift. [Figure 7-29]

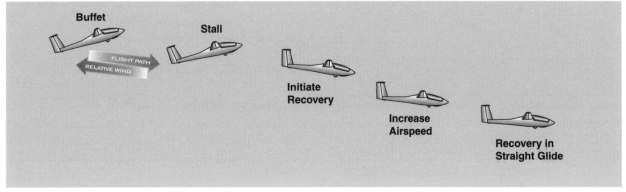

Figure 7-29. Stall recovery.

If stalls are practiced or encountered in a self-launch glider, the maximum allowable power should be applied during the stall recovery to increase the self-launch glider's speed and assist in reducing the wing's angle of attack. Generally, the throttle should be promptly, but smoothly, advanced to the maximum allowable power. Although stall recoveries should be practiced without, as well as with the use of power, in self-launch gliders during actual stalls the application of power is an integral part of the stall recovery. Usually, the greater the power applied, the less the loss of altitude. Maximum allowable power applied at the instant of a stall usually does not cause overspeeding of an engine equipped with a fixed-pitch propeller, due to the heavy air load imposed on the propeller at slow airspeeds. However, it will be necessary to reduce the power as airspeed is gained after the stall recovery so the airspeed does not become excessive. When performing intentional stalls, the tachometer indication should never be allowed to exceed the red radial line (maximum allowable RPM) as marked on the instrument.

Whether in a glider or self-launched glider, wings level, straight flight should be regained with coordinated use of all controls. The first few practices should consist of approaches to stalls, with recovery initiated as soon as the first buffeting or partial loss of control is noted. In this way, the pilot can become familiar with the indications of an approaching stall without fully stalling the glider.

Stall accidents usually result from an inadvertent stall at a low altitude in which a recovery was not accomplished prior to contact with the surface. As a preventive measure, stalls should be practiced at an altitude that allows recovery at no lower than 1,500 feet AGL.

Different types of gliders have different stall characteristics. Most gliders are designed so the wings stall progressively outward from the wing roots (where the wing attaches to the fuselage) to the wingtips. This is the result of designing the wings so the wingtips have a smaller angle of incidence than the wing roots. Such a design feature causes the wingtips to have a smaller angle of attack than the wing roots during flight.

Exceeding the critical angle of attack causes a stall. Since the wing roots will exceed the critical angle before the wingtips, they will stall first. The wings are designed in this manner so aileron control will be available at high angles of attack (slow airspeed) and give the glider more stable stalling characteristics. When the glider is in a stalled condition, the wingtips continue to provide some degree of lift, and the ailerons still have some control effect. During recovery from a stall, the return of lift begins at the tips and progresses toward the roots. Thus, the ailerons can be used to level the wings.

Using the ailerons requires finesse to avoid an aggravated stall condition. For example, if the right wing dropped during the stall and excessive aileron control was applied to the left to raise the wing, the aileron that was deflected downward (right wing) would produce a greater angle of attack (and drag). Possibly, a more complete stall would occur at the tip because the critical angle of attack would be exceeded. The increase in drag created by the high angle of attack on that wing might cause the airplane to yaw in that direction. This adverse yaw could result in a spin unless directional control was maintained by rudder, and/or the aileron control was sufficiently reduced.

Even though excessive aileron pressure may have been applied, a spin will not occur if directional (yaw) control is maintained by timely application of coordinated rudder pressure. Therefore, it is important that the rudder be used properly during both the entry and the recovery from a stall. The primary use of the rudder in stall recoveries is to counteract any tendency of the glider to yaw or slip. The correct recovery technique would be to decrease the pitch attitude by applying forward elevator pressure to reduce the angle of attack and while simultaneously maintaining directional control with coordinated use of the aileron and rudder.

Due to engineering design variations, the stall characteristics for all gliders cannot be specifically described; however, the similarities found in gliders are noteworthy enough to be considered. The factors that affect the stalling characteristics of the glider are weight and balance, bank and pitch attitude, coordination, and drag. The pilot should learn the effect of the stall characteristics of the glider being flown and the proper correction. It should be reemphasized that a stall can occur at any airspeed, in any attitude, or at any power setting in the case of a self-launch glider, depending on the total number of factors affecting the particular glider.

Whenever practicing stalls while turning, a constant bank angle should be maintained until the stall occurs. After the stall occurs coordinated control inputs should be made to return the glider to level flight.

ADVANCED STALLS
Advanced stalls include secondary, accelerated, and crossed-control stalls. These stalls are extremely useful for pilots to expand their knowledge of stall/spin awareness.

SECONDARY STALL

This stall is called a secondary stall because it may occur after a recovery from a preceding stall. It is caused by attempting to hasten the completion of a stall recovery before the glider has regained sufficient flying speed and the critical angle of attack is again exceeded. When this stall occurs, the back-elevator pressure should again be released just as in a normal stall recovery. When sufficient airspeed has been regained, the glider can then be returned to wings-level, straight flight. This stall usually occurs when the pilot uses abrupt control input to return to wings-level, straight flight after a stall or spin recovery.

ACCELERATED STALLS

Though the stalls already discussed normally occur at a specific airspeed, the pilot must thoroughly understand that all stalls result solely from attempts to fly at excessively high angles of attack. During flight, the angle of attack of a glider wing is determined by a number of factors, the most important of which are the airspeed, the gross weight of the glider, and the load factors imposed by maneuvering.

At gross weight, the glider will consistently stall at the same indicated airspeed if no acceleration is involved. The glider will, however, stall at a higher indicated airspeed when excessive maneuvering loads are imposed by steep turns, pull-ups, or other abrupt changes in its flight path. Stalls entered from such flight situations are called "accelerated maneuver stalls," a term that has no reference to the airspeeds involved.

Stalls that result from abrupt maneuvers tend to be more rapid or severe than the unaccelerated stalls, and because they occur at higher-than-normal airspeeds, they may be unexpected by pilots. Failure to take immediate steps toward recovery when an accelerated stall occurs may result in a complete loss of flight control, possibly causing a spin.

Accelerated maneuver stalls should not be performed in any glider in which the maneuver is prohibited in the GFM/POH. If they are permitted, they should be performed with a bank of approximately 45°, and in no case at a speed greater than the glider manufacturer's recommended airspeeds or the design maneuvering speed specified for the glider. The design maneuvering speed is the maximum speed at which the glider can be stalled or the application of full aerodynamic control will not exceed the glider's limit load factor. At or below this speed, the glider is designed so that it stalls before the limit load factor can be exceeded.

The objective of demonstrating accelerated stalls is not to develop competency in setting up the stall, but rather to learn how they may occur and to develop the ability to recognize such stalls immediately, and to take prompt, effective recovery action. It is important that recoveries are made at the first indication of a stall, or immediately after the stall has fully developed; a prolonged stall condition should never be allowed.

A glider will stall during a coordinated turn as it does from straight flight except the pitching and rolling actions tend to be more sudden. If the glider is slipping toward the inside of the turn at the time the stall occurs, it tends to roll rapidly toward the outside of the turn as the nose pitches down because the outside wing stalls before the inside wing. If the glider is skidding toward the outside of the turn, it will have a tendency to roll to the inside of the turn because the inside wing stalls first. If the coordination of the turn at the time of the stall is accurate, the glider's nose will pitch away from the pilot just as it does in a straight flight stall, since both wings stall simultaneously.

Glider pilots enter an accelerated stall demonstration by establishing the desired flight attitude, then smoothly, firmly, and progressively increasing the angle of attack until a stall occurs. Because of the rapidly changing flight attitude, sudden stall entry, and possible loss of altitude, it is extremely vital that the area be clear of other aircraft and the entry altitude be adequate for safe recovery.

Actual accelerated stalls most frequently occur during turns in the traffic pattern close to the ground or while maneuvering during soaring flight. The demonstration of accelerated stalls is accomplished by exerting excessive back-elevator pressure. Most frequently, it would occur during improperly executed steep turns, stall and spin recoveries, and pullouts from steep dives. The objectives are to determine the stall characteristics of the glider and develop the ability to instinctively recover at the onset of a stall at other-than-normal stall speed or flight attitudes. An accelerated stall, although usually demonstrated in steep turns, may actually be encountered any time excessive back-elevator pressure is applied and/or the angle of attack is increased too rapidly.

From straight flight at maneuvering speed or less, the glider should be rolled into a steep banked (maximum 45°) turn and back-elevator pressure gradually applied. After the bank is established, back-elevator pressure should be smoothly and steadily increased. The resulting apparent centrifugal force pushes the pilot's body down in the seat, increases the wing loading, and decreases the airspeed. Back-elevator pressure should be firmly increased until a definite stall occurs.

When the glider stalls, recovery should be made promptly by releasing back-elevator pressure. If the turn is uncoordinated, one wing may tend to drop suddenly, causing the glider to roll in that direction. If this occurs, the glider should be returned to wings-level, straight flight with coordinated control pressure.

A glider pilot should recognize when an accelerated stall is imminent and take prompt action to prevent a completely stalled condition. It is imperative that a prolonged stall, excessive airspeed, excessive loss of altitude, or spin be avoided.

CROSSED-CONTROL STALL
The objective of a crossed-control stall demonstration maneuver is to show the effect of improper control technique and to emphasize the importance of using coordinated control pressures whenever making turns. This type of stall occurs with the controls crossed—aileron pressure applied in one direction and rudder pressure in the opposite direction, and the critical angle of attack is exceeded. [Figure 7-30]

This is a stall that is most likely to occur during a poorly planned and executed base-to-final approach turn, and often is the result of overshooting the centerline of the runway during that turn. Normally, the proper action to correct for overshooting the runway is to increase the rate of turn by using coordinated aileron and rudder. At the relatively low altitude of a base-to-final approach turn, improperly trained pilots may be apprehensive of steeping the bank to increase the rate of turn. Rather than steeping the bank, they hold the bank constant and attempt to increase the rate of turn by adding more rudder pressure in an effort to align with the runway.

The addition of rudder pressure on the inside of the turn causes the speed of the outer wing to increase, creating

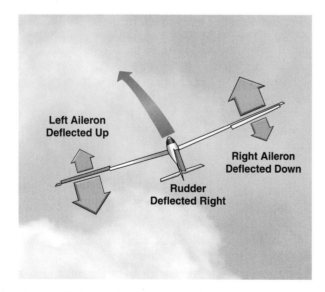

Left Aileron Deflected Up

Right Aileron Deflected Down

Rudder Deflected Right

Figure 7-30. Crossed-control approach to a stall.

greater lift on that wing. To keep that wing from rising and to maintain a constant angle of bank, opposite aileron pressure is required. The added inside rudder pressure will also cause the nose to lower in relation to the horizon. Consequently, additional back-elevator pressure would be required to maintain a constant-pitch attitude. The resulting condition is a turn with rudder applied in one direction, aileron in the opposite direction, and excessive back-elevator pressure—a pronounced cross-control condition.

Since the glider is in a skidding turn during the cross-control condition, the wing on the outside of the turn speeds up and produces more lift than the inside wing; thus, the glider starts to increase its bank. The down aileron on the inside of the turn helps drag that wing back, slowing it up and decreasing its lift. This further causes the glider to roll. The roll may be so fast that it is possible the bank will be vertical or past vertical before it can be stopped.

For the demonstration of the maneuver, it is important that it be entered at a safe altitude because of the possible extreme nose down attitude and loss of altitude that may result. Before demonstrating this stall, the pilot should clear the area for other air traffic. While the gliding attitude and airspeed are being established, the glider should be re-trimmed. When the glide is stabilized, the glider should be rolled into a medium-banked turn to simulate a final approach turn that would overshoot the centerline of the runway. During the turn, excessive rudder pressure should be applied in the direction of the turn but the bank held constant by applying opposite aileron pressure. At the same time, increased back-elevator pressure is required to keep the nose from lowering.

All of these control pressures should be increased until the glider stalls. When the stall occurs, releasing the control pressures, simultaneously decreasing the angle of attack initiates the recovery. In a cross-control stall, the glider often stalls with little warning. The nose may pitch down, the inside wing may suddenly drop, and the glider may continue to roll to an inverted position. This is usually the beginning of a spin. It is obvious that close to the ground is no place to allow this to happen.

Recovery must be made before the glider enters an abnormal attitude (vertical spiral or spin); it is a simple matter to return to wings-level, straight flight by coordinated use of the controls. The pilot must be able to recognize when this stall is imminent and must take immediate action to prevent a completely stalled condition. It is imperative that this type of stall not occur during an actual approach to a landing, since recovery may be impossible prior to ground contact due to the low altitude.

COMMON ERRORS

- Improper pitch and bank control during straight-ahead and turning stalls.
- Rough or uncoordinated control procedures.
- Failure to recognize the first indications of a stall.
- Failure to achieve a stall.
- Poor recognition and recovery procedures.
- Excessive altitude loss or airspeed or encountering a secondary stall during recovery.

SPINS

A spin may be defined as an aggravated stall that results in what is termed "autorotation" wherein the glider follows a downward corkscrew path. As the glider rotates around a vertical axis, the rising wing is less stalled than the descending wing, creating a rolling, yawing, and pitching motion. The glider is basically being forced downward by rolling, yawing, and pitching in a spiral path. [Figure 7-31]

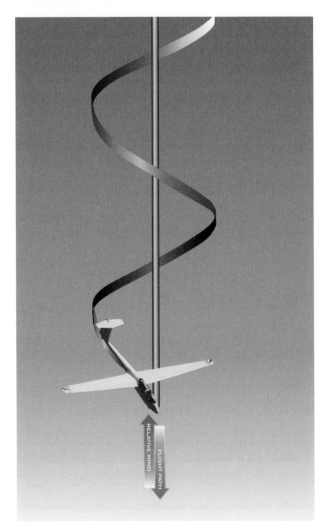

Figure 7-31. Autorotation of spinning glider.

The autorotation results from an unequal angle of attack on the glider's wings. The rising wing has a decreasing angle of attack, in which the relative lift increases and the drag decreases. In effect, this wing is less stalled. Meanwhile, the descending wing has an increasing angle of attack, past the wing's critical angle of attack (stall) where the relative lift decreases and drag increases.

A spin is caused when the glider's wing exceeds its critical angle of attack (stall) with a side slip or yaw acting on the glider at, or beyond, the actual stall. During this uncoordinated maneuver, a pilot may not be aware that a critical angle of attack has been exceeded until the glider yaws out of control toward the lowering wing. If stall recovery is not initiated immediately, the glider may enter a spin.

If this stall occurs while the glider is in a slipping or skidding turn, this can result in a spin entry and rotation in the direction that the rudder is being applied, regardless of which wingtip is raised.

Many gliders have to be forced to spin and require good judgment and technique to get the spin started. These same gliders may be put into a spin accidentally by mishandling the controls in turns, stalls, and flight at minimum controllable airspeeds. This fact is additional evidence of the necessity for the practice of stalls until the ability to recognize and recover from them is developed.

Often a wing drops at the beginning of a stall. When this happens, the nose will attempt to move (yaw) in the direction of the low wing. This is when use of the rudder is important during a stall. The correct amount of opposite rudder must be applied to keep the nose from yawing toward the low wing. By maintaining directional control and not allowing the nose to yaw toward the low wing before stall recovery is initiated, a spin will be averted. If the nose is allowed to yaw during the stall, the glider will begin to skid in the direction of the lowered wing and will enter a spin.

A glider must be stalled in order to enter a spin; therefore, continued practice of stall recognition will help the pilot develop a more instinctive and prompt reaction in recognizing an approaching spin. It is essential to learn to apply immediate corrective action any time it is apparent the glider is approaching spin conditions. If it is impossible to avoid a spin, the pilot should immediately execute spin recovery procedures.

The flight instructor should demonstrate spins and spin recovery techniques with emphasis on any special spin procedures or techniques required for a particular glider. Before beginning any spin operations, the following items should be reviewed.

- GFM/POH limitations section, placards, or type certification data sheet, to determine if the glider is approved for spins.
- Weight and balance limitations.
- Proper recommended entry and recovery procedures.
- The requirements for parachutes. It would be appropriate to review current Title 14 of the Code of Federal Regulations (14 CFR) part 91 for the latest parachute requirements.

A thorough glider preflight should be accomplished with special emphasis on excess or loose items that may affect the weight, CG, and controllability of the glider. Slack or loose control cables (particularly rudder and elevator) could prevent full anti-spin control deflections and delay or preclude recovery in some gliders.

Prior to beginning spin training, the flight area, above and below the glider, must be clear of other air traffic. Clearing the area may be accomplished while slowing the glider for the spin entry. All spin training should be initiated at an altitude high enough for a completed recovery at or above 1,500 feet AGL.

There are four phases of a spin: entry, incipient, developed, and recovery.

ENTRY PHASE
In the entry phase, the pilot provides the necessary elements for the spin, either accidentally or intentionally. The entry procedure for demonstrating a spin is similar to a stall. As the glider approaches a stall, smoothly apply full rudder in the direction of the desired spin rotation while applying full back (up) elevator to the limit of travel. Always maintain the ailerons in the neutral position during the spin procedure unless the GFM/POH specifies otherwise.

INCIPIENT PHASE
The incipient phase takes place between the time the glider stalls and rotation starts until the spin has fully developed. This change may take up to two turns for most gliders. Incipient spins that are not allowed to develop into a steady-state spin are the most commonly used in the introduction to spin training and recovery techniques. In this phase, the aerodynamic and inertial forces have not achieved a balance. As the incipient spin develops, the indicated airspeed should be near or below stall airspeed.

The incipient spin recovery procedure should be commenced prior to the completion of 360° of rotation. The pilot should apply full rudder opposite the direction of rotation.

DEVELOPED PHASE
The developed phase occurs when the glider's angular rotation rate, airspeed, and vertical speed are stabilized while in a flight path that is nearly vertical. This is when glider aerodynamic forces and inertial forces are in balance, and the attitude, angles, and self-sustaining motions about the vertical axis are constant or repetitive. The spin is in equilibrium.

RECOVERY PHASE
The recovery phase occurs when the angle of attack of the wings drops below the critical angle of attack and autorotation slows. Then the nose drops below the spin pitch attitude and rotation stops. This phase may last for a quarter turn to several turns.

To recover, control inputs are initiated to disrupt the spin equilibrium by stopping the rotation and stall. To accomplish spin recovery, the manufacturer's recommended procedures should be followed. In the absence of the manufacturer's recommended spin recovery procedures, the following general spin recovery procedures are recommended.

Step 1—Position the ailerons to neutral. Ailerons may have an adverse effect on spin recovery. Aileron control in the direction of the spin may speed up the rate of rotation and delay the recovery. Aileron control opposite the direction of the spin may cause the down aileron to move the wing deeper into the stall and aggravate the situation. The best procedure is to ensure that the ailerons are neutral. If the flaps are extended prior to the spin, they should be retracted as soon as possible after spin entry.

Step 2—Apply full opposite rudder against the rotation. Make sure that full (against the stop) opposite rudder has been applied.

Step 3—Apply a positive and brisk, straight forward movement of the elevator control past neutral to break the stall. This should be done immediately after full rudder application. The forceful movement of the elevator will decrease the excessive angle of attack and break the stall. The controls should be held firmly in this position. When the stall is "broken," the rotation stops.

Step 4—After spin rotation stops, neutralize the rudder. If the rudder is not neutralized at this time, the ensuing increased airspeed acting upon a deflected rudder will cause a yawing or skidding effect. Slow and overly cautious control movements during spin recovery must be avoided. In certain cases it has been found that such movements result in the glider continuing to spin indefinitely, even with anti-spin inputs. A brisk and positive technique, on the other hand, results in a more positive spin recovery.

Step 5—Begin applying back-elevator pressure to raise the nose to level flight. Caution must be used not to apply excessive back-elevator pressure after the rotation stops. Excessive back-elevator pressure can cause a secondary stall and result in another spin. Care should be taken not to exceed the "G" load limits and airspeed limitations during recovery.

It is important to remember that the above-spin recovery procedures are recommended for use only in the absence of the manufacturer's procedures. Before any pilot attempts to begin spin training, the pilot must be familiar with the procedures provided by the manufacturer for spin recovery.

The most common problems in spin recovery include pilot confusion in determining the direction of spin rotation and whether the maneuver is a spin versus spiral. If the airspeed is increasing, the glider is no longer in a spin but in a spiral. In a spin, the glider is stalled and the airspeed is at or below stalling speed.

COMMON ERRORS
- Failure to clear area before spins.
- Failure to establish proper configuration prior to spin entry.
- Failure to recognize conditions leading to a spin.
- Failure to achieve and maintain stall during spin entry.
- Improper use of controls during spin entry, rotation, and/or recovery.
- Disorientation during spin.
- Failure to distinguish a spiral dive and a spin.
- Excessive speed or secondary stall during spin recovery.
- Failure to recovery with minimum loss of altitude.

MINIMUM SINK AIRSPEED
Minimum sink airspeed is defined as the airspeed at which the glider loses the least amount of altitude in a given period of time. Minimum sink airspeed varies with the weight of the glider. Glider manufacturers publish the altitude loss in feet per minute or meters per second (e.g. 122 ft/min or 0.62 m/sec) at a specified weight. Flying at minimum sink airspeed results in maximum duration in the absence of convection in the atmosphere.

The minimum sink airspeed given in the GFM/POH is based on the following conditions.
- The glider is wings-level and flying a straight flight path; load factor is 1.0 G.
- The glider flight controls are perfectly coordinated.
- Wing flaps are set to zero degrees and air brakes are closed and locked.
- The wing is free of bugs or other contaminants.
- The glider is at a manufacturer-specified weight.

While flying in a thermalling turn, the proper airspeed is the minimum sink airspeed appropriate to the load factor, or G-load, that the glider is undergoing. The glider's stall speed increases with load factor. The minimum sink speed needs to be increased with an increase in load factor. For example, if a glider stall speed is 34 knots and the wings-level minimum sink airspeed is 40 knots, consider the following for thermalling.

- In a 30° banked turn, load factor is 1.2 Gs. The approximate square root of 1.2 is 1.1. Thirty-four knots times 1.1 yields a 37 knots stall speed. The minimum sink speed is still above the stall speed but by only approximately 3 knots. The margin of safety is decreasing and the pilot should consider increasing the minimum sink speed by a factor proportionate to the stall speed increase, in this case 44 knots.

- In a 45° banked turn, load factor is 1.4 Gs. The approximate square root of 1.4 is 1.2. Thirty-four knots times 1.2 yields a 41 knots stall speed. The minimum sink speed is now below the stall speed. If the pilot increases the minimum sink speed proportionately to the stall airspeed, the new speed would be 48 knots, a 7 knot safety factor.

- In a 60° banked turn, load factor is 2.0 Gs. The approximate square root of 2.0 is 1.4. Thirty-four knots times 1.4 yields a 48 knots stall speed. The minimum sink speed is now below the stall speed. The pilot should increase the minimum sink speed proportionately to 56 knots, yielding an 8 knot safety factor.

Minimum sink airspeed is always slower than best L/D airspeed at any given operating weight. If the operating weight of the glider is noticeably less than maximum gross weight, then the actual minimum sink airspeed at that operating weight will be slower than that published.

COMMON ERRORS

- Improper determination of minimum sink speed.
- Failure to maintain proper pitch attitude and airspeed control.

BEST GLIDE AIRSPEED

Best glide (Lift/Drag) **airspeed** is defined as the airspeed that results in the least amount of altitude loss over a given distance. This allows the glider to glide the greatest distance in still air. This performance is expressed as glide ratio. The manufacturer publishes the best glide airspeed for specified weights and the resulting glide ratio. For example, a glide ratio of 36:1 means that the glider will loose 1 foot of altitude for every 36 feet of forward movement in still air at this airspeed. The glide ratio will decrease at airspeeds above or below best glide airspeed. The best glide speed can be found from the glider polars in Chapter 5—Performance Limitations.

COMMON ERRORS

- Improper determination of best glide airspeed for given condition.
- Failure to maintain proper pitch attitude and airspeed control.

SPEED-TO-FLY

Speed-to-fly refers to the optimum airspeed for proceeding from one source of lift to another. Speed-to-fly depends on the following.

1. The rate-of-climb the pilot expects to achieve in the next thermal or updraft.
2. The rate of ascent or descent of the air mass through which the glider is flying.
3. The glider's inherent sink rate at all airspeeds between minimum sink airspeed and never exceed airspeed.
4. Headwind or tailwind.

The object of speed-to-fly is to minimize the time and/or altitude required to fly from the current position to the next thermal. Speed-to-fly information is presented to the pilot in one or more of the following ways.

- By placing a speed-to-fly ring (MacCready ring) around the variometer dial.
- By using a table or chart.
- By using an electronic flight computer that displays the current optimum speed-to-fly.

The pilot determines the speed-to-fly during initial planning and than constantly updates this information in flight. The pilot must be aware of changes in the flying conditions in order to be successful in conducting cross-country flights or during competition.

COMMON ERRORS

- Improper determination of speed-to-fly.
- Failure to maintain proper pitch attitude and airspeed control.

TRAFFIC PATTERNS

The pilot must be familiar with the approach and landing traffic pattern at the local gliderport/airport because the approach actually starts some distance away. Most gliderports/airports use an initial point (IP) from which to begin the approach for each landing area. The IP may be located over the center of the gliderport/airport or at a remote location near the traffic pattern. As shown in Figure 7-32, the sequence of a normal approach is from over the IP to the downwind leg, base leg, final approach, flare, touchdown, roll-out, and stop. Once the landing roll is completed, it is important to clear the active runway as soon as possible to allow other pilots to land safely.

Once over the IP, the pilot flies along the downwind leg of the planned landing pattern. The pilot should plan to be over the IP at an altitude of 800 to 1,000 feet AGL or as recommended by the local field operating procedures. During this time it is important to look for other aircraft and to listen on the communications radio, if one is installed, for other aircraft in the vicinity of the gliderport/airport. Glider pilots should be aware of other activities located at the gliderport/airport, and it is important that they are familiar with good operating practices established in the FAA *Aeronautical Information Manual* and Advisory Circulars. Glider operations usually establish the patterns for their operation with other activities in mind. Pilots new to a gliderport/airport should obtain a thorough checkout before conducting any flights.

Pilots should complete the landing checklist prior to the downwind leg. A good landing checklist is known as **FUSTALL**.

- Flaps—Set (if applicable).
- Undercarriage—Down and locked (if applicable).
- Speed—Approach speed established.
- Trim—Set.
- Air brakes (spoilers/dive brakes)—Checked for correct operation.
- Landing area—Look for wind, other aircraft, and personnel.
- Land the glider.

This checklist can be modified as necessary for any glider.

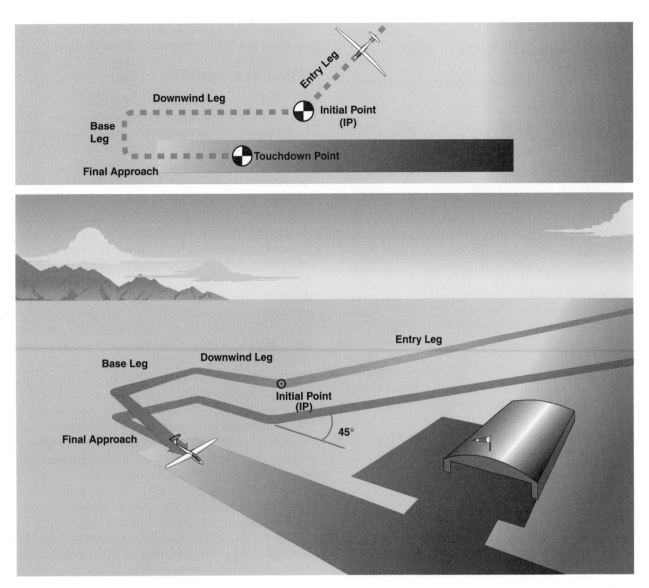

Figure 7-32. Traffic pattern.

After accomplishing the checklist, concentrate on judging your approach angle and staying clear of other aircraft while monitoring your airspeed. Medium turns should be used in the traffic pattern. The approach should be made using spoilers/dive brakes as necessary to dissipate excess altitude. Use the elevator to control the approach speed.

Strong crosswinds, tailwinds, or high sink rates that are encountered in the traffic pattern will require the pilot to modify the individual pattern leg. A strong tailwind or headwind will require a shortening or lengthening of the leg respectively. A sudden encounter with a high sink rate may require the pilot to turn toward the landing area sooner than normal. The pilot should not conduct a 360° turn once established on the downwind leg. Throughout the traffic pattern the pilot should be constantly aware of the approach speed.

When at an appropriate distance from the IP, the pilot should maneuver the glider to enter the downwind leg.

The distance from downwind leg to the landing area should be approximately $1/4$ to $1/2$ mile. This will vary at different locations. On the downwind, leg the glider should be descending to arrive abeam the touchdown point at an altitude between 500 and 600 feet AGL. On downwind leg, the groundspeed will be higher due to the tailwind. The pilot should use the spoilers/dive brakes as necessary to arrive at this altitude. The pilot should also monitor the gliders position with reference to the touchdown area. If the wind is pushing the glider away from or toward the touchdown area, the pilot should stop the drift by establishing a wind correction angle into the wind. Failure to do so will affect the point where the base leg should be started.

The base leg should be started when the touchdown point is approximately 45° over the pilot's shoulder looking back at the touchdown area. Once established on the base leg, the pilot should scan the extended final approach path in order to detect any aircraft that might be on long final approach to the landing area in use. The turn to base leg should be timely in order to keep the point of intended touchdown area within easy gliding range. The pilot should adjust the turn to correct for wind drift encountered on the base leg. On base leg, the pilot should adjust the spoilers/dive brakes, as necessary, to position the glider at the desired glide angle.

The turn onto the final approach is made so as to line up with the centerline of the touchdown area. The pilot should adjust the spoilers/dive brakes as necessary to fly the desired approach angle to the aim point. The selected aim point should be prior to the touchdown point to accommodate the landing flair. The pilot flairs the glider at or about three to five feet AGL and the glider floats some distance until it touches down.

When within three to five feet of the ground, begin the flare with slight back elevator. As the airspeed decreases, the pilot holds the glider in a level or tail low attitude so as to touchdown at the slowest possible speed while the glider still is under aerodynamic control. After touchdown the pilot should concentrate on rolling out straight down the centerline of the touchdown area.

Tracking down the centerline of the touchdown area is an important consideration in gliders. The long, low wingtips of the glider are susceptible to damage from runway border markers, runway light stanchions, or taxiway markers. Turning off the runway should be done only if and when the pilot has the glider under control.

Landing in high, gusty winds or turbulent conditions may require higher approach airspeeds to improve controllability and provide a safer margin above stall airspeed. A rule of thumb is to add $1/2$ the gust factor to the normal approach airspeed. This increased approach airspeed affords better penetration into the headwind on final approach. The adjusted final approach airspeed should not be greater than the maneuvering speed (V_A) or maximum turbulence penetration speed (V_B), whichever is lower.

CROSSWIND LANDINGS

Crosswind landings require a crabbing or slipping method to correct for the effects of the wind on the final approach. Additionally, the pilot must land the glider without placing any unnecessary side load on the landing gear.

The crab method requires the pilot to point the nose of the glider into the wind and fly a straight track along the desired ground path. The stronger the wind, the greater the crab angle. Prior to flare, the pilot must be prepared to align the glider with the landing area. The pilot should use the rudder to align the glider prior to touchdown and deflect the ailerons into the wind to control the side drift caused by the crosswind.

In the slip method, the pilot uses rudder and ailerons to slip the glider into the wind to prevent drifting downwind of the touchdown area. The disadvantage of the slip method is that the sink rate of the glider increases, forcing the pilot to adjust the spoilers/dive brakes, as necessary, to compensate for this additional sink rate.

Whether the pilot selects the slip or crab method for crosswind landing is personal preference. The important action is to stabilize the approach early enough on final so as to maintain a constant approach angle and airspeed to arrive at the selected touchdown point.

COMMON ERRORS

- Improper glide path control.
- Improper use of flaps, spoilers/dive brakes.
- Improper airspeed control.
- Improper correction of crosswind.
- Improper procedure for touchdown/landing.
- Poor directional control during/after landing.
- Improper use of wheel brakes.

SLIPS

A slip is a descent with one wing lowered. It may be used for either of two purposes, or both of them combined. A slip may be used to steepen the approach path without increasing the airspeed, as would be the case if the spoilers/dive brakes were inoperative or to clear an obstacle. It can also be used to make the glider move sideways through the air to counteract the drift which results from a crosswind.

Formerly, slips were used as a normal means of controlling landing descents to short or obstructed fields, but they are now primarily used in the performance of crosswind landings and short/off-field landings.

With the installation of effective spoilers/dive brakes on modern gliders, the use of slips to steepen or control the angle of descent is no longer a common procedure. However, the pilot still needs skill in performance of forward slips to correct for possible errors in judgment of the landing approach.

The primary purpose of forward slips is to dissipate altitude without increasing the glider's airspeed, particularly in gliders not equipped with flaps or those with inoperative spoilers/dive brakes. There are many circumstances requiring the use of forward slips, such as in a landing approach over obstacles and in making off-field landings. It is always wise to allow an extra margin of altitude for safety in the original estimate of the approach. In the latter case, if the inaccuracy of the approach is confirmed by excess altitude when nearing the boundary of the selected field, slipping may dissipate the excess altitude.

The use of slips has definite limitations. Some pilots may try to lose altitude by violent slipping rather than by smoothly maneuvering and exercising good judgment and using only a slight or moderate slip. In off-field landings, this erratic practice invariably will lead to trouble since enough excess speed may result in preventing touching down anywhere near the touchdown point, and very often will result in overshooting the entire field.

The forward slip is a slip in which the glider's direction of motion continues the same as before the slip was begun. [Figure 7-33] If there is any crosswind, the slip will be much more effective if made into the wind. Assuming the glider is originally in straight flight, the wing on the side that the slip is to be made should be lowered by using the ailerons. Simultaneously, the glider's nose must be yawed in the opposite direction by applying opposite rudder so the glider's longitudinal axis is at an angle to its original flight path. The degree to which the nose is yawed in the opposite direction from the bank should be such that the original ground track is maintained. The nose should also be raised as necessary to prevent the airspeed from increasing.

If a slip is used during the last portion of a final approach, the longitudinal axis of the glider must be aligned with the runway just prior to touchdown so the glider touches down headed in the direction in which it is moving. This requires timely action to discontinue the slip and align the glider's longitudinal axis with its direction of travel over the ground well before the instant of touchdown. Failure to accomplish this imposes severe sideloads on the landing gear and imparts violent ground looping tendencies.

Discontinuing the slip is accomplished by leveling the wings and simultaneously releasing the rudder pressure while readjusting the pitch attitude to the normal glide attitude. If the pressure on the rudder is released abruptly, the nose will swing too quickly into line and the glider will tend to acquire excess airspeed.

Because of the location of the pitot tube and static vents, airspeed indicators in some gliders may have considerable error when the glider is in a slip. The pilot must be aware of this possibility and recognize a properly performed slip by the attitude of the glider, the sound of the airflow, and the feel of the flight controls.

A sideslip, [Figure 7-34] as distinguished from a forward slip, is one during which the glider's longitudinal axis remains parallel to the original flight path, but in which the flight path changes direction according to the steepness of the bank. The sideslip is important in counteracting wind drift during crosswind landings and is discussed in crosswind landing section of this chapter.

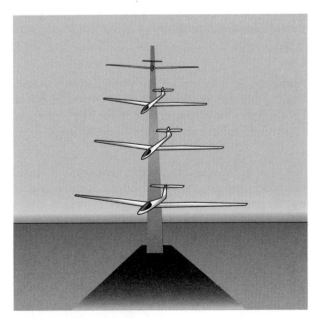

Figure 7-33. Forward slip.

Figure 7-34. Side slip.

COMMON ERRORS

- Improper glide path control.
- Improper use of slips.
- Improper airspeed control.
- Improper correction for crosswind.
- Improper procedure for touchdown/landing.
- Poor directional control during/after landing.
- Improper use of brakes.

DOWNWIND LANDINGS

Downwind landings present special hazards and should be avoided when an into-the-wind landing is available. However, factors such as gliderport/airport layout, presence of insurmountable obstacles, such as high terrain at one end of the runway, runway slope or grade, or a launch failure at low altitude can require you to make a downwind landing. The pilot must use the normal approach airspeed during a downwind landing. Any airspeed in excess only causes the approach area and runway needed for approach and landing to increase.

The tailwind increases the touchdown groundspeed and lengthens the landing roll. The increased distance for landing can be determined by dividing the actual touchdown speed by the normal touchdown speed, and squaring the result. For example, if the tailwind is 10 knots and the normal touchdown speed is 40 knots, the actual touchdown speed is 50 knots. This touchdown speed is 25 percent more than the normal speed, a factor of 1.25. A factor of 1.25 squared equals 1.56. This means the landing distance will increase 56 percent over the normal landing distance.

On downwind approaches, a shallower approach angle should be used, depending on obstacles in the approach path. Use the spoilers/dive brakes and perhaps a forward slip as necessary to achieve the desired glide path.

After touchdown, use the wheel brake to reduce groundspeed as soon as is practical. This is necessary to maintain aerodynamic control of the glider.

COMMON ERRORS

- Improper glide path control.
- Improper use of slips.
- Improper airspeed control.
- Improper correction of crosswind.
- Improper procedure for touchdown/landing.
- Poor directional control during/after landing.
- Improper use of wheel brakes.

AFTER-LANDING AND SECURING

After landing, move or taxi the glider clear of all runways. If the glider is to be parked for a short interval between flights, choose a spot that does not inconvenience other gliderport/airport users. Protect the glider from wind by securing a wingtip with a weight or by tying it down. Consult the manufacturer's handbook for the recommended methods for securing the glider. Remember that even light winds can cause gliders to move about, turn sideways, or cause the higher wing in a parked glider to slam down onto the ground. Because gliders are particularly vulnerable to wind effects, the glider should be secured any time it is unattended.

When the glider is done flying for the day, move it to the tiedown area. Secure the glider in accordance with the recommendation in the GFM/POH. The tiedown anchors should be strong and secure. Apply external control locks to the glider flight control surfaces. Control locks should be large, well marked, and brightly painted. If a cover is used to protect the pitot tube, the cover should be large and brightly colored. If a canopy cover is used, secure it so that the canopy cover does not scuff the canopy in windy conditions.

If the glider is stored in a hangar, be careful while moving the glider to avoid damaging it or other aircraft in the hangar. Chock the main wheel and tailwheel of the glider when it is in position in the hangar. If stored in a wings-level position, put a wing stand under each wingtip. If stored with one wing high, place a weight on the lowered wing to hold it down.

If the glider is to be disassembled and stored in a trailer, tow the glider to the trailer area and align the fuselage with the long axis of the trailer. Collect all tools, dollies, and jigs required to disassemble and stow the glider. Secure the trailer so that loading the glider aboard does not move or upset the trailer or trailer doors. Follow the disassembly checklist in the GFM/POH. Stow the glider components securely in the trailer. When the glider has been stowed and secured, collect all tools and stow them properly. Close trailer doors and hatches. Secure the trailer against wind and weather by tying it down properly.

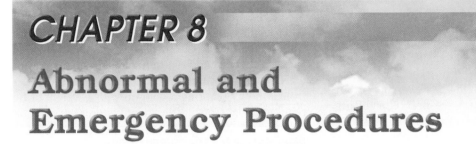

CHAPTER 8
Abnormal and Emergency Procedures

Training for abnormal and emergency procedures is an essential element in becoming a glider pilot. Knowledge of procedures for coping with control problems and instrument or equipment malfunction is especially important in soaring activities. Knowing how to use emergency equipment and survival gear is a practical necessity.

PORPOISING

Porpoising is a general term that refers to pitch oscillations that can occur in gliders. In most cases, pilots induce these oscillations through over-controlling the glider as they attempt to stop the oscillations from occurring in the first place.

PILOT—INDUCED OSCILLATIONS

The instability of a glider's attitude that arises when the pilot fails to recognize the lag time inherent in controlling the glider is known as a **pilot-induced oscillation** (PIO). Typically, PIOs occur when the glider fails to respond instantly to control input and the pilot quickly increases the pressure on the controls. By the time the pilot judges that the glider is responding satisfactorily, the extra control pressures have resulted in such a vigorous response that the glider overshoots the desired flight attitude. Alarmed, the pilot moves the controls rapidly in the opposite direction, overcompensating for the mistake. The undesired glider motion slows, stops for an instant, and then reverses. The alarmed pilot maintains significant control pressures to try to increase the rate of response. The glider, now in rapid motion in the desired direction in response to heavy-handed control inputs, again shoots past the desired attitude as the now thoroughly alarmed pilot jerks the flight controls in the opposite direction. Unless the pilot understands that these oscillations are the direct result of over-controlling the glider, it is unlikely that the oscillations will cease. More likely, they will increase in intensity until there is a complete loss of control.

Although pilot-induced oscillations can occur at any time, these situations arise most commonly during primary training. They tend to disappear as pilot experience grows because pilots gain familiarity with the lag time inherent in the flight controls. These types of oscillations may also occur when a pilot is making flights in unfamiliar types of gliders. For this reason, particular care must be taken when the pilot is preparing to fly a single seat glider in which the pilot has no prior experience. When checking out in a new type of single seat glider, the lag time of the flight controls must be learned without the obvious benefit of having an experienced glider flight instructor aboard during flight to offer advice or, if necessary, to intervene. While most PIO discussions are devoted to pitch oscillations, consideration will be given to roll and yaw induced oscillations.

The first step toward interrupting the PIO cycle is to recognize the lag time inherent in the glider's response. Any change in glider flight attitude takes an appreciable amount of time to accomplish as the flight controls take affect, and the mass of the glider responds to the pilot's control inputs. The second step is to modify control inputs to avoid over-controlling the glider. The correct technique is to pressure the controls until the glider begins to respond in the desired direction, then ease off the pressure. As the glider nears the desired attitude, center the appropriate flight control so that overshooting does not occur.

PILOT-INDUCED PITCH OSCILLATIONS DURING LAUNCH

Pilot-induced oscillations are most likely to occur during launch because the glider's lag time changes rapidly as the glider accelerates. During the first moments of the takeoff roll, aerodynamic control is poor, the control feel of the glider is very sluggish, and lag time is great. As the glider gains speed, aerodynamic response improves; control feel becomes crisper, and lag time decreases. When the glider has acquired safe flying speed, lag time is short, the controls feel "normal," and pilot-induced oscillations become much less likely.

FACTORS INFLUENCING PIOS

The pitch effect of the towhook/towline combination characteristic of the glider being flown, which may cause uncommanded pitch excursions, contributes to PIOs during aerotow launch. In addition, the propwash and wing vortices of the towplane, through which the glider must pass if there is little or no crosswind, affect the flight attitude and control response of the glider. To minimize the influence of the towplane's wake, use a towline of adequate length—200 feet is the minimum length for normal operations. A longer towline provides more isolation from towplane wake during aerotow launch. Short towlines, on the other hand, keep the glider closer to the towplane and its turbulent wake, complicating the problem of controlling the glider.

There are several techniques that reduce the likelihood and severity of PIOs during aerotow launch. Do not try to lift off until confident that flying speed and good aerodynamic control have been achieved. Also, just after the moment of liftoff, allow the glider to rise several feet above the runway before stabilizing the altitude of the glider. Two to three feet is high enough that minor excursions in pitch attitude, if corrected promptly, do not result in the glider smacking back to the ground, but not high enough for you to lose sight of the towplane below the nose of the glider. Although visually attractive to onlookers, the practice of trying to stabilize the glider just a few inches above the ground provides little margin for error if a PIO occurs.

IMPROPER ELEVATOR TRIM SETTING

The elevator trim control position also contributes to PIOs in pitch attitude. The takeoff checklist includes a check to confirm that the flight controls including elevator trim are properly set for takeoff. If the trim is properly set for takeoff, elevator pressure felt through the control stick is normal and the likelihood of PIO is reduced. If the elevator trim is set incorrectly, however, elevator pressure felt through the control stick may contribute to PIOs. If the trim is set excessively nose-down, the pilot needs to hold back pressure on the control stick to achieve and maintain the desired pitch attitude during launch and climb-out. If the trim is set excessively nose-up, the pilot needs to hold forward pressure. The more pressure that is needed, the more likely it is that the pilot will over-control the glider.

Although all gliders exhibit these tendencies if the trim is improperly set, the effect is most pronounced on those gliders with an aerodynamic elevator trim tab or an anti-servo tab on the elevator. The effect usually is less pronounced on those glider fitted with a simple spring system elevator trim. Regardless of the type of elevator trim installed in the glider, error prevention is superior to error correction. Use a comprehensive pre-takeoff checklist and set the elevator trim in the appropriate position prior to launch to help prevent PIOs attributable to elevator trim miss-use. [Figure 8-1]

IMPROPER WING FLAPS SETTING

The likelihood of PIOs increases if the wing flaps are not correctly set in the desired takeoff position. For the majority of flap-equipped gliders, most Glider Flight Manuals/Pilot Operating Handbook (GFM/POH) recommend that flaps be set at zero degrees for takeoff (check the GFM/POH for the manufacturer recommendations). If the flaps are incorrectly set to a positive flap setting, which increases wing camber and wing lift, the glider tends to rise off the runway prematurely, perhaps even before the elevator control is sufficient to control the pitch attitude. Attempting to prevent the glider from ballooning high above the runway, the pilot may exert considerable forward pressure on the control stick. As the glider continues to accelerate, this forward pressure on the control stick exerts a rapidly increasing nose-down force on the glider due to the increasing airflow over the elevator. When the glider eventually pitches down, the pilot may exert considerable back pressure on the stick to arrest the descent. PIOs are likely to result. If allowed to continue, a hard landing may result, with potential for glider damage and personal injury.

If the wing flaps are incorrectly set to a negative flap setting, decreasing wing camber and wing lift, then takeoff may be delayed so long that the towplane will lift off and begin to climb out while the glider is still rolling down the runway, unable to get airborne. Powerful back pressure on the stick may eventually assist the glider in leaving the runway, but the relatively high airspeed at liftoff translates into a very effective elevator, and ballooning may occur as a result of the elevator position. The pilot, startled once again by the magnitude of this pitch excursion, tries to correct by

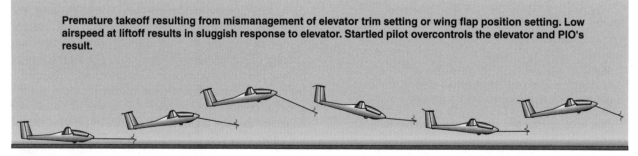

Premature takeoff resulting from mismanagement of elevator trim setting or wing flap position setting. Low airspeed at liftoff results in sluggish response to elevator. Startled pilot overcontrols the elevator and PIO's result.

Figure 8-1. Premature takeoffs and PIOs.

applying considerable forward pressure on the control stick. A series of PIOs may result. If the PIOs continue, a hard landing may occur.

PILOT-INDUCED ROLL OSCILLATIONS DURING LAUNCH

Pilot-induced roll oscillations occur primarily during launch, particularly via aerotow. As the towpilot applies full throttle, the glider moves forward, balanced laterally on its main wheel. If a wingtip begins to drop toward the ground before the glider achieves significant speed, aileron control is marginal and considerable stick displacement must be applied to elicit a response from the glider. As the glider accelerates, the control response improves and the latency of response from the glider shortens. As acceleration continues, the pilot must recognize the quickening response of the glider to avoid over-controlling the glider. [Figure 8-2]

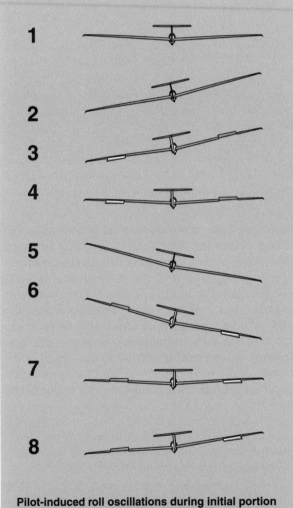

Pilot-induced roll oscillations during initial portion of takeoff ground roll. Momentum of long, massive glider wings tends to overshoot desired wings-level condition. This tendency is aggravated if the pilot holds corrective aileron pressure too long.

Figure 8-2. Pilot-induced roll oscillations during takeoff roll.

Although roll oscillations can develop during ground launch operations, they occur less often than during aerotow operations because excellent aerodynamic control of the glider is quickly achieved thanks to the rapid acceleration. Since control improves as acceleration increases, operations that use a powerful winch or launch vehicle are less likely to be hampered by oscillations.

Wing mass also affects roll oscillations. If the wings do not stay level, the pilot applies considerable aileron pressure to return the wings to level attitude. Because of the large mass and considerable aerodynamic damping that long-winged gliders exhibit, there is a considerable lag time from the moment pressure is applied until the moment the wings are level again. Inexperienced pilots maintain considerable pressure on the ailerons until the wings are level, then release the pressure. The wings continue their rolling moment due to their mass, length, and momentum about the longitudinal axis of the glider. The pilot senses this momentum too late, and applies considerable pressure in the opposite direction in another attempt to level the wings.

After a time, the wings respond and roll back to level, whereupon the pilot centers the ailerons once again. As before, the momentum of the wings about the longitudinal axis is considerable, and the wings continue their motion in roll. This series of PIOs may continue until one wingtip contacts the ground, possibly with considerable force, causing wing damage or a groundloop and an aborted launch. To reduce the likelihood of this type of roll oscillation, anticipate the momentum of the glider wings about the longitudinal axis and reduce aileron control pressure as the wings approach the level position.

PILOT-INDUCED YAW OSCILLATIONS DURING LAUNCH

Pilot-induced yaw oscillations are usually caused by overcontrolling the rudder. As with roll oscillations, the problem is the failure of the pilot to recognize that the glider is accelerating and has considerable momentum. If the glider is veering away from the towplane, rudder application in the appropriate direction helps correct the situation. If the rudder pressure is held too long, the large yaw momentum of the glider wings and fuselage results in overshooting the desired yaw position and veering off in the opposite direction. The alarmed pilot now applies considerable rudder pressure in the direction opposite from the original rudder pressure. As the glider continues to accelerate, the power of the rudder increases and the lag time decreases. In extreme cases, the glider may veer off the runway and collide with runway border markers, airport lights, parked glider, or other obstacles. The cure for this type of yaw oscillation is to anticipate the momentum of the glider wings and fuselage about the vertical axis and reduce rudder pedal pressure when the nose of the glider begins to yaw in the desired direction in response to rudder inputs. [Figure 8-3]

When a wingtip contacts the ground during takeoff roll, an uncommanded yaw results. The drag of the wingtip on the ground induces a yaw in the direction of the grounded wingtip. The yaw usually is mild if the wingtip is on smooth pavement but much more

Yaw momentum of the mass of the glider's wings and fuselage contributes to overshooting the desired heading. This tendency is aggravated if the pilot holds corrective rudder pressure too long.

Figure 8-3. Pilot-induced yaw oscillations during takeoff roll.

vigorous if the wingtip is dragging through tall grass. If appropriate aileron pressure fails to raise the wingtip off the ground quickly, the only solution is to release the towline and abort the takeoff attempt before losing all control of the glider.

The greater the mass of the wings and the longer the wingspan, the more momentum the glider will exhibit whenever roll or yaw oscillations arise. Some very high performance gliders feature remarkably long and heavy wings, meaning once in motion, they tend to remain in motion for a considerable time. This is true not only of forward momentum, but yaw and roll momentum as well. The mass of the wings, coupled with the very long moment arm of large-span wings, results in substantial lag times in response to aileron and rudder inputs during the early portion of the takeoff roll and during the latter portion of the landing roll-out. Even highly proficient glider pilots find takeoffs and landings in these gliders to be challenging. Many of these gliders are designed for racing or cross-country flights and have provisions for adding water ballast to the wings. Adding ballast increases mass, which results in an increase in lag time.

If there is an opportunity to fly such a glider, study the GFM/POH thoroughly prior to flight. It is also a good idea to seek out instruction from an experienced pilot/flight instructor in what to expect during takeoff roll and landing rollout in gliders with long/heavy wings.

GUST-INDUCED OSCILLATIONS

Gusty headwinds can induce pitch oscillations because the effectiveness of the elevator varies due to changes in the speed of the airflow over the elevator. Crosswinds also can induce yaw and roll oscillations. A crosswind from the right, for instance, tends to weathervane the glider into the wind, causing an uncommanded yaw to the right. Right crosswind also tends to lift the upwind wing of the glider. When crosswinds are gusty, these effects vary rapidly as the speed of the crosswind varies.

Local terrain can have a considerable effect on the wind. Wind blowing over and around obstacles can be gusty and chaotic. Nearby obstacles, such as hangars, groves or lines of trees, hills, and ridges can have a pronounced effect on low altitude winds, particularly on the downwind side of the obstruction. In general, the effect of an upwind obstacle is to induce additional turbulence and gustiness in the wind. These conditions are usually found from the surface to an altitude of three hundred feet or more. If flight in these conditions cannot be avoided, then the general rule during takeoff is to achieve a faster than normal speed prior to liftoff. The additional speed increases the responsiveness of the controls and simplifies the problem of correcting for turbulence and gusts. This provides a measure of protection against PIOs. The additional speed also provides a safer margin above stall airspeed. This is very desirable on gusty days because variations in the headwind component will have a considerable effect on indicated airspeed.

VERTICAL GUSTS
DURING HIGH-SPEED CRUISE

Although PIOs occur most commonly during launch, they can occur during cruising flight, even when cruising at high speed. Turbulence usually plays a role in this type of PIO, as does the elasticity and flexibility of the glider structure. An example is an encounter with an abrupt updraft during wings-level high-speed cruise. The upward-blowing gust increases the angle of attack of the main wings, which bend upward very quickly, storing elastic energy in the wing spars. For a moment, the G-loading in the cabin is significantly greater than one G. Like a compressed coil spring seeking release, the wing spars reflex downward, lofting the fuselage higher. When the fuselage reaches the top of this motion, the wing spars are now storing elastic energy in the downward direction, and the fuselage is sprung downward in response to the release of elastic energy in the wing spars. The pilot now experiences reduced G, accompanied perhaps by a head bang against the top of the canopy. During these excursions, the weight of the pilot's hand and arm on the control stick may cause the control stick to move a significant distance forward or aft. With positive G the increased apparent weight of the pilot's arm tends to move the control stick aft, further increasing the angle of attack of the main wing and increasing the positive G factor as a result, in a type of vicious circle. During negative G the reduced apparent weight of the pilot's arm tends to result in forward stick motion, reducing the angle of attack and reducing the G factor still further; once again, in a sort of vicious circle. In short, the effect of rapid alternations in load factor is to increase the intensity of load factor variations. One protection against this is to slow down when cruising through turbulent air. Another protection is to brace both arms and use both hands on the control stick when cruising through turbulent air at high speed. It is worth noting that some glider designs incorporate a parallelogram control stick linkage to reduce the tendency toward PIOs during high-speed cruise.

PILOT-INDUCED PITCH
OSCILLATIONS DURING LANDING

Instances of PIO may occur during the landing approach in turbulent air for the same reasons previously stated. Landing the glider involves interacting with ground effect during the flare and keeping precise control of the glider even as airspeed decays and control authority declines. A pilot can cause a PIO by over-controlling the elevator during the flare, causing the glider to balloon well above the landing surface even as airspeed is decreasing. If the pilot reacts by pushing the stick well forward, the glider will soon be diving for the ground with a fairly rapid rate of descent. If the pilot pulls the control stick back to arrest this descent while still in possession of considerable airspeed, the glider balloons again and the PIO cycle continues. If airspeed is low when the pilot pulls back on the stick to avoid a hard landing, there is not likely to be sufficient lift available to arrest the descent. A hard or a nose-first landing may result.

To reduce ballooning during the flare, stabilize the glider at an altitude of 3 or 4 feet, and then begin the flare anew. Do not try to force the nose of the glider down on to the runway. If airspeed during the ballooning is slow and the ballooning takes the glider higher than a normal flare altitude, it may be necessary to reduce the extension of the spoilers/dive breaks in order to moderate the descent rate of the glider. Care must be taken to avoid abrupt changes. Partial retraction of the spoilers/dive breaks allows the wing to provide a bit more lift despite decaying airspeed.

Another source of PIOs during the approach to landing is a too abrupt adjustment of the spoilers/dive breaks setting. The spoilers/dive breaks on most modern gliders provide a very large amount of drag when fully deployed, and they reduce the lift of the wing considerably. Over-controlling the spoilers/dive breaks during the approach to land can easily lead to oscillations in pitch attitude and airspeed. The easiest way to guard against these oscillations is to make smooth adjustments in the spoilers/dive breaks setting whenever spoilers/dive breaks adjustment is necessary. This becomes particularly important during the landing flare just prior to touchdown. If the spoilers/dive breaks are extended further with anything less than a very smooth and sure hand, the resultant increase in sink rate may cause the glider to contact the runway suddenly. This can lead to a rebound into the air, setting the stage for a series of PIOs. As before, the cure is to stabilize the glider then resume the flare. If the spoilers/dive breaks are retracted abruptly during the flare, the glider will likely balloon into the air. Pilot reaction may result in over-controlling and PIOs may result. During the flare, it is best to leave the spoilers/dive breaks extension alone unless the glider balloons excessively. If you must adjust the spoilers/dive breaks, do so with smooth, gentle motion.

GLIDER INDUCED OSCILLATIONS

PITCH INFLUENCE OF THE
GLIDER TOWHOOK POSITION

The location of the glider's aerotow towhook influences pitch attitude control of the glider during aerotow operations. During these operations, the towline is under considerable tension. If the towline is connected to a glider towhook located more or less directly on the longitudinal axis of the glider, the towline tension has little effect on the pitch attitude of the glider. This is the case when the towhook is located in the most forward part of the gliders nose, such as in the air vent intake hole. This is the ideal location for the aerotow hook for most gliders.

The towhook on many gliders is located below or aft of this ideal location. In particular, many European gliders have the towhook located on the belly of the glider, just forward of the main landing gear, far below the longitudinal axis of the glider. The glider's center of mass is well above the location of the towhook in this position. In fact, virtually all of the glider's mass is above the towhook. The mass of the glider has inertia and resists acceleration when the towline tension increases. In these bellyhook-equipped gliders, an increase in tension on the towline causes an uncommanded pitch-up of the glider nose as shown in Figure 8-4. Decrease in towline tension results in an uncommanded pitch-down.

Rapid changes in towline tension, most likely to occur during aerotow in turbulent air, cause these effects in alternation. Naturally, on days when good lift is available, the aerotow will be conducted in turbulent air. The potential for inducing pitch oscillations is obvious, as rapid alternations in towline tension induce rapid changes in the pitch attitude of the glider. To maintain a steady pitch attitude during aerotow in a bellyhook-equipped glider, the pilot must be alert to variations in towline tension and adjust pressure on the control stick to counteract the pitch effect of variations in towline tension.

SELF-LAUNCH GLIDER OSCILLATIONS DURING POWERED FLIGHT
Gliders equipped with an extended pod engine and propeller located high above the glider's longitudinal axis exhibit a complex relationship between power setting and pitch attitude. When power changes are made, the location of the thrust line of the propeller in this location has a noticeable effect on pitch attitude. The changing speed of the propwash over the elevator causes considerable variation in elevator effectiveness, modifying pitch attitude still further. Prior to flight, study the GFM/POH carefully to discover what these undesired effects are and how to counteract them. When throttle settings must be changed, it is good practice to move the throttle control smoothly and gradually. This gives the pilot time to recognize and counteract the effect the power setting change has on pitch attitude. In most self-launched gliders, the effect is greatest when flying at or near minimum controllable airspeed (MCA). Self-launch glider pilots avoid slow flight when flying at low altitude under power. [Figure 8-5]

Self-launch gliders may also be susceptible to PIOs during takeoff roll, particularly those with a pylon engine mounted high above the longitudinal axis. The high thrust line and the propeller wash influence on the air flow over the self-launch glider's elevator may tend to cause considerable change in the pitch attitude of the glider when power changes are made.

NOSEWHEEL GLIDER OSCILLATIONS DURING LAUNCHES AND LANDINGS
Many tandem two-seat fiberglass gliders, and some single-seat fiberglass gliders as well, feature a three-wheel landing gear configuration. The main wheel is equipped with a traditional large pneumatic tire; the tailwheel and the nosewheel are equipped with smaller pneumatic tires. During taxi operations, if the pneumatic nosewheel remains in contact with the ground, any bump will compress the nosewheel tire. When the pneumatic nosewheel tire rebounds, an uncommanded pitch-up occurs. If the pitch-up is sufficient, as is likely to be the case after hitting a bump at fast taxi speeds, the tailwheel will contact the runway, compress, and rebound. This can result in porpoising, as the nosewheel and tailwheel alternate in hitting the runway, compressing, and rebounding. In extreme cases, the fuselage of the glider may be heavily damaged.

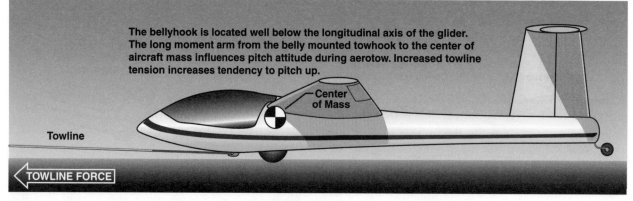

Figure 8-4. Effect of increased towline on pitch altitude of bellyhook-equipped glider during aerotow.

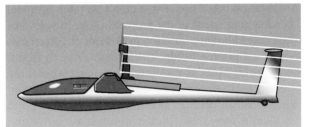

The pod mounted engine thrust line is high above the longitudinal axis of the motorglider. Moment arm of the engine pod affects pitch attitude. Power increase applies nose-down moment.

Propeller wash flows over elevator. Power increase provides higher propwash velocity and increases elevator authority. Power decrease produces propwash velocity and reduces elevator authority. Study the motorglider flight manual to learn the intricacies of the pitch-power relationship.

Figure 8-5. Pitch attitude power setting relationships for self-launch glider with engine pod.

During takeoff roll, the best way to avoid porpoising in a nosewheel-equipped glider is to use the elevator to lift the nosewheel off the runway as soon as practicable, then set the pitch attitude so the glider's main wheel is the only wheel in contact with the ground. To avoid porpoising during landing, hold the glider off during the flare until the mainwheel and tailwheel touch simultaneously. During rollout, use the elevator to keep the nosewheel off the ground for as long as possible.

TAILWHEEL/TAILSKID EQUIPPED GLIDER OSCILLATIONS DURING LAUNCHES AND LANDINGS

Some two-seat gliders, self-launch gliders, and single-seat gliders have a tailwheel. When loaded and ready for flight, these gliders have the mainwheel and the tailwheel or tailskid in contact with the ground. In these gliders, the center of gravity is aft of the main wheel(s). Because of this, any upward thrust on the main landing gear tends to pitch the nose of the glider upward unless the tail wheel or tailskid is in contact with the ground and prevents the change in pitch attitude.

Upward thrust on the main landing gear can occur in numerous circumstances. One cause is a bump in the runway surface during takeoff or landing roll. If the resultant pitch-up is vigorous enough, it is likely that the glider will leave the ground momentarily. If airspeed is slow, the elevator control is marginal. As the pilot reacts to the unexpected bounce or launch, overcontrolling the elevator will result in a PIO. [Figure 8-6]

Improper landing technique in a tailwheel glider also can lead to upward thrust on the main landing gear and subsequent PIOs. Landing a tailwheel glider in a nose-down attitude, or even in a level pitch attitude, can lead to trouble. If the main wheel contacts the ground before the tailwheel or tailskid, the compression of the pneumatic tire and its inevitable rebound will provide significant upward thrust. The glider nose may pitch up, the angle of attack will increase, and the glider will become airborne. As before, overcontrol of the elevator leads to PIOs.

To prevent this type of PIO, do not allow the glider to settle onto the landing surface with a nose-down attitude or with excess airspeed. During the landing flare, hold the glider off a few inches above the ground with gentle backpressure on the control stick as necessary. The speed will decay and the pitch attitude will gradually change to a slightly nose-up pitch attitude. The ideal touchdown is simultaneous gentle contact of main wheel and tailwheel or tailskid. Delaying the touchdown just a small amount results in the tailwheel or tailskid contacting the landing surface an instant before the mainwheel. This type of landing is very acceptable and desirable for almost all tailwheel gliders because it makes a rebound into the air very unlikely. Consult the GFM/POH for the glider being flown for further information about recommended procedure for touchdown.

OFF-FIELD LANDING PROCEDURES

The possibility of an off-field landing is present on virtually every cross-country soaring flight, even when

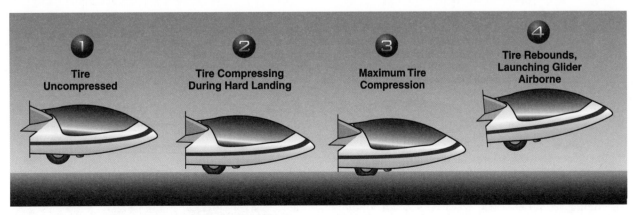

1. Tire Uncompressed
2. Tire Compressing During Hard Landing
3. Maximum Tire Compression
4. Tire Rebounds, Launching Glider Airborne

Figure 8-6. Pneumatic tire rebound during hard landing.

flying in a self-launch glider. If the engine or power system fails and there is no airport within gliding range, then an off-field landing may be inevitable. It should be noted that many glider pilots who were not flying cross-country have faced the necessity of performing an off-field landing. Root causes of off-field landings while engaged in soaring in the vicinity of the launching airport include rapid weather deterioration, a significant change in wind direction, unanticipated amounts of sinking air, disorientation, or lack of situational awareness. In these situations, it usually is safer to make a precautionary off-field landing than it is to attempt a low, straight-in approach to the airport. If the glide back to the airport comes up short for any reason, the landing is likely to be poorly executed and may result in damage to the glider or injury to the pilot.

On cross-country soaring flights, off-field landings are not usually considered emergency landings. As a matter of fact, they are expected and are considered while preparing for flight. On the other hand, if equipment failure leads to the necessity of performing an off-field landing, then the landing can be characterized or described as an emergency landing. Whatever the reason for the off-field landing, each glider pilot must be prepared at all times to plan and execute the landing safely.

Unlike airport landings, no off-field landing is entirely routine. An extra measure of care must be undertaken to achieve a safe outcome. The basic ingredients for a successful off-field landing are awareness of wind direction, wind strength at the surface, and approach path obstacles. The glider pilot must be able to identify suitable landing areas, have the discipline to select a suitable landing area while height remains to allow sufficient time to perform a safe approach and landing, and the ability to consistently make accurate landings in the glider type being flown. These ingredients can be summarized as follows:

- Recognize the possibility of imminent off-field landing.

- Select a suitable area, then a suitable landing field within that area.

- Plan your approach with wind, obstacles, and local terrain in mind.

- Execute the approach, land, and then stop the glider as soon as possible.

The most common off-field landing planning failure is denial. The pilot, understandably eager to continue the flight and return to an airport, is often reluctant to initiate planning for an off-field landing because to do so, in the pilot's mind, will probably result in such a landing. Better, the pilot thinks, to concentrate on continuing the flight and finding a way to climb back up and fly away. The danger of this false optimism is that there will be little or no time to plan an off-field landing if the attempt to climb away does not succeed. It is much better and safer to thoroughly understand the techniques for planning an off-field landing and to be prepared for the occurrence at any time.

Wind awareness, knowing wind direction and intensity, is key when planning an off-field landing. Heading downwind offers a greater geographical area to search than flying upwind. A tailwind during downwind cruise results in a greater range, headwind during upwind cruise reduces the range. Wind awareness is also essential to planning the orientation and direction of the landing approach. Visualize the wind flowing over and around the intended landing area. Remember that the area downwind of hills, buildings, and other obstructions will probably be turbulent at low altitude. Also, be aware that landing into wind shortens landing rolls.

Decision heights are altitudes at which pilots take critical steps in the off-field landing process. If the terrain below is suitable for landing, select a general area no lower than 2,000 feet above ground level (AGL). Select the intended landing field no lower than 1,500 feet AGL. At 1,000 feet AGL, commit to flying the approach and landing off-field. If the terrain below is not acceptable for an off-field landing, the best course of action is to move immediately toward more suitable terrain.

For many pilots there is a strong temptation during the off-field landing process to select a landing location based primarily on the ease of retrieval. The convenience of an easy retrieval is of little consequence if the landing site is unsuitable and results in damage to the glider or injury to the pilot. Select the landing site with safety foremost in mind. During an off-field landing approach, the precise elevation of the landing site normally will not be available to the pilot. This renders the altimeter more or less useless. Fly the approach and assess the progress by recognizing and maintaining the angle that puts the glider at the intended landing spot safely. If landing into strong headwind, the approach angle is steep. If headwind is light or non-existent, the approach angle is shallower unless landing over an obstacle. When landing with a tailwind (due to slope or one-way entry into the selected field due to terrain or obstacles) the angle will be shallower. Remember to clear each visible obstacle with safe altitude, clearing any wires by a safe margin.

Select a field of adequate length and, if possible, one with no visible slope. Any slope that is visible from the air is likely to be steep. Slope can often be assessed by the color of the land. High spots often are lighter in color than low spots because soil moisture tends to collect in low spots, darkening the color of the soil there. If level landing areas are not available and the landing must be made on a slope, it is better to land uphill than downhill. Even a slight downhill grade during landing flare allows the glider to float prior to touchdown, which may result in collision with objects on the far end of the selected field.

Knowledge of local vegetation and crops is also very useful. Tall crops are generally more dangerous to land in than low crops. Know the colors of local seasonal vegetation to help identify crops and other vegetation from the air. Without exception, avoid discontinuities such as lines or crop changes. Discontinuities usually exist because a fence, ditch, irrigation pipe, or some other obstacle to machinery or cultivation is present.

Other obstacles may be present in the vicinity of the chosen field. Trees and buildings are easy to spot, but power and telephone lines and poles are harder to see from pattern altitude. Take a careful look around to find them. Power lines and wires are nearly impossible to see from pattern altitude; assume every pole is connected by wire to every other pole. Also assume that every pole is connected by wire to every building, and that every building is connected by wire to every other building. Plan your approach to over fly the wires that may be present, even if you cannot see them. The more you see of the landing area during the approach, the fewer unpleasant surprises there are likely to be.

The recommended approach procedure is to fly the following legs in the pattern.

• Crosswind leg on the downwind side of the field.

• Upwind leg.

• Crosswind leg on the upwind side of the field.

• Downwind leg.

• Base leg.

• Final approach.

This approach procedure provides the opportunity to see the intended landing area from all sides. Use every opportunity while flying this approach to inspect the landing area and look for obstacles or other hazards. [Figure 8-7]

Landing over an obstacle or a wire requires skill and vigilance. The first goal in landing over an obstacle is to clear the obstacle! Next, you must consider how the obstacle effects the length of landing area that is actually going to be available for touchdown, rollout, and stopping the glider. If an obstacle is 50 feet high, the first 500 feet or so of the landing area will be over

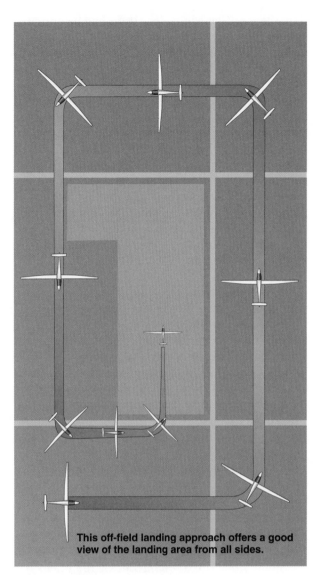

This off-field landing approach offers a good view of the landing area from all sides.

Figure 8-7. Off-field landing approach.

flown as you descend to flare and land. If the field selected has obstacles on the final approach path, remember that the field will have to be long enough to accommodate the descent to flare altitude after clearing the obstacle.

Hold the glider off during the flare and touch down at the lowest safe speed manageable. After touchdown, use the wheelbrake immediately and vigorously to stop the glider as soon as possible. Aggressive braking helps prevent collision with small stakes, ditches, rocks, or other obstacles that cannot easily be seen, especially if the vegetation in the field is tall.

AFTER LANDING OFF-FIELD

OFF-FIELD LANDING WITHOUT INJURY
If uninjured, tend to personal needs then secure the glider. Make contact with the retrieval crew or emergency crew as promptly as possible. If the wait is likely to be long, use the daylight to remove all items necessary

for darkness and cold. It is worth remembering that even a normal retrieval can take many hours if the landing was made in difficult terrain or in an area served by relatively few roads. Use a cell phone to call 911 if nervous about personal safety. To help identify your position, relay the GPS coordinates, if available, to ease the job for the retrieval crew or rescue personnel. It is a good idea to write down the GPS coordinates if the GPS battery is exhausted or if the GPS receiver shuts down for any reason. Use the glider two-way radio to broadcast your needs on the international distress frequency 121.5 MHz. Many aircraft, including civil airliners, routinely monitor this frequency. Their great height gives the line-of-sight aviation transceiver tremendous range when transmitting to, or receiving from, these high altitude aircraft. Once contact has been made with outsiders to arrange for retrieval, take care of minor items such as collecting any special tools that are needed for glider de-rigging or installing gust locks on the glider's flight controls.

OFF-FIELD LANDING WITH INJURY

If injured, tend to critical injuries first. At the first opportunity make contact with emergency response personnel, with other aircraft, or any other source of assistance you can identify. Use the glider radio, if operable, to broadcast a Mayday distress call on the emergency frequency 121.5 MHz. Many in-flight aircraft routinely monitor this frequency. Also try any other frequency likely to elicit a response. Some gliders have an Emergency Locator Transmitter (ELT) on board. If the glider is equipped with an ELT and assistance is needed, turn it on. The ELT broadcasts continuous emergency signals on 121.5 MHz. Search aircraft can home in on this signal, reducing the time spent searching for your exact location. If the two-way radio is operable and you want to transmit a voice message on 121.5 MHz, turn the ELT switch to OFF in order for the voice message to be heard. If cell phone coverage is available, dial 911 to contact emergency personnel. If possible, include a clear description of your location. If the glider is in a precarious position, secure it if possible but do not risk further personal injury in doing so. If it is clearly not safe to stay with the glider, move to a nearby location for shelter but leave clear written instructions, in a prominent location in the glider, detailing where to find you.

It is best, if at all possible, to stay with the glider. The glider bulk is likely to be much easier to locate from the air than is an individual person. The pilot may be able to obtain a measure of protection from the elements by crawling into the fuselage, crawling under a wing, or using the parachute canopy to rig a makeshift tent around the glider structure. After attending to medical needs and contacting rescue personnel, attend to clothing, food, and water issues. The pilot should make every attempt to conserve energy.

SYSTEMS AND EQUIPMENT MALFUNCTIONS

FLIGHT INSTRUMENT MALFUNCTIONS

Instrument failures can result from careless maintenance practices and from internal or external causes. Removal and replacement of the airspeed indicator but failure to connect the instrument correctly to pitot and static lines is an example of careless maintenance. A clogged pitot tube due to insect infestation or water ingress is an example of external cause of instrument failure.

AIRSPEED INDICATOR MALFUNCTIONS

If the airspeed indicator appears to be erratic or inaccurate, fly the glider by pitch attitude. Keep the nose of the glider at the proper pitch attitude for best glide or minimum sink airspeed. Additional cues to airspeed include control "feel" and wind noise. At very low airspeeds, control feel is very mushy and wind noise is generally low. At higher airspeeds, control feel is crisper and wind noise takes on a more insistent hissing quality. The sound of the relative wind can be amplified, and made more useful in airspeed control, by opening the sliding window installed in the canopy and by opening the air vent control. During the landing approach, maintain adequate airspeed using cues other than the airspeed indicator. Fly the approach with an adequate margin above stall airspeed. If conditions are turbulent or the wind is gusty, additional airspeed is necessary to penetrate the convection and to ensure adequate control authority. If in doubt, it is better to be 10 knots faster than optimum airspeed than it is to be 10 knots slower.

ALTIMETER MALFUNCTIONS

Altimeter failure may result from internal instrument failure or from external causes such as water ingress in the static lines. Regardless of the cause, it is important to maintain sufficient altitude to allow a safe glide to a suitable landing area. During the approach to land without a functioning altimeter, it is necessary to rely on perception of maintaining a safe gliding angle to the target landing area. The primary risk to safety is entering the approach from an altitude that is lower than normal. It is better to enter the approach from a normal height, or even from a higher-than-normal height. During the approach, judge the angle to the target area frequently. If the angle is too steep, apply full spoilers/dive breaks to steepen the descent path. If necessary, apply a forward slip or turning slip to lose additional altitude. If the approach angle is beginning to appear shallow, close the spoilers/dive breaks and, if necessary, modify the approach path to shorten the distance necessary to glide to make it to the target landing area.

Static line contamination affects both the altimeter and the airspeed indicator. If it is suspected either instrument is malfunctioning because of static line contamination, remember that the indications of the other instrument(s) connected to the static line may also be incorrect. Use the external cues described above to provide multiple cross-checks on the indications of all affected instruments. If in doubt about the accuracy of any instrument, it is best to believe the external cues and disregard the instrument indications. After landing and prior to the next flight, have an aviation maintenance professional evaluate the instrument system.

It is essential that a glider pilot be familiar with the procedures for making a safe approach without a functioning airspeed indicator or altimeter. An excellent opportunity to review these procedures is when accompanied by a glider flight instructor during the flight review.

VARIOMETER MALFUNCTIONS
Variometer failure can make it difficult for the pilot to locate and exploit sources of lift. If an airport is nearby, a precautionary landing should be made so the source of the problem can be uncovered and repaired. If no airport is nearby, search for cues to sources of lift. Some cues may be external, such as a rising smoke column, a cumulus cloud, a dust devil, or a soaring bird. Other sources are internal, such as the altimeter. Use the altimeter to gauge rate of climb or descent in the absence of a functioning variometer. Tapping the altimeter with the forefinger often overcomes internal friction in the altimeter, allowing the hand to move upward or downward. The direction of the movement gives an idea of the rate of climb or descent over the last few seconds. When lift is encountered, stay with it and climb.

COMPASS MALFUNCTIONS
Compass failure is rare but it does occur. If the compass performs poorly or not at all, cross-check your position with aeronautical charts and with electronic methods of navigation, such as GPS, if available. The position of the sun, combined with knowledge of the time of day, can help in orientation also. Section lines and major roads often provide helpful cues to orientation as well.

GLIDER CANOPY MALFUNCTIONS
Canopy-related emergencies are often the result of pilot error. The most likely cause is failure to lock the canopy in the closed position prior to takeoff. Regardless of the cause, if the canopy opens unexpectedly during any phase of flight, the first duty is to fly the glider. It is important to maintain adequate airspeed while selecting a suitable landing area.

GLIDER CANOPY OPENS UNEXPECTEDLY
If the canopy opens while on aerotow, it is vital to maintain a normal flying attitude to avoid jeopardizing the safety of the glider occupants and the safety of the tow-plane pilot. Only when the glider pilot is certain that glider control can be maintained should any attention

be devoted to trying to close the canopy. If flying a two-seat glider with a companion aboard, concentrate on flying the glider while the other person attempts to close and lock the canopy. If the canopy cannot be closed, the glider may still be controllable. Drag will be higher than normal, so when flying the approach it is best to plan a steeper-than-normal descent path. The best prevention against unexpected opening of the canopy is proper use of the pre-takeoff checklist.

BROKEN GLIDER CANOPY
If the canopy plexiglas is damaged or breaks during flight the best response is to land as soon as practicable. Drag will be increased if the canopy is shattered, so plan a steeper-than-normal descent path during the approach.

FROSTED GLIDER CANOPY
Extended flight at high altitude or in low ambient temperatures may result in obstructed vision as moisture condenses as frost on the inside of the canopy. Open the air vents and the side window to ventilate the cabin and to evacuate moist air before the moisture can condense on the canopy. Descend to lower altitudes or warmer air to reduce the frost on the canopy. Flight in direct sunlight helps diminish the frost on the canopy.

WATER BALLAST MALFUNCTIONS
Water ballast systems are relatively simple and major failures are not very common. Nevertheless, ballast system failures can threaten the safety of flight. One example of ballast failure is asymmetrical tank draining (one wing tank drains properly but the other wing tank does not). The result is a wing-heavy glider that may be very difficult to control during slow flight and during the latter portion of the landing rollout. Another example is leakage. Some water ballast systems drain into a central pipe that empties out through the landing gear wheel well. If the drain connections from either wing leak significantly, water from the tanks can collect in the fuselage. If the water flows far forward or far aft in the fuselage, pitch control of the glider may be severely degraded. Pitch control can be augmented by flying at mid to high airspeeds, giving the elevator more control authority to correct for the out-of-balance situation and affording time to determine whether the water can be evacuated from the fuselage. If pitch control is dangerously degraded, then abandoning the glider may be the safest choice. The best prevention for water ballast problems are regular maintenance and inspection combined with periodic tests of the system and its components.

RETRACTABLE LANDING GEAR MALFUNCTIONS
Landing gear difficulties can arise from several causes. Landing gear failures arising from mechanical malfunction of the gear extension mechanism generally

cannot be resolved during flight. Fly the approach at normal airspeed. If the landing gear is not extended, the total drag of the glider is less than it is normally during an approach with the landing gear extended. It may be necessary to use more spoiler/dive break than normal during the approach. Try to land on the smoothest surface available. Allow the glider to touch down at a slightly faster airspeed than would be used if the landing gear were extended. This helps avoid a tailwheel-first landing, and a hard thump of the glider onto the runway. Avoiding the hard thump will help to avoid back injury. The glider will make considerable noise as the glider slides along the runway, and wingtip clearance above the ground will be much reduced. Keep the wings level for as long as possible. Try to keep the glider going as straight as possible using the rudder to yaw the glider. The primary goal is to avoid collision with objects on the ground or along the runway border. Accept the fact that minor damage to the glider is inevitable if the gear cannot be extended and locked. Concentrate on personal safety during the approach and landing. Any damage to the glider can be repaired after an injury-free landing.

PRIMARY FLIGHT CONTROL SYSTEMS

Failure of any primary flight control system presents a serious threat to safety. The most frequent cause of control system failures is incomplete assembly of the glider in preparation for flight. To avoid this, use a written checklist to guide each assembly operation and inspect every connection and safety pin thoroughly. Do not allow interruptions during assembly. If interruption is unavoidable, start the checklist again from the very beginning. Perform a positive control check with the help of a knowledgeable assistant. Do not assume that any flight surface and flight control is properly installed and connected during the post-assembly inspection. Instead, assume that every connection is suspect. Inspect and test until certain that every component is ready for flight.

ELEVATOR MALFUNCTIONS

The most serious control system malfunction is a failure of the elevator flight control. Causes of elevator flight control failure include the following.

- An improper connection of the elevator control circuit during assembly.
- An elevator control lock that was not removed before flight.
- Separation of the elevator gap seal tape.
- Interference of a foreign object with free and full travel of the control stick or elevator circuit.
- A lap belt or shoulder harness in the back seat that was used to secure the control stick and not removed prior to flight.
- A structural failure of the glider due to over-stressing or flutter.

To avoid a failure, ensure that control locks are removed prior to flight, that all flight control connections have been completed properly and inspected, that all safety pins have been installed and latched properly. Ensure that a positive control check against resistance applied has been performed.

If the elevator irregularity or failure is detected early in the takeoff roll, release the towline (or reduce power to idle), maneuver the glider to avoid obstacles, and use the brakes firmly to stop the glider as soon as possible.

If the elevator control irregularity or failure is not noticed until after takeoff, a series of complicated decisions must be made quickly. If the glider is close to the ground and has a flat or slightly nose low pitch attitude, releasing the towline (or reducing power to zero) is the best choice. If this is an aerotow launch, consider the effect the glider has on the safety of the towpilot. If there is sufficient elevator control during climb, then it is probably best to stay with the launch and achieve as high an altitude as possible. If wearing a parachute, high altitude gives more time to abandon the glider and deploy the parachute.

If the decision is to stay with the glider and continue the climb, experiment with the effect of other flight controls on the pitch attitude of the glider. These include the effects of various wing flap settings, spoilers/dive breaks, elevator trim system, and raising or lowering the landing gear. If flying a self-launch glider, experiment with the effect of power settings on pitch attitude.

If aileron control is functioning, bank the glider and use the rudder to moderate the attitude of the nose relative to the horizon. When the desired pitch attitude is approached, adjust the bank angle to maintain the desired pitch attitude. Forward slips may have a predictable effect on pitch attitude and can be used to moderate it. Usually, a combination of these techniques is necessary to regain some control of pitch attitude. While these techniques may be a poor substitute for the glider elevator itself, they are better than nothing. If an altitude sufficient to permit bailing out and using a parachute is achieved, chances of survival are good because parachute failures are exceedingly rare.

Elevator gap seal tape, if in poor condition, can degrade elevator responsiveness. If the adhesive that bonds the gap seal leading edge to the horizontal stabilizer begins to fail, the leading edge of the gap seal may be lifted up by the relative wind. This will provide, in effect, a small spoiler that disturbs the airflow over the elevator just aft of the lifted seal. Elevator blanking occurring across a substantial portion of the span of the elevator seriously degrades pitch attitude control. In extreme cases, elevator authority may be compromised so drastically that the glider elevator will be useless. The pilot may be forced to resort to alternate methods to control pitch attitude as described above. Bailing out may be the safest alternative. Inspection of the gap seal bonds for all flight control surfaces prior to flight is the best prevention.

AILERON MALFUNCTIONS

Aileron failures can cause serious control problems. Causes of aileron failures include the following.

- An improper connection of the aileron control circuit during assembly.

- An aileron control lock that was not removed before flight.

- A separation of the aileron gap seal tape.

- An interference of a foreign object with free and full travel of the control stick or aileron circuit.

- A seat belt or shoulder harness in the back seat that was used to secure the control stick and not removed prior to flight.

- A structural failure and/or aileron flutter.

These failures can sometimes be counteracted successfully. Part of the reason for this is that there are two ailerons. If one aileron is disconnected or locked by an external control lock, the degree of motion still available in the other aileron may exert some influence on bank angle control. Use whatever degree of aileron available to maintain control of the glider. The glider may be less difficult to control at medium to high airspeeds than at low airspeeds.

If the ailerons are not functioning adequately and roll control is compromised, the secondary effect of the rudder can be used to make gentle adjustments in the bank angle so long as a safe margin above stall speed is maintained. The primary effect of the rudder is to yaw the glider. The secondary effect of the rudder is subtler and takes longer to assert itself. In wings-level flight, if left rudder is applied, the nose yaws to the left. If the pressure is held, the wings begin a gentle bank to the left. If right rudder pressure is held and applied, the glider yaws to the right, then begins to bank to the right. This bank effect is a secondary effect of the rudder. If the pilot must resort to using the rudder to bank the glider wings, keep all banks shallow. The secondary effect of the rudder works best when the wings are level or held in a very shallow bank, and is enhanced at medium to high airspeeds. Try to keep all banks very shallow. If the bank angle becomes excessive, it will be difficult or impossible to recover to wings-level flight using the rudder alone. If the bank is becoming too steep, use any aileron influence available, as well as all available rudder to bring the wings back to level. If a parachute is available and the glider becomes uncontrollable at low airspeed, the best chance to escape serious injury may be to bail out of the glider from a safe altitude.

RUDDER MALFUNCTIONS

Rudder failure is extremely rare because removing and installing the vertical fin/rudder combination is not part of the normal sequence of rigging and de-rigging the glider (as it is for the horizontal stabilizer/elevator and for the wing/aileron combinations). Poor directional control is so obvious to the pilot from the very beginning of the launch that, if rudder malfunction is suspected, the launch can be aborted early.

Rudder malfunctions most likely occur due to failure to remove the rudder control lock prior to flight or when an unsecured object in the cockpit interferes with the free and full travel of the rudder pedals. Preflight preparation must include removal of all flight control locks and safe stowage of all items on board. The pre-takeoff checklist includes checking all primary flight controls for correct, full travel prior to launch.

Although rudder failure is quite rare, the consequences are serious. If a control lock causes the problem, it is possible to control the glider airspeed and bank attitude but directional control is compromised due to limited rudder movement. In the air, some degree of directional control can be obtained by using the adverse yaw effect of the ailerons to yaw the glider. During rollout from an aborted launch or during landing rollout, directional control can sometimes be obtained by deliberately grounding the wingtip toward the direction of desired yaw. Putting the wingtip on the ground for a fraction of a second causes a slight yaw in that direction; holding the wingtip firmly on the ground usually causes a vigorous yaw or groundloop in the direction of the grounded wingtip.

Careless stowage of cockpit equipment can result in rudder pedal interference at any time during a flight. During soaring flight, if an object is interfering with or jamming the rudder pedals, attempt to remove it. If removal is not possible, attempt to deform, crush, or dislodge the object by applying force on the rudder pedals. It also may be possible to dislodge the object by varying the load factor, but be careful that dislodging the object does not result in its lodging in a worse place, where it could jam the elevator or aileron controls. If the object can not be retrieved and stowed, a precautionary landing may be required.

SECONDARY FLIGHT CONTROL SYSTEMS

Secondary flight control systems include the elevator trim system, wing flaps, and spoilers/dive brakes. Problems with any of these systems can be just as serious as problems with primary controls.

ELEVATOR TRIM MALFUNCTIONS

Compensating for a malfunctioning elevator trim system is usually as simple as applying pressure on the control stick to maintain the desired pitch attitude, then bringing the flight to safe conclusion. Inspect and repair the trim system prior to the next flight.

SPOILER/DIVE BRAKE MALFUNCTIONS

Spoiler/dive brake system failures can arise from rigging errors or omissions, environmental factors, and mechanical failures. Interruptions or distractions during glider assembly can result in failure to properly connect control rods to one or both spoilers/dive brakes. Proper use of a comprehensive checklist reduces the likelihood of assembly errors. If neither of these spoilers/dive brakes are connected, then one or both of the spoilers/dive brakes may deploy at any time and retraction will be impossible. This is a very hazardous situation for several reasons. One reason is that the spoilers/dive brakes are likely to deploy during the launch or the climb, causing a launch emergency. Another reason is that the spoilers/dive brakes might deploy asymmetrically: one spoiler/dive brake retracted, the other spoiler/dive brake extended. This results in a yaw tendency and a roll tendency that does not arise when the spoilers/dive brakes deploy symmetrically. The final reason is that it will not be possible to correct the situation by retracting the spoiler/dive brake(s) because the failure to connect the controls properly usually means that pilot control of the spoiler/dive brake has been lost.

If asymmetrical spoiler/dive brake extension occurs and the extended spoiler/dive brake cannot be retracted, several choices must be made. Roll and yaw tendencies due to asymmetry must be overcome or eliminated. One way to solve this problem is to deploy the other spoiler/dive brake, relieving the asymmetry. The advantages include immediate relief from yaw and roll tendencies and protection against stalling with one spoiler/dive brake extended and the other retracted, which could result in a spin. The disadvantage of deploying the other spoiler/dive brake is that the glide ratio is reduced.

If the spoiler/dive brake asymmetry arises during launch or climb, the best choice is to abort the launch, extend the other spoiler/dive brakes to relieve the asymmetry, and make a precautionary or emergency landing.

Environmental factors include cold or icing during long, high altitude flights, such as might occur during a mountain wave flight. The cold causes contraction of all glider components. If the contraction is uneven, the spoilers/dive brakes may bind and be difficult or impossible to deploy. Icing can also interfere with operation of the spoilers/dive brakes. High heat, on the other hand, causes all glider components to expand. If the expansion is uneven, the spoilers/dive brakes may bind in the closed position. This is most likely to occur while the glider is parked on the ground in direct summer sunlight. The heating can be very intense, particularly for a glider with wings painted a color other than reflective white.

Mechanical failures can cause asymmetrical spoiler/dive brake extension. For example, the spoiler/dive brake extend normally during the pre-landing checklist but only one spoiler/dive brake retracts on command. The other spoiler/dive brake remains extended, due perhaps to a broken weld in the spoiler/dive brake actuator mechanism, a defective control connector, or other mechanical failure. If a decision is made to fly with one spoiler/dive brake extended and the other retracted, the wing with the extended spoiler/dive brake creates less lift and more drag than the other wing. The glider yaws and banks toward the wing with the extended spoiler/dive brake. Aileron and rudder are required to counteract these tendencies. To eliminate any possibility of entering a stall/spin, maintain a safe margin above stall airspeed. If the decision to deploy the other spoiler/dive brake is made to relieve the asymmetry, controlling the glider will be much easier but gliding range will be reduced due to the additional drag of the second spoiler/dive brake. This may be a significant concern if the terrain is not ideal for landing the glider. Nevertheless, it is better to make a controlled landing, even in less than ideal terrain, than it is to stall or spin.

MISCELLANEOUS FLIGHT SYSTEM MALFUNCTIONS

TOWHOOK MALFUNCTIONS

Towhooks can malfunction just like any other mechanical device. Failure modes include uncommanded towline release and failure to release on command. Pilots must be prepared to abort any towed launch, whether ground or aerotow launch, at any time. Uncommanded towline release must be anticipated prior to every launch. Assess the wind and the airport environment, and then form an emergency plan prior to launch. If the towhook fails to release on command, try to release the towline again after removing tension from the line. Pull the release handle multiple times under varying conditions of towline tension. If the towrope still cannot release, alert the towpilot and follow the emergency procedures described in Chapter 7—Flight Maneuvers and Traffic Patterns.

OXYGEN SYSTEM MALFUNCTIONS

Oxygen is essential for flight safety at high altitude. If a suspected or detected failure in any component of the oxygen system, descend immediately to an altitude where supplemental oxygen is not essential for continued safe flight. Remember that the first sign of oxygen deprivation is a sensation of apparent well being. Problem-solving capability is diminished. If the pilot has been deprived of sufficient oxygen, even for a short interval, critical thinking capability has been compromised. Do not be lulled into thinking that the flight can safely continue at high altitude. Descend immediately and breathe normally at these lower altitudes for a time to restore critical oxygen to the bloodstream. Try to avoid hyperventilation, which will prolong the diminished critical thinking capability. Give enough time to recover critical thinking capability before attempting an approach and landing.

DROGUE CHUTE MALFUNCTIONS

Some gliders are equipped with a drogue chute to add drag during the approach to land. This drag supplements the drag the spoilers/dive breaks provide. The drogue chute is packed and stowed in the aft tip of the fuselage or in a special compartment in the base of the rudder. Drogue chutes are very effective when deployed properly and make steep approaches possible. The drogue chute is deployed and jettisoned on pilot command, such as would be necessary if the drag of the glider was so great that the glider would not otherwise have the range to make it to the spot of intended landing. There are several failure modes for drogue chutes. If it deploys accidentally or inadvertently during takeoff roll or during climb, the rate of climb will be seriously degraded and it must be jettisoned. During the approach to land, an improperly packed or damp drogue chute may fail to deploy on command. If this happens, use the rudder to sideslip for a moment, or fan the rudder several times to yaw the tail of the glider back and forth in rapid alternation. Make certain to have safe flying speed before attempting the slip or fanning the rudder. Either technique increases the drag on the tailcone that pulls the parachute out of the compartment.

If neither technique deploys the drogue chute, the drogue canopy may deploy at a later time during the approach without further control input from the pilot. This will result in a considerable increase in drag. If this happens, be prepared to jettison the drogue chute immediately if sufficient altitude to glide to the intended landing spot has not been reached.

Another possible malfunction is when the drogue chute evacuates the chute compartment, but fails to inflate fully. If this happens, the canopy will "stream" like a twisting ribbon of nylon, providing only a fraction of

the drag that would occur if the canopy had fully inflated. Full inflation is unlikely after streaming occurs, but if it does occur, drag will increase substantially. If in doubt regarding the degree of deployment of the drogue chute, the safest option may be to jettison the drogue.

SELF-LAUNCH GLIDERS

In addition to the standard flight control systems found on all gliders, self-launch gliders have multiple systems to support flight under power. These systems may include, but are not limited to the following.

- Fuel tanks, lines, and pumps.

- Engine and/or propeller extension and retraction systems.

- Electrical system including engine starter system.

- Lubricating oil system.

- Engine cooling system.

- Engine throttle controls.

- Propeller blade pitch controls.

- Engine monitoring instruments and systems.

The complexity of these systems demands thorough familiarity with the GFM/POH for the self-launch glider being flown. Any malfunction of these systems can make it impossible to resume powered flight.

SELF-LAUNCH GLIDER ENGINE FAILURE DURING TAKEOFF OR CLIMB

Engine failures are the most obvious source of equipment malfunction in self-launch gliders. Engine failures can be subtle (a very slight power loss at full throttle) or catastrophic and sudden (engine crankshaft failing during a full power takeoff). High on the list of possible causes of power problems are fuel contamination or exhaustion.

To provide adequate power, the engine system must have fuel and ignition, as well as adequate cooling and lubrication. Full power operation is compromised if any of these requirements are not satisfied. Monitor the engine temperature, oil pressure, fuel pressure, and RPM carefully to ensure engine performance is not compromised. Warning signs of impending difficulty include excess engine temperatures, excess engine oil temperatures, low oil pressure, low RPM despite high throttle settings, low fuel pressure, and engine missing or backfiring. Abnormal engine performance may be a precursor to complete engine failure. Even if total engine failure does not occur, operation with an engine that cannot produce full power translates into an inability to climb or perhaps an inability to hold altitude despite application of full throttle. The best course of action, if airborne, is to make a precautionary landing and discover the source of the trouble after safely on the ground.

Regardless of the type of engine failure, the pilot's first responsibility is to maintain flying airspeed and adequate control of the glider. If power failure occurs, lower the nose as necessary to maintain adequate airspeed. Pilots flying self-launch gliders with a pod-mounted external engine above the fuselage need to lower the nose much more aggressively in the event of total power loss than those with an engine mounted in the nose. In the former, the thrust of the engine during full power operations tends to provide a nose-down pitching moment. If power fails, the nose-down pitching moment disappears and is replaced by a nose-up pitching moment due to the substantial parasite drag of the engine pod high above the longitudinal axis of the fuselage. Considerable forward motion on the control stick may be required to maintain flying airspeed. If altitude is low, there is not enough time to stow the engine and reduce the drag that it creates. Land the glider with the engine extended. Glide ratio in this configuration will be poor due to the drag of the extended engine and propeller. The authoritative source for information regarding the correct sequence of pilot actions in the event of power failure is contained in the GFM/POH. The pilot must be thoroughly familiar with its contents to operate a self-launch glider safely.

If the power failure occurs during launch or climb, time to maneuver may be limited. Concentrate on flying the glider and selecting a suitable landing area. Remember that the high drag configuration of the glider may limit the distance of the glide without power. Keep turns to a minimum and land the glider as safely as you can. Do not try to restart the engine while at very low altitude because it distracts from the primary task of maintaining flying airspeed and making a safe precautionary landing. Even if you could manage to restore power in the engine system, chances are that full power will not be available. The problem that caused the power interruption in the first place is not likely to solve itself while trying to maneuver from low altitude and climb out under full power. If the problem recurs, as it is likely to do, the pilot may place the glider low over unlandable terrain with limited gliding range and little or no engine power to continue the flight. Even if the engine continues to provide limited power, flight with partial power may quickly put the glider in a position in which the pilot is unable to clear obstacles such as wires, poles, hangars, or nearby terrain. If a full-power takeoff or climb is interrupted by power loss, it is best to make a precautionary landing. The pilot can sort out the power system problems after returning safely to the ground.

INABILITY TO RE-START A SELF-LAUNCH GLIDER ENGINE WHILE AIRBORNE

Power loss during takeoff roll or climb are serious problems, but they are not the only types of problems that may confront the self-launch glider pilot. Other engine failures include an engine that refuses to start in response to airborne start attempts. This is a serious problem if the terrain below is unsuitable for a safe off-field landing.

One of the great advantages of the self-launch glider is the option to terminate a soaring flight by starting the engine and flying to an airport/gliderport for landing. Nearly all self-launch gliders have a procedure designed to start the engine while airborne. This procedure would be most valuable during a soaring flight with engine off during which the soaring conditions have weakened. The prospect of starting the engine and flying home safely is ideal under such conditions. As a precaution an airborne engine start should be attempted at an altitude high enough so that if a malfunction occurs there will be sufficient time to take corrective action. If the engine fails to start promptly, or fails to start at all, there may be little time to plan for a safe landing. If there is no landable area below, then failure to start the engine will result in an emergency off-field landing in unsuitable terrain. Glider damage and personal injury may result. To avoid these dangers, self-launch glider pilots should never allow themselves to get into a situation that can only be resolved by starting the engine and flying up and away. It is best to always keep a landable field within easy gliding range. There are many reasons that a self-launch glider engine may fail to start or fail to provide full power in response to efforts to resume full-power operations while airborne. These include lack of fuel or ignition, low engine temperature due to **cold soak**, low battery output due to low temperatures or battery exhaustion, fuel vapor lock, lack of propeller response to blade pitch controls, and other factors. It is important for the pilot to have an emergency plan in the event that full engine power is not available during any phase of flight.

SELF-LAUNCH GLIDER PROPELLER MALFUNCTIONS

Propeller failures include propeller damage and disintegration, propeller drive belt or drive gear failure, or failure of the variable blade pitch control system. To perform an air-driven engine restart, for example, many self-launch gliders require that the propeller blades be placed in a particular blade pitch position. If the propeller blades can not be properly adjusted, then the propeller will not deliver enough torque to turn the engine over. The result is a failure to obtain an air-driven engine start.

SELF-LAUNCH GLIDER ELECTRICAL SYSTEM MALFUNCTIONS

An electrical system failure in a self-launch glider may make it impossible to control the propeller pitch if the propeller is electrically controlled. It may also result in the inability to deploy a pod engine successfully for an air re-start attempt. Self-launch gliders that require a functioning electric starter for an air re-start will be unable to resume flight under power. If an airport is within gliding range, an on-airport precautionary landing can be made. If there is no airport within gliding range and the flight can be safely continued without electrical power, the pilot may be able to soar to the vicinity of an airport and land safely. If no airport is within gliding range and flight cannot be sustained without power, an emergency off-airport landing has to be made.

Some self-launch gliders are occasionally used for night flight, cruising under power and operating the necessary aeronautical lighting. If an electrical system failure occurs during night operations, pilots of nearby aircraft are not able to see the self-launch glider due to the extinguished position lights. Inside the cockpit, it is difficult or impossible to see the flight instruments or electrical circuit breakers. Carry a flashlight for such an emergency. Check the circuit breakers and reset any breaker that has overloaded unless the smell of smoke is present or any other indication of an overheating circuit.

[Figure 8-8] Head directly for the nearest airport and prepare for a precautionary landing there. The aviation transceiver installed in the instrument panel may not function if electrical failure is total, so it is a good idea to have a portable battery-operated aviation two-way radio aboard for use in such an emergency.

IN-FLIGHT FIRE

In-flight fires are the most serious emergencies a pilot can encounter. If a fire has ignited, or if there is a smell of smoke or any similar smell, do everything possible to reduce the possibilities that the fire spreads and land as soon as possible. The self-launch glider GFM/POH is the authoritative source for emergency response to suspected in-flight fire. The necessary procedures are.

• reduce throttle to idle;

• shut off fuel valves;

• shut off engine ignition;

• land immediately and stop as quickly as possible; and

• evacuate the self-launch glider immediately.

After landing, get far away from the glider. Keep onlookers away from the glider as well. The principal danger after evacuating the glider is that the fuel will ignite and explode, with the potential to injure personnel at considerable distance from the glider.

EMERGENCY EQUIPMENT AND SURVIVAL GEAR

Emergency equipment and survival gear is essential for safety of flight for all soaring flights.

SURVIVAL GEAR ITEM CHECKLISTS

Checklists help to assemble the necessary equipment in an orderly manner. The essentials for survival include reliable and usable supplies of water, food, and air or oxygen. Maintenance of an acceptable body temperature, which is difficult to manage in extreme cold or extreme heat, is also important. Blankets and appropriate seasonal clothing help to ensure safe body temperatures.

Figure 8-8. Self-launch glider circuit breakers.

FOOD AND WATER

An adequate supply of water and food (high-energy foods such as energy bars, granolas, and dried fruits are usually best) are of utmost importance during cross-country flight. Water from ballast tanks can be used in an emergency if free of contaminants such as antifreeze. Water and food should be available and reachable during the entire flight. Pilot relief for urination should also be easy to access and use.

CLOTHING

Pilots also need seasonal clothing that is appropriate to the local environment, including hat or cap, shirts, sweaters, pants, socks, walking shoes, space blanket, gloves or mittens. Layered clothing provides flexibility to meet the demands of the environment. Desert areas may be very hot in the day and very cold at night. Prolonged exposure to either condition can be debilitating. Layered clothing traps air between layers, increasing heat retention. The parachute canopy can be used as an effective layered garment when wrapped around the body to conserve body heat or to provide relief from excessive sunlight. Eye protection such as sunglasses are more than welcome if conditions during the day are bright, as they often are on good soaring days.

COMMUNICATION

Communication can be electronic, visual, or audible. Radios, telephones, and cell phones are electronic methods. Signal mirrors, flashlight or light beacons at night, signal fire flames at night, signal smoke during daylight hours, signal flares, and prominent parachute canopy displays are visual methods. Shouting and other noisemaking activities are audible methods but usually have very limited range.

Coin, cash, or credit cards are often necessary to operate pay phones. Charged batteries are required to operate cell phones, two-way radios, and emergency locator transmitters. Batteries are also necessary to operate flashlights or position lights on the glider for signal purposes. A list of useful telephone numbers aids rapid communication. The aviation transceiver can be tuned to broadcast and receive on the emergency frequency 121.5 MHz or any other useable frequency that will elicit a response. The ELT can be used to provide a continuous signal on 121.5 MHz. The parachute canopy and case can be employed to lay out a prominent marker to aid recognition from the air by other aircraft. Matches and a combustible material can provide flame for recognition by night and provide smoke that may be seen during daylight hours.

NAVIGATION EQUIPMENT

Aviation charts help to navigate during flight and help pinpoint the location when an off-airport landing is made. Sectional charts have the most useful scale for cross-country soaring flights. Local road maps (with labeled roads) should be carried in the glider during all cross-country flights. Local road maps make it much easier to give directions to the ground crew, allowing them to arrive as promptly as possible. GPS coordinates also help the ground crew if they are equipped with a GPS receiver and appropriate charts and maps. Detailed GPS maps are commercially available and make GPS navigation by land easier for the ground crew.

MEDICAL EQUIPMENT

Compact, commercially made medical or first aid kits are widely available. These kits routinely include bandages, medical tape, painkillers and other medicines, disinfectants, a tourniquet, matches, a knife or scissors, bug and snake repellent, and other useful items. Ensure that the kit contains medical items suitable to the environment in which you are operating. Stow the kit so it is secure from in-flight turbulence but is accessible after an emergency landing, even if injured.

STOWAGE

Stowing equipment properly means securing all equipment to protect occupants and ensure integrity of all flight controls and glider system controls. Items carried aboard must be secure even in the event that severe in-flight turbulence is encountered. Items must also remain secured in the event of a hard or off-field landing. No item carried in the glider should have any chance of coming loose in flight to interfere with the flight controls. Stowed objects should be adequately secured to prevent movement during a hard landing.

OXYGEN SYSTEM

The oxygen system is a life support system during flights at high altitude. Ensure that all components of the system are in working condition and that the bottle has a sufficient charge of aviators' breathing oxygen. The oxygen bailout bottle should be in good condition and in an easy-to-reach position should the need to abandon the glider at very high altitude arise. The bailout bottle is most commonly stowed aboard the glider when embarking on high-altitude flights in mountain wave conditions.

PARACHUTE

The parachute should be clean, dry, and be stored in a cool place when not in use. The parachute must have been inspected and repacked within the allowable time frame. For synthetic canopy parachutes this interval is 120 days.

CHAPTER 9
Soaring Weather

Glider pilots face a multitude of decisions, starting with the decision to take to the air. Pilots must determine if weather conditions are safe, and whether the conditions will support soaring flight. Gliders, being powered by gravity, are always sinking through the air. Therefore, glider pilots must seek air that rises faster than the sink rate of the glider to enable prolonged flight. Glider pilots refer to rising air as lift, not to be confused with the lift created by the wing.

THE ATMOSPHERE

The atmosphere is a mixture of gases surrounding the Earth. Without it, there would be no weather (wind, clouds, precipitation) or protection from the sun's rays. Though this protective envelope is essential to life, it is extraordinarily thin. When compared to the radius of the Earth, 3,438 nautical miles, the vertical limit of the atmosphere represents a very small distance. Although there is no specific upper limit to the atmosphere—it simply thins to a point where it fades away into space—the layers up to approximately 164,000 feet (about 27 nautical miles) contain 99.9 percent of atmospheric mass. At that altitude, the atmospheric density is approximately one-thousandth the density of that at sea level. [Figure 9-1]

COMPOSITION

The Earth's atmosphere is composed of a mixture of gases, with small amounts of water, ice, and other particles. Two gases, nitrogen (N_2) and oxygen (O_2), comprise approximately 99 percent of the gaseous content of the atmosphere; the other one percent is composed of various trace gases. Nitrogen and oxygen are both considered permanent gases, meaning their proportions remain the same to approximately 260,000 feet. Water vapor (H_2O), on the other hand, is considered a variable gas. Therefore, the amount of water in the atmosphere depends on the location and the source of the air. For example, the water vapor content over tropical areas and oceans accounts for as much as four percent of the gases displacing nitrogen and oxygen. Conversely, the atmosphere over deserts and at high altitudes exhibits less than one percent of the water vapor content. [Figure 9-2]

Although water vapor exists in the atmosphere in small amounts as compared to nitrogen and oxygen, it has a significant impact on the production of weather. This is because it exists in two other physical states: liquid (water) and solid (ice). These two states of water contribute to the formation of clouds, precipitation, fog, and icing, all of which are important to aviation weather. In addition, by absorbing the radiant energy from the Earth's surface, water vapor reduces surface cooling, causing surface temperatures to be warmer.

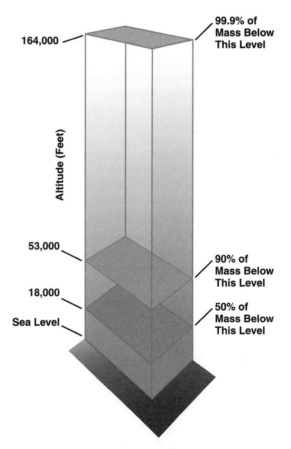

Figure 9-1. Atmospheric mass by altitude.

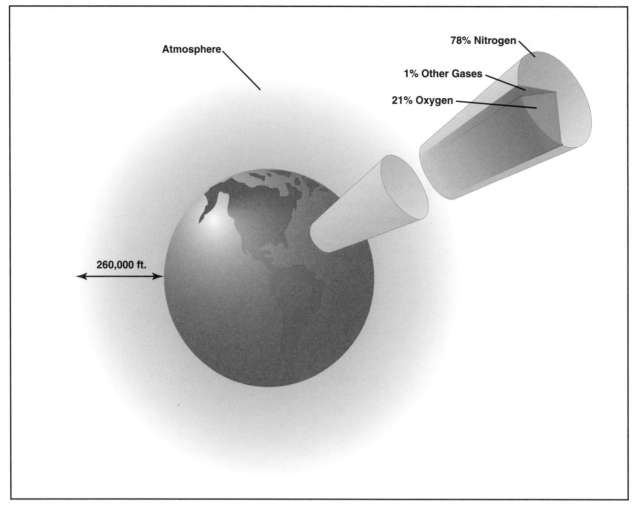

Figure 9-2. The composition of the atmosphere.

PROPERTIES

The state of the atmosphere is defined by fundamental variables, namely temperature, density, and pressure. These variables change over time and, combined with vertical and horizontal differences, lead to daily weather conditions.

TEMPERATURE

The temperature of a gas is the measure of the average kinetic energy of the molecules of that gas. Fast moving molecules are indicative of high kinetic energy and warmer temperatures. Conversely, slow moving molecules reflect lower kinetic energy and lower temperatures. Air temperature is commonly thought of in terms of whether it feels hot or cold. For quantitative measurements, the Celsius scale is used in aviation, although the Fahrenheit scale is still used in some applications.

DENSITY

The density of any given gas is the total mass of molecules in a specified volume, expressed in units of mass per volume. Low air density means a fewer number of

air molecules in a specified volume while high air density means a greater number of air molecules in the same volume. Air density affects aircraft performance, as noted in Chapter 5–Glider Performance.

PRESSURE

Molecules in a given volume of air not only posses a certain **kinetic energy** and density, but they also exert force. The force per unit area defines pressure. At the Earth's surface, the pressure exerted by the atmosphere is due to its weight. Therefore, pressure is measured in terms of weight per area. For example, atmospheric pressure is measured in pounds per square inch (lb./in.^{2}). From the outer atmosphere to sea level, a typical value of atmospheric pressure is 14.7 lb./in.^{2} This force measured at sea level is commonly reported as 29.92 inches of mercury (in. Hg.) (from the level of mercury at standard sea-level pressure in a mercurial barometer). In aviation weather reports, the common reporting unit is millibars. When 29.92 in. Hg. is converted, it becomes 1013.2 millibars. The force created by the moving molecules act equally in all directions when measured at a given point.

Dry air behaves almost like an "ideal" gas, meaning it obeys the gas law given by P/DT = R, where P is pressure, D is density, T is temperature, and R is a constant. This law states that the ratio of pressure to the product of density and temperature must always be the same. For instance, at a given pressure if the temperature is much higher than standard, then the density must be much lower. Air pressure and temperature are usually measured, and using the gas law, density of the air can be calculated and used to determine aircraft performance under those conditions.

STANDARD ATMOSPHERE

Using a representative vertical distribution of these variables, the standard atmosphere has been defined and is used for pressure altimeter calibrations. Since changes in the static pressure can affect pitot-static instrument operation, it is necessary to understand basic principles of the atmosphere. To provide a common reference for temperature and pressure, a definition for the standard atmosphere, also called International Standard Atmosphere (ISA), has been established. In addition to affecting certain flight instruments, these standard conditions are the basis for most aircraft performance data. At sea level, the standard atmosphere consists of a barometric pressure of 29.92 in. Hg., (1013.2 millibars) and a temperature of 15°C (59°F). This means that under the standard conditions, a column of air at sea level weighs 14.7 lb./in.^{2}.

Since temperature normally decreases with altitude, a standard **lapse rate** can be used to calculate temperature at various altitudes. Below 36,000 feet, the standard temperature lapse rate is 2°C (3.5°F) per 1,000 feet of altitude change. Pressure does not decrease linearly with altitude, but for the first 10,000 feet, 1 in.Hg. for each 1,000 feet approximates the rate of pressure change. It is important to note that the standard lapse rates should only be used for flight planning purposes with the understanding that large variations from standard conditions can exist in the atmosphere. [Figure 9-3]

LAYERS OF THE ATMOSPHERE

The Earth's atmosphere is divided into four strata or layers: troposphere, stratosphere, mesosphere, and thermosphere. These layers are defined by the temperature change with increasing altitude. The lowest layer, called the troposphere, exhibits an average decrease in temperature from the Earth's surface to about 36,000 feet above mean sea level (MSL). The troposphere is deeper in the tropics and shallower in Polar Regions. It also varies seasonally, being higher in the summer and lower in the winter months.

Almost all of the Earth's weather occurs in the troposphere as most of the water vapor and clouds are found

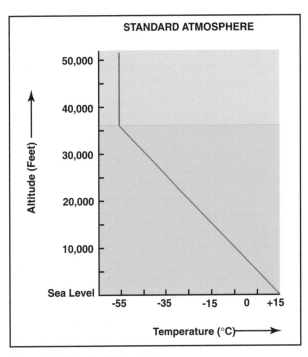

Figure 9-3. Standard Atmosphere.

in this layer. The lower part of the troposphere interacts with the land and sea surface, providing thermals, mountain waves, and sea-breeze fronts. Although temperatures decrease as altitude increases in the troposphere, local areas of temperature increase (inversions) are common.

The top of the troposphere is called the tropopause. The pressure at this level is only about ten percent of MSL (0.1 atmospheres) and density is decreased to about 25 percent of its sea-level value. Temperature reaches its minimum value at the tropopause, approximately -55° Celsius (–67°F). For pilots this is an important part of the atmosphere because it is associated with a variety of weather phenomena such as thunderstorm tops, clear air turbulence, and jet streams. The vertical limit altitude of the tropopause varies with season and with latitude. The tropopause is lower in the winter and at the poles; it is higher in the summer and at the equator.

The tropopause separates the troposphere from the stratosphere. In the stratosphere, the temperature tends to first change very slowly with increasing height. However, as altitude increases the temperature increases to approximately 0° Celsius (32°F) reaching its maximum value at about 160,000 feet MSL. Unlike the troposphere where the air moves freely both vertically and horizontally, the air within the stratosphere moves mostly horizontally.

Gliders have reached into the lower stratosphere using mountain waves. At these altitudes, pressurization becomes an issue, as well as the more obvious breathing oxygen requirements. Layers above the stratosphere, the mesosphere and thermosphere, have some interesting features that are normally not of importance to glider pilots. However, interested pilots might refer to any general text on weather or meteorology.

SCALE OF WEATHER EVENTS

When preparing forecasts, meteorologists consider atmospheric circulation on many scales. To aid the forecasting of short- and long-term weather, various weather events have been organized into three broad categories called the scales of circulations. The size and life span of the phenomena in each scale is roughly proportional, so that larger size scales coincide with longer lifetimes. The term microscale refers to features with spatial dimensions of 1/10th to 1 nautical mile and lasting for seconds to minutes. An example is an individual **thermal**. Mesoscale refers to horizontal dimensions of 1 to 1,000 nautical miles and lasting for many minutes to weeks. Examples include mountain waves, sea-breeze fronts, thunderstorms, and fronts. Research scientists break down the mesoscale into further subdivisions to better classify various phenomena. Macroscale refers to horizontal dimensions greater than 1,000 nautical miles and lasting for weeks to months. These include the long waves in the general global circulation and the jetstreams imbedded within those waves. [Figure 9-4]

Smaller-scale features are imbedded in larger scale features. For instance, a microscale thermal may be just one of many in a mesoscale **convergence** line, like a sea-breeze front. The sea-breeze front may occur only under certain synoptic conditions, which is controlled by the macroscale circulations. The scales interact, with feedback from smaller to larger

scales and vice versa, in ways that are not yet fully understood by atmospheric scientists. Generally, the behavior and evolution of macroscale features is more predictable, with forecast skill decreasing as scale diminishes. For instance, forecasts up to a few days for major events, such as a trough with an associated cold front have become increasingly accurate. However, nobody would attempt to forecast the exact time and location of an individual thermal an hour ahead of time. Since most of the features of interest to soaring pilots lies in the smaller mesoscale and microscale range, prediction of soaring weather is a challenge.

Soaring forecasts should begin with the macroscale, that is, identifying large-scale patterns that produce good soaring conditions. This varies from site to site, and depends, for instance, on whether the goal is thermal, ridge, or wave soaring. Then, mesoscale features should be considered. This may include items, such as the cloudiness and temperature structure of the airmass behind a cold front, as well as the amount of rain produced by the front. Understanding lift types, and environments in which they form, is the first step to understanding how to forecast soaring weather.

THERMAL SOARING WEATHER

A thermal is a rising mass of buoyant air. Thermals are the most common updraft used to sustain soaring flight. In the next sections, several topics related to thermal soaring weather are explored, including thermal structure, **atmospheric stability**, the use of **atmospheric soundings**, and **air masses** conducive to thermal soaring.

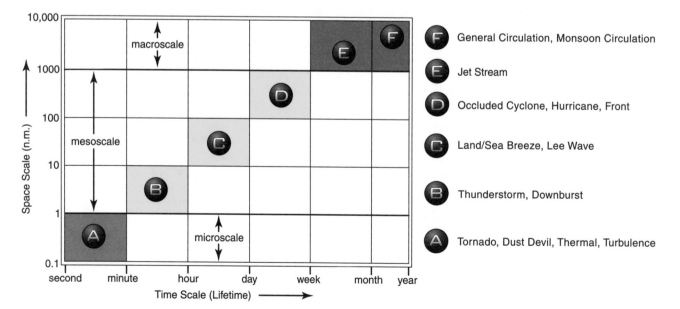

Figure 9-4. Scale of circulation—horizontal dimensions and life spans of associated weather events.

Convection refers to an energy transfer involving mass motions. Thermals are convective currents and are one means by which the atmosphere transfers heat energy vertically. **Advection** is the term meteorologists use to describe horizontal transfer, for instance, cold-air advection after the passage of a cold front. As a note of caution, meteorologists sometimes are careless with the use of the word "convection" and use it to mean "deep convection," that is, thunderstorms.

Unfortunately, there is often a fine meteorological line between a warm, sunny day with plenty of thermals, and a warm, sunny day that is stable and produces no thermals. To the earthbound general public, it matters little–either is a nice day. Glider pilots, however, need a better understanding of these conditions and must often rely on their own forecasting skills.

THERMAL SHAPE AND STRUCTURE

Two primary conceptual models exist for the structure of thermals, the bubble model and the column or plume model. Which model best represents thermals encountered by glider pilots is a topic of ongoing debate among atmospheric scientists. In reality, thermals fitting both conceptual models likely exist. A blend of the models, such as individual strong bubbles rising within one plume, may be what occurs in many situations. It must be kept in mind, these models attempt to simplify a complex and often turbulent phenomenon, so that many exceptions and variations are to be expected while actually flying in thermals. Many books, articles, and Internet resources are available for further reading on this subject.

The bubble model describes an individual thermal resembling a vortex ring, with rising air in the middle and descending air on the sides. The air in the middle of the vortex ring rises faster than the entire thermal bubble. The model fits occasional reports from glider pilots. At times, one glider may find no lift, when only 200 feet below another glider that climbs away. At other times, one glider may be at the top of the bubble climbing only slowly, while a lower glider climbs rapidly in the stronger part of the bubble below. [Figure 9-5]

More often, a glider flying below another glider circling in a thermal is able to contact the same thermal and climb, even if the gliders are displaced vertically by a 1,000 feet or more. This suggests the column or plume model of thermals is more common. [Figure 9-6]

Which of the two models best describes thermals depends on the source or reservoir of warm air near the surface. If the heated area is rather small, one single bubble may rise and take with it all the warmed surface air. On the other hand, if a large area is heated and one spot acts as the initial trigger, surrounding warm air

Figure 9-5. The bubble or vortex ring model of a thermal.

flows into the relative void left by the initial thermal. The in-rushing warm air follows the same path, creating a thermal column or plume. Since all the warmed air near the surface is not likely to have the exact same temperature, it is easy to envision a column with a few or several imbedded bubbles. Individual bubbles within a thermal plume may merge, while at other times, two adjacent and distinct bubbles seem to exist side by side. No two thermals are exactly alike since the thermal sources are not the same.

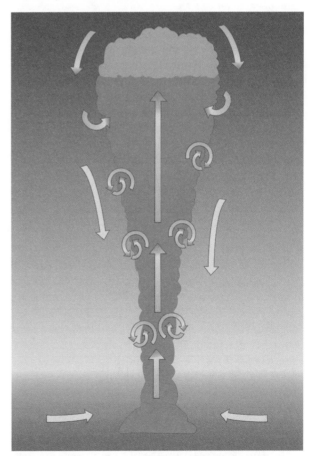

Figure 9-6. The column or plume model of a thermal.

Whether the thermal is considered a bubble or column, the air in the middle of the thermal rises faster than the air near the sides of the thermal. A horizontal slice through an idealized thermal provides a bulls-eye pattern. Real thermals usually are not perfectly concentric; techniques for best using thermals are discussed in the next chapter. [Figure 9-7]

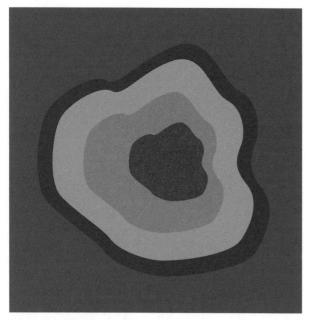

Figure 9-7. Cross-section through a thermal. Darker green is stronger lift, red is sink.

The diameter of a typical thermal cross section is on the order of 500–1,000 feet, though the size varies considerably. Typically, due to mixing with the surrounding air, thermals expand as they rise. Thus, the thermal column may actually resemble a cone, with the narrowest part near the ground. Thermal plumes also tilt in a steady wind and can become quite distorted in the presence of vertical shear. If vertical shear is strong enough, thermals can become very turbulent or become completely broken apart. A schematic of a thermal lifecycle in wind shear is shown in Figure 9-8.

ATMOSPHERIC STABILITY

Stability in the atmosphere tends to hinder vertical motion, while instability tends to promote vertical motion. A certain amount of instability is desirable for glider pilots, since without it, thermals would not develop. If the air is moist enough, and the atmospheric instability deep enough, thunderstorms and associated hazards can form. Thus, an understanding of atmospheric stability and its determination from available weather data is important for soaring flight and safety. As a note, the following discussion is concerned with vertical stability of the atmosphere. Other horizontal atmospheric instabilities, for instance, in the evolution of large-scale cyclones, are not covered here.

Generally, a stable dynamic system is one in which a displaced element will return to its original position. An unstable dynamic system is one in which a displaced element will accelerate further from its original position. In a neutrally stable system, the displaced element neither returns to nor accelerates from its original position. In the atmosphere, it is easiest to use a parcel of air as the displaced element. The behavior of a stable or unstable system is analogous to aircraft stability discussed in Chapter 3–Aerodynamics of Flight.

For simplicity, assume first that the air is completely dry. Effects of moisture in atmospheric stability are considered later. A parcel of dry air that is forced to rise expands due to decreasing pressure and cools in the process. By contrast, a parcel of dry air that is forced to descend is compressed due to increasing pressure and warms. If there is no transfer of heat between the surrounding, ambient air, and the displaced parcel, the process is called adiabatic. Assuming adiabatic motion, a rising parcel cools at a lapse rate of 3°C (5.4°F) per 1,000 feet, known as the **dry adiabatic lapse rate (DALR)**. As discussed below, on a thermodynamic chart, parcels cooling at the DALR are said to follow a **dry adiabat**. A parcel warms at the DALR as it descends. In reality, heat transfer often occurs. For instance, as a thermal rises, the circulation in the thermal itself (recall the bubble model) mixes in surrounding air. Nonetheless, the DALR is a good approximation.

The DALR represents the lapse rate of the atmosphere when it is neutrally stable. If the ambient lapse rate in some layer of air is less than the DALR (for instance, 1°C per 1,000 feet), then that layer is stable. If the lapse rate is greater than the DALR, it is unstable. An unstable lapse rate usually only occurs within a few hundred feet of the heated ground. When an unstable layer develops aloft, the air quickly mixes and reduces the lapse rate back to DALR. It is important to note that the DALR is not the same as the standard atmospheric lapse rate of 2°C per 1,000 feet. The standard atmosphere is a stable one.

Another way to understand stability is to imagine two scenarios, each with a different temperature at 3,000 feet above ground level (AGL), but the same temperature at the surface, nominally 20°C. In both scenarios, a parcel of air that started at 20°C at the surface has cooled to 11°C by the time it has risen to 3,000 feet at the DALR. In the first scenario, the parcel is still warmer than the surrounding air, so it is unstable and the parcel keeps rising—a good thermal day. In the second scenario, the parcel is cooler than the surrounding air, so it is stable and will sink. The parcel in the second scenario would need to be forced to 3,000 feet AGL by a mechanism other than convection, being

Figure 9-8. Life cycle of a typical thermal with cumulus cloud.

lifted up a mountainside or a front for instance. [Figure 9-9]

Figure 9-9 also illustrates factors leading to instability. A stable atmosphere can turn unstable in one of two ways. First, if the surface parcel warmed by more than 2°C (greater than 22°C), the layer to 3,000 feet would then become unstable in the second scenario. Thus, if the temperature of the air aloft remains the same, warming the lower layers causes instability and better thermal soaring. Second, if the air at 3,000 feet is cooler, as in the first scenario, the layer becomes unstable. Thus, if the temperature on the ground remains the same, cooling aloft causes instability and better thermal soaring. If the temperature aloft and at the surface warm or cool by the same amount, then the stability of the layer remains unchanged. Finally, if the air aloft remains the same, but the surface air-cools (for instance due to a very shallow front) then the layer becomes even more stable.

An **inversion** is a layer in which the temperature warms as altitude increases. Inversions can occur at any altitude and vary in strength. In strong inversions, the temperature can rise as much as 10°C over just a few hundred feet of altitude gain. The most notable effect of an inversion is to cap any unstable layer below. Along with trapping haze or pollution below, they also effectively provide a cap to any thermal activity.

So far, only completely dry air parcels have been considered. However, moisture in the form of water vapor is always present in the atmosphere. As a moist parcel of air rises, it cools at the DALR until it reaches its **dew point**, at which time the air in the parcel begins to condense. During the process of condensation, heat (referred to as latent heat) is released to the surrounding air. Once saturated, the parcel continues to cool, but since heat is now added, it cools at a rate slower than the DALR. The rate at which saturated air-cools with height is known as the **saturated adiabatic lapse rate (SALR)**. Unlike the DALR, the SALR varies substantially with altitude. At lower altitudes, it is on the order

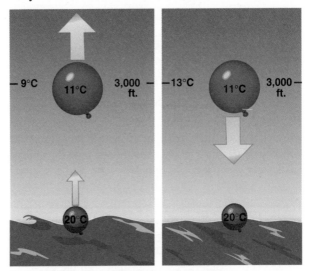

Figure 9-9. Stable and unstable parcels of air.

of 1.2°C per 1,000 feet, whereas in mid levels it increases to 2.2°C per 1,000 feet. Very high up, above about 30,000 feet, little water vapor exists to condense, and the SALR approaches the DALR.

UNDERSTANDING SOUNDINGS

The so-called Skew-T/Log-P (or simply Skew-T for short) is an example of the **thermodynamic diagram** most commonly used in the United States. The Skew-T part of the name comes from the fact that temperature lines on the chart are slanted, while the Log-P is a reminder that pressure does not decrease linearly in the atmosphere. A temperature and dewpoint sounding presented on a Skew-T shows a record of the current atmospheric stability, moisture content, and winds versus altitude. Given surface forecast temperatures, the potential for thermal soaring, including the likelihood of cumulus and/or over-development can then be forecast. Using Skew-T diagrams to their fullest potential requires practice. [Figure 9-10]

There are five sets of lines on a standard Skew-T. Other types of thermodynamic charts, for instance the Tephigram often used in Great Britain, have the same lines, but with a somewhat different presentation. The colors and actual number of lines vary, but the main diagram components should always be present. The following discussion refers to the Skew-T in Figure 9-10.

Horizontal blue lines indicate pressure levels and are labeled every 100 millibars (mb) along the left side of the diagram. On this diagram, the approximate height (in feet) of each pressure level in the standard atmosphere is shown on the right. The actual height of each pressure level varies from day to day. Slanted (skewed) blue lines indicate temperature and are labeled every 10°C along the right side of the isotherm. Thin red lines slanted at an angle almost perpendicular to the temperature lines indicate dry adiabats. (An air parcel following a dry adiabat is changing temperature with height at the DALR.) Thin green lines curving in the same direction as, but at a different angle to, the dry adiabats represent saturated adiabats. (An air parcel that is saturated follows a saturated adiabat is changing temperature with height at the SALR.) The thin orange lines slanting in the same

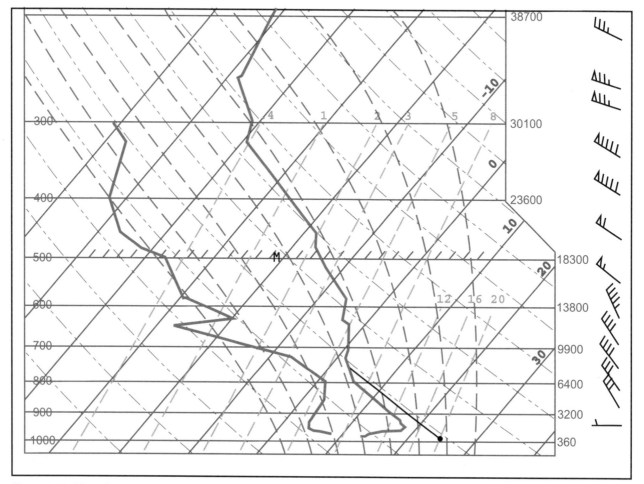

Figure 9-10. Skew-T from an actual sounding.

direction, but at an angle to the temperature lines represent the ratio of water vapor to dry air, called the **mixing ratio**. Lines of constant mixing ratio are labeled in grams of water vapor per kilogram of dry air, abbreviated g/kg.

Over the continental United States, several dozen sounding balloons are launched twice daily, at 00 and 12 Universal Coordinated Time (UTC). These sounding balloons record temperature, humidity, and winds at several mandatory levels, as well as "significant" levels, where notable changes with height occur. In Figure 9-10, the actual temperature sounding (shown in bold red), the actual dew-point temperature (shown in bold green), and the winds aloft (shown in wind barbs on the right side) for this day are shown.

The basic analysis for forecasting the potential for dry thermals based on a sounding is achieved by answering the question, "At what levels is a parcel of air rising from the surface warmer than the ambient air?" Assume on this day, the surface temperature is forecast to reach 23°C. This point is marked on the Skew-T; the parcel of air at 23°C is warmer than the surrounding air and starts to rise at the DALR. When the parcel has risen along a dry adiabat (parallel to the slanted red line) to 900 mb (3,200 feet), it has cooled to 17.2°C, which is warmer than the surrounding air at 15°C. Continuing upward along the dry adiabat, at about 780 mb (7,100 feet) the air parcel and surrounding air are at the same temperature, and the air no longer rises due to its buoyancy. The **Thermal Index (TI)** at each level is defined as the temperature of the air parcel having risen at the DALR subtracted from the ambient temperature. Experience has shown that a TI should be -2 for thermals to form and be sufficiently strong for soaring flight. Larger negative numbers favor stronger conditions, while values of 0 to –2 may produce few or no thermals. On this day, with a surface temperature of 23°C, the TI is found to be 15–17.2 or -2.2 at 900 mb, sufficient for at least weak thermals to this level. At 780 mb, the TI is 0, and as mentioned, the expectation is that this would be the approximate top of thermals.

Thermal strength is difficult to quantify based on the TI alone since many factors contribute to thermal strength. For instance, in the above example, the TI at 800 mb (6,400 feet) was –1. The thermal may or may not weaken at this level depending on the thermal size and the amount of vertical wind shear. These factors tend to mix in ambient air and can decrease the thermal strength.

It is important to remember that the TI calculated as above is based on a forecast temperature at the surface. If the forecast temperature is incorrect, the analysis above produces poor results. As a further example, assume that on this day the temperature only reached 20°C. From a point on the surface at 20°C and following a dry adiabat upwards, the TI reaches 0 only 1,000 feet AGL, making the prospects for workable thermals poor. On the other hand, if temperatures reached 25°C on this day, thermals would reach about 730 mb (8,800 feet), be stronger, and have more negative TI values.

The previous analysis of the morning sounding calculated the TI and maximum thermal height based upon a maximum afternoon temperature. In reality, the sounding evolves during the day. It is not untypical for a morning sounding to have an inversion as shown in Figure 9-10. A weaker inversion on another day is shown in Figure 9-11. This sounding was taken at 12 UTC, which is 05 local time (LT) at that location. The surface temperature was 13°C at the time of the sounding. A shallow inversion is seen near the surface with a nearly isothermal (no temperature change) layer above. Two hours after the sounding was taken (07 LT), the surface temperature had risen to only 14°C. By 09 LT, the temperature had risen to 17°C. The line labeled "09" shows how the sounding should look at this time. It was drawn by taking the surface temperature at that time, and following the DALR until TI is 0, which is the same as intercepting the ambient temperature. Lines at other times are drawn in a similar fashion. At 10 LT, the TI becomes 0 at about 2,200 feet AGL, so the first thermals may be starting. By 12 LT, at 25°C, thermals should extend to 4,000 feet AGL. Because of the isothermal layer, thermal heights increased steadily until about 16 LT, when temperatures reached 31°C, at which time they reached about 8,000 feet AGL. Understanding this evolution of the convective layer can help predict when thermals will first form, as well as if and when they might reach a height satisfactory for an extended or cross-country flight. [Figure 9-11, on next page]

The analysis presented thus far has neglected the possibility of cumulus clouds, for which the orange slanted mixing ratio lines on the Skew-T need to be considered. The assumption that a rising parcel conserves its mixing ratio is also needed. For instance, if an air parcel has a mixing ratio of 8 g/kg at the surface, it will maintain that value as it rises in a thermal. Typically, this is true, though factors, such as mixing with much drier air aloft can cause errors.

Refer to the sounding in Figure 9-12. The temperature on this day reached 26°C during the afternoon. In order to determine if cumulus clouds would be present, draw a line from 26°C at the surface parallel to a red dry adiabat as before. Draw a second line from the surface

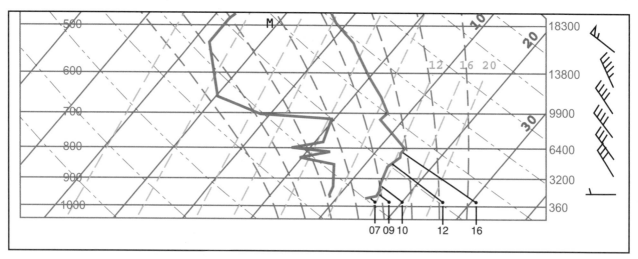

Figure 9-11. Skew-T from an actual sounding.

dew point temperature parallel to the orange mixing ratio lines. The two lines intersect at a point before the parcel has a zero TI. This is the base of the cumulus, called the **convective condensation level (CCL)**. In this case, cloudbase occurs at about 750 mb (8,100 feet). Since the parcel is saturated above this level, it no longer cools at the DALR, but at the SALR. Next, from the CCL, draw a line parallel to a saturated adiabat until it intersects the original sounding temperature curve. This shows the maximum cumulus height, at about 670 mb (11,000 feet). [Figure 9-12]

The above analysis leads to a rule of thumb for estimating the CCL. The temperature and dew point converge at about 4.4°F per 1,000 feet of altitude gain. This is the same as saying for every degree of surface temperature and dew point spread in Fahrenheit, multiply by 225 feet to obtain the base of the convective cloud (if any). Since aviation surface reports are reported in degrees Centigrade, convert the data by multiplying every degree of surface temperature and dew point spread in degrees Centigrade by 400 feet. For example, if the reported temperature

is 28°C and the reported dew point is 15°C, we would estimate cloud base as (28 – 15) x 400 = 5200 feet AGL.

Notice that in Figure 9-12, the dew point curve shows a rapid decrease with height from the surface value. As thermals form and mixing begins, it is likely that the drier air just above the surface will be mixed in with the moister surface air. A more accurate estimate of the CCL is found by using an average dew point value in the first 50 mb rather than the actual surface value. This refinement can change the analyzed CCL by as much as 1,000 feet.

The second example, Figure 9-11, would only produce dry thermals, even at this day's maximum temperature of 32°C. Following a line parallel to a mixing ratio line from the surface dew point, the height of any cumulus would be almost 12,000 feet AGL, while at 32°C, thermals should only reach 9,000 feet AGL. The elevated inversion at 9,000 to 10,000 feet AGL effectively caps thermal activity there.

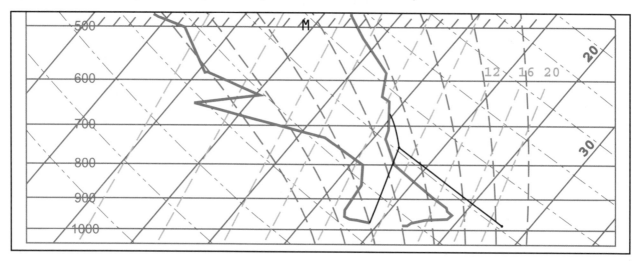

Figure 9-12. Skew-T from an actual sounding.

It is also important to recognize the limitations of a sounding analysis. The sounding is a single snapshot of the atmosphere, taken at one time in one location. (This is not absolutely true since the sounding balloon rises at about 1,000 feet per minute (fpm), so it takes about 30 minutes to reach 30,000 feet, during which time it has also drifted with the winds aloft from the launch point). The analysis is limited by how well the sounding is representative of the greater area. This may or may not be a factor depending on the larger-scale weather situation, and in any case, tends to be less valid in regions of mountainous terrain. In addition, the upper air patterns can change during the day due to passing fronts or smaller-scale, upper-air features. For example, local circulation patterns near mountains can alter the air aloft over nearby valleys during the day. A temperature change aloft of only a few degrees also can make a large difference. Despite these limitations, the sounding analysis is still an excellent tool for soaring pilots.

In recent years, with the advent of the Internet, soundings from numerical weather model forecasts have become available in graphical form, like the Skew-T. Thus, forecast soundings are available for a variety of locations (far more numerous than the observational sounding network) and at many intervals over the forecast cycle. The advantage of using model forecast soundings is a dramatic increase in both space and time resolution. For instance, maps of the predicted thermal tops can be made over a large (e.g., multi-state) area from model data spaced every 10 miles or closer. Great detail in the forecast distribution of thermals is available. In addition, model output can be produced far more frequently than every 12 hours. For instance, hourly model soundings can be produced for a location. This is a tremendous potential aide to planning both local and cross-country flights. The disadvantage is that these forecasts are not real data. They are a model forecast of what the real atmosphere *should* do. Model forecasts of critical items, such as temperatures at the surface and aloft, are often inaccurate. Thus, the model-forecast soundings are only as good as the model forecast. Fortunately, models show continual improvement, so this new tool should become more useful in the future.

AIR MASSES CONDUCIVE TO THERMAL SOARING

Generally, the best air masses for thermals are those with cool air aloft, with conditions dry enough to allow the sun's heating at the surface, but not too dry so cumulus form. Along the West Coast of the continental United States, these conditions are usually found after passage of a pacific cold front. Similar conditions are found in the eastern and mid-west United States, except the source air for the cold front is from polar continental regions, such as the interior of Canada. In both cases, high pressure building into the region is favorable, since it is usually associated with an inversion aloft, which keeps cumulus from growing into rain showers or thundershowers. However, as the high pressure builds after the second or third day, the inversion has often lowered to the point that thermal soaring is poor or no longer possible. This can lead to warm and sunny, but very stable conditions, as the soaring pilot awaits the next cold front to destabilize the atmosphere. Fronts that arrive too close together can also cause poor post-frontal soaring, as high clouds from the next front keep the surface from warming enough. Very shallow cold fronts from the northeast (with cold air only one or two thousand feet deep) often have a stabilizing effect along the Plains directly east of the Rocky Mountains. This is due to cool low-level air undercutting warmer air aloft advecting from the west.

In the desert southwest, the Great Basin, and intermountain west, good summertime thermal soaring conditions are often produced by intense heating from below, even in the absence of cooling aloft. This dry air mass with continental origins produces cumulus bases 10,000 feet AGL or higher. At times, this air will spread into eastern New Mexico and western Texas as well. Later in the summer, however, some of these regions come under the influence of the North American Monsoon, which can lead to widespread and daily late-morning or early afternoon thundershowers.

CLOUD STREETS

Cumulus clouds are often randomly distributed across the sky, especially over relatively flat terrain. Under the right conditions, however, cumulus can become aligned in long bands, called **cloud streets**. These are more or less regularly spaced bands of cumulus clouds. Individual streets can extend 50 miles or more while an entire field of cumulus streets can extend hundreds of miles. The spacing between streets is typically three times the height of the clouds. Cloud streets are aligned parallel to the wind direction, thus they are ideal for a downwind cross-country flight. Glider pilots can often fly many miles with little or no circling, sometimes achieving glide ratios far exceeding the still-air value.

Cloud streets usually occur over land with cold-air outbreaks, for instance, following a cold front. Brisk surface winds and a wind direction remaining nearly constant up to cloud base are favorable cloud street conditions. Wind speed should increase by 10 to 20 knots between the surface and cloud base, with a maximum somewhere in the middle of or near the top of the convective layer. Thermals should be capped by a notable inversion or stable layer.

A vertical slice through an idealized cloud street illustrates a distinct circulation, with updrafts under the

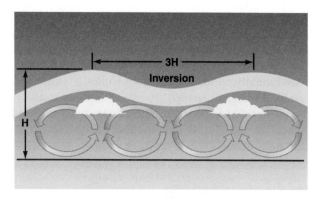

Figure 9-13. Circulation across a cloud street.

clouds and downdrafts in between. Due to the circulation, sink between streets may be stronger than typically found away from cumulus. [Figure 9-13]

Thermal streets, with a circulation like Figure 9-13, may exist without cumulus clouds. Without clouds as markers, use of such streets is more difficult. A glider pilot flying upwind or downwind in consistent sink

should alter course crosswind to avoid inadvertently flying along a line of sink between thermal streets.

THERMAL WAVES

Figure 9-14 shows a wave-like form for the inversion capping the cumulus clouds. If the winds above the inversion are perpendicular to the cloud streets and increasing at 10 kts per 5,000 feet or more, waves called cloud-street waves can form in the stable air above. Though usually relatively weak, thermal waves can produce lift of a 100 to 500 fpm and allow smooth flight along streets above the cloud base. [Figure 9-14]

So-called cumulus waves also exist. These are similar to cloud-street waves, except the cumulus clouds are not organized in streets. Cumulus waves require a capping inversion or stable layer and increasing wind above cumulus clouds. However, directional shear is not necessary. Cumulus waves may also be short-lived, and difficult to work for any length of time. An exception is when the cumulus is anchored to some feature, such as a ridge line or short mountain range. In these

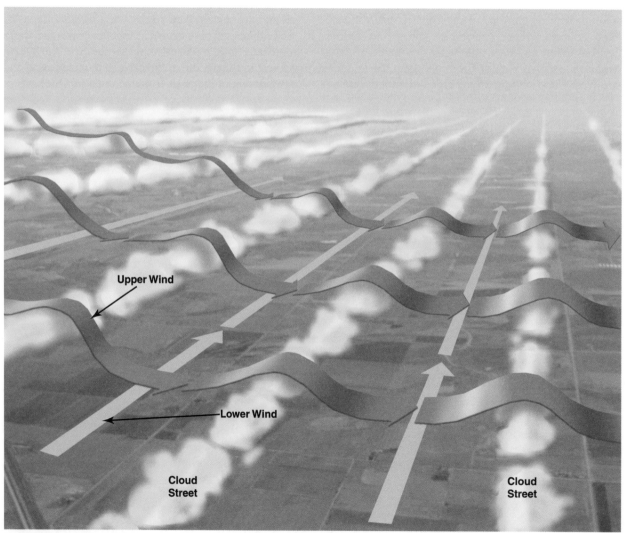

Figure 9-14. Cloud street wave.

cases, the possible influence of the ridge or mountain in creating the wave lift becomes uncertain. Further discussion of atmospheric waves appears later in this chapter. As a final note, thermal waves can also form without clouds present.

THUNDERSTORMS

An unstable atmosphere can provide great conditions for thermal soaring. If the atmosphere is too moist and unstable, however, **cumulonimbus (Cb)** or thunderclouds can form. Thunderstorms are local storms produced by Cb and are accompanied by lightning, thunder, rain, **graupel** or hail, strong winds, turbulence, and even tornadoes. Not all precipitating, large cumulo-form clouds are accompanied by lightning and thunder, although their presence is usually an indication that conditions are ripe for full-blown thunderstorms. Forecasters sometimes use the term "deep convection" to refer to convection that rises to high levels, which usually means thunderstorms. The tremendous amount of energy associated with Cb stems from the release of latent heat as condensation occurs with the growing cloud.

Thunderstorms can occur any time of year, though they are more common during the spring and summer seasons. They can occur anywhere in the continental United States but are not common along the immediate West Coast, where on average only about one per year occurs. During the summer months, the desert southwest, extending northeastward into the Rocky Mountains and adjacent Great Plains, experiences an average of 30 to 40 thunderstorms annually. Additionally, in the southeastern United States, especially Florida, between 30 and 50 thunderstorms occur in an average year. Thunderstorms in the cool seasons usually occur in conjunction with some forcing mechanism, such as a fast moving cold front or a strong upper-level trough. [Figure 9-15]

The lifecycle of an air-mass or ordinary thunderstorm consists of three main stages: cumulus, mature, and dissipating. We will use the term "ordinary" to describe this type of thunderstorm consisting of a single Cb, since other types of thunderstorms (described below) can occur in a uniform large-scale air mass. The entire lifecycle takes on the order of an hour, though remnant cloud from the dissipated Cb can last substantially longer.

The cumulus stage is characterized by a cumulus growing to a towering cumulus (Tcu), or **cumulus congestus**. During this stage, most of the air within the cloud is going up. The size of the updraft increases, while the cloud base broadens to a few miles in diameter. Since the cloud has increased in size, the strong updraft in the middle of the cloud is not susceptible to entrainment of dryer air from the outside. Often, other

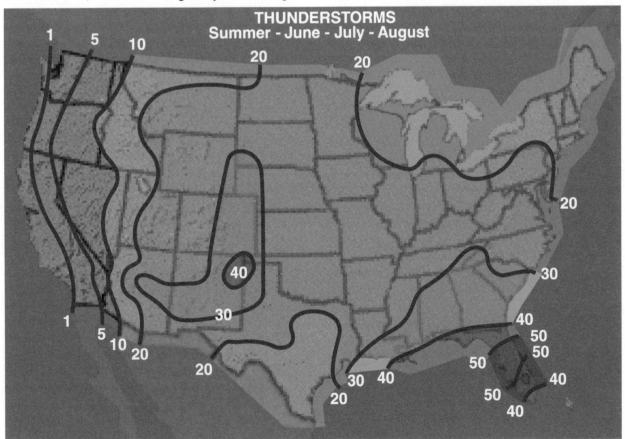

Figure 9-15. Thunderstorm frequency in the summertime.

smaller cumulus in the vicinity of the Tcu are suppressed by general downward motion around the cloud. Towards the end of the cumulus stage, downdrafts and precipitation begin to form within the cloud. On some days, small cumulus can be around for hours, before Tcu form, while on other days, the air is so unstable that almost as soon as any cumulus form, they become Tcu. [Figure 9-16]

As the evolution of the thunderstorm continues, it reaches its mature stage. By this time, downdrafts reach the ground and spread out in what are known as **downbursts** or **microbursts**. These often lead to strong and sometimes damaging surface winds. Lightning and thunder form along with precipitation (rain, graupel, or hail) below cloud base, which has now increased to several miles in diameter. It may become difficult to discern cloud from precipitation after this stage. The cloud top reaches to the tropopause, or nearly so, and sometimes strong cells even extend into the stratosphere. The cloud top forms a cirrus anvil indicating the mature stage. The direction in which the anvil streams provides an estimate of the direction of thunderstorm movement. Often organized circulations form within the Cb and the longevity of the thunderstorm partly depends on the nature of those circulations. The greatest storm intensity and hazards (discussed below) are attained during the mature stage.

The precipitation and downdrafts in an ordinary thunderstorm are eventually responsible for its demise, as the supply of heat and moisture is cut off, leading to the dissipating stage. As the Cb dissipates, the mid-level cloud becomes more stratiform (spread out). Remnant cloud can linger for some time after the storm begins to dissipate, especially the upper-level cirrus anvil, which consists mostly of ice. In hazy conditions, or with Cb imbedded in widespread cloudiness, judging the stage of the Cb lifecycle can be difficult.

Thunderstorms frequently last longer than an hour. As an ordinary thunderstorm reaches its mature stage, cool and sometimes quite strong surface outflows are created by Cb downdrafts reaching the ground and spreading out. The outflows can act as a focus for lifting warm, moist air that may still be ahead of the advancing storm. New cells form in the direction of storm movement, for instance, a Cb moving eastward will generate new storms on the east side. The new cell undergoes a mature and dissipating stage as it progresses towards the back of what has become a cluster of Cb. This is an example of a **multi-cell thunderstorm**, which, depending on the vertical shear of the wind, will continue to regenerate new cells as long as unstable air exists ahead of the moving storm. Multi-cell thunderstorms can last for several hours and travel 100 miles or more. As usual when dealing with weather phenomena, there is no clear distinction between an ordinary and multi-cell thunderstorm. For instance, a thunderstorm may last one to two hours after having undergone regeneration two or three times. Pilots need to closely watch apparently dissipating thunderstorms for new dark, firm bases that indicate a new cell forming. In addition, outflow from one Cb may flow several miles before encountering an area where the air is primed for lifting given an extra boost. The relatively cool air in the outflow can provide that boost, leading to new a Cb, which is nearby, but not connected to the original Cb. [Figure 9-17]

Another type of thunderstorm is the **supercell**. These huge and long-lasting storms are usually associated with severe weather: strong surface winds exceeding 50 knots, hail at least $3/4$ inch in diameter, and/or tornadoes. Supercells can occur anywhere in the United States, but are most common in the southern Great Plains. They differ from ordinary thunderstorms in two ways. First supercells are much larger in size. Second, they form in an unstable environment with

Figure 9-16. Lifecycle of an ordinary thunderstorm (A) cumulus stage, (B) mature stage, (C) dissipating stage.

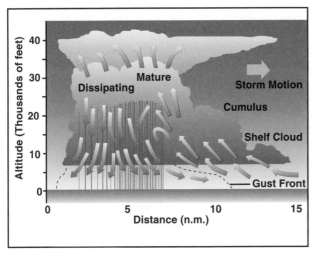

Figure 9-17. Multi-cell thunderstorm.

large vertical direction and speed shear, which causes the updraft to be tilted or even twisted so that is located away from the main downdraft. This leads to an organized circulation within the storm, hence the longevity of a supercell. These dangerous storms should be avoided. [Figure 9-18]

Thunderstorms sometimes exist in clusters, known to meteorologists as **Mesoscale Convective Systems (MCS)**. Most commonly, MCSs form east of the Rocky Mountains in the spring and summer months. **Squall lines** are MCSs that are organized in a line or arc, sometimes hundreds of miles long. A cold front or upper-level trough advancing on unstable air can be the forcing mechanism for squall-line development. Strong lift can be found ahead of advancing squall line and some extended cross-country flights have been made using them. Unfortunately, they come with all the dangers of severe thunderstorms, so their use is not recommended. Another type of MCS has a similar name, the Mesoscale Convective Complex (MCC), which form as a cluster of storms not along any distinct line or arc. When viewed from satellite, MCCs reveal a circular or elliptical shape to the cirrus anvil, which can be a few hundred miles across. Severe thunderstorms are often embedded within the MCC. Fortunately, the huge cirrus shield tends to suppress thermals away from the thunderstorm, so soaring pilots should not have the opportunity to approach an MCS. However, since they can contain severe weather, the forecast of a possible MCS or other severe thunderstorm may inspire the glider pilot to avoid leaving a glider outside overnight if other options are available, e.g., an enclosed trailer. Securing the trailer extra well would also be advisable.

Using the Skew-T and a morning sounding, the possibility of thunderstorms can be predicted. Figure 9-19 illustrates a late-spring morning sounding from the southeast United States. The temperature and dew point are within about a degree below a shallow surface inversion, indicating the likelihood of haze and the possibility of fog. In addition, a shallow layer

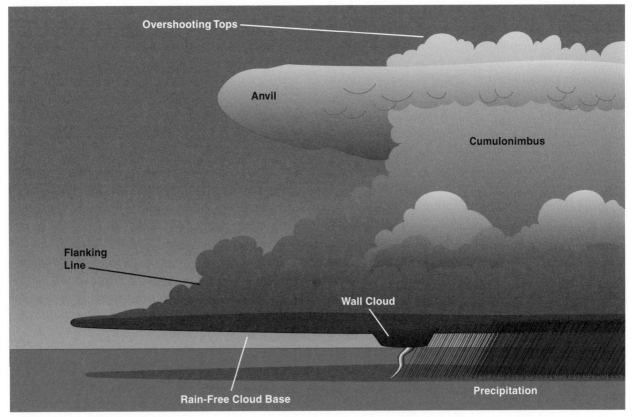

Figure 9-18. Supercell thunderstorm. Air enters on left into the bottom of the storm and exits at top towards the reader.

where temperature and dew point coincide are also located at about 12,000 feet, indicating a thin, mid-level cloud.

As the day warms to 28°C, cumulus should form at about 2,500 feet AGL, using the same analysis as before. By the time surface the temperature reaches 31°C, the CCL should be around 4,000 feet AGL. Recall that once condensation occurs, the parcel follows the SALR. Following parallel to the nearest saturated adiabat from the CCL, the parcel does not intersect the ambient temperature line again until almost 40,000 feet. Thunderstorms are possible if the surface temperature reaches 31°C. [Figure 9-19]

Two common indices are routinely reported using this type of analysis, the Lifted Index (LI) and the K-Index (KI). The LI is determined by subtracting the tempera-

ture of a parcel that has been lifted (as in Figure 9-19) to 500 mb from the temperature of the ambient air. This index does not give the likelihood of occurrence; rather it gives an indication of thunderstorm severity *if* they occur. In the example above, LI would be given by –9 – (-4) = -5. Looking at Figure 9-20, a LI of –5 indicates moderately severe thunderstorms if they develop. [Figure 9-20]

The KI is used to determine the probability of thunderstorm occurrence and uses information about temperature and moisture at three levels. It is given by the equation KI = (T850 – T500) + Td850 – (T700-Td700). Here, T stands for temperature, Td is the dew point, and 500, 700, or 850 indicate the level in mb. All values are obtained from a morning sounding. In the above example, using values from the sounding KI = (16 –[-9]) + 12 – (6 –0) = 31. This indicates about a

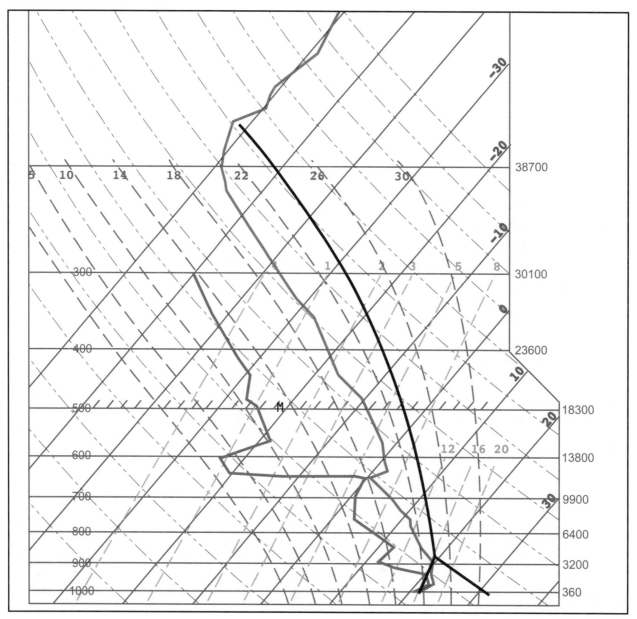

Figure 9-19. Skew-T from an actual sounding for a thunderstorm day.

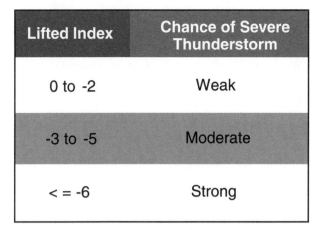

Lifted Index	Chance of Severe Thunderstorm
0 to -2	Weak
-3 to -5	Moderate
< = -6	Strong

Figure 9-20. Lifted Index (LI) vs. thunderstorm severity.

60 percent probability that thunderstorms will occur. [Figure 9-21] As discussed below, charts showing both the LI and KI for all the sounding sites in the continental United States are produced daily.

Thunderstorms have several hazards, including turbulence, strong up and down drafts, strong shifting surface winds, hail, icing, poor visibility and/or low ceilings, lightning, and even tornadoes. Once a cloud has grown to be a Cb, hazards are possible, whether or not there are obvious signs. Since thermal soaring weather can rapidly deteriorate into thunderstorm weather, recognition of each hazard is important. Knowledge of the many hazards may inspire the pilot to land and secure the glider when early signs of thunderstorm activity appear—the safest solution.

Moderate turbulence is common within several miles of a thunderstorm and it should be expected. Severe or even extreme turbulence (leading to possible structural failure) can occur anywhere within the thunderstorm

K Index	Thunderstorm Probability (%)
<15	near 0
15 to 20	20
21 to 25	20 to 40
26 to 30	40 to 60
31 to 35	60 to 80
36 to 40	80 to 90
>40	near 100

Figure 9-21. K-Index (KI) vs. probability of thunderstorm occurrence.

itself. The inside of a thunderstorm is no place for glider pilots of any experience level. Outside of the storm, severe turbulence is common. One region of expected turbulence is near the surface gust front as cool outflow spreads from the storm. Violent updrafts can be followed a second or two later by violent downdrafts, with occasional side gusts adding to the excitement–not a pleasant proposition while in the landing pattern. At somewhat higher altitudes, but below the base of the Cb, moderate to severe turbulence can also be found along the boundary between the cool outflow and warm air feeding the Cb. Unpredictable smaller-scale turbulent gusts can occur anywhere near a thunderstorm, so recognizing and avoiding the gust front does not mean safety from severe turbulence.

Large and strong up and downdrafts accompany thunderstorms in the mature stage. Updrafts under the Cb base feeding into the cloud can easily exceed 1,000 fpm. Near the cloud base, the distance to the edge of the cloud can be deceptive; trying to avoid being inhaled into the cloud by strong updrafts can be difficult. In the later cumulus and early mature stage, updrafts feeding the cloud can cover many square miles. As the storm enters its mature stage, strong downdrafts, called downbursts or microbursts, can be encountered, even without very heavy precipitation present. Downbursts can also cover many square miles with descending air of 2,000 fpm or more. A pilot unlucky enough to fly under a forming downburst, which may not be visible, could encounter sink of 2,000 or 3,000 fpm, possibly more in extreme cases. If such a downburst is encountered at pattern altitude, it can cut the normal time available to the pilot for planning the approach. For instance, a normal three-minute pattern from 800 feet AGL to the ground happens in a mere 19 seconds in 2,500 fpm sink!

When a downburst or microburst hits the ground, the downdraft spreads out leading to strong surface winds, that is, thunderstorm outflow referred to earlier. Typically, the winds strike quickly and give little warning of their approach. While soaring, pilots should keep a sharp lookout between the storm and the intended landing spot for signs of a wind shift. Blowing dust, smoke, or wind streaks on a lake indicating wind from the storm are clues that a gust front is rapidly approaching. Thunderstorm outflow winds are usually 20 to 40 knots for a period of 5 to 10 minutes before diminishing. However, winds can easily exceed 60 knots, and in some cases, with a slow-moving thunderstorm, strong winds can last substantially longer. Although damaging outflow winds usually do not extend more than 5 or 10 miles from the Cb, winds of 20 or 30 knots can extend 50 miles or more from large thunderstorms.

Hail is possible with any thunderstorm and can exist as part of the main rain shaft. Hail can also occur many miles from the main rain shaft, especially under the thunderstorm anvil. Pea-sized hail usually will not damage a glider, but hail with a severe storm (3/4 inch diameter or larger) can dent metal gliders or damage the gelcoat on composite gliders, whether on the ground or in the air.

Icing is generally only a problem within a cloud, especially at levels where the outside temperature is around –10°C. Under these conditions, super-cooled water droplets (that is, water droplets existing in a liquid state at below 0°C) can rapidly freeze onto wings and other surfaces. At the beginning of the mature stage, early precipitation below cloud base may be difficult to see. At times, precipitation can even be falling through an updraft feeding the cloud. Snow, graupel, or ice pellets falling from the forming storm above can stick to the leading edge of the wing, causing degradation in performance. Rain on the wings can be a problem since some airfoils can be adversely affected by water.

Poor visibility due to precipitation and possible low ceilings as the air below the thunderstorm is cooled is yet another concern. Even light or moderate precipitation can reduce visibility dramatically. Often, under a precipitating Cb, there is no distinction between precipitation and actual cloud.

Lightning in a thunderstorm occurs in-cloud, cloud-to-cloud (in the case of other nearby storms, such as a multicell storm), or cloud-to-ground. Lightning strikes are completely unpredictable, and cloud-to-ground strikes are not limited to areas below the cloud. Some strikes emanate from the side of the Cb and travel horizontally for miles before turning abruptly towards the ground. In-flight damage to gliders has included burnt control cables and blown off canopies. In some cases, strikes have caused little more than mild shock and cosmetic damage. On the other extreme, a composite training glider in Great Britain suffered a strike that caused complete destruction of one wing; fortunately, both pilots parachuted to safety. In that case, the glider was two or three miles from the thunderstorm. Finally, ground launching, especially with a metal cable, anywhere near a thunderstorm should be avoided.

Severe thunderstorms can sometimes spawn tornadoes, which are rapidly spinning vortices, generally a few hundred to a few thousand feet across. Winds can exceed 200 mph. Tornadoes that do not reach the ground are called funnel clouds. By definition, tornadoes form from severe thunderstorms. Obviously, they should be avoided on the ground or in the air.

WEATHER FOR SLOPE SOARING

Slope or ridge soaring refers to using updrafts produced by the mechanical lifting of air as it encounters the upwind slope of a hill, ridge, or mountain. Slope soaring requires two ingredients: elevated terrain and wind.

Slope lift is the easiest lift source to visualize. When it encounters topography, wind is deflected either horizontally, vertically, or in some combination of the two. Not all topography produces good slope lift. Individual or isolated hills do not produce slope lift because the wind tends to deflect around the hill, rather than over it. A somewhat broader hill with a windward face at least a mile or so long, might produce some slope lift, but the lift will be confined to a small area. The best ridges for slope soaring are at least a few miles long.

Slope lift can extend to a maximum of two or three times the ridge height. However, the pilot may only be able to climb to ridge height. As a general rule, the higher the ridge above the adjacent valley, the higher the glider pilot can climb. Ridges only one or two hundred feet high can produce slope lift. The problem with very low ridges is maintaining safe maneuvering altitude, as well as sufficient altitude to land safely in the adjacent valley. Practically speaking, 500 to 1,000 feet above the adjacent valley is a minimum ridge height. [Figure 9-22]

In addition to a ridge being long and high enough, the windward slope needs to be steep enough as well. An ideal slope is on the order of 1 to 4. Shallower slopes do not create a vertical wind component strong enough to compensate for the glider's sink rate. Very steep, almost vertical slopes, on the other hand, may not be

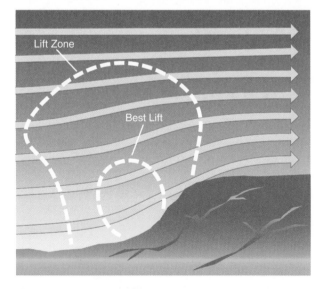

Figure 9-22. Slope soaring.

ideal either. Such slopes create slope lift, but can produce turbulent eddies along the lower slope or anywhere close to the ridge itself. In such cases, only the upper part of the slope may produce updrafts, although steeper slopes do allow a quick escape to the adjacent valley. [Figure 9-23]

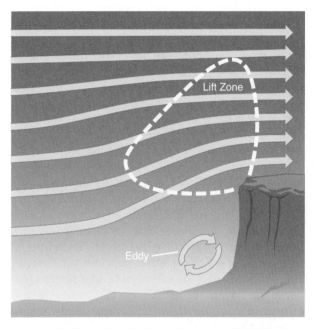

Figure 9-23. Slope lift and eddy with near-vertical slope.

A ridge upstream can block the wind flow, so that no low-level flow occurs upwind of an otherwise promising ridge, and hence no updraft. Additionally, if lee waves are produced by an upstream ridge or mountain, slope lift can be enhanced or destroyed, depending on the wavelength of the lee waves. Locally, the downdraft from a thermal just upwind of the ridge can cancel the slope lift for a short distance. The bottom line: never assume slope lift is present. Always have an alternative.

Just as the flow is deflected upward on the windward side of a ridge, it is deflected downward on the lee side of a ridge.[Figure 9-24] This downdraft can be alarmingly strong—up to 2,000 fpm or more near a steep ridge with strong winds (A). Even in moderate winds, the downdraft near a ridge can be strong enough to make penetration of the upwind side of the ridge impossible. Flat-topped ridges also offer little refuge, since sink and turbulence can combine to make an upwind penetration impossible (B). Finally, an uneven upwind slope, with ledges or "steps," require extra caution since small-scale eddies along with turbulence and sink can form there (C).

Three-dimensional effects are important as well. For instance, a ridge with cusps or bowls may produce better

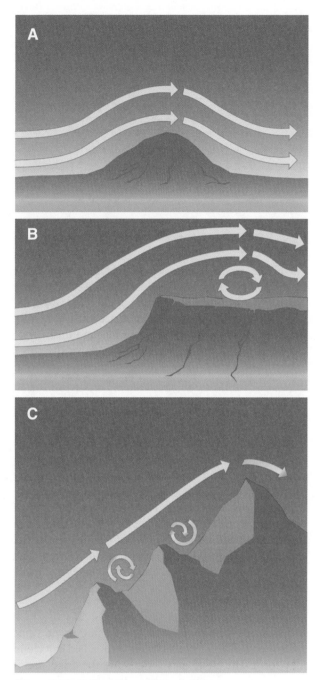

Figure 9-24. Airflow along different ridges.

lift in upwind-facing bowls if the wind is at an angle from the ridge. However, sink may be encountered on the lee side of the bowl. If crossing ridges in windy conditions, always plan for heavy sink on the lee side and make sure an alternative is available. [Figure 9-25]

Depending on the slope, wind speed should be 10-15 knots and blowing nearly perpendicular to the ridge. Wind directions up to 30° or 40° from perpendicular may still produce slope lift. Vertical wind shear is also a consideration. High ridges may have little or no wind along the lower slopes, but the upper parts of the ridge may be in winds strong enough to produce slope lift there.

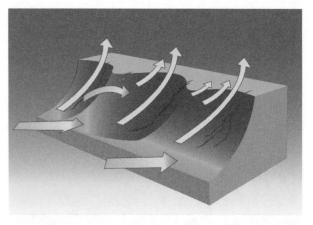

Figure 9-25. Three-dimensional effects of oblique winds and bowls.

The area of best lift varies with height. Below the ridge crest, the best slope lift is found within a few hundred feet next to the ridge, again depending on the slope and wind strength. As mentioned, very steep ridges require extra speed and caution, since eddies and turbulence can form even on the upwind side. Above the ridge crest, the best lift usually is found further upwind from the ridge the higher one climbs. [Figure 9-22]

When the air is very stable, and the winds are sufficient but not too strong, slope lift can be very smooth, enabling safe soaring close to the terrain. If the air is not stable, thermals may flow up the slope. Depending on thermal strength and wind speed, the thermal may rise well above the ridge top, or it may drift into the lee downdraft and break apart. Downdrafts on the sides of thermals can easily cancel the slope lift; hence, extra speed and caution is required when the air is unstable, especially below the ridge crest near the terrain. The combination of unstable air and strong winds can make slope soaring unpleasant or even dangerous for the beginning glider pilot.

Moisture must be considered. If air rising in the slope lift is moist and cools sufficiently, a so-called cap cloud may form. The cloud may form above the ridge, and if the air moistens more with time, the cloud will slowly lower onto the ridge and down the upwind slope, limiting the usable height of the slope lift. Since the updraft forms the cloud, it is very easy to climb into the cap cloud—obviously a dangerous situation. Under certain conditions, a morning cap cloud may rise as the day warms, then slowly lower again as the day cools.

WAVE SOARING WEATHER
Where there is wind and stable air, there is the likelihood of waves in the atmosphere. Most of the waves that occur throughout the atmosphere are of no use to the glider pilot. However, often mountains or ridges produce waves downstream, the most powerful of which have lifted gliders to 49,000 feet. Indirect measurements show waves extending to heights around

100,000 feet. If the winds aloft are strong and widespread enough, mountain lee waves can extend the length of the mountain range. Pilots have achieved flights in mountain wave using three turn points of over 2,000 km. Another type of wave useful to soaring pilots is generated by thermals, which were discussed in the previous section.

A common analogy to help visualize waves created by mountains or ridges uses water flowing in a stream or small river. A submerged rock will cause ripples (waves) in the water downstream, which slowly dampen out. This analogy is useful, but it is important to realize that the atmosphere is far more complex, with vertical shear of the wind and vertical variations in the stability profile. Wind blowing over a mountain will not always produce downstream waves.

Mountain wave lift is fundamentally different from slope lift. Slope soaring occurs on the upwind side of a ridge or mountain, while mountain wave soaring occurs on the downwind side. (Mountain wave lift sometimes tilts upwind with height. Therefore, at times near the top of the wave, the glider pilot may be almost directly over the mountain or ridge that has produced the wave). The entire mountain wave system is also more complex than the comparatively simple slope soaring scenario.

MECHANISM FOR WAVE FORMATION
Waves form in stable air when a parcel is vertically displaced and then oscillates up and down as it tries to return to its original level, illustrated in Figure 9-26. In the first frame, the dry parcel is at rest at its equilibrium level. In the second frame, the parcel is displaced upward along a DALR, at which point it is cooler than the surrounding air. The parcel accelerates downward toward its equilibrium level, but due to momentum, it overshoots the level and keeps going down. The third frame shows that the parcel is now warmer than the surrounding air, and thus starts upward again. The process continues with the motion damping out. The number of oscillations depends on the initial parcel displacement and the stability of the air. In the lower part of the figure, wind has been added, illustrating the wave pattern that the parcel makes as it oscillates vertically. If there were no wind, a vertically displaced parcel would just oscillate up and down, while slowly damping, at one spot over the ground, much like a spring. [Figure 9-26]

The lower part of Figure 9-26 also illustrates two important features of any wave. The **wavelength** is the horizontal distance between two adjacent wave crests. Typical mountain wavelengths vary considerably, between 2 and 20 miles. The **amplitude** is half the vertical distance between the trough and crest of the wave. Amplitude varies with altitude and is smallest near the

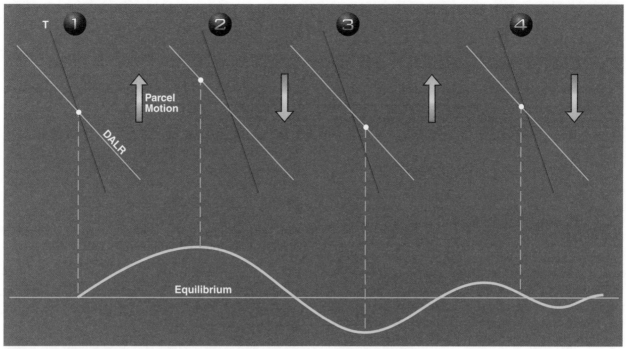

Figure 9-26. Parcel displaced vertically and oscillating around its equilibrium level.

surface and at upper levels. As a note, mountain lee waves are sometimes simply referred to as mountain waves, lee waves, and sometimes, standing waves.

In the case of mountain waves, it is the airflow over the mountain that displaces a parcel from its equilibrium level. This leads to a two-dimensional conceptual model, which is derived from the experience of many glider pilots along with post-flight analysis of the weather conditions. Figure 9-27 illustrates a mountain with wind and temperature profiles. Note the increase in wind speed (blowing from left to right) with altitude

and a stable layer near mountaintop with less stable air above and below. As the air flows over the mountain, it descends the lee slope (below its equilibrium level if the air is stable) and sets up a series of oscillations downstream. The wave flow itself is usually incredibly smooth. Beneath the smooth wave flow is what is known as a low-level turbulent zone, with an imbedded rotor circulation under each crest. Turbulence, especially within the individual rotors is usually moderate to severe, and on occasion can become extreme. [Figure 9-27]

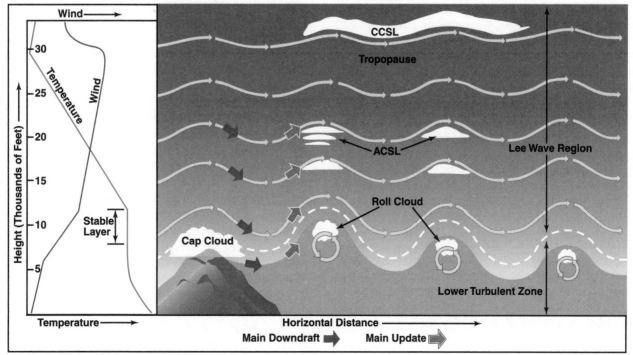

Figure 9-27. Mountain lee wave system.

This conceptual model is often quite useful and representative of real mountain waves, but many exceptions exist. For instance, variations to the conceptual model occur when the topography has many complex, three-dimensional features, such as individual higher peak, large ridges or spurs at right angles to the main range. Variations can occur when a north-south range curving to become oriented northeast-southwest. In addition, numerous variations of the wind and stability profiles are possible.

Turbulence associated with lee waves deserves respect. Low-level turbulence can range from unpleasant too dangerous. Glider pilots refer to any turbulence under the smooth wave flow above as **"rotor"**. The nature of rotor turbulence varies from location to location as well as with different weather regimes. At times, rotor turbulence is widespread and fairly uniform, that is, it is equally rough everywhere below the smooth wave flow. At other times, uniformly moderate turbulence is found, with severe turbulence under wave crests. On occasion, no discernable turbulence is noted except for moderate or severe turbulence within a small-scale rotor under the wave crest. Typically, the worst turbulence is found on the leading edge of the primary rotor. Unfortunately, the type and intensity of rotor turbulence is difficult to predict. However, the general rule of thumb is that higher amplitude lee waves tend to have stronger rotor turbulence.

Clouds associated with the mountain wave system are also indicated in Figure 9-27. A **cap cloud** flowing over the mountain tends to dissipate as the air forced down the mountain slope warms and dries. The first (or primary) wave crest features a roll or rotor cloud with one or more **lenticulars** (or lennies using glider terminology) above. Wave harmonics further downstream (secondary, tertiary, etc.) may also have lennies and/or rotor clouds. If the wave reaches high enough altitudes, lennies may form at cirrus levels as well. It is important to note that the presence of clouds depends on the amount of moisture at various levels. The entire mountain wave system can form in completely dry conditions with no clouds at all. If only lower level moisture exists, only a cap cloud and rotor clouds may be seen with no lennies above as in Figure 9-28(A). On other days, only mid-level or upper-level lennies are seen with no rotor clouds beneath them. When low and mid levels are very moist, a deep rotor cloud may form, with lennies right on top of the rotor cloud, with no clear air between the two cloud forms. In wet climates, the somewhat more moist air can advect in, such that the gap between the cap cloud and primary rotor closes completely, stranding the glider on top of the clouds (B). Caution is required when soaring above clouds in very moist conditions.

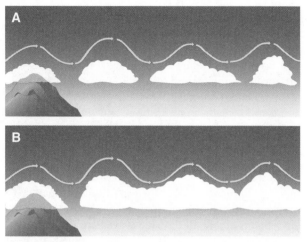

Figure 9-28. Small Foehn Gap under most conditions.

Suitable terrain is required for mountain wave soaring. Even relatively low ridges of 1,000 feet or less vertical relief can produce lee waves. Wave amplitude depends partly on topography shape and size. The shape of the lee slope, rather than the upwind slope is important. Very shallow lee slopes are not conducive to producing waves of sufficient amplitude to support a glider. A resonance exists between the topography width and lee wavelength that is difficult to predict. One particular mountain height, width, and lee slope is not optimum under all weather conditions. Different wind and stability profiles favor different topography profiles. Hence, there is no substitute for experience at a particular soaring site when predicting wave-soaring conditions. Uniform height of the mountaintops along the range is also conducive to better-organized waves.

The weather requirements for wave soaring include sufficient wind and a proper stability profile. Wind speed should be at least 15 to 20 knots at mountaintop level with increasing winds above. The wind direction should be within about 30° of perpendicular to the ridge or mountain range. The requirement of a stable layer near mountaintop level is more qualitative. A sounding showing a DALR, or nearly so, near the mountaintop would not likely produce lee waves even with adequate winds. A well-defined inversion at or near the mountaintop with less stable air above is best.

Weaker lee waves can form without much increase in wind speed with height, but an actual decrease in wind speed with height usually caps the wave at that level. When winds decrease dramatically with height, for instance, from 30 to 10 knots over two or three thousand feet, turbulence is common at the top of the wave. On some occasions, the flow at mountain level may be sufficient for wave, but then begins to decrease with altitude just above the mountain, leading to a phenomenon called **"rotor streaming."** In this case, the air downstream of the mountain breaks up and becomes turbulent, similar to rotor, with no lee waves above.

Lee waves experience **diurnal effects**, especially in the spring, summer, and fall. Height of the topography also influences diurnal effects. For smaller topography, as morning leads to afternoon, and the air becomes unstable to heights exceeding the wave-producing topography, lee waves tend to disappear. On occasion, the lee wave still exists but more height is needed to reach the smooth wave lift. Toward evening as thermals again die down and the air stabilizes, lee waves may again form. During the cooler season, when the air remains stable all day, lee waves are often present all day, as long as the winds aloft continue. The daytime dissipation of lee waves is not as notable for large mountains. For instance, during the 1950s Sierra Wave Project, it was found that the wave amplitude reached a maximum in mid- to late afternoon, when convective heating was a maximum. Rotor turbulence also increased dramatically at that time.

Topography upwind of the wave-producing range can also create problems, as illustrated in Figure 9-29. In the first case (A), referred to as destructive interference, the wavelength of the wave from the first range is out of phase with the distance between the ranges. Lee waves do not form downwind of the second range despite winds and stability aloft being favorable. In the second case (B), referred to as constructive interference, the ranges are in phase, and the lee wave from the second range has a larger amplitude than it might otherwise.

Isolated small hills or conical mountains do not form "classic" lee waves. In some cases, they do form waves emanating at angle to the wind flow similar to water waves created by the wake of a ship. A single peak may only require a mile or two in the dimension perpendicular to the wind for high-amplitude lee waves to form,

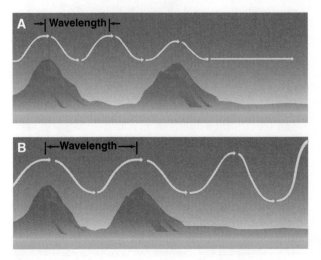

Figure 9-29. Constructive and destructive interference.

though the wave lift will be confined to a relatively small area in these cases.

LIFT DUE TO CONVERGENCE

Convergence lift is most easily imagined as easterly and westerly winds meet. When the air advected by the two opposing winds meet, it must go up. Air does not need to meet "head on" to go up, however. Wherever air piles up, it leads to convergence and rising air. [Figure 9-30]

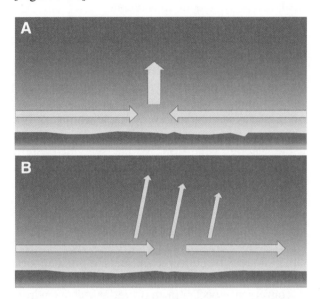

Figure 9-30. Convergence examples. (A) Wind from different directions. (B) Wind slows and "piles up."

Examples of converging air leading to rising air have already been discussed though not specifically referred to as convergence. In Figure 9-17, convergence along the outflow leads to air rising into the multi-cell thunderstorm. In Figure 9-13, the circulation associated with cloud streets leads to convergence under the cumulus. A synoptic-scale example of convergence is found along cold fronts. Convergence can occur along distinct, narrow lines (convergence or shear lines), as in Figure 9-30 (A), or can cause lifting over an area several miles across (**convergence zones**), as in Figure 9-30 (B). At times convergence lines produce steady lift along a line many miles long, while at other times they simply act as a focus for better and more frequent thermals.

One type of convergence line commonly found near coastal areas is the so-called sea-breeze front. Inland areas heat during the day, while the adjacent sea maintains about the same temperature. Inland heating leads to lower pressure, drawing in cooler sea air. As the cooler air moves inland, it behaves like a miniature shallow cold front, and lift forms along a convergence line. Sometimes consistent lift can be found along the sea-breeze front while at other times it acts as a trigger for a line of thermals. If the inland air is quite unstable, the sea-breeze front can act as a focus for a line of thunderstorms. Additionally, since the air on the coast side of the sea-breeze front is rather cool, passage of the front can spell the end of thermal soaring for the day.

Sea air often has a higher dew point than drier inland air. As shown in Figure 9-31, a "curtain" cloud sometimes forms, marking the area of strongest lift. Due to the mixing of different air along the sea-breeze front, at times the lift can be quite turbulent. At other times, weak and fairly smooth lift is found.

Several factors influence the sea-breeze front character (e.g., turbulence, strength, and speed of inland penetration, including the degree of inland heating and the land/sea temperature difference). For instance, if the land/sea temperature difference at sunrise is small and overcast cirrus clouds prevent much heating; only a weak sea-breeze front, if any, will form. Another factor is the synoptic wind flow. A weak synoptic onshore flow may cause quicker inland penetration of the sea-breeze front, while a strong onshore flow may prevent the sea-breeze front from developing at all. On the other hand, moderate offshore flow will generally prevent any inland penetration of the sea-breeze front.

Other sources of convergence include thunderstorm outflow boundaries already mentioned. Since this type of convergence occurs in an overall unstable environment, it can quickly lead to new thunderstorms. More subtle convergence areas form the day after ordinary thunderstorms have formed. If an area has recently been subject to spotty heavy rains, wet areas will warm more slowly than adjacent dry areas. The temperature contrast can give rise to a local convergence line, which acts similar to a sea-breeze front, and may be marked by a line of cumulus.

Convergence can also occur along and around mountains or ridges. In Figure 9-32(A), flow is deflected around a ridgeline and meets as a convergence line on the lee side of the ridge. The line may be marked by cumulus or a boundary with a sharp visibility contrast. The latter occurs if the air coming around one end of the ridge flows past a polluted urban area such as in the Lake Elsinore soaring area in southern California. In very complex terrain, with ridges or ranges oriented at different angles to one another, or with passes between high peaks, small-scale convergence zones can be found in adjacent valleys depending on wind strength and direction. Figure 9-32(B) illustrates a smaller-scale convergence line flowing around a single hill or peak and forming a line of lift stretching downwind from the peak.

Convergence also can form along the top of a ridgeline or mountain range. In Figure 9-33, drier synoptic-scale winds flow up the left side of the mountain, while a more moist valley breeze flows up the right side of the slope. The two flows meet at the mountain top and form lift along the entire range. If cloud is present, the air from the moist side condenses first often forming one cloud with a well-defined "step," marking the convergence zone.

As a final example, toward evening in mountainous terrain as heating daytime abates, a cool **katabatic** or drainage wind flows down the slopes. The flow down the slope converges with air in the adjacent valley to form an area of weak lift. Sometimes the convergence is not strong enough for general lifting, but acts as a trigger for the last thermal of the day. In narrow valleys, flow down the slope from both sides of the valley can converge and cause weak lift. [Figure 9-34]

Figure 9-31. Sea-breeze front.

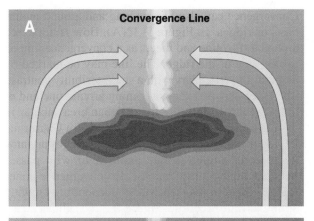

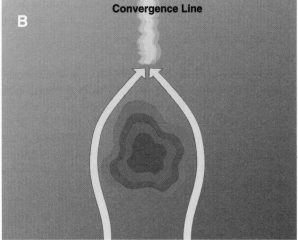

Figure 9-32. Convergence induced by flow around topography.

Many local sites in either flat or mountainous terrain have lines or zones of lift that are likely caused or enhanced by convergence. Chapter 10–Soaring Techniques covers locating and using convergence.

OBTAINING WEATHER INFORMATION

One of the most important aspects of flight planning is obtaining reliable weather information. Fortunately,

Figure 9-33. Mountain-top convergence.

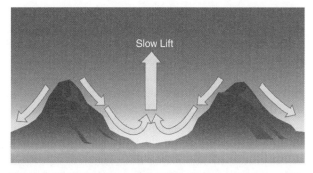

Figure 9-34. Convergence induced by flow around topography.

pilots have several outlets to receive reliable weather reports and forecasts to help them determine if a proposed flight can be completed safely. For VFR flights, federal regulations only require pilots to gather weather reports and forecasts if they plan to depart the airport vicinity. Nevertheless, it is always a good idea to be familiar with the current and expected weather anytime a flight is planned. Preflight weather information sources include Automated Flight Service Stations (AFSS) and National Weather Service (NWS) telephone briefers, the Direct User Access Terminal System (DUATS), and the Internet. In addition, a multitude of commercial venders provide custom services.

The following pages give a comprehensive synopsis of available weather services and products. For complete details, refer to the current version of AC 00-45, *Aviation Weather Services*.

AUTOMATED FLIGHT SERVICE STATIONS

Automated flight service stations (AFSS) are a primary source of preflight weather information. A briefing can be obtained from an AFSS, 24 hours a day by calling the toll free number, 1-800-WX BRIEF. The National Weather Service may also provide pilot weather briefings. Telephone numbers for NWS facilities and additional numbers for AFSSs can be found in the *Airport/Facility Directory* (A/FD) or the U.S. Government section of the telephone directory under Department of Transportation, Federal Aviation Administration, or Department of Commerce, National Weather Service.

PREFLIGHT WEATHER BRIEFING

To obtain a briefing, certain background information must be supplied to the weather specialist: type of flight planned (VFR or IFR), aircraft number or pilot's name, aircraft type, departure airport, route of flight, destination, flight altitude(s), estimated time of departure (ETD), and estimated time enroute (ETE). At many gliderports the operator or dispatcher will obtain the weather reports and forecasts from the AFSS or NWS at various times throughout the day and post them on a bulletin board for easy reference.

Weather briefers do not actually predict the weather, they simply translate and interpret weather reports and forecasts within the vicinity of the airport, route of flight, or the destination airport, if the flight is a cross-country. A pilot may request one of three types of briefings — standard, abbreviated, or outlook.

A standard briefing is the most complete weather briefing and should be requested when a preliminary briefing has not been obtained or when the proposed flight is a cross-country. When a standard briefing is requested the following information will be provided by the briefer.

ADVERSE CONDITIONS—This includes the type of information that might influence the go, no-go decision.

VFR FLIGHT RECOMMENDATION—If the weather specialist indicates that VFR flight is not recommended, it means that, in the briefer's judgment, it is doubtful that the flight can be conducted under VFR conditions. Although, the final go, no-go decision, does rest with the pilot.

SYNOPSIS—This is a broad overview of the major weather systems or airmasses that will affect the flight.

CURRENT CONDITIONS—This information is a rundown of existing conditions including pertinent hourly, pilot, and radar weather reports. It is normally omitted when the departure time is more than 2 hours in the future.

ENROUTE FORECAST—This information summarizes the forecast conditions along the route of flight for cross-country flights and is omitted for local flights.

DESTINATION FORECAST—For cross-country flights, the briefer will provide the forecast for the destination airport for 1 hour before and after the estimated time of arrival (ETA).

WINDS AND TEMPERATURES ALOFT—This can be of particular interest to soaring pilots. This is summary of the winds along a route of flight. At the pilots request, the weather briefer can interpolate wind direction and speed between levels and reporting stations for various altitudes. Temperature is also provided only on request.

NOTICES TO AIRMEN—The briefer will supply notices to airman (NOTAM) information pertinent to the proposed flight. However, information, which has already been published in the NOTAM publication, is only provided on request.

AIR TRAFFIC CONROL DELAYS—This information advises of any known Air Traffic Control (ATC) delays. Soaring pilots don't normally need this information, unless they are flying a self-launch glider and the flight will terminate at an airport with a control tower.

OTHER INFORMATION—Upon request the briefer can provide other information, such as density altitude data, military operations areas (MOA), military training routes (MTR) within 100 nautical miles of the fight plan area.

An abbreviated briefing is used to update weather information from a previous briefing or when requesting specific information. This allows the briefer to limit the search for weather data to that information that has changed or can have a significant impact on the proposed flight. The briefer will automatically include adverse weather conditions, both present or forecast.

For a flight with a departure time of 6 or more hours away, an outlook briefing should be requested. This briefing provides forecast information appropriate to the proposed flight in order to help make a go no-go decision. An outlook briefing is designed for planning purposes only and a standard briefing should be requested just before the departure time to acquire current conditions and the latest forecasts.

DIRECT USER ACCESS TERMINAL SYSTEM
The FAA-funded direct user access terminal system (DUATS), allows pilots with a current medical certificate to receive weather briefings and file flight plans directly via personal computer and modem. The information on DUATS sites is presented in textual format, which requires some skill and practice to interpret. Information for the current DUATS providers can be found in the *Aeronautical Information Manual (AIM)*.

ON THE INTERNET
Weather related information can be found on the Internet including sites directed toward aviation. These sites can be found using a variety of Internet search engines. It is import to verify the timeliness and source of the weather information provided by the Internet sites to ensure the information is up-to-date and accurate. Pilots should exercise caution when accessing weather information on the Internet especially if the information cannot be verified. One source of accurate weather information is the National Weather Service site located at: www.nws.noaa.gov.

INTERPRETING WEATHER CHARTS, REPORTS, AND FORECASTS

Knowing how and where to gather weather information is important but the ability to interpret and understand the information requires additional knowledge and practice. Weather charts and reports are merely records of observed atmospheric conditions at certain locations at specific times. Trained observers using electronic instruments, computers, and personal observations produce the weather products necessary for pilots to determine if a flight can be conducted safely. This same information can be used by soaring pilots to determine where they can find lift and how long the lift will be usable for soaring flight.

GRAPHIC WEATHER CHARTS

Reports of observed weather are graphically depicted in a number of weather products. Among them are the surface analysis chart, weather depiction chart, radar summary chart, and composite moisture stability chart.

SURFACE ANALYSIS CHART

A surface analysis chart is a computer-generated graphic that covers the 48 contiguous states and adjacent areas, for the valid time shown on the chart. The chart is prepared and disseminated every 3 hours by human observers.

A review of this chart provides a picture of the atmospheric pressure patterns at the earth's surface. [Figure 9-35] In addition, the chart depicts the amount of sky cover, the velocity and direction of the wind, the temperature, humidity, dewpoint, and other important weather data at specific locations. The observations from these locations are plotted on the chart to aid in analyzing and interpreting the surface weather features. [Figure 9-36, on next page.]

WEATHER DEPICTION CHART

The weather depiction chart provides an overview of favorable and adverse weather conditions for the chart time and is an excellent resource to help determine general weather conditions during flight planning. Information plotted on this chart is derived from aviation routine weather reports (METARs). Like the surface chart, the weather depiction chart is prepared and transmitted by computer every 3 hours and is valid at the time the data is plotted.

On this chart, a simplified station model is used to depict the type of weather, amount of sky cover, the height of the cloud base or ceiling, obstructions to vision, and visibility. Unlike the station model on a surface analysis chart, a bracket symbol is placed to the right of the circle to indicate an observation made by

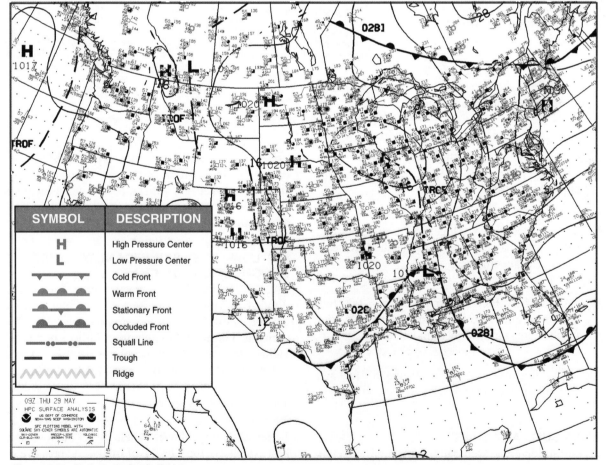

Figure 9-35. Surface Analysis Chart.

WIND
Symbols extending out from the station circle give wind information. The symbol shows the general true direction of the surface wind and the velocity in knots. The absence of a wind symbol and a double circle around the station means calm wind. True wind direction is shown by the orientation of the wind pointer. Velocity is indicated by barbs and/or pennants attached to the wind pointer. One short barb is 5 knots, a longer barb is 10 knots, and a pennant is 50 knots. For example, the wind pointer in the sample station model shows the wind is from the northwest at 15 knots.

TEMPERATURE
Temperature is shown in degrees Fahrenheit. For example, the temperature at the sample station is 34°F.

PRESENT WEATHER
Over 100 symbols are available to depict the present weather. Decoding information for these symbols is available in various FAA publications and at flight service stations. In this example, continuous snowfall is occurring.

DEWPOINT
Dewpoint is shown in degrees Fahrenheit. In the example, the dewpoint is 32°F.

STATION IDENTIFIER
The station identifier is shown to the lower left of the station model. This observation is from KABI, or Abilene Regional Airport.

SKY COVER
Sky cover is depicted in the center of the station model. The eight possible symbols are shown below.

Clear | Few | Scattered | Broken | Breaks in Overcast | Overcast | Obscured | Missing or Partial Obscuration

CLOUDS
Low cloud symbols are placed below the station model, while middle and high cloud symbols are placed immediately above it. A typical station model may include only one cloud type; seldom are more than two included. Decoding information for these symbols is available in various FAA publications and at flight service stations.

SEA LEVEL PRESSURE
Sea level pressure is shown in three digits to the nearest tenth of a millibar (hPa). For 1000 mb or greater, add a 10 to the 3 digits. For less than 1000 mb, add a 9 to the 3 digits. In this example, the sea level pressure is 1014.7 mb (hPa).

PRESSURE CHANGE/TENDENCY
The pressure change in tenths of millibars over the past 3 hours is shown below the sea level pressure. The tendency of pressure change is depicted using a symbol to the right of the change. In the example, pressure has increased 2.8 mb (hPa) over the past 3 hours, and is increasing more slowly or holding steady. Other symbols may be decoded using information available in various FAA publications and at flight service stations.

PRECIPITATION
The precipitation over the last 6-hour period is given to the nearest hundredths of an inch. In the example, 0.45 inch of precipitation has fallen in the last 6 hours.

34
** **
32
KABI
147
28
.45

Figure 9-36. Station Model and Explanation.

an automated system only. [Figure 9-37] The observed ceiling and visibility for a general area is shown for IFR, MVFR, and VFR.

IFR—Ceilings less than 1,00 feet and/or visibility less than 3 miles are depicted in the hatched area outlined by a smooth line.

MVFR (Marginal VFR)—Ceiling 1,000 to 3,000 feet and/or visibility 3 to 5 miles is depicted in a non-hatched area outlined by a smooth line.

VFR—No ceiling or ceiling greater than 3,000 feet and visibility greater than 5 miles are not outlined.

RADAR SUMMARY CHART
The computer-generated radar summary chart is produced 35 minutes past each hour and depicts a collection of radar weather reports (SDs). This chart displays areas and type of precipitation, intensity, coverage, echo top, and cell movement. In addition, an area of severe weather is plotted if they are in effect when the chart is valid. [Figure 9-38]

U.S. LOW-LEVEL SIGNIFICANT WEATHER PROGNOSTICATION CHART
The low-level significant weather prognostic chart is divided into two forecast periods. The two panels on the left show the weather prognosis for a 12-hour period and those on the right for a 24-hour period. The valid times and titles for each panel are shown in the lower left corner of the respective panel.

The two upper panels depict cloud cover, altitudes of the freezing level, and areas where turbulence can be expected. The two lower panels depict the forecasters best estimate of the location of frontal and pressure systems, as well as the areas and types of precipitation. It

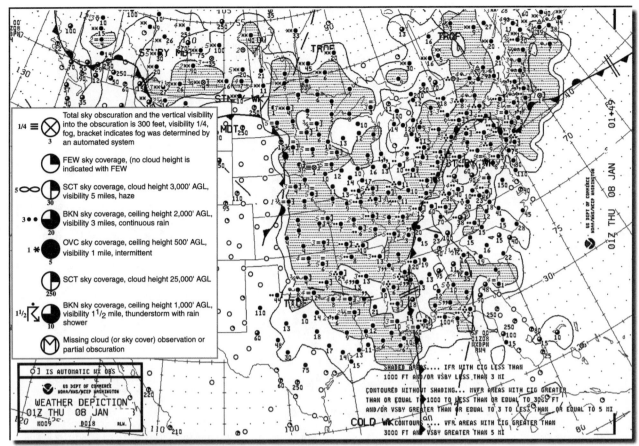

Figure 9-37. Weather Depiction Chart.

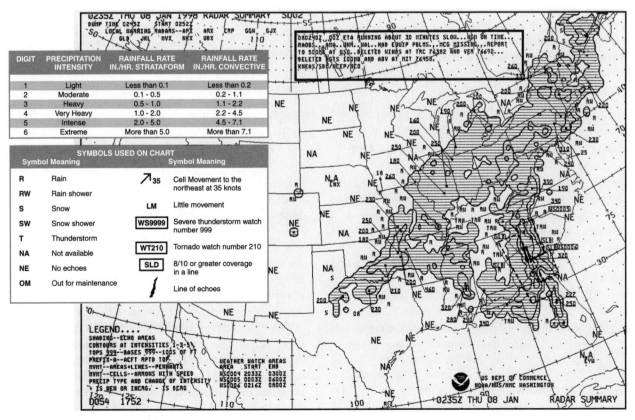

Figure 9-38. Radar Summary Chart.

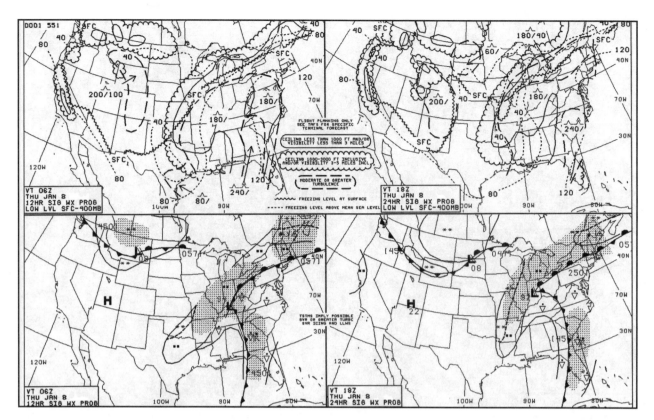

Figure 9-39. U.S. Low-Level Significant Weather Prognostic Chart.

is important to remember that a prognostic chart is a forecast and actual conditions may vary due to a number of factors. [Figure 9-39]

An area that is expected to have continuous of intermittent precipitation is enclosed by a solid line. If only showers are expected, the area is enclosed with a dot-dash pattern. Areas where precipitation is expected to cover one-half or more of the area is shaded. On the prognostic chart, special symbology is used to indicate various types of precipitation and how it will occur. [Figure 9-40]

WINDS AND TEMPERATURES ALOFT CHART

The winds and temperatures aloft chart (FD) is a 12-hour chart that is issued at 0000Z and 1200Z daily. It is primarily used to determine expected wind direction and velocity, and temperatures for the altitude of a planned cross-country flight. The chart contains eight panels that correspond to forecast levels—6,000; 9,000; 12,000; 18,000; 24,000; 30,000; 34,000; and 39,000 feet MSL. Soaring pilots planning to attempt a proficiency award for altitude should be aware that the levels below 18,000 feet are in true altitude, and levels 18,000 feet and above are reported in pressure altitude.

The predicted winds are depicted using an arrow from the station circle pointing in the direction of the wind. The second digit of the wind direction is given near the outer end of the arrow. Pennants and barbs are used to depict wind speed in much the same manner as the surface

analysis chart. When calm winds are expected the arrow is eliminated and 99 is entered below the station circle. Forecast temperatures are shown as whole degrees Celsius near the station circle. In the example, the temperature is 3° Celsius and the wind is 160° at 25 knots. [Figure 9-41]

COMPOSITE MOISTURE STABILITY CHART

The composite moisture stability chart is a four-panel chart, which depicts stability, **precipitable water**, freezing level, and average relative humidity. It is a computer-generated chart derived from upper-air observation data and is available twice daily with a valid time of 0000Z and 1200Z. This chart is useful for determining the characteristics of a particular weather system with regard to atmospheric stability, moisture content and possible hazards to aviation hazards, such as thunderstorms and icing. [Figure 9-42]

The stability panel located in the upper left corner of the chart outlines areas of stable and unstable air. [Figure 9-43] The numbers on this panel resemble fractions, the top number is the lifted index (LI), and the lower number is the K index (KI). The lifted index is the difference between the temperature of a parcel of air being lifted from the surface to the 500-millibar level (approximately 18,000 feet MSL) and the actual temperature at the 500-millibar level. If the number is positive, the air is considered stable. For example, a lifted index of +8 is very stable, and the likelihood of severe thunderstorms is weak. Conversely, an index of

SYMBOL	MEANING	SYMBOL	MEANING	SYMBOL	MEANING
	Showery precipitation (thunderstorms/rain-showers) covering half or more of the area.		Rain Shower		Severe Turbulence
	Continuous precipitation (rain) covering half or more of the area.		Snow Shower		Moderate Icing
					Severe Icing
	Showery precipitation (snow showers) covering less than half of the area.		Thunderstorms		Rain
			Freezing Rain		Snow
			Tropical Storm		Drizzle
	Intermittent precipitation (drizzle) covering less than half of the area.		Hurricane (Typhoon)		
			Moderate Turbulence		

Figure 9-40. Prognostic Chart Symbology.

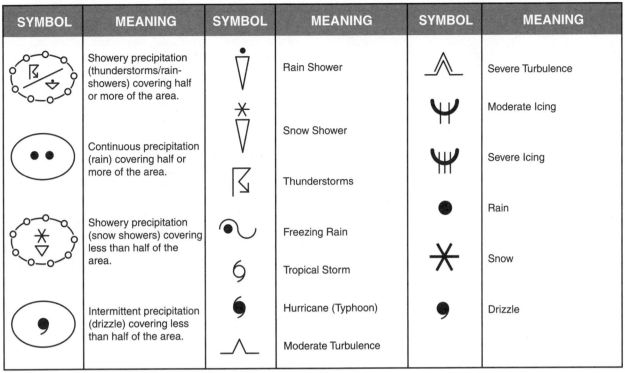

Figure 9-41. Winds and Temperatures Aloft (FD) chart.

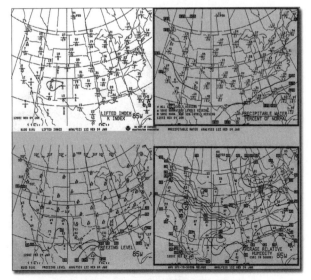

Figure 9-42. Composite Moisture Stability Chart.

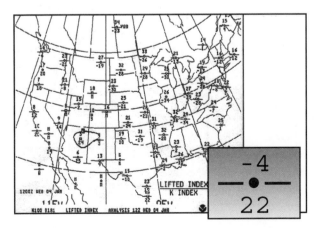

Figure 9-43. Stability Panel.

THUNDERSTORM POTENTIAL			
LIFTED INDEX (LI)	SEVERE POTENTIAL	K INDEX	AIRMASS THUNDERSTORM PROBABILITY
0 to -2	Weak	<15	near 0%
		15-19	20%
		20-25	21-40%
-3 to -5	Moderate	26-30	41-60%
		31-35	61-80%
≤ -6	Strong	36-40	81-90%
		>40	near 100%

Figure 9-44. Thunderstorm Potential.

–6 or less is considered very unstable, and severe thunderstorms are likely to occur. A zero index is neutrally stable. [Figure 9-44]

The K index indicates whether the conditions are favorable for airmass thunderstorms. The K index is based on temperature, low-level moisture, and saturation. A K index of 15 or less would be forecast as a 0 percent probability for airmass thunderstorms, and an index of 40 or more would be forecast as 100 percent probability.

The chart shows relative instability in two ways. First, the station circle is darkened when the lift index is zero or less. Second, solid lines are used to delineate areas which have an index of +4 or less at intervals of 4 (+4, 0, -4, -8). The stability panel is an important preflight planning tool because the relative stability of an airmass is indicative of the type of clouds that can be found in a given area. For example, if the airmass is

stable, a pilot can expect smooth air and given sufficient moisture, steady precipitation. On the other hand, if the airmass is unstable convective turbulence and showery precipitation can be expected.

The lower left panel of the chart is the freezing level panel. [Figure 9-45] This panel plots the observed freezing level data gathered from upper air observations. When the freezing level (0° Celsius isotherm) is at the surface, it is shown as a dashed contour line. The abbreviation "BF" is used to indicate a station that is reporting a temperature below freezing. As the freezing level increases in height, it is depicted on the chart as a solid line. These isotherms, lines of equal temperature, are given in 4,000-foot intervals but are labeled in hundreds of feet MSL. For example, an isotherm labeled 40 indicates that the freezing level is at 4,000 feet MSL. Since the freezing level panel plots an overall view of the isotherms, it is easy to determine at which altitude structural icing is probable. An inversion, with warm air above the freezing level is indicated by multiple crossings of 0° Celsius isotherms.

The precipitable water panel, located in the upper right corner of the composite moisture stability chart, graphically depicts the atmospheric water vapor available for condensation. The coverage for this panel is from the surface to the 500-millibars level. The top number in the station model represents the amount of precipitable water in hundredths of an inch. The lower number is the percent of normal value for the month. For example, when the value is .68/205, there is 68 hundredths of an inch of precipitable water, which is 205 percent of the normal (above average) for any day during the month. When a station symbol is darkened, the precipitable water value at the station is 1 inch or more. Isopleths are also plotted on the chart for every 1/4-inch. To differentiate the isopleths, a heavier line is used to indicate 1/2-inch of precipitable water. [Figure 9-46]

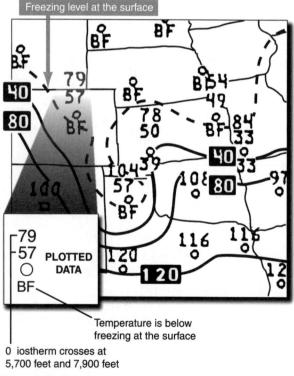

Figure 9-45. Freezing Level Panel.

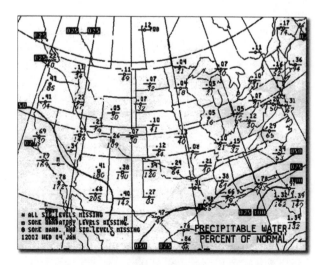

Figure 9-46. Precipitable Water Panel.

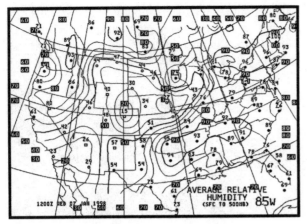

Figure 9-47. Average Relative Humidity Panel.

This panel is used primarily by meteorologists who are concerned with predicting localized flooding. However, when used with reference to the other panels it adds credibility to the prediction and probability of severe weather.

In the lower right corner of the composite moisture stability chart is the average relative humidity panel. The values for each station are plotted as a percentage and are valid from the surface to the 500-millibar level. For quick reference isohumes are drawn and labeled for every 10 percent, with heavier isohumes drawn for 10, 50, and 90 percent. When the stations is reporting humidity higher than 50 percent, the station symbol is darkened. If relative humidity data is missing, an "M" is placed above the station symbol. [Figure 9-47]

For flight planning, this chart is useful for determining average air saturation at altitudes from the surface to 18,000 feet MSL. Average relative humidity of 50 percent or higher is frequently associated with areas of clouds and possible precipitation. However, an area with high humidity may or may not be indicative of high water vapor content (precipitable water). For example, Kansas City may have the same relative humidity as New Orleans, but if the precipitable water value were .13 inches in Kansas City and .66 inches in New Orleans, greater precipitation would be expected in New Orleans.

While each panel of the composite moisture stability chart provides important information for predicting weather over a wide area of the United States, it is more important to reference all four panels to develop the best weather picture.

PRINTED REPORTS AND FORECASTS

Weather reports and forecasts are beneficial in numerous ways. For example, predictions of warm temperatures signal the beginning of thermal soaring in the northern climates, if it were only that simple. Printed reports and forecasts provide much more information to help pilots

decide if a flight can be conducted safely. To that end, wide varieties of weather products are available to assist pilots in that decision-making process.

PRINTED WEATHER REPORTS

In the simplest of terms, a weather report is a record of observed weather conditions at a particular location and time. Weather information gathered by trained observers, radar systems, and pilots is disseminated in a variety of reports. The types of reports pilots are likely to encounter include aviation routine weather reports, radar weather reports, and pilot reports.

AVIATION ROUTINE WEATHER REPORT

An aviation routine weather report (METAR) is a weather observer's interpretation of weather conditions at the time of the observation. This report is used by the aviation community and the National Weather Service to determine the flying category of the airport where the observation is made. Based on the observed weather conditions, this determination dictates whether the pilots will operate under visual flight rules (VFR), marginal visual flight rules (MVFR), or instrument flight rules (IFR) in the vicinity of the airport. Additionally, the METAR is used to produce an aviation terminal forecast (TAF).

Although, the code that makes-up a METAR is used worldwide, some variations of the code used in the United States exist in other countries. In the United States, temperature and dewpoint are reported in degrees Celsius, using current units of measure for the remainder of the report.

A METAR consists of a sequence of observed weather conditions or elements, if an element is not occurring or cannot be observed at the time of the observation, the element is omitted from the report. The elements of the report are separated by a space except temperature and dewpoint, which are separated by a slash (/). A non-routine METAR report, referred to as a SPECI report, is issued any time the observed weather meets the SPECI criteria. The SPECI criteria includes initial volcanic eruptions and the beginning or ending of thunderstorms as well as other hazardous weather conditions.

The METAR for Los Angles in Figure 9-48 was given on the 14th day of the month, at 0651 UTC. When a METAR is derived from a totally automated weather observation station, the modifier AUTO follows the date/time element. The wind was reported to be 140° at 21 knots with gusts to 29 knots. The reported surface visibility is 1 statute mile. Runway visual range (RVR) is based on the visual distance measured by a machine looking down the runway. In the example above, the runway visual range for runway 36 left is 4,500 feet variable to 6,000 feet. The weather phenomena is rain

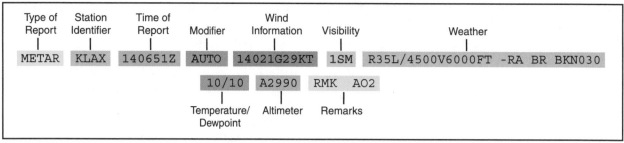

Figure 9-48. Typical Aviation Routine Weather Report (METAR) as generated in the United States.

(RA) and mist (BR), note the minus sign preceding the RA indicates light rain is falling. The sky condition element indicates there are broken clouds at 3,000 feet above the ground. Temperature and dewpoint are reported in a two-digit format in whole degrees Celsius separated by a slash. In the example, the temperature is 10°C and the dewpoint is 10°C. The altimeter setting is reported in inches and hundredths of inches of mercury using a four-digit format prefaced by an A and is reported as 29.90 in. Hg. The Remarks element is included in a METAR or SPECI when it is appropriate. If the reporting station is automated, AO1 or AO2 will be noted. Certain remarks are included to enhance or explain weather conditions that are considered significant to flight operations. The types of information that

may be included are wind data, variable visibility, beginning and ending times of a particular weather phenomenon, pressure information, and precise temperature/dewpoint readings. Refer to Appendix A at the end of this chapter for further explanation of TAF and METAR codes and references.

PILOT REPORTS
Of all of the weather reports available to pilots, PIREPs provide the most timely weather information for a particular route of flight. The advantage for pilots is significant because unforecast adverse weather conditions, such as low in-flight visibility, icing conditions, wind shear, and turbulence can be avoided along a route of flight. When significant conditions are reported or forecast, ATC facilities are required to solicit PIREPs. When unexpected weather conditions are encountered, pilots should not wait for ATC to request a PIREP of conditions, but offer them to aid other pilots. [Figure 9-49]

Another type of PIREP is an AIREP (ARP) or air report. These reports are disseminated electronically and are used almost exclusively by commercial airlines. However, pilots may see AIREPs when accessing weather information on the Internet.

RADAR WEATHER REPORTS
Radar weather reports (SDs), derived from selected radar locations are an excellent source of information about precipitation and thunderstorms. [Figure 9-50] The report describes the type, intensity, intensity trend, and height of the echo top of precipitation. [Figure 9-51] If the base of the precipitation is considered significant, it is also included in the report. All heights are reported in hundreds of feet MSL.

PRINTED FORECASTS
Everyday, National Weather Service Offices prepare a variety of forecasts using past weather observations and computer modeling. Weather specialists develop printed forecasts for more than 2,000 forecasts for airports, over 900 route forecasts, which are intended for flight planning purposes. The printed forecasts pilots need to become familiar with include the aviation terminal forecast, aviation area forecast, and the winds and temperatures aloft forecast.

PIREP FORM	
Pilot Weather Report ➡ = Space Symbol	

3-Letter SA Identifier 1. UA ➡ _____ UUA ➡ _____	
— — ➡	Routine Report Urgent Report
2. /OV ➡	Location: In relation to a NAVAID
3. /TM ➡	Time: Coordinated Universal Time
4. /FL ➡	Altitude/Flight Level: Essential for turbulence and icing reports
5. /TP ➡	Aircraft Type: Essential for turbulence and icing reports
Items 1 through 5 are mandatory for all PIREPs	
6. /SK ➡	Sky Cover: Cloud height and coverage (scattered, broken, or overcast)
7. /WX ➡	Flight Visibility and Weather: Flight visibility, precipitation, restrictions to visibility, etc.
8. /TA ➡	Temperature (Celsius): Essential for icing reports
9. /WV ➡	Wind: Direction in degrees and speed in knots
10. /TB ➡	Turbulence: Turbulence intensity, whether the turbulence occurred in or near clouds, and duration of turbulence
11. /IC ➡	Icing: Intensity and Type
12. /RM ➡	Remarks: For reporting elements not included or to clarify previously reported items

Figure 9-49. PIREP Form.

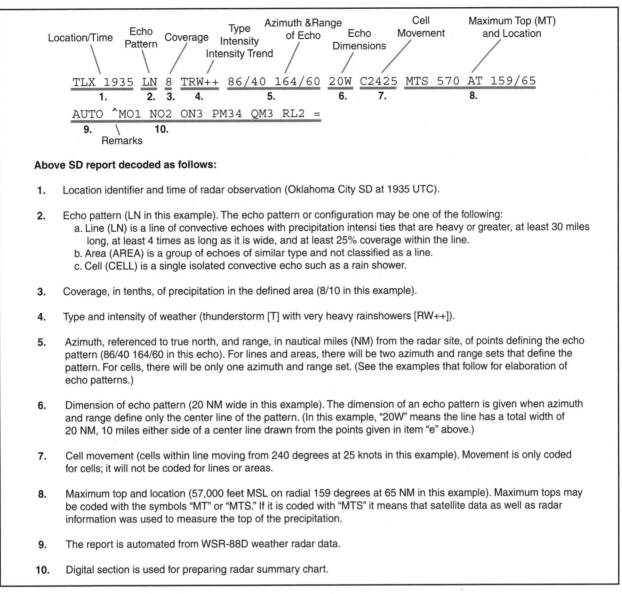

Figure 9-50. Sample Radar Weather Report.

TERMINAL AERODROME FORECAST

The terminal aerodrome forecast (TAF) is derived from weather data and observations at a specific airport. It is a concise statement of expected weather conditions within a five statute mile radius of the center of the air-

SYMBOL	INTENSITY
-	Light
(none)	Moderate
+	Heavy
++	Very Heavy
X	Intense
XX	Extreme

Figure 9-51. Intensity and intensity trend symbols.

port's runway complex. Normally valid for a 24-hour period, TAFs are scheduled for dissemination four times a day at 0000Z, 0600Z, 1200Z, and 1800Z. Each TAF contains the International Civil Aviation Organization (ICAO) station identifier, time and date of issuance, valid period, and the body of the forecast. With a few exceptions, the coding used in a TAF is similar to that found in a METAR.

The TAF for Pierre, South Dakota [Figure 9-52] was issued on the eleventh day of the month at 1140Z. This TAF is valid from 1200Z to 1200Z on the 11-day of the month. The first three digits of the surface wind forecast indicate direction and the following two indicate speed in knots (KT). In this case, the winds are 130° at 12 knots. P6SM indicates the visibility is forecast to be greater than 6 statute miles. BKN100 forecasts a broken layer of clouds at 10,000 feet AGL. The temporary (TEMPO) change group is used when fluctuations of

```
TAF
KPIR 111140Z 111212 13012KT P6SM BKN100 TEMPO 1214 5SM BR
  FM0000 14012KT P6SM BKN080 OVC150 PROB40 0004 3SM TSRA BKN030CB
  FM0400 14008KT P6SM SCT040
  BECMG 0810 32007KT=
```

Figure 9-52. Terminal Aerodrome Forecast.

wind, visibility, weather, or sky conditions are expected to last for less than one hour at a time, and expected to occur during less than half the time period. The four digits following the temporary code give the expected beginning and ending hours during which the conditions will prevail. In the example, reduced visibility due to mist is expected to prevail between 1200 hours and 1400 hours. The from (FM) change group is used to describe a rapid and significant change in the forecast weather that is expected to occur in less than an hour. When a gradual change in the forecast weather is expected over a period of about 2-hours, the becoming (BECMG) group is used. The probability-forecast group is used when there is less than a 50 percent chance of thunderstorms or precipitation. In the example, PROB40 indicates that between 0000Z and 0400Z there is a 40 to 50 percent chance of a moderate rain showers associated with a thunder-storm, 3 statute miles visibility, and broken cloud layer at 3,000 feet AGL. The CB following the sky condition stands for cumulonimbus clouds.

AVIATION AREA FORECAST

An aviation area forecast (FA) covers general weather conditions over several states or a known geographical area and is a good source of information for enroute weather. It also helps determine the weather conditions at airports, which do not have Terminal Aerodrome Forecasts. FAs are issued three times a day in the 48

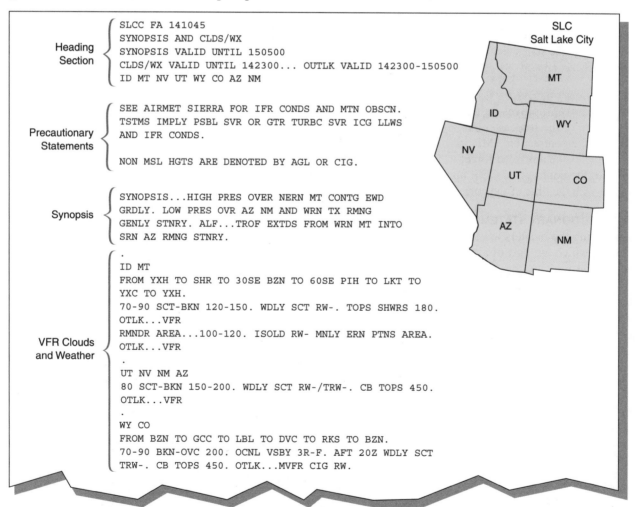

Figure 9-53. Aviation Area Forecast.

contiguous states, and amended as required. NWS offices issue FAs for Hawaii and Alaska; however, the Alaska FA uses a different format. An additional specialized FA may be issued for the Gulf of Mexico by the National Hurricane Center in Miami, Florida.

The FA consists of several sections: a communications and product header section, a precautionary statement section, and two weather sections (synopsis and VFR clouds and weather). Each area forecast covers an 18-hour period. [Figure 9-53]

COMMUNICATIONS AND PRODUCT HEADERS
Refer to figure 9-53 for the following discussion. In the heading SLCC FA 141045, the SLC identifies the Salt Lake City forecast area, C indicates the product contains clouds and weather forecast, FA means area forecast, and 141045 is the date time group and indicates that the forecast was issued on the 14th day of the month at 1045Z. Since these forecasts times are rounded to the nearest full hour, the valid time for the report begins at 1100Z. The synopsis is valid until 18 hours later, which is shown as the 15th 0500Z. The clouds and weather section forecast is valid for 12-hour period, until 2300Z on the 14th. The outlook portion is valid for six hours following the forecast, from 2300Z on the 14th to 0500Z on the 15th. The last line of the header lists the states that are included in the Salt Lake City forecast area.

Amendments to FAs are issued whenever the weather significantly improves or deteriorates based on the judgment of the forecaster. An amended FA is identified by the contraction AMD in the header along with the time of the amended forecast. When an FA is corrected, the contraction COR appears in the heading, along with the time of the correction.

PRECAUTIONARY STATEMENTS
Following the headers are three precautionary statements, which are part of all FAs. The first statement alerts the pilot to check the latest AIRMET Sierra, which describes areas of mountain obscuration which may be forecast for the area. The next statement is a reminder that thunderstorms imply possible severe or greater turbulence, severe icing, low-level wind shear, and instrument conditions. Therefore, when thunderstorms are forecast, these hazards are not included in the body of the FA. The third statement points out that heights, which are not MSL, are noted by the letters AGL (above ground level) or CIG (ceiling). All heights are expressed in hundreds of feet.

SYNOPSIS
The synopsis is a brief description of the location and movement of fronts, pressure systems, and circulation patterns in the FA area over an 18-hour period. When appropriate, forecasters may use terms describing ceilings and visibility, strong winds, or other phenomena.

In the example, high pressure over northeastern Montana will continue moving gradually eastward. A low-pressure system over Arizona, New Mexico, and western Texas will remain generally stationary. Aloft (ALF), a trough of low pressure extending from western Montana into southern Arizona is expected to remain stationary.

VFR CLOUDS AND WEATHER
The VFR clouds and weather portion is usually several paragraphs long and broken down by states or geographical regions. It describes clouds end weather, which could affect VFR operations over an area of 3,000 square miles or more. The forecast is valid for 12 hours, and is followed by a 6-hour categorical outlook (18 hours in Alaska).

When the surface visibility is expected to be six statute miles or less, the visibility and obstructions to vision are included the forecast. When precipitation, thunderstorms, and sustained winds of 20 knots or are forecast, they will be included in this section. The term OCNL (occasional) is used when there is a 50 percent or greater probability, but for less than 1/2 of the forecast period, of cloud or visibility conditions which could affect VFR flight. The area covered by showers or thunderstorms is indicated by the terms ISOLD (isolated), meaning single cells. WDLY SCT (widely scattered, less then 25 percent of the area), SCT or AREAS (25 to 54 percent of the area), and NMRS or WDSPRD (numerous or widespread, 55 percent or more of the area).

The outlook follows the main body of the forecast, and gives a general description of the expected weather using the terms VFR, IFR, or MVFR (marginal VFR). A ceiling less than 1,000 feet and/or visibility less than 3 miles is considered IFR. Marginal VFR areas are those with ceilings from 1,000 to 3,000 feet and/or visibility between 3 and 5 miles. Abbreviations are used to describe causes of IFR or MVFR weather.

In the example shown above, the area of coverage in the specific forecast for Wyoming and Colorado is identified using three-letter designators. This area extends from Bozeman, Montana to Gillette, Wyoming to Liberal, Kansas to Dove Creek, Wyoming to Rocksprings, Wyoming, and back to Bozeman. As mentioned previously under the header, the valid time begins on the 14th day of the month at 1100Z for a 12-hour period. A broken to overcast cloud layer begins between 7,000 to 9,000 feet MSL, with tops extending to 20,000 feet. Since visibility and wind information is omitted, the visibility is expected to be greater than 6 statute miles and the wind less than 20 knots. However, the visibility (VSBY) is forecast to be occasionally 3 miles in light rain and fog (3R-F). After 2000Z, widely scattered thunderstorms with light rain showers are expected, with cumulonimbus (CB) cloud tops to 45,000 feet. The 6-hour categorical outlook covers the period from 2300Z on the 14th to 0500 on the 15th. The forecast is for marginal VFR weather due to ceilings (CIG) and rain showers (RW).

CONVECTIVE OUTLOOK CHART

The convective outlook chart (AC), is a two-panel chart that forecasts general thunderstorm activity for the valid period of the chart. ACs describe areas in which there is a risk of severe thunderstorms. Severe thunderstorm criteria include winds equal to or greater than 50 knots at the surface or hail equal to or greater than 3/4 inch in diameter, or tornadoes. Convective outlooks are useful for planning flights within the forecast period. Both panels of the convective outlook chart qualify the risk of thunderstorm activity at three levels, as well as areas of general thunderstorm activity.

Slight (SLGT)—implies well-organized severe thunderstorms are expected but in small numbers and/or low coverage.

Moderate (MDT)—implies a greater concentration of severe thunderstorms, and in most cases greater magnitude of severe weather.

High (HIGH)—means a major severe weather outbreak is expected, with a greater coverage of severe weather with a likelihood of violent tornadoes and/or damaging high winds.

General thunderstorm activity is identified on the chart by a solid line with an arrowhead at one end. This indicated that the area of general thunderstorm activity is expected to the right of the line from the direction of the arrowhead.

The left panel [Figure 9-54] describes specific areas of probable thunderstorm activity for day-1 of the outlook. The day-1 panel is issued five times daily, starting a 0600Z and is valid from 1200Z that day until 1200Z

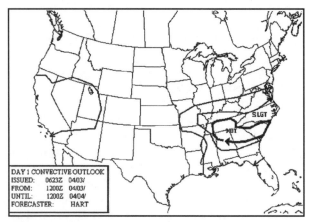

Figure 9-54. Day-1 panel of the Convective Outlook Chart.

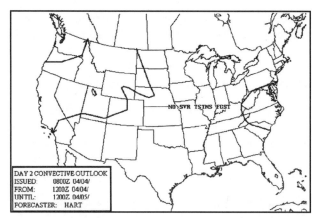

Figure 9-55. Day-2 panel of the Convective Outlook Chart.

the day after. The other issuance times are 1300Z, 1630Z, 2000Z, and 0100Z and are valid until 1200Z the day after the original issuance day.

The right panel [Figure 9-55] is the day-2 chart, it is issued twice daily. The initial issue is 0830Z standard time, 0730Z daylight time and is updated at 1730Z. The valid time of the chart is from 1200Z following the original issue of the day-1 chart until 1200Z of the next day. For example, if the day-1 chart is issued on Monday it is valid until 1200Z on Tuesday, subsequently the day-2 chart is valid from 1200Z Tuesday until 1200Z on Wednesday.

WINDS AND TEMPERATURES ALOFT FORECAST

A winds and temperatures aloft forecast (FD) provides an estimate of wind direction relation to true north, wind speed in knots and the temperature in degrees Celsius for selected altitudes. Depending on the station elevation, winds and temperatures are usually forecast for nine levels between 3,000 and 39,000 feet. Information for two additional levels (45,000 foot and 53,000 foot) may be requested from a FSS briefer or NWS meteorologist but is not included on an FD. [Figure 9-56]

The heading begins with the contraction FD, followed by the four-letter station identifier. The six digits are the day of the month and the time of the transmission. The next two lines indicate the time of the observation and the valid time for the forecast. In the example, the observation was taken on the 15th day of the month at 1200Z, is valid at 1800Z, and is intended to be used between 1700Z and 2100Z on the same day.

The first two numbers indicate the true direction from which the wind is blowing. For example, 1635-08 indicates the wind is from 160° at 35 knots and the temperature is –8°C. Determining the wind direction and speed and temperature requires interpolation between two levels. For instance, to determine the wind direc-

```
FD KWBC 151640

BASED ON 151200Z DATA

VALID 151800Z FOR USE 1700-2100Z TEMPS NEG ABV 24000

FD    3000    6000     9000      12000     18000     24000     30000

ALA                    2420      2635-08   2535-18   2444-30   245945

AMA           2714     2725+00   2625-04   2531-15   2542-27   265842

DEN                    2321-04   2532-08   2434-19   2441-31   235347

HLC           1707-01  2113-03   2219-07   2330-17   2435-30   244145
```

Figure 9-56. Winds and Temperatures Aloft Forecast.

tion and speed for a flight at 7,500 feet over Hill City (HLC), a good estimate of the wind at 7,500 feet is 190° at 10 knots with a temperature of -2C.

Wind speed between 100 and 199 knots are encoded, so direction and speed can be represented by four digits. This is done by adding 50 to the two-digit wind direction; and subtracting 100 from the velocity. For example, a wind of 270° at 101 knots is coded as 7701 (27 + 50 = 77 for wind direction and 101 – 100 = 0l for wind speed). A code of 9900 indicates light and variable winds (less than five knots). However, wind speeds of 200 knots or more are encoded as 199.

It is important to note that temperatures are not forecast for the 3,000-foot level or for any level within 2,500 feet of the station elevation. Likewise, wind groups are omitted when the level is within 1,500 feet of the station elevation. For example, the station elevation at Denver (DEN) is over 5,000 feet, so the forecast for the lower two levels is omitted.

TRANSCRIBED WEATHER BROADCASTS

A transcribed weather broadcast (TWEB) contains recorded weather information concerning expected sky cover, cloud tops, visibility, weather, and obstructions to vision in a route format. This information is transmitted over selected navigation aids such as very high frequency omni-directional ranges (VORs) and non-directional radio beacons (NDBs). At some locations, the information is only broadcast locally and is limited to items, such as the hourly weather for the transmitting station and up to five adjacent stations, local NOTAM information, the local TAF, and potential hazardous conditions.

When a TWEB is available along a route of flight, it is particularly useful for timely in-flight weather information. At some locations, telephone access to the recording is also available (TEL-TWEB), providing an additional source of preflight information. The telephone numbers for this service are listed in the *A/FD*. A circled "T" inside the communication boxes of selected NDBs and VORs on National Aeronautical Charting Office (NACO) enroute and sectional charts identifies the TWEB availability. In the regions where there has been high utilization of TWEB, the FSS puts the TWEB on a recording called Telephone Information Briefing Service (TIBS). It can be accessed prior to flight by calling 1-800-WX-BRIEF, then choosing TIBS from the menu.

APPENDIX A—KEY FOR TAF AND METAR

KEY to AERODROME FORECAST (TAF) and AVIATION ROUTINE WEATHER REPORT (METAR) (FRONT)

TAF TAF KPIT 091730Z 091818 15005KT 5SM HZ FEW020 WS010/31022KT
FM 1930 30015G25KT 3SM SHRA OVC015 TEMPO 2022 1/2SM +TSRA OVC008CB
FM0100 27008KT 5SM SHRA BKN020 OVC040 PROB40 0407 1SM - RA BR
FM1015 18005KT 6SM -SHRA OVC020 BECMG 1315 P6SM NSW SKC

METAR KPIT 091955Z COR 22015G25KT 3/4SM R28L/2600FT TSRA OVC010CB
18/16 A2992 RMK SLP045 T01820159

FORECAST	REPORT	EXPLANATION
TAF	METAR	Message type : TAF-routine or TAF AMD-amended forecast, METAR-hourly, SPECI-special or TESTM-non-commissioned ASOS report
KPIT	KPIT	ICAO location indicator
091730Z	091955z	Issuance time: ALL times in UTC "Z", 2-digit date, 4-digit time
091818		Valid period: 2-digit date, 2-digit beginning, 2-digit ending times
	COR	In U.S. METAR: CORrected of; or AUTOmated ob for automated report with no human intervention; omitted when observer logs on
15005KT	22015G25KT	Wind: 3 digit true-north direction , nearest 10 degrees (or VaRiaBle); next 2-3 digits for speed and unit, KT (KMH or MPS); as needed, Gust and maximum speed; 00000KT for calm; for METAR, if direction varies 60 degrees or more, Variability appended, e.g. 180V260
5SM	3/4SM	Prevailing visibility; in U.S., Statute Miles & fractions; above 6 miles in TAF Plus6SM. (Or, 4-digit minimum visibility in meters and as required, lowest value with direction)
	R28L/2600FT	Runway Visual Range: R: 2-digit runway designator Left, Center, or Right as needed; "/"; Minus or Plus in U.S., 4-digit value, FeeT in U.S., (usually meters elsewhere); 4-digit value Variability 4-digit value (and tendency Down, Up or No change)
HZ	TSRA	Significant present, forecast and recent weather: see table (on back)
FEW020	OVC 010CB	Cloud amount, height and type: SKy Clear 0/8, FEW >0/8-2/8, SCaTtered 3/8-4/8, BroKeN 5/8-7/8, OVerCast 8/8; 3-digit height in hundreds of ft; Towering Cumulus or CumulonimBus in METAR; in TAF, only CB Vertical Visibility for obscured sky and height "VV004". More than 1 layer may be reported or forecast. In automated METAR reports only, CLeaR for "clear below 12,000 feet"
18/16		Temperature: degrees Celsius; first 2 digits, temperature "Z" last 2 digits, dew-point temperature; Minus for below zero, e.g., M06
A2992	A2992	Altimeter setting: indicator and 4 digits; in U.S., Δ-inches and hundredths; (Q-hectoPascals, e.g. Q1013)

KEY to AERODROME FORECAST (TAF) and AVIATION ROUTINE WEATHER REPORT (METAR) (BACK)

FORECAST	REPORT	EXPLANATION
WS010/31022KT		In U.S. TAF, non-convective low-level (≤ 2,000 ft) Wind Shear; 3-digit height (hundreds of ft); "/"; 3-digit wind direction and 2-3 digit wind speed above the indicated height, and unit, KT
	RMK SLP045 T01820159	In METAR, ReMarK indicator & remarks. For example: Sea-Level Pressure in hectoPascals & tenths, as shown: 1004.5 hPa; Temp/dew-point in tenths °C, as shown: temp. 18.2°C, dew-point 15.9°C
FM1930		FroM and 2-digit hour and 2-digit minute beginning time: indicates significant change. Each FM starts on a new line, indented 5 spaces
TEMPO 2022		TEMPOrary: changes expected for <1 hour and in total, < half of 2-digit hour beginning and 2-digit hour ending time period
PROB40 0407		PROBability and 2-digit percent (30 or 40): probable condition during 2-digit hour beginning and 2-digit hour ending time period
BECMG 1315		BECoMinG: change expected during 2-digit hour beginning and 2-digit hour ending time period

Table of Significant Present, Forecast and Recent Weather- Grouped in categories and used in the order listed below; or as needed in TAF, No Significant Weather.

QUALIFIER

INTENSITY OR PROXIMITY

'-' Light   " no sign" Moderate   '+' Heavy

VC Vicinity: but not at aerodrome; in U.S. METAR, between 5 and 10SM of the point(s) of observation; in U.S. TAF, 5 to 10SM from center of runway complex (elsewhere within 8000m)

DESCRIPTOR

| MI | Shallow | BC | Patches | PR | Partial | TS | Thunderstorm |
| BL | Blowing | SH | Showers | DR | Drifting | FZ | Freezing |

WEATHER PHENOMENA

PRECIPITATION

DZ	Drizzle	RA	Rain	SN	Snow	SG	Snow grains
IC	Ice Crystals	PL	Ice Pellets	GR	Hail	GS	Small hail/snow pellets
UP	Unknown precipitation in automated observations						

OBSCURATION

| BR | Mist (≥5/8SM) | FG | Fog (<5/8SM) | FU | Smoke | VA | Volcanic ash |
| SA | Sand | HZ | Haze | PY | Spray | DU | Widespread dust |

OTHER

| SQ | Squall | SS | Sandstorm | DU | Duststorm | PO | Well developed dust/sand whirls |
| FC | Funnel cloud | +FC | tornado/waterspout | | | | |

- Explanations in parentheses "( )" indicate different worldwide practices.
- Ceiling is not specified; defined as the lowest broken or overcast layer, or the vertical visibility.
- NWS TAFs exclude turbulence, icing & temperature forecasts; NWS METARs exclude trend forecasts

January 1999
Aviation Weather Directorate

Department of Transportation
FEDERAL AVIATION ADMINISTRATION

CHAPTER 10
Soaring Techniques

Soaring flight, maintaining or gaining altitude rather than slowly gliding downward, is the reason most glider pilots take to the sky. After learning to stay aloft for two or more hours at a time, the urge to set off **cross country** often overcomes the soaring pilot. The goal is the same whether on a cross-country or a local flight—to use available updrafts as efficiently as possible. This involves finding and staying within the strongest part of the updraft. This chapter covers the basic soaring techniques.

In the early 1920s, soaring pilots discovered the ability to remain aloft using updrafts caused by wind deflected by the very hillside from which they had launched. This allowed time aloft to explore the air. Soon afterward, they discovered thermals in the valleys adjacent to the hills. In the 1930s, mountain waves, which were not yet well understood by meteorologists, were discovered leading pilots to make the first high altitude flights. Thermals are the most commonly used type of lift for soaring flight, since they can occur over flat terrain and in hilly country. Therefore, we will begin with thermal soaring techniques.

As a note, glider pilots refer to rising air as lift. This is not the lift generated by the wings as was discussed in Chapter 3—Aerodynamics of Flight. The use of this term may be unfortunate, but in reality it rarely causes confusion when used in the context of updrafts. This chapter refers to lift as the rising air within an updraft and sink as the descending air in downdrafts.

THERMAL SOARING

When locating and utilizing thermals for soaring flight, called thermalling, glider pilots must constantly be aware of any nearby lift indicators. Successful thermalling requires several steps: locating the thermal, entering the thermal, **centering** the thermal, and finally leaving the thermal. Keep in mind that every thermal is unique in terms of size, shape, and strength.

In the last chapter, we learned that if the air is moist enough and thermals rise high enough, cumulus clouds, or Cu (pronounced 'q') form. Glider pilots seek Cu in their developing stage, while the cloud is still being built by a thermal underneath it. The base of the Cu should be sharp and well defined. Clouds that have a fuzzy appearance are likely well past their prime and will probably have little lift left or even sink as the cloud dissipates. [Figure 10-1]

Judging which clouds have the best chance for a good thermal takes practice. On any given day, the lifetime of an individual Cu can differ from previous days, so it becomes important to observe their lifecycle on a particular day. A good looking Cu may already be dissipating by the time you reach it. Soaring pilots refer to such Cu as rapid or quick cycling, meaning they form, mature, and dissipate in a short time. The lifetime of Cu often varies during a given day as well; quick cycling Cu early in the day will often become well formed and longer lived as the day develops.

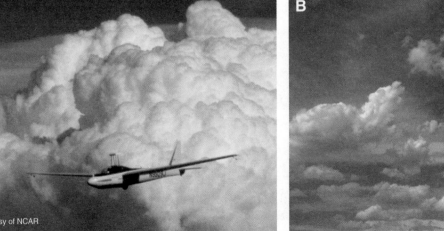

Courtesy of NCAR

Figure 10-1. Photographs of (A) mature cumulus likely producing good lift, and (B) dissipating cumulus.

Sometimes Cu cover enough of the sky that seeing the cloud tops becomes difficult. Hence, glider pilots should learn to read the bases of Cu. Generally, a dark area under the cloud base indicates a deeper cloud; therefore, a higher likelihood of a thermal underneath. Also, several thermals can feed one cloud, and it is often well worth the deviation to those darker areas under the cloud. At times, an otherwise flat cloud base under an individual Cu has wisps or tendrils of cloud hanging down from it, producing a particularly active area. Cloud hanging below the general base of a Cu indicate that that air is more moist, and hence more buoyant. Note the importance of distinguishing features under Cu that indicate potential lift from virga. Virga is rain or snow from the cloud base that is not yet reaching the ground and often signals that the friendly Cu has grown to cumulus congestus or thunderstorms. [Figure 10-2] Another indicator that one area of Cu may provide better lift is a concave region under an otherwise flat cloud base. This indicates air that is especially warm, and hence more buoyant, which means stronger lift. This can cause problems for the unwary pilot, since the lift near cloud base often dramatically increases, for instance from 400 to 1,000 (fpm). When trying to leave the strong lift in the concave area under the cloud, pilots can find themselves climbing rapidly with cloud all around—another good reason to abide by required cloud clearances.

After a thermal rises from the surface and reaches the **Convective Condensation Level (CCL)**, a cloud begins to form. At first, only a few wisps form. Then the cloud grows to a cauliflower shape. The initial wisps of Cu in an otherwise blue (cloudless) sky indicate where an active thermal is beginning to build a cloud. When crossing a blue hole (a region anywhere from a few miles to several dozen miles of cloud-free sky in an otherwise Cu-filled sky), diverting to an initial wisp of Cu is often worthwhile. On some days, when only a few thermals are reaching the CCL, the initial wisps may be the only cloud markers around. The trick is to get to the wisp when it first forms, in order to catch the thermal underneath.

Lack of Cu does not necessarily mean lack of thermals. If the air aloft is cool enough and the surface temperature warms sufficiently, thermals will form whether or not enough moisture exists for cumulus formation. These blue or dry thermals, as they are called, can be just as strong as their Cu-topped counterparts. Glider pilots can find blue thermals, without Cu markers, by gliding along until stumbling upon a thermal. With any luck, other blue thermal indicators exist, making the search less random.

One indicator of a thermal is another circling glider. Often the glint of the sun on wings is all you will see, so finding other gliders thermalling requires keeping a good lookout, which glider pilots should be doing anyway. Circling birds are also good indicators of thermal activity. Thermals tend to transport various aerosols, such as dust, upward with them. When a thermal rises to an inversion it disturbs the stable air above it and spreads out horizontally, thus depositing some of the aerosols at that level. Depending on the sun angle and the pilot's sunglasses, haze domes can indicate dry thermals. If the air contains enough moisture, haze domes often form just before the first wisp of Cu.

On blue, cloudless days, gliders and other airborne indicators are not around to mark thermals. In such cases, you must pay attention to clues on the ground. First, think about your previous flight experiences. It is worth noting where thermals have been found previously since certain areas tend to be consistent thermal sources. Remember that weather is fickle, so there is never a guarantee that a thermal will exist in the same place. In addition, if a thermal has recently formed, it will take time for the sun to reheat the area before the next thermal is triggered. Glider pilots new to a soaring location should ask the local pilots about favored spots—doing so might save the cost of a tow. Glider pilots talk about **house thermals**, which are simply thermals that seem to form over and over in the same spot or in the same area.

Stay alert for other indicators, as well. In drier climates, **dust devils** mark thermals triggering from the ground. In hilly or mountainous terrain, look for sun-facing slopes. Unless the sun is directly overhead, the heating of a sun-facing slope is more intense than that over

Figure 10-2. Photographs of (A) cumulus congestus, (B) cumulonimbus (Cb), (C) virga.

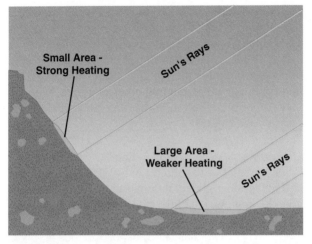

Figure 10-3. Sun's rays are concentrated in a smaller area on a hillside than on adjacent flat ground.

adjacent flat terrain because the sun's radiation strikes the slope at more nearly right angles. [Figure 10-3] Also, cooler air usually pools in low-lying areas overnight; therefore, it takes longer to heat up during the morning. Finally, slopes often tend to be drier than surrounding lowlands, and hence tend to heat better. Given the choice, it usually pays to look to the hills for thermals first.

Whether soaring over flat or hilly terrain, some experts suggest taking a mental stroll through the landscape to look for thermals. Imagine strolling along the ground where warmer areas would be found. For instance, walking from shade into an open field the air suddenly warms. A town surrounded by green fields will likely heat more than the surrounding farmland. Likewise, a yellowish harvested field will feel warmer than an adjacent wet field with lush green vegetation. Wet areas tend to use the sun's radiation to evaporate the moisture rather than heat the ground. Thus, a field with a rocky outcrop might produce better thermals. Rocky outcrops along a snowy slope will heat much more efficiently than surrounding snowfields. Though this technique works better when at lower altitudes, it can also be of use at higher altitudes in the sense of avoiding cool-looking areas, such as a valley with many lakes.

Wind also has important influences not only on thermal structure, but on thermal location as well. Strong winds at the surface and aloft often break up thermals, making them turbulent and difficult or impossible to work at all. Strong shear can break thermals apart and effectively cap their height even though the local sounding indicates that thermals should extend to higher levels. On the other hand, as discussed in Chapter 9—Soaring Weather, moderately strong winds without too much wind shear will sometimes organize thermals into long

streets, a joyous sight when they lie along a cross-country course line. [Figure 10-4]

In lighter wind conditions, consideration of thermal drift is still important, and search patterns should become "slanted." For instance, in Cu-filled skies, glider pilots need to search upwind of the cloud to find a thermal. How far upwind depends on the strength of the wind, typical thermal strength on that day, and distance below cloud base (the lower the glider, the further upwind the gliders needs to be). Add to this the fact that wind speed does not always increase at a constant rate with height, and/or the possibility that wind direction also can change dramatically with height, and the task can be challenging.

Wind speed and direction at cloud base can be estimated by watching the cloud shadows on the ground. With all the variables, it is sometimes difficult to estimate exactly where a thermal should be. Pay attention to where thermals appear to be located in relation to clouds on a given day, and use this as the search criteria for other clouds on that day. If approaching Cu from the downwind side, expect heavy sink near the cloud. Head for the darkest, best defined part of the cloud base, then continue directly into the wind. Depending on the distance below cloud base, just about the time of passing upwind of the cloud, fly right into the lift forming the cloud. If approaching the cloud from a cross-wind direction (for instance, heading north with westerly winds), try to estimate the thermal location from others encountered that day. If only reduced sink is found, there may be lift nearby, so a short leg upwind or downwind may locate the thermal.

Of course, thermals drift with the wind on blue days as well, and similar techniques are required to locate thermals using airborne or ground-based markers. For instance, if heading toward a circling glider but at a

Figure 10-4. Photograph of cloud streets.

thousand feet lower, estimate how much the thermal is tilted in the wind and head for the most likely spot upwind of the circling glider. [Figure 10-5] When in need of a thermal, pilots might consider searching on a line upwind or downwind once abeam the circling glider. This may or may not work; if the thermal is a bubble rather than a column, the pilot may be below the bubble. It is easy to waste height while searching in sink near one spot, rather than leaving and searching for a new thermal. Remember that a house thermal will likely be downwind of its typical spot on a windy day. Only practice and experience enable glider pilots to consistently find good thermals.

As a note, cool stable air can also drift with the wind. Avoid areas downwind of known stable air, such as large lakes or large irrigated regions. On a day with Cu, stable areas can be indicated by a big blue hole in an otherwise Cu-filled sky. If the area is broad enough, a detour upwind of the stabilizing feature might be in order. [Figure 10-6]

When the sky is full of Cu, occasional gliders are marking thermals, and dust devils move across the landscape, the sky becomes glider pilot heaven. If gliding in the upper part of the height band, it is best to focus on the Cu, and make choices based on the best clouds. Sometimes lower altitudes will cause glider pilots to go out of synch with the cloud. In that circumstance, use the Cu to find areas that appear generally active, but then start focusing more on ground-based indicators, like dust devils, a hillside with sunshine on it, or a circling bird. When down low, accept weaker climbs. Often the day cycles again, and hard work is rewarded.

When searching for lift, use the best speed to fly, that is, best L/D speed plus corrections for sink and any

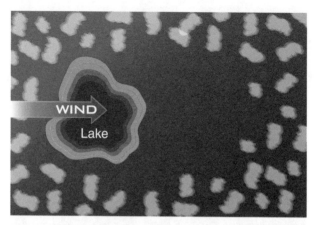

Figure 10-6. Blue hole in a field of cumulus downwind of a lake.

wind. This technique allows glider pilots to cover the most amount of ground with the available altitude.

Once a thermal has been located, enter it properly, so as not to lose it right away. The first indicator of a nearby thermal is often, oddly enough, increased sink. Next a positive G-force will be felt, which may be subtle or obvious depending on the thermal strength. The "seat-of-the-pants" indication of lift is the quickest, and is far faster than any variometer, which has a small lag. Speed should have been increased in the sink adjacent to the thermal, hence as the positive G-force increases, reduce speed to between L/D and minimum sink. Note the trend of the variometer needle (should be an upswing) or the audio variometer going from the drone to excited beeping, and at the right time in the anticipated lift, begin the turn. If everything has gone perfectly, the glider will roll into a coordinated turn, at just the right bank angle, at just the right speed, and be perfectly centered perfectly. In reality, it rarely works that well.

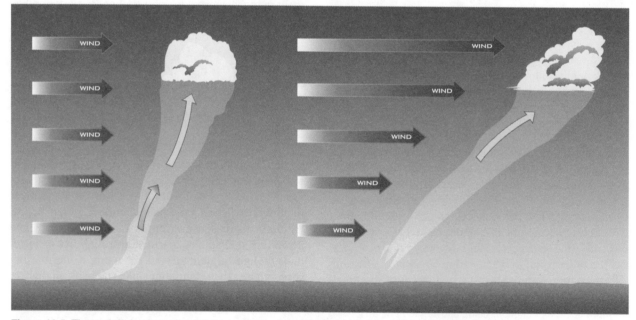

Figure 10-5. Thermal tilt in shear that (a) does not change with height, and that (b) increases with height.

Before going further, what vital step was left out of the above scenario? *CLEAR BEFORE TURNING!* The variometer is hypnotic upon entering lift, especially at somewhat low altitudes. This is exactly where pilots forget that basic primary step before any turn—looking around first. An audio variometer helps avoid this.

To help decide which way to turn, determine which wing is trying to be lifted. For instance, when entering the thermal and the glider is gently banking to the right, *CLEAR LEFT,* then turn left. A glider on its own tends to fly away from thermals. [Figure 10-7] As the glider flies into the first thermal, but slightly off center, the stronger lift in the center of the thermal banks the glider right, away from the thermal. It then encounters the next thermal with the right wing toward the center and is banked away from lift to the left, and so on. Avoid letting thermals bank the glider even slightly. Sometimes the thermal-induced bank is subtle, so be light on the controls and sensitive to the air activity. At other times there is no indication on one wing or another. In this case, take a guess, *CLEAR,* then turn. As a note, new soaring pilots often get in the habit of turning in a favorite direction, to the extreme of not being able to fly reasonable circles in the other direction. If this happens, make an effort to thermal in the other direction half the time—being proficient in either direction is important, especially when thermalling with traffic.

Optimum climb is achieved when proper bank angle and speed are used after entering a thermal. The shallowest possible bank angle at minimum sink speed is

ideal. Thermal size and associated turbulence usually do not allow this. Large-size, smooth, and well-behaved thermals can be the exception in some parts of the country. Consider first the bank angle. The glider's sink rate increases as the bank angle increases. However, the sink rate begins to increase more rapidly beyond about a 45° bank angle. Thus, a 40° compared to a 30° bank angle may increase the sink rate less than the gain achieved from circling in the stronger lift near the center of the thermal. As with everything else, this takes practice, and the exact bank angle used will depend on the typical thermal, or even a specific thermal, on a given day. Normally bank angles in excess of 50° are not needed, but exceptions always exist. It may be necessary, for instance, to use banks of 60° or so to stay in the best lift. Thermals tend to be smaller at lower levels and expand in size as they rise higher. Therefore, a steeper bank angle is required at lower altitudes, and shallower bank angles can often be used while climbing higher. Remain flexible with techniques throughout the flight.

If turbulence is light and the thermal is well-formed, use the minimum sink speed for the given bank angle. This should optimize the climb because the glider's sink rate is at its lowest, and the turn radius is smaller. As an example, for a 30° bank angle, letting the speed increase from 45 to 50 knots increases the diameter of the circle by about 100 feet. In some instances, this can make the difference between climbing or not. Some gliders can be safely flown several knots below minimum sink speed. Even though the turn radius is smaller, the increased sink rate may offset any gain achieved by being closer to strong lift near the thermal center.

There are two other reasons to avoid thermalling speeds that are too slow: the risk of a stall and lack of controllability. Distractions while thermalling can increase the risk of an inadvertent stall and include, but are not limited to: studying the cloud above or the ground below (for wind drift, etc.), quickly changing bank angles without remaining coordinated while centering, thermal turbulence, or other gliders in the thermal. Stall recovery should be second nature, so that if the signs of an imminent stall appear while thermalling, recovery is instinctive. Depending on the stall characteristics of the particular glider or in turbulent thermals, a spin entry is always possible. Glider pilots should carefully monitor speed and nose attitude at lower altitudes. Regardless of altitude, when in a thermal with other gliders below, maintain increased awareness of speed control and avoid any stall/spin scenario. Controllability is a second, though related, reason for using a thermalling speed greater than minimum sink. The bank angle may justify a slow speed, but turbulence in the thermal may make it difficult or impossible to maintain the desired quick responsiveness, especially in aileron control, in

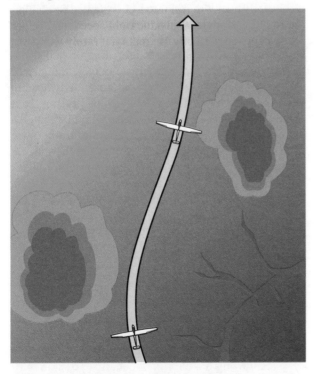

Figure 10-7. Effect of glider being allowed to bank on its own when encountering thermals.

order to properly remain in the best lift. Using sufficient speed will ensure that the pilot, and not the thermal turbulence, is controlling the glider.

Soaring pilots' opinions differ regarding how long to wait after encountering lift and before rolling into the thermal. Some pilots advocate flying straight until the lift has peaked. Then, they start turning, hopefully back into stronger lift. It is imperative not to wait too long after the first indication that the thermal is decreasing for this maneuver. Other pilots favor rolling into the thermal before lift peaks, thus avoiding the possibility of losing the thermal by waiting too long. Turning into the lift too quickly will cause the glider to fly back out into sink. There is no one right way; the choice depends on personal preference and the conditions on a given day. Timing is everything and practice is key.

Usually upon entering a thermal, the glider is in lift for part of the circle and sink for the other part. It is rare to roll into a thermal and immediately be perfectly centered. The goal of centering the thermal is to determine where the best lift is and move the glider into it for the most consistent climb. One centering technique is known as the "270° correction." [Figure 10-8] In this case, the pilot rolls into a thermal and almost immediately encounters sink, an indication of turning the wrong way. Complete a 270° turn, straighten out for a few seconds, and if lift is encountered again, turn back into it in the same direction. Avoid reversing the direction of turn. The distance flown while reversing turns is more than seems possible and can lead away from the lift completely. [Figure 10-9]

Figure 10-9. Possible loss of thermal while trying to reverse directions of circle.

Often stronger lift exists on one side of the thermal than on the other, or perhaps the thermal is small enough that lift exists on one side and sink on the other, thereby preventing a climb. There are several techniques and variations to centering. One method involves paying close attention to where the thermal is strongest, for instance, toward the northeast or toward some feature on the ground. To help judge this, note what is under the high wing when in the best lift. On the next turn, adjust the circle by either straightening or shallowing the turn toward the stronger lift. Anticipate things a bit and begin rolling out about 30° before actually heading towards the strongest part. This allows rolling back toward the strongest part of the thermal rather than flying through the strongest lift and again turning away from the thermal center. Gusts within the thermal can cause airspeed indicator variations; therefore, avoid "chasing the ASI." Paying attention to the nose attitude helps pilots keep their focus outside the cockpit. How long a glider remains shallow or straight depends on the size of the thermal. [Figure 10-10]

Other variations include the following. [Figure 10-11]

1.   Shallow the turn slightly (by maybe 5° or 10°) when encountering the weaker lift, then as stronger lift is encountered again (feel the positive g, variometer swings up, audio variometer starts to beep) resume the original bank angle. If shallowing the turn too much, it is possible to fly completely away from the lift.

Figure 10-8. The 270° centering correction.

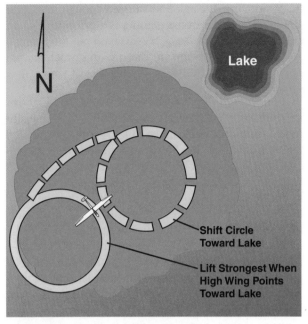

Figure 10-10. Centering by shifting the circle turn toward stronger lift.

2. Straighten or shallow the turn for a few seconds 60° after encountering the weakest lifts or worst sink indicated by the variometer. This allows for the lag in the variometer since the actual worst sink occurred a couple of seconds earlier than indicated. Resume the original bank angle.

3. Straighten or shallow the turn for a few seconds when the stronger seat-of-the-pants surge is felt. Then resume the original bank. Verify with the variometer trend (needle or audio).

For the new glider pilots, it is best to become proficient using one of the above methods first, and then experi-

ment with other methods. As an additional note, thermals often deviate markedly from the conceptual model of concentric gradients of lift increasing evenly toward the center. For instance, it sometimes feels as if two (or more) nearby thermal centers exist, making centering difficult. Glider pilots must be willing to constantly adjust, and re-center the thermal to maintain the best climb.

In addition to helping pilots locate lift, other gliders can help pilots center a thermal as well. If a nearby glider seems to be climbing better, adjust the turn to fly within the same circle. Similarly, if a bird is soaring close by, it is usually worth turning toward the soaring bird. Along with the thrill of soaring with a hawk or eagle, it usually leads to a better climb.

Collision avoidance is of primary importance when thermalling with other gliders. The first rule calls for all gliders in a particular thermal to circle in the same direction. The first glider in a thermal establishes the direction of turn and all other gliders joining the thermal should turn in the same direction. Ideally, two gliders in a thermal at the same height or nearly so should position themselves across from each other so they can best maintain visual contact. [Figure 10-12] When entering a thermal, strive to do so in a way that will not interfere with gliders already in the thermal, and above all, in a manner that will not cause a hazard to other gliders. An example, of a dangerous entry, is pulling up to bleed off excess speed in the middle of a crowded thermal. A far safer technique is to bleed off speed before reaching the thermal and joining the thermal at a "normal" thermalling speed. Collision avoidance, not optimum aerodynamic efficiency, is the priority when thermalling with other gliders. Announcing to the other

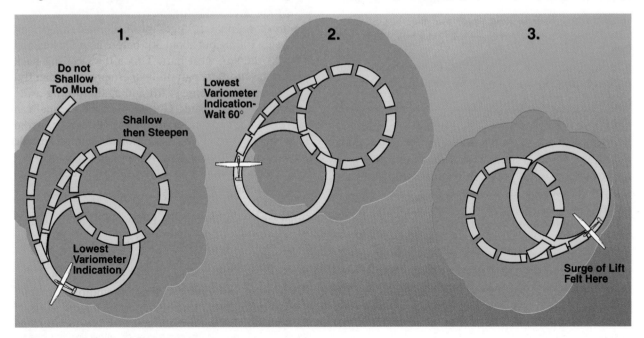

Figure 10-11. Other centering corrections.

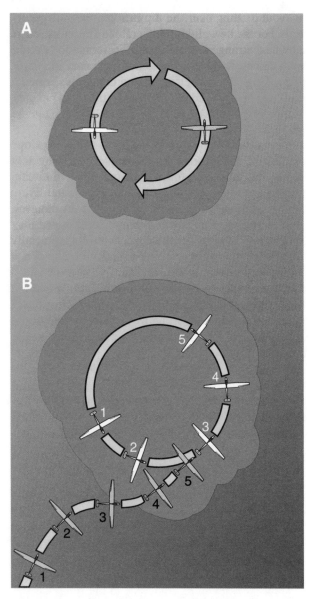

Figure 10-12. Proper positioning with two gliders at the same altitude. Numbers represent each glider's position at that time.

fic positioning. It cannot be stressed enough that collision avoidance when thermalling is a priority! Mid-air collisions can sometimes be survived but only with a great deal of luck. Unsafe thermalling practices not only endangers your own safety but that of your fellow glider pilots. [Figure 10-13]

Leaving a thermal properly can also save you some altitude. While circling, scan the full 360° of sky with each thermalling turn. This first allows the pilot to continually check for other traffic in the vicinity. Second, it helps the pilot analyze the sky in all directions in order to decide where to go for the next climb. It is better to decide where to go next while still in lift rather than losing altitude in sink after leaving a thermal. Exactly when to leave depends on the goals for the climb—whether the desire is to maximize altitude for a long glide or leave when lift weakens in order to maximize time on a cross-country flight. In either case, be ready to increase speed to penetrate the sink often found on the edge of the thermal, and leave the thermal in a manner that will not hinder or endanger other gliders.

The preceding pages describe techniques for locating thermals, as well as entering, centering, and leaving thermals. Exceptions to normal or typical thermals are numerous. For instance, instead of stronger sink at the edge of a thermal, weak lift sometimes continues for a distance after leaving a thermal. Glider pilots should be quick to adapt to whatever the air has to offer at the

glider(s) on the radio when entering the thermal enhances collision avoidance. [Figure 10-12]

Different types of gliders in the same thermal may have different minimum sink speeds, and it may be difficult to remain directly across from another glider in a thermal. Avoid putting yourself in a situation where you cannot see the other glider, or the other glider cannot see you. Radio communication is helpful. Too much talking clogs the frequency, and may make it impossible for a pilot to broadcast an important message. Do not fly directly above or below another glider in a thermal since differences in performance, or even minor changes in speed can lead to larger than expected altitude changes. If you lose sight of another glider in a thermal and cannot establish position via a radio call, leave the thermal. After 10 or 20 seconds, come back around to rejoin the thermal, hopefully with better traf-

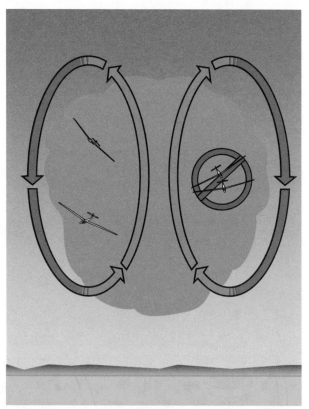

Figure 10-13. When thermalling, avoid flying in another glider's blind spot, or directly above or below another glider.

time. Just as the mechanics of simply flying the glider become second nature with practice, so do thermalling techniques. Expect to land early because anticipated lift was not there on occasion—it is part of the learning curve.

If **thermal waves** are suspected, climb in the thermal near cloud base, then head toward the upwind side of the Cu. Often, only very weak lift, barely enough to climb at all, is found in smooth air upwind of the cloud. Once above cloud base and upwind of the Cu, climb rates of a few hundred fpm can be found. Climbs can be made by flying back and forth upwind of an individual Cu, or by flying along cloud streets if they exist. If no clouds are present, but waves are suspected, climb to the top of the thermal and penetrate upwind in search of smooth, weak lift. Without visual clues, thermal waves are more difficult to work. Thermal waves are most often stumbled upon as a pleasant surprise when their presence is furthest from the pilot's mind.

RIDGE AND SLOPE SOARING

Efficient slope soaring (also called ridge soaring) is fairly easy; simply fly in the updraft along the upwind side of the ridge (see Figure 9-20). The horizontal distance from the ridge will vary with height above the ridge, since the best lift zone tilts upwind with height above the ridge. Even though the idea is simple, traps exist for both new and expert glider pilots. Obtain instruction when first learning to slope soar.

Avoid approaching from the upwind side perpendicularly to the ridge. Instead, approach the ridge at a shallower angle, so that a quick egress away from the ridge is possible should lift not be contacted. While flying along the ridge, a crab angle is necessary to avoid drifting too close to the ridge or, if gliding above the ridge,

to avoid drifting over the top into the lee-side downdraft. For the new glider pilot, crabbing along the ridge may be a strange sensation, and it is easy to become uncoordinated while trying to point the nose along the ridge. This is both inefficient and dangerous, since it leads to a skid toward the ridge. [Figure 10-14]

In theory, to obtain the best climb, it is best to slope soar at minimum sink speed. However, flying that slowly may be unwise for two reasons. First, minimum sink speed is relatively close to stall speed, and flying close to stall speed near terrain has obvious dangers. Second, maneuverability at minimum sink speed may be inadequate for proper control near terrain, especially if the wind is gusty and/or thermals are present. When gliding at or below ridge top height, fly faster than minimum sink speed—how much faster depends on the glider, terrain, and turbulence. When the glider is at least several hundred feet above the ridge and shifting upwind away from it in the best lift zone, reduce speed. If in doubt, fly faster!

Slope soaring comes with several procedures to enable safe flying and to allow many gliders on the same ridge. The rules are:

1.   make all turns away from the ridge;

2.   do not fly directly above or below another glider;

3.   pass another glider on the ridge side, anticipating that the other pilot will make a turn away from the ridge; and

4.   the glider with its right side to the ridge has the right of way. [Figure 10-15]

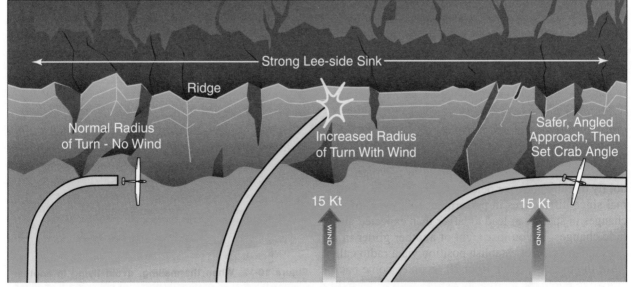

Figure 10-14. Flying with a wind increases the turn radius over the ground, so approach the ridge at a shallow angle.

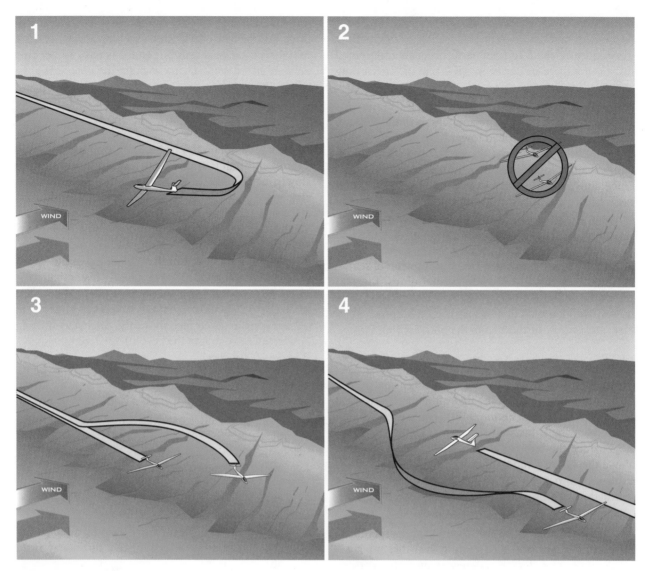

Figure 10-15. Ridge rules.

These procedures deserve some comment.

Procedure #1: A turn toward the ridge is dangerous, even if gliding seemingly well away from the ridge. The ground speed on the downwind portion of the turn will be difficult to judge properly, and striking the ridge is a serious threat. Even if above the ridge, it will be easy to finish the turn downwind of the ridge in heavy sink.

Procedure #2: Gliders spaced closely together in the vertical are in each other's blind spots. A slight change in climb-rate between the gliders can lead to a collision.

Procedure #3: Sometimes the glider to be passed is so close to the ridge that there is inadequate space to pass between the glider and the ridge. In that case, either turn back in the other direction (away from the ridge) if traffic permits, or fly upwind away from the ridge and rejoin the slope lift as traffic allows. When soaring outside of the United States, be aware that this rule may differ.

Procedure #4: Federal Aviation Regulations call for aircraft approaching head-on to both give way to the right. A glider with the ridge to the right may not have room to move in that direction. The glider with its left side to the ridge should give way. When piloting the glider with its right side to the ridge, make sure the approaching glider sees you and is giving way in plenty of time. In general, gliders approaching head-on are difficult to see; therefore, extra vigilance is needed to avoid collisions while slope soaring.

If the wind is at an angle to the ridge, bowls or spurs extending from the main ridge can create better lift on the upwind side and sink on the downwind side. If at or near the height of the ridge, it may be necessary to detour around the spur to avoid the sink, then drift back into the bowl to take advantage of the better lift. After passing such a spur, do not make abrupt turns toward the ridge (Rule #1), and as always, consider what the general flow of traffic is doing. If soaring hundreds of feet above a spur, it may be possible to fly over it and increase speed in any sink. This requires caution, since a thermal in the upwind bowl, or even an imperceptible increase in the wind, can cause greater than anticipated sink on the downwind side. Always have an escape route or, if in any doubt, detour around. [Figure 10-16]

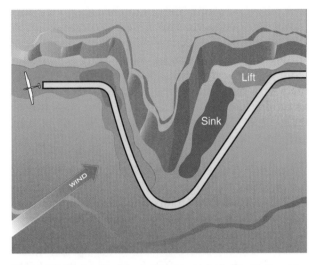

Figure 10-16. Avoid sink on the downwind side of spurs by detouring around them.

It is not uncommon for thermals to exist with slope lift. Indeed, slope soaring can often be used as a "save" when thermals have temporarily shut down. Working thermals from slope lift requires special techniques. When a thermal is encountered along the ridge, a series of S-turns can be made into the wind. Drift back to the thermal after each turn if needed and, of course, never continue the turn to the point that the glider is turning toward the ridge. Speed is also important, since it is easy to encounter strong sink on the sides of the thermal. It is very likely that staying in thermal lift through the entire S-turn is not possible. The maneuver takes practice, but when done properly, a rapid climb in the thermal can be made well above the ridge crest, where thermalling turns can begin. Even when well above the ridge, caution is needed to ensure the climb is not too slow as to drift into the lee-side sink. Before trying S-turns make sure it will not interfere with other traffic along the ridge. [Figure 10-17]

A second technique for catching thermals when slope soaring is to head upwind away from the ridge. This works best when Cu mark potential thermals and aide timing. If no thermal is found, the pilot should cut the search short while still high enough to dash back downwind to the safety of the slope lift. [Figure 10-18]

As a final note, caution is also needed to avoid obstructions when slope soaring. These primarily include wires, cables, and power lines, all of which are very

Figure 10-17. One technique for catching a thermal from ridge lift.

difficult to see. Aeronautical charts show high-tension towers that, of course, have many wires between them. Soaring pilots familiar with the area should be able to provide useful information on any problems with the local ridge.

Figure 10-18. Catching a thermal by flying upwind away from the slope lift.

WAVE SOARING

Almost all high-altitude flights are made using mountain lee waves. As covered in Chapter 9—Soaring Weather, lee wave systems can contain tremendous turbulence in the rotor, while the wave flow itself is usually unbelievably smooth. In more recent years, the use of lee waves for cross-country soaring has lead to flights exceeding 1,500 miles, with average speeds over 100 mph. [Figure 10-19]

PREFLIGHT PREPARATION

The amount of preflight preparation depends on the height potential of the wave itself. Let us assume that the pilot is planning a flight above 18,000 feet MSL during the winter. (Pilots planning wave flights to much lower altitudes can reduce the list of preparation items accordingly.)

For flights above 14,000 feet MSL, the CFRs state that required crewmembers must use supplemental oxygen. Pilots must be aware of their own physiology; however, it may be wise to use oxygen at altitudes well below 14,000 feet MSL. In addition, signs of hypoxia should be known. The U.S. Air Force in cooperation with the FAA provides a one-day, high-altitude orientation and chamber ride for civilian pilots. The experience is invaluable for any pilot contemplating high altitude soaring and is even required by many clubs and operations as a prerequisite. Before any wave flight, it is important to be thoroughly familiar with the specific oxygen system that will be used, as well as its adequacy for potential heights. The dangers of oxygen deprivation should not be taken lightly. At around 20,000 feet MSL pilots might have only 10 minutes of "useful consciousness." By 30,000 feet MSL, the timeframe for "useful consciousness" decreases to one minute or less! For planned flights above 25,000 feet MSL, an emergency oxygen back-up or **bailout bottle** should be carried.

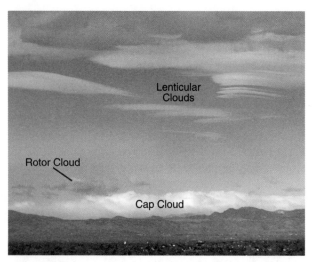

Figure 10-19. Rotor and cap clouds with lenticulars above.

Proper clothing is a must since temperatures of –30° to –60°C may be encountered at altitude. Proper preparation for the cold is especially difficult since temperatures on the ground are often pleasant on wave soaring days. Sunshine through the canopy keeps the upper body amazingly warm for a time, but shaded legs and feet quickly become cold. Frostbite is a very real threat. After an hour or two at such temperatures, even the upper body can become quite cold. Layered, loose-fitting clothing aides in insulating body heat. Either wool gloves or light fitting gloves with mittens over them work best for the hands. Mittens make tasks such as turning radio knobs difficult. For the feet, two or three pair of socks (inner silk, outer wool) with an insulated boot is recommended.

Within the continental United States, Class A airspace lies between 18,000 and 60,000 feet MSL (FL 180 to FL 600). Generally, flights in Class A must be conducted under Instrument Flight Rules (IFR). However, several clubs and glider operations have established so-called "Wave Windows". These are special areas, arranged in agreement with Air Traffic Control (ATC), in which gliders are allowed to operate above 18,000 feet MSL under VFR operations. Wave windows have very specific boundaries. Thus, to maintain this privilege, it is imperative to stay within the designated window. On any given day, the wave window may be opened to a specific altitude during times specified by ATC. Each wave window has its own set of procedures agreed upon with ATC. All glider pilots should become familiar with the procedures and required radio frequencies.

True Airspeed (TAS) becomes a consideration at higher altitudes. To avoid the possibility of flutter, some gliders require a reduced indicated never-exceed speed as a function of altitude. For instance, at sea level the POH for one common two-seat glider, the V_{NE}, is 135 knots. However, at 19,000 feet MSL it is only 109 knots. Study the glider's POH carefully for any limitations on indicated airspeeds.

There is always the possibility of not contacting the wave. Sink on the downside of a lee wave can be high—2,000 fpm or more. In addition, missing the wave often means a trip back through the turbulent rotor. The workload and stress levels in either case can be high. To reduce the workload, it is a good idea to have minimum return altitudes from several locations calculated ahead of time. In addition, plan for some worse case scenarios. For instance, consider what off-field landing options are available if the planned minimum return altitude proves inadequate.

A normal preflight of the glider should be performed. In addition, check the lubricant that has been used on control fittings. Some lubricants can become very stiff when cold. Also, check for water from melting snow or a recent rain in the spoilers or dive brakes. Freezing water in the spoilers or drive brakes at altitude can make them difficult to open. Checking the spoilers or dive brakes occasionally during a high climb helps avoid this problem. A freshly charged battery is recommended, since cold temperatures can reduce battery effectiveness. Check the radio and accessory equipment, such as a microphone in the oxygen mask even if it is not generally used. As mentioned, the oxygen system is vital. Other specific items to check depend on the system being used. A checklist such as PRICE is often helpful. The acronym PRICE stands for:

- Pressure—Check pressure in the oxygen bottle.

- Regulator—Check at all settings.

- Indicator—Check flow meters or flow-indicator blinkers.

- Connections—Check for solid connections, possible leaks, cracks in hoses, etc.

- Emergency—Check that the system is full and properly connected.

A briefing with the towpilot is even more important before a wave tow. Routes, minimum altitudes, rotor avoidance (if possible), anticipated tow altitude, and eventualities should the rotor become too severe, are among topics that are best discussed on the ground prior to flight.

After all preparations are complete, it is time to get in the glider. Some pilots may be using a parachute for the first time on wave flights, so make sure you are familiar with its proper fitting and use. The parachute fits on top of clothing that is much bulkier than for normal soaring, so the cockpit can suddenly seem quite cramped. It will take several minutes to get settled and organized. Make sure radio and oxygen are easily accessible. If possible, the oxygen mask should be in place, since the climb in the wave can be very rapid. At the very least, the mask should be set up so that it is ready for use in a few seconds. All other gear (e.g., mittens, microphone, maps, barograph, etc.) should be securely stowed in anticipation of the rotor. Check for full, free rudder movement, since footwear is likely larger than what you normally use. In addition, given the bulky cold-weather clothing, check to make sure the canopy clearance is adequate. The pilot's head has broken canopies in rotor turbulence so seat and shoulder belts should be tightly secured. This may be difficult to achieve with the extra clothing and accessories, but take the time to make sure everything is secure. There will not be time to attend to such matters once the rotor is encountered.

GETTING INTO THE WAVE

There are two possibilities for getting into the wave: soaring into it or being towed directly into it. Three main wave entries while soaring are: thermalling into the wave, climbing the rotor, and transitioning into the wave from slope soaring.

At times, an unstable layer at levels below the mountaintop is capped by a strong, stable layer. If other conditions are favorable, the overlying stable layer may support lee waves. On these days, it is sometimes possible to largely avoid the rotor and thermal into the wave. Whether lee waves are suspected or not, near the thermal top the air may become turbulent. At this point, attempt a penetration upwind into smooth wave lift. A line of cumulus downwind of and aligned parallel to the ridge or mountain range is a clue that waves may be present. [Figure 10-20]

Figure 10-20. Thermalling into wave.

Another possibility is to tow into the upside of the rotor, then climb the rotor into the wave. This can be rough, difficult, and prone to failure. The technique is to find a part of the rotor that is going up and try to stay in it. The rotor lift is usually stationary over the ground. Either "figure-8" in the rotor lift to avoid drifting downwind, fly several circles with an occasional straight leg, or fly straight into the wind for several seconds until lift diminishes. Then circle to reposition in the lift. Which choice works depends on the size of the lift and the wind strength. Since rotors have rapidly changing regions of very turbulent lift and sink, simple airspeed and bank angle control can become difficult. This wave-entry technique is not for new pilots.

Depending on the topography near the soaring site, it may be possible to transition from slope lift into a lee wave that is created by upwind topography as shown in Figure 9-27. In this case, climb as high as possible in slope lift, then penetrate upwind into the lee wave. When the lee waves are in phase with the topography, it is often possible to climb from slope to wave lift without the rotor. At times, the glider pilot may not realize wave has been encountered until they find lift steadily increasing as they climb from the ridge. Climbing in slope lift and then turning downwind to encounter possible lee waves produced downwind of the ridge is generally not recommended. Even with a tailwind, the lee-side sink can put the glider on the ground before the wave is contacted.

Towing into the wave can be accomplished by either towing ahead of the rotor or through the rotor. Avoiding the rotor completely will generally increase the towpilot's willingness to perform future wave tows. If possible, tow around the rotor and then directly into the wave lift. This may be feasible if the soaring site is located near one end of the wave-producing ridge or mountain range. A detour around the rotor may require more time on tow, but it's well worth the diversion. [Figure 10-21]

Often, a detour around the rotor is not possible and a tow directly through the rotor is the only route to the wave. The rotor turbulence is, on rare occasion, only light. However, moderate to severe turbulence is usually encountered. The nature of rotor turbulence differs from turbulent thermal days, with sharp, chaotic horizontal and vertical gusts along with rapid accelerations and decelerations. At times, the rotor can become so rough that even experienced pilots may elect to remain on the ground. Any pilot inexperienced in flying through rotors should obtain instruction before attempting a tow through rotor.

When towing through a rotor, being out of position is normal. Glider pilots must maintain position horizontally and vertical as best they can. Pilots should also be

aware that an immediate release may be necessary at any time if turbulence becomes too violent. Slack-producing situations are common, due to a rapid deceleration of the towplane. The glider pilot must react quickly to slack if it occurs and recognize that slack is about to occur and correct accordingly. The vertical position should be the normal high-tow. Any tow position that is lower than normal runs the risk of the slack line coming back over the glider. On the other hand, care should be taken to tow absolutely no higher than normal to avoid a forced release should the towplane suddenly drop. Gusts may also cause an excessive bank of the glider, and it may take a moment to roll back to level. Full aileron and rudder deflection, held for a few seconds, is sometimes needed.

Progress through the rotor is often indicated by noting the trend of the variometer. General down swings are replaced by general upswings, usually along with increasing turbulence. The penetration into the smooth wave lift can be quick, in a matter of few seconds, while at other times it can be more gradual. Note any lenticulars above—a position upwind of the clouds helps confirm contact with the wave. If in doubt, tow a few moments longer to be sure. Once confident about having contacted the wave lift, make the release. If heading more or less crosswind, the glider should release and fly straight or with a crab angle. If flying directly into the wind, the glider should turn a few degrees to establish a crosswind crab angle. The goal is

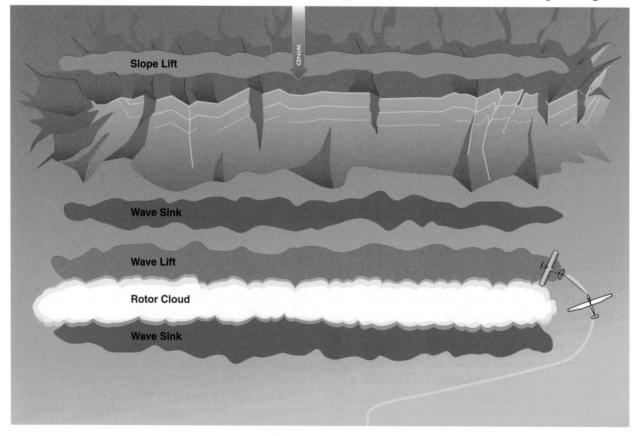

Figure 10-21. If possible, tow around the rotor directly into the wave.

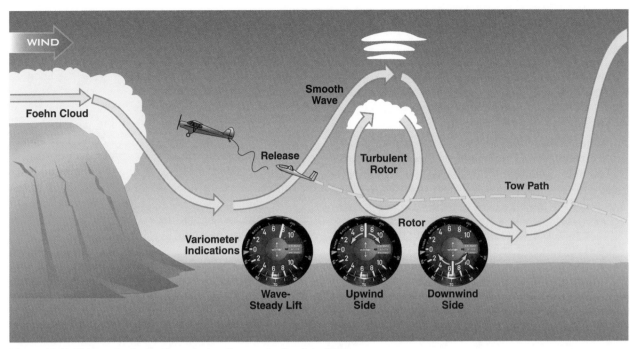

Figure 10-22. Variometer indications during the penetration into the wave.

to avoid drifting downwind and immediately lose the wave. After release, the towplane should descend and/or turn away to separate from the glider. Possible non-standard procedures need to be briefed with the towpilot before takeoff. [Figures 10-22 and 10-23]

FLYING IN THE WAVE

Once the wave has been contacted, the best techniques for utilizing the lift depends on the extent of the lift (especially in the direction along the ridge or mountain range producing the wave) and the strength of the wind. The lift may initially be weak. In such circumstances, be patient and stay with the initial slow climb. Patience is usually rewarded with better lift as the climb contin-

ues. At other times, the variometer may be pegged at 1,000 fpm directly after release from tow.

If the wind is strong enough (40 knots or more), find the strongest portion of the wave and point into the wind, and adjust speed so that the glider remains in the strong lift. The best lift will be found along the upwind side of the rotor cloud or just upwind of any lenticulars. In the best-case scenario, the required speed will be close to the glider's minimum sink speed. In quite strong winds, it may be necessary to fly faster than minimum sink to maintain position in the best lift. Under those conditions, flying slower will allow the glider to drift downwind (fly backwards over the ground!) and into the down side of the wave. This can be a costly mistake since it will be difficult to penetrate

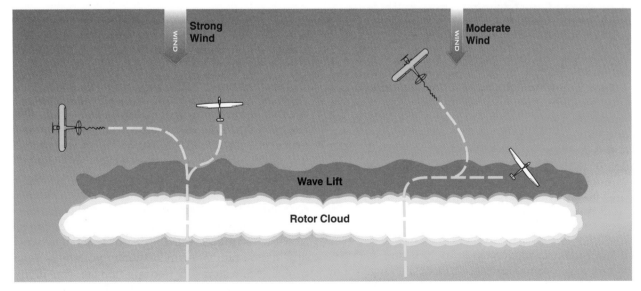

Figure 10-23. Possible release and separation on a wave tow.

back into the strong headwind. When the lift is strong, it is easy to drift downwind while climbing into stronger winds aloft, so it pays to be attentive to the position relative to rotor clouds or lenticulars. If no clouds exist, special attention is needed to judge wind drift by finding nearby ground references. It may be necessary to increase speed with altitude to maintain position in the best lift. Often the wind is strong, but not quite strong enough for the glider to remain stationary over the ground, so that the glider slowly moves upwind out of the best lift. If this occurs, turn slightly from a direct upwind heading, drift slowly downwind into better lift, and turn back into the wind before drifting too far. [Figure 10-24]

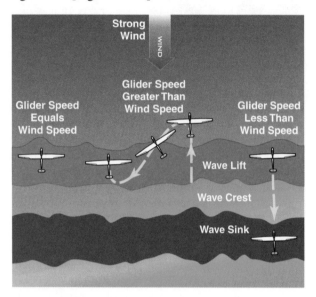

Figure 10-24. Catching a thermal by flying upwind away from the slope lift.

Oftentimes, the wave lift is not perfectly stationary over the ground since small changes in wind speed and/or stability can alter the wavelength of the lee wave within minutes. If lift begins to decrease while climbing in the wave, one of these things has occurred: the glider is nearing the top of the wave, the glider has moved out of the best lift, or the wavelength of the lee wave has changed. In any case, it is time to explore the area for better lift, and it is best to search upwind first. Searching upwind first allows the pilot to drift downwind back into the up part of the wave if he or she is wrong. Searching downwind first can make it difficult or impossible to contact the lift again if sink on the downside of the wave is encountered. In addition, caution is needed to avoid exceeding the glider's maneuvering speed or rough-air redline, since a penetration from the down side of the wave may put the glider back in the rotor. [Figure 10-25]

If the winds are moderate (20 to 40 knots), and the wave extends along the ridge or mountain range for a few miles, it is best to fly back and forth along the wave

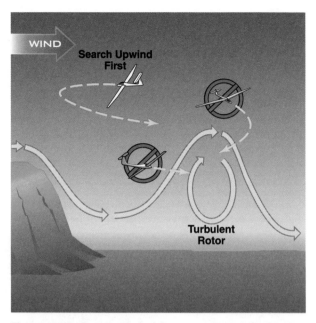

Figure 10-25. Search upwind first to avoid sink behind the wave crest or the rotor.

lift while crabbing into the wind. This technique is similar to slope soaring, using the rotor cloud or lenticular as a reference. All turns should be into the wind to avoid ending up on the down side of the wave or back into the rotor. Once again, it is easy to drift downwind into sink while climbing higher and searching for better lift should be done upwind first. When making an upwind turn to change course 180°, remember that the heading change will be less, depending on the strength of the wind. Note the crab angle needed to stay in lift on the first leg, and assume that same crab angle after completing the upwind turn. This will prevent the glider from drifting too far downwind upon completing the upwind turn. With no cloud, ground references are used to maintain the proper crab angle, and avoid drifting downwind out of the lift. While climbing higher into stronger winds, it may become possible to transition from crabbing back and forth to a stationary upwind heading. [Figure 10-26]

Weaker winds (15 to 20 knots) sometimes require different techniques. Lee waves from smaller ridges can form in relatively weak winds, on the order of only 15 knots. Wave lift from larger mountains will rapidly decrease when climbing to a height where winds aloft diminish. As long as the lift area is big enough, use a technique similar to that used in moderate winds. Near the wave top, there sometimes remains only a small area that still provides lift. In order to attain the maximum height; fly shorter "figure-8" patterns within the remaining lift. If the area of lift is so small that consistent climb is not possible, a series of circles can be flown with an occasional leg into the wind to avoid drifting too far downwind. Another possibility is an oval-shaped pattern—fly straight into the wind in lift, and as it diminishes, fly a quick 360° turn to reposi-

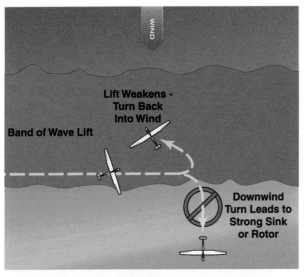

Figure 10-26. Proper crabbing to stay in lift and effects of upwind turn (correct) or downwind turn (incorrect).

tion. These last two techniques do not work as well in moderate winds, and not at all in strong winds since it is too easy to end up downwind of the lift and into heavy sink. [Figure 10-27]

In the discussion thus far, we have assumed a climb in the primary wave. It is also possible to climb in the secondary or tertiary lee wave (if they exist on a given day) and then penetrate into the next wave upwind. The success of this depends on wind strength, clouds, the intensity of sink downwind of wave crests, and the performance of the glider. Depending on the height attained in the secondary or tertiary lee wave, a trip through the rotor of the next wave upwind is a distinct possibility. Caution is needed if penetrating upwind at high speed. The transition into the downwind side of the rotor can be as abrupt as on the upwind side, so speed should be reduced at the first hint of turbulence. In any case, expect to lose surprising amounts of alti-

tude while penetrating upwind through the sinking side of the next upwind wave. [Figure 10-28]

If a quick descent is needed or desired, the sink downwind of the wave crest can be used. Sink can easily be twice as strong as lift encountered upwind of the crest. Eventual descent into downwind rotor is also likely. Sometimes the space between a rotor cloud and overlying lenticulars is inadequate and a transition downwind cannot be accomplished safely. In this case, a crosswind detour may be possible if the wave is produced by a relatively short ridge or mountain range. If clouds negate a downwind or crosswind departure from the wave, a descent on the upwind side of the wave crest will be needed. Spoilers or dive brakes may be used to descend through the updraft, followed by a transition under the rotor cloud and through the rotor. A descent can be achieved by moving upwind of a very strong wave lift if spoilers or dive brakes alone do not allow a quick enough descent. A trip back through the rotor is at best unpleasant. At worst it can be dangerous if the transition back into the rotor is done with too much speed. In addition, strong wave lift and lift on the upwind side of the rotor may make it difficult to stay out of the rotor cloud. This wave descent requires a

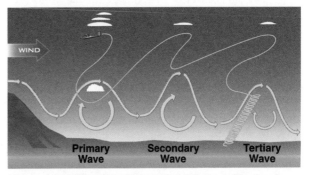

Figure 10-28. Possible flight path while transitioning from the tertiary into the secondary and then into the primary.

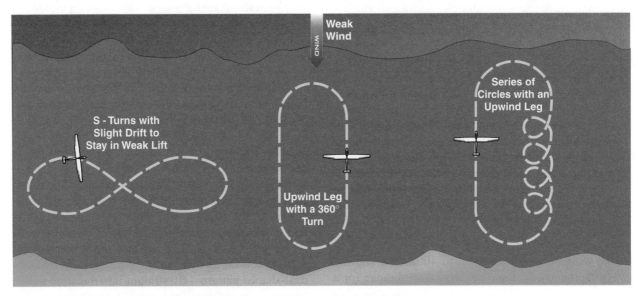

Figure 10-27. Techniques for working lift near the top of the wave in weak winds.

good deal of caution and emphasizes the importance of an exit strategy before climbing too high in the wave, keeping in mind that conditions and clouds can rapidly evolve during the climb.

Some of the dangers and precautions associated with wave soaring have already been mentioned. Those and others are summarized below.

- If any signs of hypoxia appear, check the oxygen system and immediately begin a descent to lower altitudes below which oxygen is not needed. Do not delay!

- Eventually, regardless of how warmly you are dressed, it will become cold at altitude. Descend well before it becomes uncomfortably cold.

- Rotor turbulence can be severe or extreme. Caution is needed on tow and when transitioning from smooth wave flow (lift or sink) to rotor. Rotors near the landing area can cause strong shifting surface winds—20 or 30 knot. Wind shifts up to 180° sometimes occur in less than a minute at the surface under rotors.

- Warm, moist exhaled air can cause frost on the canopy, restricting vision. Opening air vents may alleviate the problem or prolong frost formation. Clear-vision panels may also be installed. If frosting cannot be controlled, descend before frost becomes a hazard.

- In "wet" waves, those associated with a great deal of cloud, beware of the gaps closing beneath the glider. If trapped above cloud, a benign spiral mode is an option, but only if this mode has been previously explored and found stable for your glider.

- Know the time of actual sunset. At legal sunset, bright sunshine is still found at 25,000 feet while the ground below is already quite dark. Even at an average 1,000 fpm descent it takes 20 minutes to lose 20,000 feet.

SOARING CONVERGENCE ZONES
Convergence zones are most easily spotted when cumulus clouds are present. They appear as a single straight or curved cloud street, sometimes well defined and sometimes not, for instance when a wind field as in Figure 9-30(B) causes the convergence. The edge of a field of cumulus can mark convergence between a mesoscale air mass that is relatively moist and/or unstable from one that is much drier and/or more stable. Often the cumulus along convergence lines have a base lower on one side than the other, similar to Figure 9-33.

With no cloud present, a convergence zone is sometimes marked by a difference in visibility across it,

which may be subtle or distinct. When there are no clues in the sky itself, there may be some on the ground. If lakes are nearby, look for wind differences on lakes a few miles apart. A lake showing a wind direction different than the ambient flow for the day may be a clue. Wind direction shown by smoke can also be an important indicator. A few dust devils, or better, a short line of them, may indicate the presence of ordinary thermals vs. those triggered by convergence. Spotting the subtle clues takes practice and good observational skills, and is often the reason a few pilots are still soaring while others are already on the ground.

The best soaring technique for this type of lift depends on the nature of the convergence zone itself. For instance, a sea-breeze front may be well-defined and marked by "curtain" clouds, in which case the pilot can fly straight along the line in fairly steady lift. A weaker convergence line often produces more lift than sink, in which case the pilot must fly slower in lift and faster in sink. An even weaker convergence line may just act as focus for more-frequent thermals, in which case normal thermal techniques are used along the convergence line. Some combination of straight legs along the line with an occasional stop to thermal is often used.

Convergence zone lift can at times be somewhat turbulent, especially if air from different sources is mixing, such as along a sea-breeze front. The general roughness may be the only clue of being along some sort of convergence line. There can also be narrow and rough (but strong) thermals within the convergence line. Work these areas like any other difficult thermals—steeper bank angles and more speed for maneuverability.

COMBINED SOURCES OF UPDRAFTS
Finally, lift sources have been categorized into four types: thermal, slope, wave, and convergence. Often, more than one type of lift exists at the same time. For instance, thermals with slope lift, thermalling into a wave, convergence zones enhancing thermals, thermal waves, and wave soaring from slope lift were all considered. In mountainous terrain, it is possible for all four lift types to exist on a single day. The glider pilot needs to remain mentally nimble to take advantage of various pieces of rising air during the flight.

Nature does not know that it must only produce rising air based on these four lift categories. Sources of lift that do not fit one of the four lift types discussed probably exist. For instance, there have been a few reports of pilots soaring in travelling waves, the source of which was not known. At some soaring sites it is sometimes difficult to classify the type of lift. This should not be a problem—simply work the mystery lift as needed, then ponder its nature after the flight.

CHAPTER 11
Cross-Country Soaring

A cross-country flight is defined as one in which the glider has flown beyond gliding distance from the local soaring site. Cross-country soaring seems simple enough in theory, but in reality, it requires a great deal more preparation and decision making than local soaring flights. Items that must be considered during cross-country flights are how good are the thermals ahead, and will they remain active? What are the landing possibilities? Which airport along the course has a runway that is favorable for the prevailing wind conditions? What effect will the headwind have on the glide? What is the best speed to fly in sink between thermals?

Flying cross-country using thermals is the basis of this chapter. A detailed description of cross-country using ridge or wave lift is beyond the scope of this chapter.

FLIGHT PREPARATION AND PLANNING
Adequate soaring skills form the basis of the pilot's preparation for cross-country soaring. Until the pilot has flown several flights in excess of two hours and can locate and utilize thermals consistently, the pilot should focus on improving those skills before attempting cross-country flights.

Any cross-country flight may end in an off-field landing, so short-field landing skills are essential. These landings should be practiced on local flights by setting up a simulated off-field landing area. Care is needed to avoid interfering with the normal flow of traffic during simulated off-field landings. The first few simulated landings should be done with an instructor, and several should be done without the use of the altimeter.

The landing area can be selected from the ground, but the best training is selecting one from the air. Landing area selection training and simulated approaches to these areas using a self-launch glider or other powered aircraft is a good investment if one is available.

Once soaring skills have been honed, pilots need to be able to find their position along a route of flight. A Sectional Aeronautical Chart, or sectional for short, is a map soaring pilots use during cross-country flights. They are updated every 6 months and contain general information, such as topography, cities, major and minor roads and highways, lakes, and other features that may stand out from the air, such as a ranch in an

otherwise featureless prairie. In addition, sectionals show the location of private and public airports, airways, restricted and warning areas, and boundaries and vertical limits of different classes of airspace. Information on airports includes field elevation, orientation and length of all paved runways, runway lighting, and radio frequencies in use. Each sectional features a comprehensive legend. A detailed description of the sectional chart is found in the *Pilot's Handbook of Aeronautical Knowledge*, FAA-H-8083-25. Figure 11-1 shows a sample sectional chart.

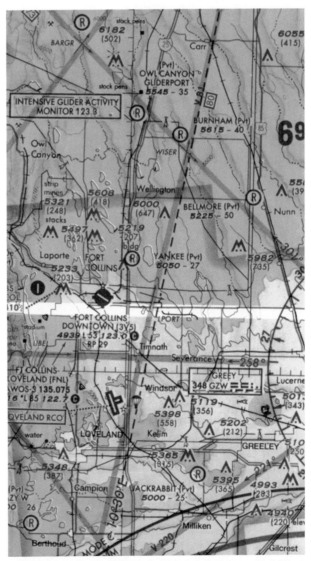

Figure 11-1. Sample area from a Sectional Aeronautical Chart.

The best place to become familiar with sectional charts is on the ground. It is instructive to fly some "virtual" cross-country flights in various directions from the local soaring site. In addition to studying the terrain (hills, mountains, large lakes) that may effect the soaring along the route, study the various lines and symbols. What airports are available on course? Do any have a control tower? Can all the numbers and symbols for each airport be identified? If not, find them on the legend. Is there Class B, C, or D airspace enroute? Are there any restricted areas? Are there airways along the flight path? Once comfortable with the sectional from ground study, it can be used on some local flights to practice locating features within a few miles of the soaring site.

Any cross-country flight may end with a landing away from the home soaring site, so pilots and crews should be prepared for the occurrence prior to flight. Sometimes an aerotow retrieve can be made if the flight terminates at an airport; however, trailer retrieval is more typical. Both the trailer and tow vehicle need a "preflight" before departing on the flight. The trailer should be roadworthy and set up for the specific glider. Stowing and towing a glider in an inappropriate trailer can lead to damage. The crew should be familiar with procedures for towing and backing a long trailer. The tow vehicle should be strong and stable enough for towing. Both radio and telephone communication options should be discussed with the retrieval crew.

Before any flight, obtain a standard briefing from the Automated Flight Service Station (AFSS). As discussed in Chapter 9—Soaring Weather, the briefer supplies general weather information for the planned route, as well as any NOTAMs, AIRMETs, or SIGMETs, winds aloft, an approaching front, or areas of likely thunderstorm activity. Depending on the weather outlook, beginners may find it useful to discuss options with more experienced cross-country pilots at their soaring site.

Many pilots have specific goals in mind for their next cross-country flight. Several options should be planned ahead based on the area and different weather scenarios. For instance, if the goal is a closed-course 300 km flight, several likely out and return or triangle courses should be laid out ahead of time, so that on the specific day, the best task can be selected based on the weather outlook. There are a number of final details that need attention on the morning of the flight, so special items should be organized and readied the day before the flight.

Lack of preparation can lead to delays, which may mean not enough of the soaring day is left to accomplish the planned flight. Even worse, poor planning

leads to hasty last minute preparation and a rush to launch—critical safety items can then be missed easily.

Inexperienced and experienced pilots alike should use checklists for various phases of the cross-country preparation in order to organize details. When properly used, checklists can help avoid oversights, such as sectionals left at home, **barograph** not turned on before take-off. Checklists also aid in making certain that safety of flight items are checked or accomplished, such as all assembly items are accomplished, and checked, oxygen turned on, drinking water in the glider, etc. Examples of checklists include the following.

- Items to take to the gliderport (food, water, battery, charts, barograph).

- Assembly (follow the Glider Flight Manual/Pilot's Operating Handbook [GFM/POH] and add items as needed).

- Pre-launch (water, food, charts, glide calculator, oxygen on, sunscreen, cell phone).

- Pre-take-off checklist itself.

Being better organized before the flight leads to less stress during the flight, thus enhancing flight safety.

PERSONAL AND SPECIAL EQUIPMENT

Many items not required for local soaring are needed for cross-country flights. Pilot comfort and physiology is even more important on cross-country flights since these flights often last longer than local flights. An adequate supply of drinking water is essential to avoid dehydration. Many pilots use the backpack drinking system with readily accessible hose and bite-valve that is often used by bicyclists. This system is easily stowed beside the pilot, allowing frequent sips of water. A relief system also may be needed on longer flights. Cross-country flights can last anywhere from two to eight hours or more, so food of some kind is also a good idea.

Several items should be carried in case there is an off-field landing. (For more details, see Chapter 8—Abnormal and Emergency Procedures.) First, a system for securing the glider is necessary, as is a land-out kit for the pilot. The kit will vary depending on the population density and climate of the soaring area. For instance, in the Great Basin in the United States, a safe landing site may be many miles from the nearest road or ranch house. Since weather is often hot and dry during the soaring season, extra water and food should be added items. Carrying good walking shoes is a good idea as well. A cell phone may prove useful for land-outs in areas with sparse telephone coverage. Some

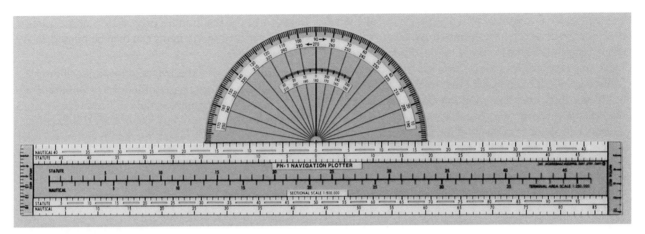

Figure 11-2. Navigational plotter.

pilots elect to carry an Emergency Locator Transmitter (ELT) in remote areas in case of mishap during an off-field landing.

Cross-country soaring requires some means of measuring distances to calculate glides to the next source of lift or the next suitable landing area. Distances can be measured using a sectional chart and navigational plotter with the appropriate scale, or by use of Global Positioning System (GPS). If GPS is used, a sectional and plotter should be carried as a backup. A plotter may be made of clear plastic with a straight edge on the bottom marked with nautical or statute miles for a sectional scale on one side and World Aeronautical Chart (WAC) scale on the other. On the top of the plotter is a protractor or semicircle with degrees marked for measuring course angles. A small reference index hole is located in the center of the semicircle. [Figure 11-2]

Glide calculations must take into account any headwind or tailwind, as well as speeds to fly through varying sink rates. Tools range widely in their level of sophistication, but all are based on the performance polar for the particular glider. The simplest glide aide is a table showing altitudes required for distance vs. wind, which can be derived from the polar. To avoid a table with too many numbers, which could be confusing, some interpolation is often needed. Another option is a circular glide calculator as shown in Figure 11-3. This tool allows the pilot to read the altitude needed for any distance and can be set for various estimated headwinds and tailwinds. Circular glide calculators also make it easy to determine whether you are actually achieving the desired glide, since heavy sink or a stronger-than-estimated headwind can cause you to lose more height with distance than was indicated by the calculator. For instance, the settings in Figure 11-3 indicate that for the estimated 10-knot headwind, 3,600 feet is required to glide 18 miles. After gliding 5 miles, you should still have 2,600 feet. Note that this only gives the altitude required to make the glide. You must

also add the ground elevation and an altitude cushion to set up the pattern.

In addition to a glide calculator, a MacCready ring on the variometer allows the pilot to easily read the speed to fly for different sink rates. MacCready rings are specific to the type of glider and are based on the glider performance polar.(See Chapter 4–Flight Instruments for a description of the MacCready ring.) Accurately flying the correct speed in sinking air, while flying slower in lift, can extend the achieved glide considerably.

Many models of electronic glide calculators now exist. Often coupled with an electronic variometer, they display the altitude necessary for distance and wind as input by the pilot. In addition, many electronic glide calculators feature speed-to-fly functions that indicate whether the pilot should fly faster or slower. Most electronic speed-to-fly directors include audio indications, so the pilot can keep eyes outside the cockpit. The pilot should have manual backups for electronic glide calculators and speed-to-fly directors in case of a low battery or other electronic system failure.

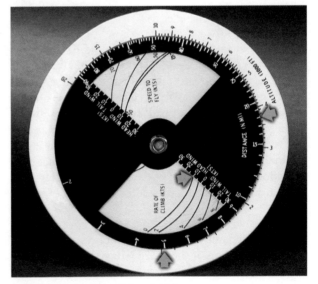

Figure 11-3. Circular glide calculator.

Other equipment may be needed to verify soaring performance for Federation Aeronautique Internationale (FAI) badge or record flights. These include turn-point cameras, barographs, and GPS flight recorders. For complete descriptions of these items, as well as badge or record rules, check the Soaring Society of America web site (www.ssa.org).

Finally, a notepad or small leg-attached clipboard on which to make notes before and during the flight is often handy. Notes prior to flight could include weather information like winds aloft forecasts or distance between turn points. In flight, noting takeoff and start time, as well as time around any turn points, is useful to gauge average speed around the course.

NAVIGATION

Airplane pilots navigate by **pilotage** (flying by reference to ground landmarks) or **dead reckoning** (computing a heading from true airspeed and wind, then estimating time needed to fly to a destination). Glider pilots use pilotage since they generally cannot remain on a course line over a long distance and do not fly one speed for any length of time. Nonetheless, it is

important to be familiar with the concepts of dead reckoning since a combination of the two methods is sometimes needed.

USING THE PLOTTER

Measuring distance with the plotter is accomplished by using the straight edge. Use the Albuquerque sectional chart and measure the distance between Portales Airport (Q34) and Benger Airport (Q54), by setting the plotter with the zero mark on Portales. Read the distance of 47 NM to Benger. Make sure to set the plotter with the sectional scale if using a sectional chart (as opposed to the WAC scale), otherwise the measurement will be off by a factor of two. [Figure 11-4]

The true heading between Portales and Benger can be determined by setting the top of the straightedge along the course line, then slide it along until the index hole is on a line of longitude intersecting the course line. Read the true heading on the outer scale, in this case, 48°. The outer scale should be used for headings with an easterly component. If the course were reversed, flying from

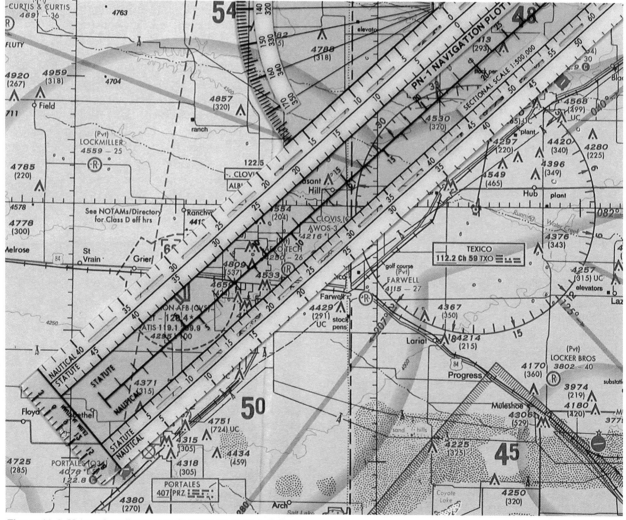

Figure 11-4. Measuring distance using the navigational plotter.

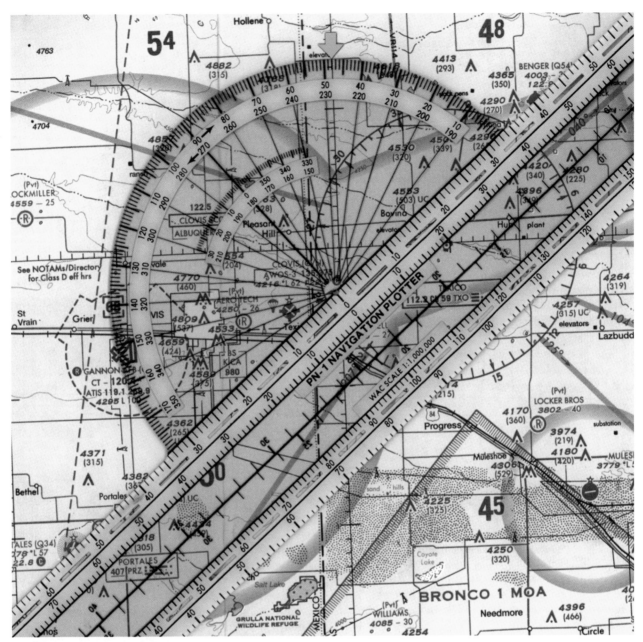

Figure 11-5. Navigational plotter.

Benger to Portales, use the inner scale, for a westerly component, to find 228°. [Figure 11-5]

A common error when first using the plotter is to read the course heading 180° in error. This error is easy to make by reading the scale marked W (270°) instead of the scale marked E (090°). For example, the course from Portales to Benger is towards the northeast, so the heading should be somewhere between 30° and 60°, therefore the true heading of 48° is reasonable.

Calculating heading and groundspeed when there is a crosswind component along the course can be done by using the wind triangle. [Figure 11-6] Suppose the course is 50°, the true airspeed (TAS) is 70 knots, and the wind at cruise altitude is 190° at 20 knots. On a sheet of paper, draw a line representing north-south. Mark a reference point midway along the north-south line, and draw a line along 50° using the plotter and label it C for course. Designate the original point along the north-south line as point A. Next, using either the WAC or sectional scale on the plotter, draw a line from the reference point A along 190°. Make this line 20 miles long and label it W for wind. Mark the end of the line point B. Set the 0-mile mark on the plotter straightedge at point B and rotate the plotter until the 70-mile mark intersects line C. The heading can be obtained from the new line (label it H) and is found to be 61°. The ground-speed is determined by measuring the distance point B and where the H line intersects line C and is found to be 84 knots.

Construction of the **wind triangle** is useful if cruising in a self-launch glider under power at a constant indicated

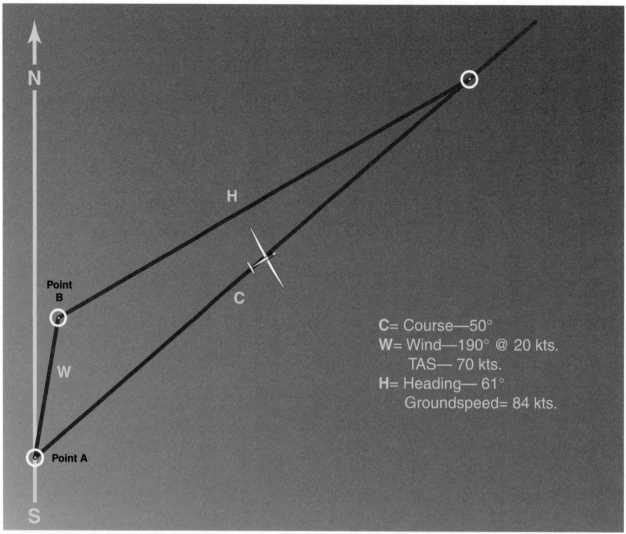

C= Course—50°
W= Wind—190° @ 20 kts.
TAS— 70 kts.
H= Heading— 61°
Groundspeed= 84 kts.

Figure 11-6. Construction of the wind triangle.

speed and altitude. This also assumes the winds at altitude do not change along the course, which is reasonable for a course of 100 miles or so. For longer distances, winds aloft may change along the course. Normal soaring flight involves glides that vary in altitude (so the winds will vary), drifting off course while thermalling, deviations from course to follow the best lift, and frequent speed variations for lift and sink. So the wind triangle is of limited use on soaring flights, and usually glider pilots simply estimate the crab angle needed for a given crosswind component. It is a useful exercise to devise a few scenarios and note the crab angle needed for varying airspeeds. For instance, cruising 60 knots will require about 20° of crab with a 20 knot direct crosswind, while only 15° is needed for the same crosswind cruising at 80 knots.

A SAMPLE CROSS COUNTRY FLIGHT

For training purposes, plan a triangle course starting at Portales Airport (Q34), with turn points at Benger Airport (Q54), and the town of Circle Back. As part of the preflight preparation, draw the course lines for the three legs. Using the plotter, determine the true heading

for each leg, then correct for variation and make written note of the magnetic heading on each leg. Use 9° easterly variation as indicated on the sectional chart (subtract easterly variations, and add westerly variations). For the first leg, the distance is 47 NM with a true heading of 48° (39° magnetic), the second leg is 38 NM at 178° true (169° magnetic) and the third leg is 38 NM at 282° true (273° magnetic). [Figure 11-7]

Assume the base of the cumulus is forecast to be 11,000 MSL, and the winds aloft indicate 320° at 10 knots at 9,000 MSL and 330° at 20 knots at 12,000 MSL. Make written note of the winds aloft for reference during the flight. Mentally note the estimated crab angle needed to remain on course along each leg. For instance, the first leg will have almost a direct crosswind from the left; on the second leg, a weaker crosswind component from the right; while the final leg will be almost directly into the wind. Knowing courses and approximate headings aids the navigation and helps avoiding getting lost, even though deviations to stay with the best lift are often needed. During the flight, if the sky ahead shows several equally promising cumu-

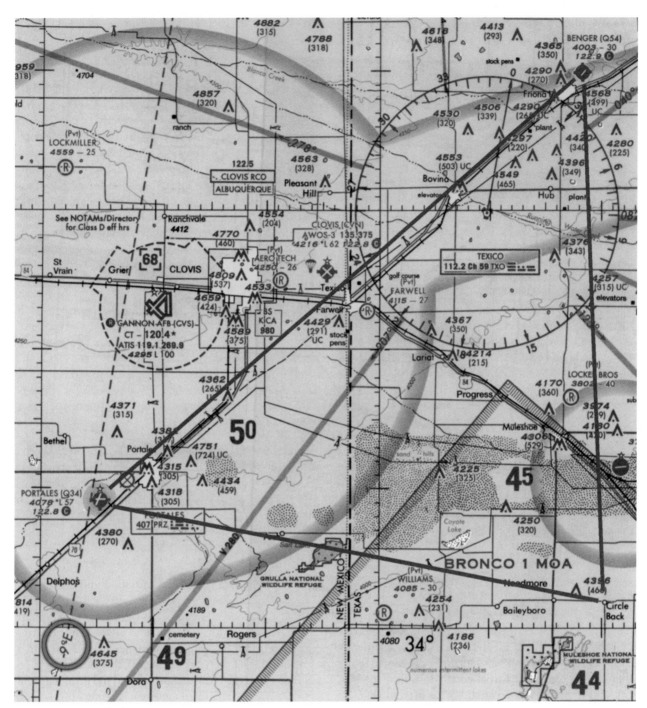

Figure 11-7. Cross-country triangle.

lus clouds, choosing the one closest to the course line makes the most sense.

As further preflight preparation, study the course line along each leg for expected landmarks. For instance, the first leg follows highway and parallel railroad tracks for several miles before the highway turns north. The town of Clovis should become obvious on the left. Note the Class D airspace around Cannon Air Force Base (AFB) just west of Clovis—this could be an issue if better clouds lead to a north of course track. Also, with the northwesterly flow, it is possible to be crossing the path of aircraft on a long final approach to the

northwest-southeast runway. Note that Clovis Airport (CVN) has parachute activity—be aware that they will drop upwind of the airport if they are active. Next the towns of Bovina and then Friona should come into view. The proximity of the Texico VOR near Bovina indicates that alertness needs to be taken for power traffic in the vicinity. The second leg has fewer landmarks. After about 25 miles, the town of Muleshoe and the airport will be straddled. Note that the Reese 1 MOA covers part of this leg of the flight and the next leg. The dimensions of the MOA can be found on the sectional chart, and the AFSS should be consulted concerning the active times of this airspace. Approaching the second turn point it is easy to confuse the towns of Circle Back and Needmore. The clues are the position of Circle Back relative to a 466 feet AGL obstruction (south and east) and the lack of a road that heads north out of Needmore. Landmarks on the third leg include power transmission lines, Coyote Lake (possibly dry), Salt Lake, the small town of Arch and a major road coming south out of Potales. About eight miles from Portales a VOR airway is crossed.

After a thorough preflight of the glider and all the appropriate equipment is stowed or in position for use in flight, it is time to go fly. Once in the air and on course, try to verify the winds aloft. Use pilotage to remain as close to the course line as soaring conditions permit. If course deviations become necessary, stay aware of the location of the course line to the next turn point. For instance, the cu directly ahead indicates lift, but the one 30° off course indicates possibly even more lift, it may be better not to deviate. If the cu left of course indicates a possible area of lift compared to the clouds ahead and only requires a 10° off course deviation, proceed towards the lift. Knowing the present location of the glider and where the course line is located is important for keeping situational awareness.

Sometimes it is necessary to determine an approximate course once already in the air. Assume a few miles before reaching the town of Muleshoe, on the second leg, the weather ahead is not as forecast and has deteriorated—there is now a shower at the third turn point (Circle Back). Rather than continuing on to a certain landing in the rain, the decision is made to cut the triangle short and try to return directly to Portales. Measure and find that Portales is about 37 miles away, and the estimated true heading is about 240°. Correct for variation (9° east) for a compass heading of about 231°. The northwesterly wind is almost 90° to the new course and requires a 10° or 20° crab to the right, so a compass heading between 250° and 270° should work, allowing for some drift in thermal climbs. With practice, the entire thought process should take little time.

The sky towards Portales indicates favorable lift conditions. However, the area along the new course includes sand hills, an area that may not have good choices for off-field landings. It may be a good idea to fly more conservatively until beyond this area and then back to where there are suitable fields for landing. Navigation, evaluation of conditions ahead, and decision-making are required until arrival back at Portales or until a safe off-field landing is completed.

NAVIGATION USING GPS

The GPS navigation systems are available as small hand-held units. (See Chapter 4—Flight Instruments for information on GPS and electronic flight computers.) Some pilots prefer to use existing flight computers for final glide and speed-to-fly information and add a hand-held GPS for navigation. A GPS system makes navigation easier. A GPS unit will display distance and heading to a specified point, usually found by scrolling through an internal database of waypoints. Many GPS units also continuously calculate and display ground speed. If TAS is also known, the headwind component can be calculated from the GPS by subtracting ground speed from TAS. Many GPS units also feature a moving map display that shows past and present positions in relation to various prominent landmarks like airports. These displays can often be zoomed in and out to various map scales. Other GPS units allow you to mark a spot for future reference. This feature can be used to mark the location of a thermal before going into a turn point, with the hopes that the area will still be active after rounding the turn point.

One drawback to GPS units is their attractiveness—it is easy to be distracted by the unit at the expense of flying the glider and finding lift. This can lead to a dangerous habit of focusing too much time inside the cockpit rather than scanning outside for traffic. Like any electronic instrument, GPS units can fail, so it is important to have a backup for navigation, such as a sectional and plotter.

CROSS–COUNTRY TECHNIQUES

The number one rule of safe cross-country soaring is never allow the glider to be out of glide range of a suitable landing area. The alternate landing area may be an airport or a farmer's field. If thermalling is required just to make it to a suitable landing area, safe cross-country procedures are not being practiced.

Before venturing beyond gliding distance from the home airport, thermalling and cross-country techniques can be practiced using small triangles or other short courses. Three examples are shown in Figure 11-8. The length of each leg depends on the performance of the glider, but they are typically small, around 5 or 10 miles each. Soaring conditions do not need to be excellent for these practice tasks but should not be so weak that it is difficult just to stay aloft. On a good day, the triangle may be flown more than once. Besides locating, entering, and centering thermals on course, altitude needed to glide to each turnpoint should be determined using a manual or electronic glide calculator with corrections for wind on each leg. If other airports are nearby, practice finding and switching to their communication frequency and listening to local traffic. As progress is made along each leg of the triangle, frequently cross check the altitude needed to return to the home airport and abandon the course if needed. Setting a minimum altitude of 1,500 feet or 2,000 feet AGL to arrive back at the home site adds a margin of safety. Every landing after a soaring flight should be an accuracy landing.

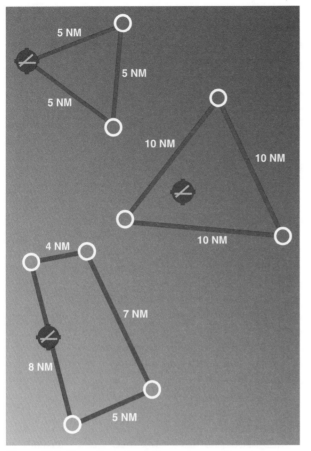

Figure 11-8. Examples of practice cross country courses

provided by the AFSS. Once aloft, estimate wind speed and direction from the track of cumulus shadows over the ground, keeping in mind that the winds at cloud level are often different than those at lower levels. On cloudless days, obtain an estimate of wind by noting drift while thermalling. If the estimate was for headwind of 10 knots but you seem to lose more height on glides than the glide calculator indicates, the headwind estimate may be too low and needs to be adjusted. When flying with GPS, determine wind speed from TAS by simple subtraction. Some flight computers automatically calculate the winds aloft while other GPS systems estimate winds by calculating the drift after several thermal turns.

It is important to develop skill in quickly determining altitude needed for a measured distance using one of the glide calculator tools. For instance, while on a cross-country flight you are over a good landing spot and the next good landing site is a distance of 12 miles into a 10-knot headwind. [Figure 11-9] The glide calculator shows that 3,200 feet is needed to accomplish the glide. Add 1,500 feet above ground to allow time to set up for an off-field landing if necessary, to make the total needed 4,700 feet. The present height is only 3,800 feet, not high enough to accomplish the 12-mile glide, but still high enough to start along course. Head out adjusting the speed based on the MacCready ring or other speed director. After two miles with no lift, altitude is almost 3,300 feet, still not high enough to glide the remaining 10 miles, but high enough to turn back to the last landing site. After

Determining winds aloft while en route can be difficult. Often an estimate is the best that can be achieved. A first estimate is obtained from winds aloft forecasts

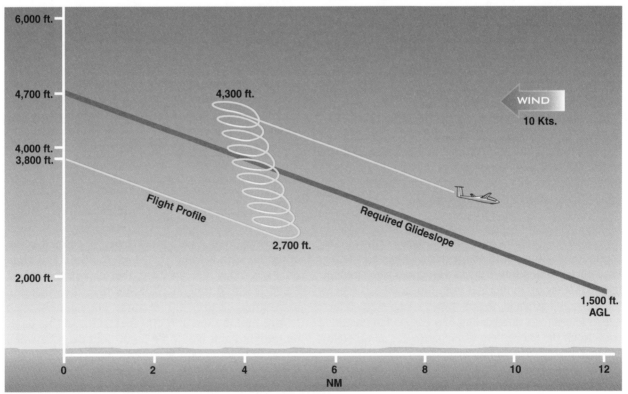

Figure 11-9. Example of a flight profile during a cross-country flight.

almost 4 miles, a 4-knot thermal is encountered at about 2,700 feet and you are able to climb to 4,300 feet. During the climb, the downwind drift of the thermal moves the glider back on course approximately a half-mile. Now there is almost 9 miles to glide to the next landing spot, and a check of the glide calculator indicates 2,400 feet needed for the glide into the 10 knot headwind, plus 1,500 feet at the destination, for a total of 3,900 feet. Now there is 400 feet above the minimum glide with a margin to plan the landing.

In the previous example, had the thermal topped at 3,600 feet (instead of 4,300 feet) there would not be enough altitude to glide the 9 miles into the 10-knot headwind. However, there would be enough height to continue further on course in hopes of finding more lift before needing to turn downwind back to the previous landing spot. Any cross-country soaring flight involves dozens of decisions and calculations such as this. In addition, safety margins may need to be more conservative if there is reason to believe the glide may not work as planned, for example, other pilots reporting heavy sink along the intended course.

On any soaring flight there is an altitude when a decision must be made to cease attempts to work thermals and commit to a landing. This is especially true of cross-country flights in which landings are often in unfamiliar places and feature additional pressures like those discussed in Chapter 8—Abnormal and Emergency Procedures. It is even more difficult on cross-country flights to switch the mental process from soaring to committing to a landing. For beginners, an altitude of 1,000 feet AGL is a recommended minimum to commit to landing. A better choice is to pick a landing site by 1,500 feet AGL, which still allows time to be ready for a thermal while further inspecting the intended landing area. The exact altitude where the thought processes should shift from soaring to landing preparation depends on the terrain. In areas of the Midwest in the United States, landable fields may be present every few miles, allowing a delay in field selection to a lower altitude. In areas of the desert southwest or the Great Basin, landing sites may be 30 or more miles apart, so focusing on a landing spot must begin at much higher altitudes above the ground.

Once committed in the pattern, do not try to thermal away again. Accidents occur due to stalls or spins from thermalling attempts in the pattern. Other accidents have occurred as pilots drifted away from a safe landing spot while trying to thermal from low altitudes. When the thermal dissipated, the pilot was too far beyond the site to return for a safe landing. It is easy to fall into this trap! In all the excitement of preparing for an off-field landing, do not forget a pre-landing checklist.

A common first cross-country flight is a 50-kilometer (32 statute miles) straight distance flight with a landing at another field. The distance is short enough that it can be flown at a leisurely pace on an average soaring day and also qualifies for part of the FAI Silver Badge. Prepare the course well and find out about all available landing areas along the way. Get to the soaring site early so there is no rush in the preflight preparations. Once airborne, take time to get a feel for the day's thermals. If the day looks good enough and height is adequate to set off on course, go! Committing to a landing away from the home field for the first time is difficult. The first landing away from the home field, whether the goal was reached or not, is a notable achievement.

SOARING FASTER AND FARTHER

Early cross-country flights, including small practice triangles within gliding range of the home field, are excellent preparation and training for longer cross-country flights. The FAI Gold Badge requires a 300-km (187 statute miles) cross-country flight, which can be straight out distance or a declared triangle or out and return flight. An average cross-country speed of 20 or 30 MPH may have been adequate for a 32-mile flight, but that average speed is too slow on most days for longer flights. Flying faster average cross-country speeds also allows for farther soaring flights.

Improvement of cross-country skills comes primarily from practice, but reviewing theory as experience is gained is also important. A theory or technique that initially made little sense to the beginner will have real meaning and significance after several cross-country flights. Post-flight self-critique is a useful tool to improve skills.

In the context of cross-country soaring, flying faster means achieving a faster average ground speed. The secret to faster cross-country lies in spending less time climbing and more time gliding. This is achieved by only using the better thermals and spending more time in lifting air and less time in sinking air. Optimum speeds between thermals are given by MacCready ring theory and/or speed-to-fly theory, and can be determined through proper use of the MacCready speed ring or equivalent electronic speed director.

On most soaring days there is an altitude range, called a **height band**, in which the thermal strength is at a maximum. Height bands can be defined as the optimum altitude range in which to climb and glide on a given day. For instance, thermals in the lowest 3,000 feet AGL may be 200-300 fpm, then increase to 500 fpm up to 5,000 feet AGL and again weaken before topping out at 6,000 feet AGL. In this case, the height band would be 2,000 feet deep between 3,000 feet and 5,000 feet AGL. Staying within the height band gives the best (fastest) climbs. Avoid stopping for weaker thermals while within the height band unless there is a good reason. On another day,

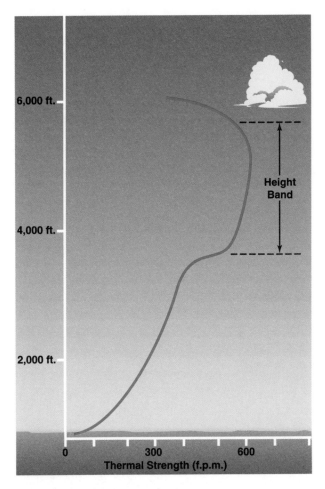

6,000 ft.

Height
Band

4,000 ft.

2,000 ft.

0   300   600
Thermal Strength (f.p.m.)

Figure 11-10. Example of the height band.

thermals may be strong from 1,000 feet to 6,000 feet AGL before weakening, which would suggest a height band 5,000 feet deep. In this case, however, depending on thermal spacing, terrain, pilot experience level, and other factors, the height band would be 2,000 feet or 3,000 feet up to 6,000 feet AGL. Avoid continuing on to the lower bounds of strong thermals (1,000 feet AGL) since failure to find a thermal there gives no extra time before committing to a landing. [Figure 11-10]

Determining the top of the height band is a matter of personal preference and experience, but a rule of thumb puts the top at an altitude where thermals drop off to 75 percent of the best achieved climb. If maximum thermal strength in the height band is 400 fpm, leave when thermals decrease to 300 FPM for more than a turn or two. The thermal strength used to determine the height band should be an average achieved climb. Many electronic variometers have an average function that display average climb over specific time intervals. Another technique involves simply timing the altitude gained over 30 seconds or 1 minute.

Theoretically, the optimum average speed is attained if the MacCready ring is set for the achieved rate-of-climb within the height band. To do this, rotate the ring

so that the index mark is at the achieved rate of climb (for instance 400 fpm) rather than at zero (the setting used for maximum distance). A series of climbs and glides gives the optimum balance between spending time climbing and gliding. The logic is that on stronger days, the extra altitude lost by flying faster between thermals is more than made up in the strong lift during climbs. Flying slower than the MacCready setting does not make the best use of available climbs. Flying faster then the MacCready setting uses too much altitude between thermals; it then takes more than the optimum amount of time to regain the altitude.

Strict use of the MacCready ring assumes that the next thermal is at least as strong as that set on the ring and can be reached with the available altitude. Efforts to fly faster must be tempered with judgement when conditions are not ideal. Factors which may require departure from the MacCready ring theory include terrain (extra height needed ahead to clear a ridge), distance to the next landable spot, or deteriorating soaring conditions ahead. If the next thermal appears to be out of reach before dropping below the height band, either climb higher, glide more slowly, or both.

To illustrate the use of speed-to-fly theory, assume there are four gliders at the same height. Ahead are three weak cumulus clouds, each produced by 200-fpm thermals, then a larger cumulus with 600 fpm under it as in Figure 11-11 on the next page.

- Pilot #1 sets his ring to 600 fpm for the anticipated strong climb under the large cumulus, but his aggressive approach has him on the ground before reaching the cloud.

- Pilot #2 sets his ring for 200 fpm and climbs under each cloud until resetting the ring to 600 fpm after climbing under the third weak cumulus, in accordance with strict speed-to-fly theory.

- Pilot #3 is conservative and sets his ring to zero for the maximum glide.

- Pilot #4 calculates the altitude needed to glide to the large cumulus using an intermediate setting of 300 fpm, and finds she can glide to the cloud and still be within the height band.

By the time Pilot #4 has climbed under the large cumulus, she is well ahead of the other two airborne pilots and is relaying retrieve instructions for Pilot #1. This example illustrates the science and art of faster cross-country soaring. The science is provided by speed-to-fly theory, while the art involves interpreting and modifying the theory for the actual conditions. Knowledge of speed-to-fly theory is important as a

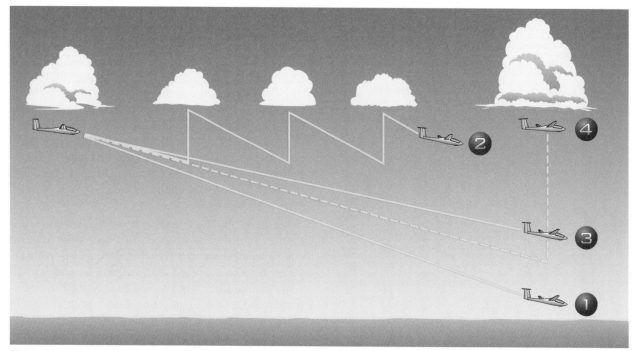

Figure 11-11. Examples of glides achieved for different MacCready ring settings.

foundation. How to apply the art of cross-country soaring stems from practice and experience.

The height band changes during the day. On a typical soaring day, thermal height and strength often increases rapidly during late morning, then both remain somewhat steady for several hours during the afternoon. The height band rises and broadens with thermal height. Sometimes the top of the height band is limited by the base of cumulus clouds. Cloud base may slowly increase by thousands of feet over several hours, in which case the height band also increases over several hours. Thermals often "shut off" rapidly late in the day, so a good rule of thumb is to stay higher late in the day. [Figure 11-12]

It is a good idea to stop and thermal when at or near the bottom of the height band. Pushing too hard can lead to an early off-field landing. At best, pushing too hard leads to lost time at lower altitudes because you are trying to climb away in weak lift.

Another way to increase cross-country speed is to avoid turning at all! A technique known as **dolphin flight** can be used to cover surprising distances on thermal days with little or no circling. The idea is to speed up in sink and slow down in lift while only stopping to circle in the best thermals. The speed-to-fly between lift areas is based on the appropriate MacCready setting. This technique is effective when thermals are spaced relatively close together, as occurs along a cloud street.

As an example, assume two gliders are flying under a cloud street with frequent thermals and only weak sink between thermals. Glider #1 conserves altitude and

stays close to cloud base by flying best L/D through weak sink. To stay under the clouds, he is forced to fly

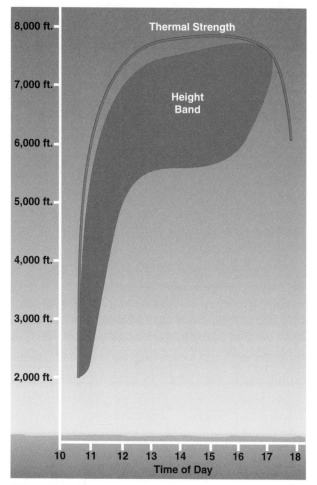

Figure 11-12. Thermal height and height band (shaded) vs. time of day.

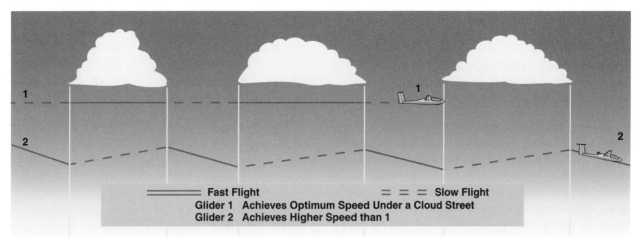

Fast Flight = = = Slow Flight
Glider 1 Achieves Optimum Speed Under a Cloud Street
Glider 2 Achieves Higher Speed than 1

Figure 11-13. Advantage of proper speed to fly under a cloud street.

faster in areas of lift, exactly opposite of flying fast in sink, slow in lift. Glider #2 uses the conditions more efficiently by flying faster in the sink and slower in lift. In a short time, Glider #2 has gained distance on Glider #1. At the end of the cloud street, one good climb quickly puts Glider #2 near cloud base and well ahead of Glider #1. [Figure 11-13]

On an actual cross-country flight, a combination of dolphin flight and classic climb and glide is frequently needed. In a previous example, the two pilots who decided not to stop and circle in the weaker thermals would still benefit from dolphin flight techniques in the lift and sink until stopping to climb in the strong lift.

SPECIAL SITUATIONS
COURSE DEVIATIONS
Diversion on a soaring cross-country flight is the norm rather than the exception. Some soaring days supply fair-weather cumulus evenly-spaced across all quadrants, but even these days cycle and it is beneficial to deviate toward stronger lift. Deviations of 10° or less add little to the total distance and should be used without hesitation to fly toward better lift. Even deviations up to 30° are well worthwhile if they lead toward better lift and/or avoid suspected sink ahead. The sooner the deviation is started, the less total distance will be covered during the deviation. [Figure 11-14]

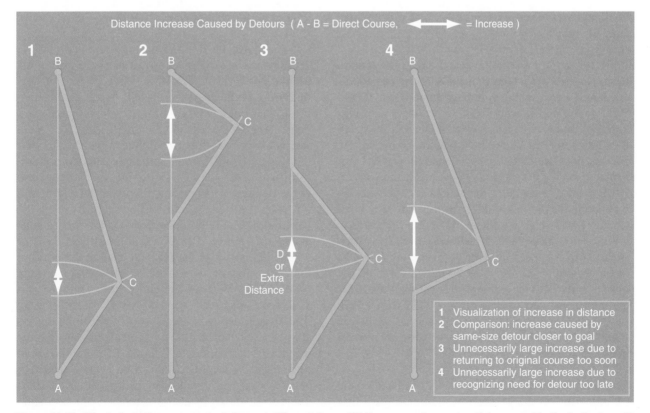

Distance Increase Caused by Detours (A - B = Direct Course, ←→ = Increase)

1 Visualization of increase in distance
2 Comparison: increase caused by same-size detour closer to goal
3 Unnecessarily large increase due to returning to original course too soon
4 Unnecessarily large increase due to recognizing need for detour too late

Figure 11-14. Effect of starting course deviations at different times. White arrows show extra distance and indicate the benefit of early course deviations.

Deviations of 45° or even 90° may be needed to avoid poor conditions ahead. An example might be a large cloudless area or a shaded area where cumulus have spread out into stratus clouds. Sometimes deviations in excess of 90° are needed to return to active thermals after venturing into potentially dead air.

Deviations due to poor weather ahead should be undertaken before the flight becomes unsafe. For instance, if cloud bases are lowering and showers developing, always have the option for a safe, clear landing area before conditions deteriorate too far. It is very easy to leave one safe landing site hoping to beat weather to the next, only to have both spots go below VFR during the glide. Thunderstorms along the course are a special hazard, since storm outflow can affect surface winds for many miles surrounding the storm. Do not count on landing at a site within 10 miles of a strong thunderstorm—sites further removed are safer. Thunderstorms ahead often warrant large course deviations, even up to 180° (i.e., retreat to safety).

LOST PROCEDURES

Navigation has become far easier with the advent of GPS. Since GPS systems are not 100 percent free from failure, pilots must still be able use the sectional chart and compass for navigation. It is important to have an alternate plan in the event of becoming lost.

As discussed earlier, preflight preparation can help in avoiding becoming lost. Spend some time studying the sectional chart for airports or other notable landmarks along the route.

If still lost after some initial searching, try to remain calm. The first priority is to make sure there is a suitable landing area within gliding distance. Then, if possible, try to find lift, even if it is weak, and climb. This buys time and gives a wider view of the area. Next, try to estimate the last known position, the course flown, and any possible differences in wind at altitude. For instance, maybe the headwind is stronger then anticipated and not as far along the course as expected. Try to pin point the present position from an estimate of the distance traveled for a given period of time and confirm it with visible landmarks by reference to the sectional chart. For instance, if at point X, averaging about 50 knots, heading north for about 30 minutes, should put you at point Y. Look again at the sectional chart for landmarks that should be nearby point Y, then search the ground for these landmarks. Thermalling while searching has the added advantage of allowing a wider area of scan while circling.

Once a landmark is located on the sectional and on the ground, confirm the location by finding a few other nearby landmarks. For instance, if that is a town below, then the highway should curve like the one shown on the chart. Does it? If lost and near a suitable landing area, make certain not to leave the area until certain of your location. Airport runways sometimes provide valuable clues. The airport name is often painted right on the runway. Failing that, the runway orientation itself may indicate the airport.

If all efforts fail, attempt a radio call to other soaring pilots in the area. A description of what is below and nearby may bring help from a fellow pilot more familiar with the area.

CROSS–COUNTRY USING A SELF-LAUNCHING GLIDER

A self-launch glider can give the pilot much more freedom in exchange for a more complex and expensive aircraft. First, a self-launch glider allows the pilot to fly from airports without a towplane or towpilot. Second, the engine can be used to avoid off-field landings and extend the flight. In theory, when low in a self-launcher, simply start the engine and climb to the next source of lift. This second advantage has pitfalls and dangers of its own and has lead to many accidents due to engine failure and/or improper starting procedures. Engines on self-launch gliders are generally not quite as reliable as those on airplanes and are susceptible to special problems. For instance, in the western United States, summer thermals often extend to altitudes where the air is cold. The self-launch engine can become **cold soaked**, after several hours of flight and may take more time to start or may fail to start altogether.

Over reliance on the engine may result in a false sense of security. This can lead pilots to glide over unlandable terrain, something they might not normally do. If the engine then fails just when needed most, the pilot has no safe place to land. Some accidents have occurred when the engine starting system was actually fully functional, but in the rush to start the engine to avoid landing, the pilot did not perform a critical task, such as switching the ignition on. Other accidents have occurred when the engine did not start right away, and while trying to solve the starting problem, the pilot flew too far from a suitable landing area. For self-launch gliders with an engine that stows in the fuselage behind the cockpit, the added drag of an extended engine can reduce the glide ratio by 50 to 75 percent![Figure 11-15]

The critical decision height to commit to an engine start on a self-launch glider is typically higher than the minimum to commit to landing of a non-powered glider. This is due to a combination of time needed to actually start the engine and extra drag during the starting process. It may take anywhere from 200 feet to 500 feet of altitude to extend and start the engine. Whereas a pure glider may commit to landing at 1,000 feet

Figure 11-15. Effect on the glide ratio of the engine being extended but not running.

AGL, the self-launch pilot will likely opt for 1,500 feet AGL, depending on the glider and landing options should the engine fail. In this sense, the self-launch glider becomes more restrictive.

Cross-country flight can also be done under power with a self-launching glider, or a combination of powered and soaring flight. For some self-launch gliders, the most efficient distance per gallon of fuel is achieved by a maximum climb under power followed by a power-off glide. Check the GFM/POH for recommendations.

Another type of glider features a sustainer engine. These engines are not powerful enough to self-launch but are able to keep the glider airborne if lift fails. The sustainer engine is typically less complex to operate than their self-launch counterparts, and can eliminate the need for a time-consuming retrieve. Pilots flying with a sustainer are susceptible to the same pitfalls as their self-launch counterparts.

HIGH–PERFORMANCE GLIDER OPERATIONS AND CONSIDERATIONS

Extended cross-country flights have been made in relatively low-performance gliders. However, on any given soaring day, a glider with a 40-to-1 glide ratio will be able to fly farther and faster than one with 20-to-1, assuming the pilots in each have similar skill levels. Often a glider pilot looks for more performance in a glider to achieve longer and faster cross-country flights.

High-performance gliders are usually more complex and somewhat more difficult to fly, but they vary considerably. Current Standard Class gliders (15-meter wingspan and no flaps) are easy to assemble and newer types are comparatively easier to fly. On the other end of the spectrum, Open Class gliders (unlimited wingspan with flaps) can feature wingspans of 24

meters or more with wings in four sections. The experience required to fly a high-performance glider can not be quantified simply in terms of a pilot's total glider hours. Types of gliders flown (low- and high-performance) must be considered.

Most high-performan ce gliders are single-seat. If a two-seat, high-performance glider is available, the pilot should obtain some instruction from an authorized flight instructor before attempting to fly a single-seat high-performance glider for the first time. Before flying any single-seat glider, pilots should thoroughly familiarize themselves with the GFM/POH, including important speeds, weight and balance issues, and all operating systems in the glider GFM/POH such as landing gear, flaps, and wheel-brake location.

As mentioned, most high-performance gliders are complex. Almost all have retractable landing gear, so pilots must make certain that "landing gear down" is on their pre-landing checklist. Most landing-gear handles are on the right side of the cockpit, but a few are on the left side, so caution is required when reaching for a handle to make sure it is not flaps or airbrakes. A common error is to neglect to retract the landing gear and then mistakenly retract it as part of the pre-landing checklist. A gear-up landing in a glider usually only causes embarrassment and minor damage. The distance between the pilot and the runway with the landing gear up is minimal, however, providing no real "cushioning" protection for the pilot in case of a hard landing.

Many high-performance gliders have flaps. A few degrees of positive flap can be used when thermalling, and some gliders have 30° or more positive flap settings for slower landing speeds. Flaps can be set to 0° for relatively slow-speed glides, while negative flap settings are available for glides at faster speeds. The

GFM/POH and glider polar provide recommended flap settings for different speeds, as well as maximum speeds allowed for different flap settings. A few high-performance gliders have no airbrakes and use only large positive flap settings for landing. This system allows for steep approaches but can be uncomfortable for a pilot who has only used spoilers or divebrakes for landing. A thorough ground briefing is required.

Many high-performance gliders have longer wingspans that require special care to avoid ground loops on take-off or landing. Runway lights and other obstructions near the runway can become a problem. If a wingtip strikes the ground before the glider has touched down, a cartwheel is a possibility, leading to extensive damage and serious injury. Gliders with long wings often have speed restrictions for dive-brake use to avoid severe bending loads at the wingtips.

The feel of the controls on high-performance gliders is light, and pilot-induced oscillations (PIOs) occur easily with the sensitive elevator. Elevator movements using the wrist only, while the forearm rests on the thigh, can aid in avoiding PIOs.

Some high-performance gliders have only one center-of-gravity (CG) tow hook either ahead of the landing gear or in the landing gear well. If the CG hook is within the landing gear well, retracting the gear on tow interferes with the towrope. Even if the glider has a nose hook, retracting the gear on tow is not recommended, since the handle is usually on the right cockpit side and switching hands to raise the gear can lead to lose of control on tow. A CG hook, as compared to a nose hook, makes a crosswind take-off more difficult since the glider can weathervane into the wind more easily. In addition, a CG hook makes the glider more susceptible to "kiting" on take-off, especially if the flying CG is near the aft limit. This can present a serious danger to the towpilot.

Most high-performance gliders are built from composites, instead of metal or wood, with a gelcoat finish. The gelcoat is susceptible to damage from exposure to ultraviolet radiation (UV) from the sun as well as prolonged exposure to moisture. At some soaring sites, pilots can keep the glider assembled in a hanger, but more frequently, the composite glider is rigged before flying and derigged after flying. The transition to high-performance gliders necessitates development of checklists and discipline during glider assembly and disassembly. Other considerations for gelcoat care include extreme cold soaking. There is evidence that flying a composite glider with a gelcoat finish to very high and cold altitudes followed by a quick descent to warmer levels can seriously reduce the life of the gelcoat. Composite gliders appear to be more susceptible to flutter than metal gliders. Flutter is a function of true airspeed, thus the GFM/POH of composite gliders sometimes present a table of the indicated V_{NE} for different heights. For instance, a popular two-seat composite glider shows 135 knots as the sea level V_{NE}, 128 knots at 10,000 feet MSL, 121 knots at 13,000 feet MSL, etc. Read the GFM/POH carefully and abide by the limits.

Many high-performance gliders have the capability of adding water ballast. A heavier glider has a higher minimum sink rate and speed; thus it has a larger circling radius. A glider with water ballast achieves the same glide ratio but at a higher speed than the same glider without water ballast. To maximize average cross-country speed on a day with strong thermals, water ballast can be used. The gain in speed between thermals outweighs the lost time due to slightly slower climbs with water ballast. If thermals are weak, ballast should not be used. If strong thermals become weak the water ballast can be dumped. In any case, water ballast should be dumped before landing because heavy wings are more difficult to keep level on the ground roll and a hard landing is more likely to lead to damage with a heavier glider. Dump times vary but are typically between two and five minutes.

Water ballast is carried in the wings in built-in tanks or water bags. The latter works well but has been known to have problems with leaks. Filling and dumping systems vary from glider to glider, and it is vital to be familiar with the ballast system as described in the GFM/POH. Filling without proper venting can lead to structural damage. Care must be taken to ensure that both wings are filled with the same amount of water. If one wing has a few extra gallons, it can be lead to ground loops and loss of control on take-off, especially in the presence of a crosswind.

Water unfortunately expands when going from liquid to solid state. The force of the water ballast freezing can be enough to split composite wing skins. If anticipating flying at levels where the temperature might be below 0°C, follow the GFM/POH recommended additive to avoid freezing.

Some gliders have a small ballast tank in the tail as well as ballast in the wings. Tail ballast is an effective means to adjust for a CG that is too far forward. It should be used with caution, however, since the position of the tail ballast tank gives it a long arm aft of the empty CG. A careless calculation can lead to too much water in the tail tank and a flying CG that is aft of the limits.

CROSS–COUNTRY USING OTHER LIFT SOURCES

Many world distance and speed records have been broken using ridge or wave lift. Under the right conditions, these lift sources can extend for hundreds of miles from sunrise to sunset. Ridge or wave lift is often more consistent than thermals, allowing long, straight stretches at high speed.

Cross-country on ridge lift poses some special problems and considerations. Often the best lift is very close to the ridge crest where the air can be quite turbulent. Great concentration is needed over several hours close to terrain in rough conditions for longer flights. On relatively low ridges, for instance in the eastern United States; ridge lift may not extend very high, so the pilot is never too far from a potential off-field landing. These are not conditions for the beginning cross-country pilot. In milder conditions, gaps in the ridge may require thermalling to gain enough height to cross the gap. Ridge lift can provide a place to temporarily wait for thermals to generate. For instance, if cumulus have spread out to form a stratus layer shading the ground and eliminating thermals, a wind facing slope can be used to maintain soaring flight until the sun returns to regenerate thermals.

Wave lift can also provide opportunities for long and/or fast cross-country flights. Most record flights have been along mountain ranges with flights in excess of 2,000 km having been flown in New Zealand and along the Andes. In the United States, speed records have been set using the wave in the lee of the Sierra Nevada Mountains. In theory, long-distance flights could also be made by climbing high in wave then gliding with a strong tailwind to the next range downwind for another climb. Special consideration to pilot physiology (cold, oxygen, etc.) and airspace restrictions are needed when considering a cross-country flight using wave.

Convergence zones can also be used to enhance cross-country speed. Even if the convergence is not a consistent line but merely acts as a focus for thermals, dolphin flight is often possible, making glides over long distances possible without thermalling. When flying low, awareness of local, small-scale convergence can help the pilot find thermal triggers to help them climb back to a comfortable cruising height.

It is possible to find ridge, thermal, wave, and even convergence lift during one cross-country flight. Optimum use of the various lift sources requires mental agility but makes for an exciting and rewarding flight.

INDEX

A

ABSOLUTE ALTITUDE, 4-7
ACUTE FATIGUE, 1-14
ADVECTION, 9-5
ADVERSE YAW, 3-12, 7-23
AERODYNAMICS, 3-1
AERONAUTICAL CHARTS, 11-1
   sectional, 11-1
   WAC, 11-3
AERONAUTICAL DECISION MAKING, 1-2
AERONAUTICAL INFORMATION MANUAL
   (AIM), 9-26
AEROTOW EMERGENCIES, 7-4
AEROTOW LAUNCH, 7-1
   launch procedures, 7-2
AILERONS, 2-2
AIR DENSITY, 3-2
AIRFOIL, 3-1
AIR MASSES, 9-4, 9-11
AIRMET, 9-37, 11-2
AIRSPACE, 11-2
AIRSPEED, 4-1, 4-2
   true, 4-2
   indicated, 4-2
   minimum control, 4-3, 4-4, 7-26
   placard, 5-5. 5-6
   maneuvering, 4-3
   L/D Speed, 4-3, 5-5
   minimum sink, 4-3, 5-5
   aero tow, 4-3
   ground launch, 4-3
   flaps extended, 4-3
   never exceed, 4-3
   indicator, 4-1
   calibrated, 4-2
AIRSPEED CONTROL, 7-26
ALCOHOL, 1-15
ALTIMETER, 4-4
ALTITUDE, 4-7, 5-1
   indicated, 4-7
   true, 4-7
   absolute, 4-7
   pressure, 4-7
   density, 4-7
AMPLITUDE, 9-20
ANGLE OF ATTACK, 3-1, 3-14

ANGLE OF BANK, 3-11
ANGLE OF INCIDENCE, 3-1
ANXIETY, 1-6
AREA FORECAST, 9-36
ARM, 5-10
ASPECT RATIO, 3-7
ASSEMBLY TECHNIQUES, 6-1
ASYMMETRICAL AIRFOIL, 3-1
ATMOSPHERE, 9-1
ATMOSPHERIC PRESSURE, 5-1
ATMOSPHERIC STABILITY, 9-4, 9-6
ATMOSPHERIC SOUNDINGS, 9-4
ATTITUDE, 4-16
ATTITUDE INDICATOR, 4-16
AUTO LAUNCH PROCEDURES, 7-11
AUTO-ROTATION, 7-31
AUTO TOW, 7-2
AUTOMATED FLIGHT SERVICE STATION, 9-25, 11-2
AVIATION AREA FORECAST, 9-36
AVIATION ROUTINE WEATHER REPORT, 9-33
AVIATION WEATHER SERVICES, 9-25
AWARDS, 11-4, 11-5
AXES, 3-8

B

BAILOUT, 10-12
BALLAST, 5-5, 5-13
BANK ANGLE, 3-11
BAROGRAPH, 11-2
BASE LEG, 7-35
BASIC FLIGHT MANEUVERS, 7-22
BERNOULLI'S PRINCIPLE, 3-3
BEST GLIDE (L/D) AIRSPEED, 5-5, 7-34
BOXING THE WAKE, 7-10

C

CALCULATOR, 11-3
CALIBRATED AIRSPEED (CAS), 4-2

N

O

P

R

S

Y

GLOSSARY

ADVECTION—The transport of an atmospheric variable due to mass motion by the wind. Usually the term as used in meteorology refers only to horizontal transport.

AILERONS—The hinged portion of the trailing edge of the outer wing used to bank or roll around the longitudinal axis.

AIR DENSITY—The mass of air per unit volume.

AIRFOIL—The surfaces on a glider that produce lift.

AIR MASS—A widespread mass of air having similar characteristics (e.g., temperature), which usually helps to identify the source region of the air. Fronts are distinct boundaries between air masses.

AMPLITUDE—In wave motion, one half the distance between the wave crest and the wave trough.

ANGLE OF ATTACK—The angle formed between the relative wind and the chord line of the wing.

ANGLE OF INCIDENCE—The angle between the chord line of the wing and the longitudinal axis of the glider. The angle of incidence is built into the glider by the manufacturer and cannot be adjusted by the pilot's movements of the controls.

ASPECT RATIO—The ratio between the wing span and the mean chord of the wing.

ASYMMETRICAL AIRFOIL—One in which the upper camber differs from the lower camber.

ATMOSPHERIC SOUNDING—A measure of atmospheric variables aloft, usually pressure, temperature, humidity, and wind.

ATMOSPHERIC STABILITY—Describes a state in which an air parcel will resist vertical displacement, or once displaced (for instance by flow over a hill) will tend to return to its original level.

BAILOUT BOTTLE—Small oxygen cylinder connected to the oxygen mask supplying several minutes of oxygen. It can be used in case of primary oxygen system failure or if an emergency bailout at high altitude became necessary.

BALLAST—Term used to describe any system that adds weight to the glider. Performance ballast employed in some gliders increases wing loading using releasable water in the wings (via integral tanks or water bags). This allows faster average cross-country speeds. Trim ballast is used to adjust the flying CG, often necessary for light-weight pilots. Some gliders also have a small water ballast tank in the tail for optimizing flying CG.

BAROGRAPH—Instrument for recording pressure as a function of time. Used by glider pilots to verify flight performance for badge or record flights.

BEST GLIDE SPEED (BEST L/D SPEED)—The airspeed that results in the least amount of altitude loss over a given distance. This speed is determined from the performance polar. The manufacturer publishes the best glide (L/D) airspeed for specified weights and the resulting glide ratio. For example, a glide ratio of 36:1 means that the glider will lose 1 foot of altitude for every 36 feet of forward movement in still air at this airspeed.

CAMBER—The curvature of a wing when looking at a cross section. A wing has upper camber on its top surface and lower camber on its bottom surface.

CAP CLOUD—Also called a foehn cloud. These are clouds forming on mountain or ridge tops by cooling of moist air rising on the upwind side followed by warming and drying by downdrafts on the lee side.

CENTERING—Adjusting circles while thermalling to provide the greatest average climb.

CENTER OF PRESSURE—The point along the wing chord line where lift is considered to be concentrated.

CENTRIFUGAL FORCE—The apparent force occurring in curvilinear motion acting to deflect objects outward from the axis of rotation. For instance, when pulling out of a dive, it is the force pushing you down in your seat.

CENTRIPETAL FORCE—The force in curvilinear motion acting toward the axis of rotation. For instance, when pulling out of a dive, it is the force that the seat exerts on the pilot to offset the centrifugal force.

CHORD LINE—An imaginary straight line drawn from the leading edge of an airfoil to the trailing edge.

CLOUD STREETS—Parallel rows of cumulus clouds. Each row can be as short as 10 miles or as long as a 100 miles or more.

COLD SOAKED—Condition of a self-launch or sustainer engine making it difficult or impossible to start in flight due to long-time exposure to cold temperatures. Usually occurs after a long soaring flight at altitudes with cold temperatures, e.g., a wave flight.

CONVECTION—Transport and mixing of an atmospheric variable due to vertical mass motions (e.g., updrafts).

CONVECTIVE CONDENSATION LEVEL (CCL)—The level at which cumulus will form from surface-based convection. Under this level, the air is dry adiabatic, and the mixing ratio is constant.

CONVENTIONAL TAIL—A glider design with the horizontal stabilizer mounted at the bottom of the vertical stabilizer.

CONVERGENCE—A net increase in the mass of air over a specified area due to horizontal wind speed and/or direction changes. When convergence occurs in lower levels, it is usually associated with upward air motions.

CONVERGENCE ZONE—An area of convergence, sometimes several miles wide, at other times very narrow. These zones often provide organized lift for many miles along the convergence zone, for instance, a sea-breeze front.

CRITICAL ANGLE OF ATTACK—Angle of attack, typically around 18°, beyond which a stall occurs. The critical angle of attack can be exceeded at any airspeed and at any nose attitude.

CROSS COUNTRY—In soaring, any flight out of gliding range of the take-off airfield. Note that this is different than the definitions in the CFRs for meeting the experience requirements for various pilot certificates and/or ratings.

CUMULUS CONGESTUS—A cumulus cloud of significant vertical extent and usually displaying sharp edges. In warm climates, these sometimes produce precipitation. Also called towering cumulus, these clouds indicate that thunderstorm activity may soon occur.

CUMULONIMBUS (CB)—Also called thunderclouds, these are deep convective clouds with a cirrus anvil and may contain any of the characteristics of a thunderstorm: thunder, lightning, heavy rain, hail, strong winds, turbulence, and even tornadoes.

DEAD RECKONING—Navigation by computing a heading from true airspeed and wind, then estimating time needed to fly to a destination.

DENSITY ALTITUDE—Pressure altitude corrected for nonstandard temperature variations. Performance charts for many older gliders are based on this value.

DEWPOINT (OR DEWPOINT TEMPERATURE)—The temperature to which a sample of air must be cooled, while the amount of water vapor and barometric pressure remain constant, in order to attain saturation with respect to water.

DIHEDRAL—The angle at which the wings are slanted upward from the root to the tip.

DIURNAL EFFECTS—A daily variation (may be in temperature, moisture, wind, cloud cover, etc.) especially pertaining to a cycle completed within a 24-hour period, and which recurs every 24 hours.

DOLPHIN FLIGHT—Straight flight following speed-to-fly theory. Glides can often be extended and average cross-country speeds increased by flying faster in sink and slower in lift without stopping to circle.

DOWNBURST—A strong, concentrated downdraft, often associated with a thunderstorm. When these reach the ground, they spread out, leading to strong and even damaging surface winds.

DRAG—The force that resists the movement of the glider through the air.

DRY ADIABAT—A line on a thermodynamic chart representing a rate of temperature change at the dry adiabatic lapse rate.

DRY ADIABATIC LAPSE RATE (DALR)—The rate of decrease of temperature with height of unsaturated air lifted adiabatically (not heat exchange). Numerically the value is 3°C or 5.4°F per 1,000 feet.

DUST DEVIL—A small vigorous circulation that can pick up dust or other debris near the surface to form a column hundreds or even thousands of feet deep. At the ground, winds can be strong enough to flip an unattended glider over on its back. Dust devils mark the location where a thermal is leaving the ground.

DYNAMIC STABILITY—A glider's motion and time required for a response to static stability.

ELEVATOR—Attached to the back of the horizontal stabilizer, the elevator controls movement around the lateral axis.

EMPENNAGE—The tail group of the aircraft usually supporting the vertical stabilizer and rudder, as well as the horizontal stabilizer and elevator, or on some aircraft, the V-Tail.

FLAPS—Hinged portion of the trailing edge between the ailerons and fuselage. In some gliders ailerons and flaps are interconnected to produce full-span "flaperons." In either case, flaps change the lift and drag on the wing.

FLUTTER—Resonant condition leading to rapid, unstable oscillations of part of the glider structure (e.g., the wing) or a control surface (e.g., elevator or aileron). Flutter usually occurs at high speeds and can quickly lead to structural failure.

FORWARD SLIP—A slide used to dissipate altitude without increasing the glider's speed, particularly in gliders without flaps or with inoperative spoilers.

GLIDER—A heavier-than-air aircraft that is supported in flight by the dynamic reaction of the air against its lifting surfaces, and whose free flight does not depend on an engine.

GRAUPEL—Also called soft hail or snow pellets, these are white, round or conical ice particles 1/8 to 1/4 inch diameter. They often form as a thunderstorm matures and indicate the likelihood of lightning.

GROUND EFFECT—A reduction in induced drag for the same amount of lift produced. Within one wingspan above the ground, the decrease in induced drag enables the glider to fly at a slower airspeed. In ground effect, a lower angle of attack is required to produce the same amount of lift.

HEIGHT BAND—The altitude range in which the thermals are strongest on any given day. Remaining with the height band on a cross-country flight should allow the fastest average speed.

HOUSE THERMAL—A thermal that forms frequently in the same or similar location.

HUMAN FACTORS—The study of how people interact with their environments. In the case of general aviation, it is the study of how pilot performance is influenced by such issues as the design of cockpits, the function of the organs of the body, the effects of emotions, and the interaction and communication with the other participants of the aviation community, such as other crewmembers and air traffic control personnel.

INDUCED DRAG—Drag that is the consequence of developing lift with a finite-span wing. It can be represented by a vector that results from the difference between total and vertical lift.

INERTIA—The tendency of a mass at rest to remain at rest, or if in motion to remain in motion, unless acted upon by some external force.

INSTRUMENT METEOROLOGICAL CONDITIONS (IMC)—Meteorological conditions expressed in terms of visibility, distance from cloud, and ceiling less than the minimum specified for Visual Meteorological Conditions (VMC). Gliders rarely fly in IMC due to instrumentation and air traffic control requirements.

INVERSION—Usually refers to an increase in temperature with height, but may also be used for other atmospheric variables.

ISOHUMES—Lines of equal relative humidity.

ISOPLETH—A line connecting points of constant or equal value.

ISOTHERM—A contour line of equal temperature.

KATABATIC—Used to describe any wind blowing down slope.

KINETIC ENERGY—Energy due to motion, defined as one half mass times velocity squared.

LAPSE RATE—The decrease with height of an atmospheric variable, usually referring to temperature, but can also apply to pressure or density.

LATERAL AXIS—An imaginary straight line drawn perpendicularly (laterally) across the fuselage and through the center of gravity. Pitch movement occurs around the lateral axis, and is controlled by the elevator.

LENTICULAR CLOUD—Smooth, lens-shaped clouds marking mountain-wave crests. They may extend the entire length of the mountain range producing the wave and are also called wave clouds or lennies by glider pilots.

LIFT—Produced by the dynamic effects of the airstream acting on the wing, lift opposes the downward force of weight.

LIMIT LOAD—The maximum load, expressed as multiples of positive and negative G (force of gravity), that an aircraft can sustain before structural damage becomes possible. The load limit varies from aircraft to aircraft.

LOAD FACTOR—The ratio of the load supported by the glider's wings to the actual weight of the aircraft and its contents.

LONGITUDINAL AXIS—An imaginary straight line running through the fuselage from nose to tail. Roll movement occurs around the longitudinal axis, and is controlled by the ailerons.

MESOSCALE CONVECTIVE SYSTEM (MCS)—A large cluster of thunderstorms with horizontal dimensions on the order of 100 miles. MCSs are sometimes organized in a long line of thunderstorms (e.g., a squall line) or as a random grouping of thunderstorms. Individual thunderstorms within the MCS may be severe.

MICROBURST—A small-sized downburst of 2.2 nautical mile or less horizontal dimension.

MINIMUM SINK AIRPSEED— Airspeed, as determined by the performance polar, at which the glider will achieve the lowest sink rate. That is, the glider will lose the least amount of altitude per unit of time at minimum sink airspeed.

MIXING RATIO— The ratio of the mass of water vapor to the mass of dry air.

MULTI-CELL THUNDERSTORM— A group or cluster of individual thunderstorm cells, with varying stages of development. These storms are often self propagating and may last for several hours.

PARASITE DRAG— Drag caused by any aircraft surface, which deflects or interferes with the smooth airflow around the airplane.

PILOTAGE— Navigational technique based on flight by reference to ground landmarks.

PILOT-INDUCED OSCILLATION (PIO)— Rapid oscillations caused by the pilot's over-controlled motions. PIOs usually occur on takeoff or landings with pitch sensitive gliders and in severe cases can lead to loss of control or damage.

PITCH ATTITUDE— The angle of the longitudinal axis relative to the horizon. Pitch attitude serves as a visual reference for the pilot to maintain or change airspeed.

PITOT-STATIC SYSTEM— Powers the airspeed altimeter and variometer by relying on air pressure differences to measure glider speed, altitude, and climb or sink rate.

PLACARDS— Small statements or pictorial signs permanently fixed in the cockpit and visible to the pilot. Placards are used for operating limitations (e.g., weight or speeds) or to indicate the position of an operating lever (e.g., landing gear retracted or down and locked).

PRECIPITABLE WATER— The amount of liquid precipitation that would result if all water vapor were condensed.

PRESSURE ALTITUDE— The height above the standard pressure level of 29.92 in. Hg. It is obtained by setting 29.92 in the barometric pressure window and reading the altimeter.

RADIANT ENERGY— Energy due to any form of electromagnetic radiation, for instance, from the sun.

RADIUS OF TURN— The amount of horizontal distance an aircraft uses to complete a turn.

RATE OF TURN— The amount of time it takes for a glider to turn a specified number of degrees.

RELATIVE WIND— The airflow caused by the motion of the aircraft through the air. Relative wind, also called relative airflow is opposite and parallel to the direction of flight.

ROTOR— A turbulent circulation under mountain-wave crests, to the lee side and parallel to the mountains creating the wave. Glider pilots use the term rotor to describe any low-level turbulent flow associated with mountain waves.

ROTOR STREAMING— A phenomenon that occurs when the air flow at mountain levels may be sufficient for wave formation, but begins to decrease with altitude above the mountain. In this case, the air downstream of the mountain breaks up and becomes turbulent, similar to rotor, with no lee waves above.

RUDDER— Attached to the back of the vertical stabilizer, the rudder controls movement about the vertical axis.

SAILPLANE— A glider used for traveling long distances and remaining aloft for extended periods of time.

SATURATED ADIABATIC LAPSE RATE(SALR)— The rate of temperature decrease with height of saturated air. Unlike the dry adiabatic lapse rate (DALR), the SALR is not a constant numerical value but varies with temperature.

SELF-LAUNCH GLIDER— A glider equipped with an engine, allowing it to be launched under its own power. When the engine is shut down, a self-launch glider displays the same characteristics as a non-powered glider.

SIDE SLIP— A slip in which the glider's longitudinal axis remains parallel to the original flight path but in which the flight path changes direction according to the steepness of the bank.

SLIP— A descent with one wing lowered and the glider's longitudinal axis at an angle to the flight path. A slip is used to steepen the approach path without increasing the airspeed, or to make the glider move sideways through the air, counteracting the drift resulting from a crosswind.

SPEED TO FLY— Optimum speed through the (sinking or rising) air mass to achieve either the furthest glide or fastest average cross-country speed depending on the objectives during a flight.

SPIN— An aggravated stall that results in the glider descending in a helical, or corkscrew, path.

SPOILERS— Devices on the tops of wings to disturb (spoil) part of the airflow over the wing. The resulting decrease in lift creates a higher sink rate and allows for a steeper approach.

SQUALL LINE— A line of thunderstorms often located along or ahead of a vigorous cold front. Squall lines may contain severe thunderstorms. The term is also used to describe a line of heavy precipitation with an abrupt wind shift but no thunderstorms, as sometimes occurs in association with fronts.

STABILATOR—A one-piece horizontal stabilizer used in lieu of an elevator.

STABILITY—The glider's ability to maintain a uniform flight condition and return to that condition after being disturbed.

STALL—Condition that occurs when the critical angle of attack is reached and exceeded. Airflow begins to separate from the top of the wing, leading to a loss of lift. A stall can occur at any pitch attitude or airspeed.

STANDARD ATMOSPHERE—A theoretical vertical distribution of pressure, temperature and density agreed upon by international convention. It is the standard used, for instance, for aircraft performance calculations. At sea level, the standard atmosphere consists of a barometric pressure of 29.92 inches of mercury (in. Hg.) or 1013.2 millibars, and a temperature of 15°C (59°F). Pressure and temperature normally decrease as altitude increases. The standard lapse rate in the lower atmosphere for each 1,000 feet of altitude is approximately 1 in. Hg. and 2°C (3.5°F). For example, the standard pressure and temperature at 3,000 feet mean sea level (MSL) is 26.92 in. Hg. (29.92 - 3) and 9°C (15°C - 6°C).

STATIC STABILITY—The initial tendency to return to a state of equilibrium when disturbed from that state.

SUPERCELL THUNDERSTORM—A large, powerful type of thunderstorm that forms in very unstable environments with vertical and horizontal wind shear. These are almost always associated with severe weather, strong surface winds, large hail, and/or tornadoes.

T-TAIL—A type of glider with the horizontal stabilizer mounted on the top of the vertical stabilizer, forming a T.

THERMAL—A buoyant plume or bubble of rising air.

THERMAL INDEX (TI)—For any given level is the temperature of the air parcel having risen at the dry adiabatic lapse rate (DALR) subtracted from the ambient temperature. Experience has shown that a TI should be -2 for thermals to form and be sufficiently strong for soaring flight.

THERMAL WAVE—Waves, often but not always marked by cloud streets, that are excited by convection disturbing an overlying stable layer. Also called convection waves.

THERMODYNAMIC DIAGRAM—A chart presenting isopleths of pressure, temperature, water vapor content, as well as dry and saturated adiabats. Various forms exist, the most commonly used in the United States being the Skew-T/Log-P.

THRUST—The forward force that propels a powered glider through the air.

TOTAL DRAG—The sum of parasite and induced drag.

TOWHOOK—A mechanism allowing the attachment and release of a towrope on the glider or towplane. On gliders, it is located near the nose or directly ahead of the main wheel. Two types of towhooks commonly used in gliders are manufactured by Tost and Schweizer.

TRIM DEVICES—Any device designed to reduce or eliminate pressure on the control stick. When properly trimmed, the glider should fly at the desired airspeed with no control pressure from the pilot (i.e., "hands off"). Trim mechanisms are either external tabs on the elevator (or stabilator) or a simple spring-tension system connected to the control stick.

TRUE ALTITUDE—The actual height of an object above mean sea level.

V-TAIL—A type of glider with two tail surfaces mounted to form a V. V-Tails combine elevator and rudder movements.

VARIOMETER—Sensitive rate of climb or descent indicator that measures static pressure between the static ports and an external capacity. Variometers can be mechanical or electrical and can be compensated to eliminate unrealistic indications of lift and sink due to rapid speed changes.

VERTICAL AXIS—An imaginary straight line drawn through the center of gravity and perpendicular to the lateral and longitudinal axes. Yaw movement occurs around the vertical axis and is controlled by the rudder.

VISUAL METEOROLOGICAL CONDITIONS (VMC)—Meteorological conditions expressed in terms of visibility, distance from cloud, and ceiling equal to or better than a specified minimum. VMC represents minimum conditions for safe flight using visual reference for navigation and traffic separation. Ceilings and visibility below VMC constitutes Instrument Meteorological Conditions (IMC).

WASHOUT—Slight twist built in towards the wingtips, designed to improve the stall characteristics of the wing.

WATER VAPOR—Water present in the air while in its vapor form. It is one of the most important of atmospheric constituents.

WAVE LENGTH—The distance between two wave crests or wave troughs.

WAVE WINDOW—Special areas arranged by Letter of Agreement with the controlling ATC wherein gliders may be allowed to fly under VFR in Class A Airspace at certain times and to certain specified altitudes.

WEIGHT—Acting vertically through the glider's center of gravity, weight opposes lift.

WIND TRIANGLE Navigational calculation allowing determination of true heading with a correction for crosswinds on course.